The History of
HENRICO COUNTY

The
History
of
HENRICO COUNTY

Louis H. Manarin (signature)

LOUIS H. MANARIN
and
CLIFFORD DOWDEY

University Press of Virginia
Charlottesville

The Henrico County Bicentennial Commission
has sponsored the publication of this work.

THE UNIVERSITY PRESS OF VIRGINIA
Copyright © 1984 by the Rector and Visitors
of the University of Virginia

First published in 1984

Library of Congress Cataloging in Publication Data

Manarin, Louis H.
  The history of Henrico County.

  Bibliography: p.
  Includes index.
  1. Henrico County (Va.)—History.   I. Dowdey, Clifford,
1904– . II. Title.
F232.H4M36   1984   975.5′453   84-7323
ISBN 0-8139-0984-8

Printed in the United States of America

This book is dedicated
to the children of
Henrico County

Contents

Contents

Illustrations

Foreword

The Henrico County Bicentennial Commission was established in the spring of 1974 as an honorary arm of the Henrico County Board of Supervisors for the purpose of planning, coordinating, and approving all aspects of the bicentennial observance in Henrico County. The commission had its first meeting in the courthouse at Twenty-fifth and Main streets on October 14, 1974.

Each member of the Board of Supervisors appointed one representative from his magisterial district. They were:

District	Supervisor	Member
Brookland	Charles M. Johnson	Robert A. Bracey
Fairfield	Linwood E. Toombs	George H. Moody
Three Chopt	George W. Jinkins, Jr.	Thomas E. Veazey
Tuckahoe	Eugene T. Rilee, Jr.	Robert F. Smart
Varina	Anthony P. Mehford	Jean Nelson Gibbons

I was elected chairman by my fellow members, and Robert A. Bracey was elected vice-chairman. James D. Clark, Jr., the county public information officer, was asked by County Manager Edward Beck to act as secretary for the commission. At a later meeting, Thomas E. Veazey was elected treasurer. Tracy Davis of J. R. Tucker High School was our youth adviser for a year.

Later, as the work of the commission increased, the supervisors appointed one additional member from each magisterial district. They were:

District	Supervisor	Member
Brookland	Charles M. Johnson	Gerald Kersey & Mrs. Hazel Tate
Fairfield	Robert N. Johnson	John A. Waldrop
Three Chopt	George W. Jinkins, Jr.	Floyd S. Tinder
Tuckahoe	Eugene T. Rilee, Jr.	Edward D. Simon
Varina	Victor W. Kreiter	Mrs. Walter Lemon

Left to right: Louis H. Manarin, Charles M. Johnson, Clifford Dowdey, Jean Nelson Gibbons, George H. Moody, Col. Charles O. Frank, Jr. *(Photo by Richard G. Gibbons)*

There have been some changes in commission pesonnel and duties since its beginning. Thomas E. Veazey died, and the commission elected John A. Waldrop as the new treasurer. Robert A. Bracey died, and George H. Moody was elected vice-chairman. Mrs. Cheryl S. Reed and the Reverend Quay F. Reiser, Jr., also served from Brookland before moving from Henrico. We also lost Brookland member Bruce Johnson when he died shortly after he was appointed. Gerald Kersey became the commission secretary when James Clark retired.

The county sent me a CETA student secretary from Highland Springs High School, Miss Ernestine Robinson, who helped with the flood of paperwork.

As we began our work our first priority was to select and approve projects. We sought official designation for Henrico County as a Bicentennial Community. Our application listing our projects was sent to the Virginia Independence Bicentennial Commission (VIBC) in Williamsburg. The VIBC sent our application on to the American Revolutionary Bicentennial Administration (ARBA) in Philadelphia for national approval. In January 1975 ARBA designated Henrico County an official Bicentennial Community.

Special Projects

Preservation of a Scenic and Historic Route

State Route 5, which joins the old capital, Williamsburg, to the present capital, Richmond, follows the James River and was an Indian trail before the settlers came to Jamestown. Many of the historical landmarks in Virginia are located along this road. The commission was successful in getting the support of many groups, and in the summer of 1975 State Route 5 was named a Scenic Virginia Byway.

Farmstead

The commission supported a live exhibit located at the Virginia State Fairgrounds. A complete pioneer farmstead was built with a barn, sheds, and a reconstructed log cabin which is believed to be over two hundred years old. This authentic exhibit, including a working family, has been used during the State Fair every year since 1975.

The Israeli Showcase

The commission endorsed a two-week festival which took place in February 1976 at the Jewish Community Center in western Henrico. The festival traced the history of the Jewish settlers in Henrico County and Richmond from earliest times. There were displays, dances, dramas, and a bazaar. This festival was the biggest commemoration of ethnic heritage in Henrico throughout the Bicentennial.

Independence Honor Roll

The commission tried in vain to find a service club in Henrico to research the names of Henrico County persons who took part in the War for Independence. However, the Appendix lists the names as compiled by the late Ann Waller Reddy.

Henrico School Committees

So that the young people of Henrico County could become directly involved in the celebration, the commission asked the Henrico County School Board to establish a School Bicentennial Committee. The group coordinated the bicentennial activities through the county school system.

The committee was headed by W. Carrington Tate, assistant principle of Henrico High School. Other members were Mrs. Jenny Nelson, elementary school librarian; Henry L. Nelson, Jr., elementary school principal; Mrs. Ann H. Friend, elementary school teacher; Warner M. Jones, visiting teacher; and I. Herbert Levenson, social director of staff development.

The group is to be congratulated on a job well done. One member, Mrs. Jenny Nelson of Baker School, produced a special Revolutionary War slide presentation with sound tape for Henrico students.

Town Meeting '76

The commission approved a town meeting for eastern Henrico headed by the Reverend Jim Athearn and sponsored by many churches, clubs, and businesses. The meeting was held on February 21, 1976, with good participation by area residents. "The Town Meeting '76" was recognized by the ARBA.

Reenactment of the First Reading of the Declaration of Independence

On August 5, 1776, a month and a day after the signing of the Declaration of Independence, a rider from Philadelphia came to the steps of Henrico County Courthouse in the town of Richmond and read the Declaration to the citizens for the first time. The commission appointed a committee to plan a suitable commemoration of this event. The committee included Robert A. Bracey, chairman; Bruce Johnson; Jean N. Gibbons; Floyd S. Tinder; and John A. Waldrop, Jr.

Committee planning resulted in a major festival with a reenactment of this reading at the new courthouse on Parham Road on August 5, 1976. The Common Glory Players of Williamsburg played the parts of the rider and citizens. The celebration included performances by the York County Fife and Drum Corps and the Fort Lee Army Band and a flyover by the Virginia Air National Guard. The 2079th USAR School acted as military escorts. More than three thousand citizens of Henrico, many of them costumed, were there to hear the reading—perhaps more people than heard it on the day two hundred years earlier.

Henrico County Historical Society

I attended a meeting of the Hanover County Historical Society at the invitation of Bruce English, chairman of the Hanover County Bicentennial Commission. After this experience, I was determined that Henrico would have its own historical society. Mrs. Joseph A. Brandon of the Varina Woman's Club offered to help. I introduced her to Mrs. Robert Foley of the Goochland County Historical Society. With expert advice from Mrs. Foley and funds provided by the Varina Woman's Club, Mrs. Brandon set up the Henrico County Historical Society and served as temporary president until the election of Col. Oliver J. Sands, Jr., at the first meeting on June 1, 1975. There were 200 charter members.

The Fort Harrison Lodge

The commission was contacted by the Veterans' Administration regarding an old stone lodge in Henrico which was slated to be torn down. The one-hundred-year-old building was in an excellent state of repair, but the federal government has a policy of tearing down all empty buildings. We voted to use the building for much needed office, storage, and meeting space. The Henrico County Historical Society was invited to use a room for their growing historical library.

The Official Henrico County Commemorative Medal

Because I am an artist, the commission requested that I design a coin-size medal to be minted in bronze and fine silver. The obverse side of the medal depicts the Indian princess Pocahontas who played a significant role in the successful settlement of the English in Henrico. After she became a Christian, Pocahontas married John Rolfe, and they had one son, Thomas. Through her influence, peace was maintained between the Indians and the English. The reverse side of the medal illustrates the landing on eastern Henrico soil just eight days after the landing at Jamestown. The landing in Henrico was led by Capt. Christopher Newport.

The medals went on sale in 1975. They were so successful that Supervisor Eugene Rilee asked the commission to reorder so that all citizens could have a chance to buy one. This was done. All profits from the sales went toward the cost of having *The History of Henrico County* researched and written.

The Lost City of Henrico

There had been a mystery in Henrico for years. What had happened to the archaeological remains of the city of Henrico after it was burned during an Indian massacre in 1622? The commission voted to make an effort to find out and try to locate the original site of Henrico City. The Governor's Advisory Board on Archaeological Surveys took an interest in the project and gave William Kelso of the Virginia Research Center for Archaeology a grant of $2,000 to conduct the initial dig at the area traditionally believed to be the site of Henrico City. Only Indian artifacts were found. Kelso believed that there was still hope of finding the site of the city. So another more extensive dig was done using commission funds and matching funds from Lone Star Industries.

The Virginia Research Center for Archaeology report to the commissioner written by Martha W. McCarthey tells us that the city or the "Town of Henrico" has been destroyed. On file with the records of the commission, this report can be read in its entirety by those wishing to do further research.

The History of Henrico

Henrico County is one of the oldest political subdivisions in Virginia. When it was established in 1611, it covered a large part of the Commonwealth extending along both sides of the James River from its junction with the Appomattox to the Blue Ridge Mountains. From Henrico territory came the counties of Goochland Albemarle, Amherst, Fluvanna, Nelson, Chesterfield, Cumberland, Buckingham, and Powhatan and part of Appomattox County as well as the cities of Richmond, Charlottesville, and Colonial Heights.

The commission was told that a history could never be written because of the many records burned by British raiders in 1781. It was learned, however, that the courthouse was not damaged during the raid and some county records were not burned. The commission voted to try to work around the loss, and a history committee was appointed to investigate the feasibility of having a history written. The members were:

Col. Charles O. Frank, Jr. Mrs. Walter Lemon
Virginia Johnson Mrs. Jenny Nelson
George H. Moody Robert F. Smart
Henry L. Nelson, Jr.

Following the recommendation of this committee, the commission voted to have a history written. Charles M. Johnson called a joint meeting of the Board of Suprevisors and the bicentennial commission. The board gave its support and agreed to help fund the history project. A contract was signed in November 1975 with Clifford Dowdey and Louis Manarin to research and write this history.

During our work for the past ten years, our commission has suffered many setbacks and problems. Four of our members have died including the latest commission vice-chairman, George Moody. This history lost one of its greatest supporters with the untimely death of Charles M. Johnson, supervisor of the Brookland District, in the summer of 1981. The commission has, however, carried *The History of Henrico*

County to a good conclusion and is pleased to wish its readers an exciting trip through Henrico's past. May our past help light the way to our future as a county.

With love to the people of Henrico, I am

Jean Nelson Gibbons, Chairman

Henrico County Bicentennial Commission

Acknowledgments

The history of a geographical-political area is a mosaic of the interactions of the people who inhabit the area, reflected in governmental, political, and social institutions that they develop as their society evolves. The economic institutions developed to utilize the natural resouces and to provide the needs of the general citizenry are overriding influences. Just as there are many factors that go into the fabric of a history of a county, so there are many sources that provide the information to tell the story. Although this book is the product of our pens, we received assistance from many who provided information on a variety of aspects of Henrico and Virginia history.

We participated in developing the general outline of the book and divided the tasks of researching and writing. Shortly after work started on the first chapter, the combined task was assumed by the surviving author after the death of Clifford Dowdey. Although he was unable to contribute directly to the final product, his influence on the development of the basic outline and theme of the history are greatfully acknowledged. It was agreed that the history would not emphasize the genealogies of Henrico famlies but the history of Henricoans, their institutions, and the events that influenced their lives.

A book is the product of the authors' efforts, but as in history, many people assisted in the effort and in many ways influenced the final product. The late William M. E. Rachal, editor of the *Virginia Magazine of History and Biography,* shared freely of his knowledge of colonial Henrico, particularly social life in the county and sources on the early coal industry. He frequently gave his time just to talk over specific events and their relationships to the general history of the colony and state. The late Prentiss Price, genealogist, shared his extensive knowledge on Henrico families and made available files of the First Families of Virginia which are now on deposit in the state archives. The authors are also indebted to the late Robert L. Scribner, compiler of the seven-volume series of Revolutionary Virginia from 1763 to 1776 and to his assitant and successor, Brent Tarter, for allowing access to the source material relating to events in Henrico during that turbulent period.

To the staff of the archives, general library, and picture collection of the Virginia State Library a debt of gratitude is owed for their professional assistance. They never tired while running down obscure references to manuscripts, early editions, and pictures. Greatful acknowledgement is also given to the staffs of the Virginia Historical Society, the Valentine Museum, the Virginia Randolph Museum, the National Archives and Records Service, and the Office of Naval History. Their assistance was especially helpful while researching the educational, economic, military, and political aspects of Henrico history. Assistance in the area of county government, particularly on the twentieth-century annexation suits, was received from Thomas Owdom, municipal librarian for the county.

Valuable assistance was also received from a number of individuals. We wish to thank former county managers E. A. Beck and Frank A. Faison for taking time out of their busy schedules to discuss events that occurred during their terms and their general observations on Henrico's history and the current status of county administration and government. The work of Barbara D. Ecton, who researched the minutes of the Board of Supervisors from 1870 to 1980, is greatfully acknowledged. Her thoroughness has contributed greatly to the text. To Carlton N. McKenney, for sharing that part of his manuscript on "Rails in Richmond" relating to activity in Henrico, we are truly indebted. His technical knowledge on the subject was extremely helpful. A special note of thanks is also due to Charles Davenport Carrington for his assistance in tracking down information on claims after the Civil War, to H. Douglas Pitts for his assistance in developing the history of schools in the county around the turn of the twentieth century, and to George Moody for sharing his knowledge about the development of Henrico's schools and educational programs during the pre– and post–World War II period.

The members of the Henrico Bicentennial Commission were particularly helpful, and we wish to express our appreciation for their encouragement and guidance. Their willingness to share their knowledge about Henrico and their personal experiences contributed significantly to the manuscript, which they willingly took time to review. No manuscript can be produced without the diligent effort of a typist. We are especially appreciative of Peggy Williamson's abilities as a typist and her acute eye to detail. Her pleasant disposition made the task easier. To John S. Salmon and to the photographic studios and laboratories credited under the pictures, the authors wish to express a debt of gratitude. Their talents provide an added dimension to the text.

As is evident, this work has been produced with the assistance of many people. We would be remiss if we failed to recognize the contribution of our families. Through it all, they have supported and encouraged us, and we thank them for being so patient with us.

Louis H. Manarin
Clifford Dowdey

The History of
HENRICO COUNTY

The James River just above where Capt. Christopher Newport erected the cross. The many rocks in the river prevented further exploration by boat. (Photograph by John S. Salmon)

CHAPTER I

A City in the Wilderness

The present geographical-political area known as Henrico County can trace its origins back to 1634. In that year, it was established as one of the eight original shires of Virginia and included all the land on both sides of the James River from Charles City County west to the mountains. In time, nine counties, part of another county, and the city of Richmond would be cut from Henrico. Today, the county is 245 square miles in size.

When the English settlers came in 1607, they discovered the tidewater area was inhabited by Indians. Algonquian tribes had moved down from the north during the sixteenth century and had occupied the coastal plains from New England to central North Carolina. By the beginning of the seventeenth century, they were restricted to the land east of the fall line. In Virginia the country west of the falls was claimed by Siouan tribes, and the Iroquoian tribes occupied the lands west and south of the Siouan tribes and near the coast south of the James.[1]

Nearly all the tribes in the Virginia Tidewater were members of a nation, or confederacy, ruled by Wahunsonacock, also known as Powhatan. When he inherited control around 1595, there were six tribes, all within fifty miles of the falls on the James. These were the Arrohattoc, Appomattoc, Mattaponi, Pamunkey, Powhatan, and Youghtanund. Within a few years, he brought at least twenty-five tribes under his control. Powhatan's empire was subdivided into tribes, or tribal divisions, and each had a well-defined territory. Each division had a governmental hierarchy consisting of the cockarouse or sachem; the werowance, or war leader; the tribal council; and the priests.[2]

Powhatan's confederacy was in reality a loose knit organization of tribes who owed allegiance to Powhatan out of respect, heredity, or fear. Power and influence depended on the energy of the leaders, and not on a form of government. With increased pressure from the hostile Siouan tribes, the arrival of the settlers gave Powhatan an opportunity to negotiate for an alliance to strengthen his position. Powhatan's confederacy served as a buffer for the English settlers, but he always sought to work out a policy with the English to insure his interest.

Within his territorial domain, Powhatan had three places of residence. His favorite was Werowocomoco, situated about ten miles from Jamestown, north of the Pamunkey River. Orapakes, at the head of the Chickahominy River, is where he lived until a few years after the English settled Jamestown. The third village, just below the falls of the James River, was known as Powhatan, which means "falls in a current." Because it was one of Powhatan's residences and a primary point of contact between the Indians and the settlers, the name was later applied to Powhatan, his tribe, and his confederacy.[3]

Powhatan was the principal Indian village within the present confines of Henrico County and was inhabited by Powhatan's own tribe. Seated on a hill opposite three islands, the village consisted of some twelve houses with cornfields around it. After visiting the town, Capt. John Smith remarked: "The place is very pleasant and strong by nature."[4]

One of Powhatan's sons, Parahunt (called Tanxpowatan or Little Powhatan by the settlers) was chief of the village. The total population of the village was about 150 in 1607; of these, 40 were warriors. Twelve miles downriver from Powhatan lived the Arrohattoc tribe, with approximately 120 members, of whom 30 were warriors.[5] These two villages were connected by a well-traveled path, as were all the villages. Near Powhatan, the main north-south trading path intersected with the path running down to Arrohattoc and eastward. A trail marked by three notches on the trees ran along the north bank of the river westward from Powhatan to the mountains.[6]

These early inhabitants of Henrico County lived in mat- or bark-covered lodges constructed close together and sometimes encircled by palisades. One English adventurer reported:

Captain John Smith trading with Powhatan Indians on the James River in 1607. (Smithsonian Institution, National Museum of Natural History).

Powhatan. From John Smith's map of Virginia, 1612.

They goe all naked, save their privityes; yet, in coole weather, they weare deare-skinns, with the hayre on, loose. Some have leather stockings up to their twists, and sandalls on their feet. Their hayre is black generally, which they weare long on the left side, tyed up on a knott; about which knott the kings and best among them have a kind of coronett of deare's hayre colored redd. Some have chaines of long, linckt copper about their necks, and some chaines of pearle. The common sort stick long fethers in this knott. . . . Their skin is tawny; not so borne, but with dying and paynting themselves, in which they delight greatly. The wemen are like the men, onely this difference—their hayre groweth long al over their heads, save clipt somewhat short afore. These do all the labour, and the men hunt and goe at their plesure. They live comonly by the water-side, in little cottages made of canes and reeds, covered with the barke of trees. They dwell, as I guesse, by families of kindred and allyance, soe fortie or fiftie in a hatto or small village; which townes are not past a myle asunder in most places. They live upon sodden wheat, beanes, and pease, for the most part; also they kill deare, take fish in their weares, and kill fowl aboundance. They eate often, and that liberally.[7]

The first encounter between the white settlers and the Indians in Henrico County occurred shortly after the colonists landed to establish the fortified settlement that became Jamestown.[8] Following instructions to explore the source of any rivers, an expedition was sent up the river the Indians called Powhatan's river, which the settlers named after their king, James I. Capt. Christopher Newport, a one-armed veteran of raids on the Spanish West Indies, commanded the party of twenty-two men, which included five gentlemen, four mariners, and fourteen sailors. Notable among these were Capt. Gabriel Archer, Capt. John Smith and George Percy, Esq.[9]

After fitting out a shallop built by the adventurers after their arrival, Captain Newport departed around noon on May 21, 1607, "with a perfect resolutyon not to returne, but either to finde the head of this ryver, the laake mentyoned by others heretofore, the sea againe, the mountaynes Apalatsi [Appalachian] or some issue." Their movements did not go unobserved by the Indians. The first night was spent at the village of the Paspeheagh tribe at the mouth of the Chickahominy River. The next day the explorers proceeded up the river to "an ilet, on which were many turkeys, and greate store of young byrdes like blackbirdes."[10] Here the men had breakfast. Before resuming their journey, they encountered eight Indians in a canoe, and after displays of friendship, one of the Indians drew a map of the river. This band of Indians preceded Newport's party as it continued up the river. The Indians upriver brought food to the riverbank as the party came in sight, and when the explorers came ashore at day's end at a place they called "Poore Cottage," the Indians entertained them. The next day, Saturday, May 23, Newport and his men proceeded up the river five miles from "Poore Cottage" and went ashore at the village of the Arrohattoc. Here they met the leader of the tribe, and later Powhatan himself came to the village. Newport's account of his explorations contains a description of the first meeting of whites and Indians on Henrico soil.

We found here a wiroans (for so they called their kyngs), who satt upon a matt of reeds, with his people about him. He caused one to be layd for Capt. Newport; gave us a deare roasted, which, according to their custome, they seethed againe. His people gave us mullberyes, sodd wheate, and beanes; and he caused his weomen to make cakes for us. He gave our captain his crowne; which was of deare's hayre, dyed redd. Certifying him of our intentyon up the ryver, he was willing to send guydes with us. This we found to be a kyng subject to Pawatah (the chief of all the kyngdomes). His name is Arahatec; the country, Arahatecoh. Now, as we satt merye banquetting with them, seeing their dauncs and taking tabacco, newes came that the greate Kyng Powatah was come: at whose presence they all rose of their matts (save the Kyng Arahatec), separated themselves aparte, in fashion of a guard; and, with a long shout, they saluated him. Him wee saluted with silence; sitting still on our matts, our captain in the myddest; but presented (as before we dyd to Kyng Arahatec) gifts of dyvers sorts—as pennyknyves, sheeres, belles, beades, glass toyes, &c.—more amply than before. Now, this king appointed five men to guyde us up the river, and sent posts before to provyde us victuall.[11]

The explorers left the village they called "Aratahec's Joye" and proceeded up the river to an island opposite the village of the Powhatans, which they called Powhatan's Tower. The scribe recorded the events.

Heere we were conducted up the hill to the kyng; with whome we found our kinde Kyng Aratahec. Thes two satt by themselves aparte from all the rest (save one who satt by Powatah; and what he was I could not gesse, but they told me he was no wiroans). Many of his company satt on either syde; and the matts for us were layde right over against the kynge's. He caused his weomen to bring us vittailes, mulberyes, strawberryes, &c; but our best entertaynment was frendly wellcome. In discoursing with him, we founde that all the kyndgomes . . . were frends with him, and, to use his owne worde, *cheisc;* which is, "all one with him or under him."

During the discussion that followed, the English convinced Powhatan of their friendly intentions, and he "moved, of his own accord, a league of fryndship."[12]

Continuing their journey, the party rowed up the river to the falls. The majestic beauty of nature's creation undisturbed by man was greeted with a sense of awe, but not without an eye for economic potential. "Here the water falles downe through great mayne rocks from ledges of rocks above, two fadome highe; in which fall it maketh divers little iletts, on which might be placed a hundred water-milnes for any uses," noted the scribe. They observed that "shippes of two hundred or three hundred toone may come to within five myle hereof, and the rest [of the way is] deep inoughe for barges or small vessells that drawe not above six foote water."[13] Captain Smith described the same scene.

We were intercepted with great craggy stones in the midst of the river, where the water falleth so rudely, and with such a violence, as not any boat can possibly passe, and so broad disperseth the streame, as there is not past five or sixe Foote at low water, and to the shore scarce passage with a barge, the water floweth foure foote, and the freshes by reason of the Rockes have left markes of the inundations 8. or 9. foote: The south side is plain low ground, and the north side high mountaines, the rockes being of a gravelly nature, interlaced with many vains of glistring spangles.[14]

With mixed feelings of "content and greefe" the men retired down river and anchored between the island and the riverbank below Powhatan's village. They were satisfied that they could go no farther by water and determined to return to the falls to find a land route around them.

Palisaded Indian town similar to Powhatan's town at the falls. From Robert Beverley, *The History of Virginia in Four Parts* (Richmond, 1855), p. 136.

Indians of the Powhatan confederation. From Robert Beverley, *The History of Virginia in Four Parts* (Richmond, 1855), p. 137.

The next day was Sunday, May 24, Whitsunday, and Captain Newport entertained Powhatan at dinner. When questioned about the river above the falls, Powhatan informed Newport that he would meet him at the falls. After the meal, Newport and his men went up the river and Powhatan met them "upon the bank by the overfall." During the discussion, Powhatan left the impression that he would not look with favor on any expedition above the falls. Newport decided not to antagonize Powhatan and returned to his boat. While the party moved downriver Powhatan and his band returned to their village on foot.

As Newport's boat moved past one of the islands, he decided to claim the land for King James I. "So, upon one of the little iletts at the mouth of the falls, he sett up a crosse, with this inscriptyon,—'Iacobus, Rex, 1607;' and his owne name belowe." A prayer for the king, which included a petition for a successful journey, was offered. Then Newport claimed the river and land for the king, and he and his men offered up a cheer for the monarch. Percy reported that they "set up a Crosse at the head of the River, naming it Kings River," and "proclaimed James King of England to have the most right unto it." To quell any fears their Indian guides might have had, Captain Newport explained that the two arms of the cross signified Powhatan and himself and the point where they united signified their league of friendship.[15]

Newport then proceeded to Powhatan's village where he went ashore to present Powhatan with a hatchet. The Indians were not completely satisfied that the colonists were only there to explore. Some believed that the explorations might result in permanent settlements. Percy related that one Indian "made answere againe very wisely of a Savage" when he explained to another Indian: "Why should you bee offended with them as long as they hurt you not, nor take anything away by force, they take but a little waste ground, which doth you nor any of us any good." The Indian chief was pleased with the explanation of the cross as described by the Indian guide, and Newport and his men departed with several shouts of recognition for Powhatan. That night the band of explorers anchored at Arrohattoc. The tribal chief was very sick from the "hott dryncks" consumed the day before and sent his regrets. The next day, May 25, the chief welcomed them with a feast. On this day the Indians showed the colonists how to plant corn and presented them with a quantity of tobacco, nuts, and berries. Newport related that "they would shew us anything we demanded; and laboured very much, by signes, to make us understand their languadg."[16] That evening Newport and his men dropped downriver, and the next day they visited several villages. Returning to Jamestown on May 27, Newport learned that hostile Indians had attacked the settlement the previous day and were still in the area.

This was the first of many exploratory missions carried out by the colonists in the first few years of the settlement. They were years of struggle for survival from the elements, Indians, and Spaniards. Although their mission was to explore and to exploit, settlement was a means to that end; a strong colony had to be planted before further exploration and settlement could be undertaken. The band of adventurers was under the authority of the Virginia Company of London, a private undertaking chartered by the crown to settle Virginia. The members of the company saw the colony as a potentially profit-making commercial, agricultural, or industrial venture. Throughout its first decade, Virginia was essentially a military post serving a trading company.

In September 1608 Captain Newport received instructions to complete the exploration of the James River above the falls. With 120 men, Newport sailed up the James to the falls and went ashore on the south bank. After a forty-mile march without reaching the headwaters of the river, he turned back. On the two-and-a-half-day march, his party encountered two Indian villages, but the natives hid their corn and refused to trade with them. The next recorded visit to the falls occurred in the spring of 1609. In an effort to gather needed supplies, Capt. John Smith, president of the governing council, dispersed the colonists. He sent Master West with twenty men up to the falls to search for food. They found nothing except a few acorns and returned to Jamestown.[17]

In early June 1609 Sir Thomas Gates sailed from England on the *Sea Venture* with a new charter. His instructions were to retain Jamestown as a port and to establish two additional plantations or settlements, one at the falls of the James River

Captain John Smith (1580–1631). During the early colonization period, Smith was very active in building defenses at the falls where the city of Richmond was later established. From Robert Alonzo Brock, *Hardesty's Historical and Geographical Encyclopedia Illustrated* (New York, 1885), opp. p. 336.

Captain John Smith showing a compass to the Indians. From Thomas Wentworth Higginson, *Young Folks' History of the United States* (New York, 1904), p. 116.

and the other near "Roanoke." A violent storm scattered his fleet during the voyage; the *Sea Venture* survived the storm only to be cast on some rocks off the coast of Bermuda. After building two small boats, the survivors continued their voyage to Virginia, arriving in May 1610. Seven of Gates's vessels had survived the storm and dropped anchor at Jamestown in August 1609 while Gates was still in Bermuda. These ships brought four hundred settlers, and their leaders challenged Smith's authority to rule. To relieve the tension and disperse the colonists in groups large enough for defense but small enough to subsist, Smith sent Capt. Francis West, twenty-two-year-old brother of Baron De La Warr, to the falls with 120 men. Capt. John Martin was sent "with near as many to Nansemond."[18]

Captain West proceeded with his men to the falls. There he purchased land from the Indians and "erected . . . a fort, calling yt Wests' Fort." West then left to return to Jamestown. When Captain Smith arrived at the falls to inspect the fort, he "found his [West's] company planted so inconsiderately in a place not only subject to the river's inundation but round environed with many intolerable inconviences." Smith negotiated with Powhatan's son, Tanxpowhatan, and purchased the village known as Powhatan. In exchange, Smith promised to protect the Indians from the Monocans and traded Henry Spelman, one of the colonists, and some pieces of copper for "the fort and houses." West's men were then ordered to move to the village, but they refused. After nine days of trying to get them to obey, Smith boarded a ship and left for Jamestown. While his ship moved downriver, West's men were attacked by the Indians; several were killed and the survivors were driven into the woods. Smith's boat was grounded, and he returned to negotiate a peace that resulted in the expulsion of six or seven of the men. He stationed the remainder of the force at Powhatan, which he described as "ready built and prettily fortified with poles and barks of trees sufficient to have defended them from all the savages of Virginia; dry houses for lodgings and near two hundred acres of ground ready to be planted; and no place we knew so strong, so pleasant and delightful in Virginia, for which we called it Non such."[19] No sooner had the men settled in than Captain West returned and moved his men back to

West's Fort. Captain Smith was wounded in an accident on his return to Jamestown, and he left the colony on October 4, 1609. After losing several men to Indian attacks, Captain West abandoned the fort and returned to Jamestown.

The effort to establish a fort at the falls was temporarily abandoned, and as winter set in, the colonists faced one of the most difficult periods in the history of the infant settlement. Food became scarce, and the combination of hunger, cold weather, and disease contributed to a high mortality rate. In October 1609 there were approximately 500 settlers. Within a six-month period, only 60 remained alive. In May 1610, Sir Thomas Gates arrived with the crew and passengers of the *Sea Venture*. With another 150 souls to provide for and little prospect of increasing the food supply, the decision was made to abandon Jamestown and the colony in early June, but just as the survivors were leaving, Baron De La Warr arrived with 300 more colonists and sufficient provisions to reestablish the colony.

Lord De La Warr brought stability to the colony by ruling with a firm hand. While governor, he established a fort "at the Falles, upon an Island invironed also with Corne ground," intending to use it as a base to send out detachments to explore for minerals. The Indians attacked the fort and killed three or four of his men. De La Warr's poor health forced him to abandon his effort, and he left in March 1611.[20]

In May 1611, Sir Thomas Dale arrived with 300 more colonists, a new code of justice, and instructions to establish a town farther up the river. On May 21 at a council meeting the decision was made to "go up unto the falls ward to search and advise upon a seate for a new towne, with 200 men, where we will set downe and build houses as fast as we may." Dale proposed to eliminate the Indian problem from the peninsula bordered by the James and York rivers by establishing posts at, or near, the Indian villages. He was convinced that "by the severall Plantations and Seates which I would make I shold so over master the subtile-mischeivous Great Powhatat, that I should leave him either no roome in his countrie to harbour in, or drawe him to a firme association with ourselves." After surveying the James up to the falls, he decided to establish two settlements on the river above Jamestown. The first site chosen, near Arrohattoc, was described as "a convenient strong, healthie and sweete seate to plant a new Towne . . . the Title and Name, which it hath pleased the Lords allreadie to appoint for it." The site of the second settlement was "tenn miles above this, to command the head of the River, and the many fruit full Islands in the same."[21]

Powhatan sent messengers to Dale to tell him not to move up the river. Ignoring the warning, Dale led an expedition to the falls, and one night while the men were at prayer, "a strange noise was heard cominge out of the corne towards the trenches . . . like an Indian 'hup hup' with an 'Oho Oho.' The men reported seeing one Indian leap over their fire. In the darkness, confusion reigned as the men sought to arm themselves against an unseen enemy. The affair lasted about fifteen minutes, and when they began to counterattack, they discovered that the Indians had retired. The only injuries were bruises received in the haste to arm themselves. This incident did not deter Dale. In August, he received reinforcements when Sir Thomas Gates arrived with some three hundred more colonists and "with a plentiful Supply of Hogs, Cattle, Fowls, &c. with a good Quantity of Ammunition, and all other Things necessary for a new Colony.[22]

Gates assumed the presidency of the governing council and assented to Dale's plans. Early in September, Dale moved up the river to establish the colony's second settlement. He had already had "timber, pales, posts and railes" prepared "for the present impaling this new Towne to secure himselfe and men from the mallice and trechery of the Indians." A part of Dale's men rowed up to the site, on present-day Farrar's Island, while a contingent under Capt. Edward Brewster marched overland. True to his word, Powhatan sent some of his warriors to attack the column. Resorting to hit-and-run tactics, the Indians under "Jacke of the Feathers" managed to harass but did not deter Captain Brewster and his men. Dale established his town, which he called Henrico in honor of Henry Frederick, Prince of Wales, James I's son, at or very near Arrohattoc "upon a neck of very high land, 3 parts thereof environed with the main River." As a defensive measure, Dale erected a log fence known as a pale across the narrow end of the neck of land to make it an island. Within ten to twelve days, the men had impaled "seven English Acres of ground for a towne." Powhatan's skilled bowmen continued to harass the Englishmen as the fort and palisade took shape, sending arrows over the walls at such a high trajectory that they dropped down on the unsuspecting men inside.[23]

Dale confidently expected that the new town would replace Jamestown as the principal seat of the colony, for the location upriver provided security from possible Spanish attack. As commander of the settlement at Henrico, Dale governed according to the new laws with stern punishment for those who violated them. His military training served him well in the presence of hostile Indians, but the harshness of Dale's rule led many settlers to leave against his orders. Some were captured and tortured by the Indians, and others were apprehended and punished by the colonists. One contemporary account noted that Dale "oppressed his whole companye with such extra-ordinarye labors by daye and watchinge by night, as maye seeme incredible to the eares of any who had not the experimentall triall thereof." The lack of shelter and hunger "made those imposed labours most insufferable."[24]

After the fence was constructed around the townsite, watchtowers were constructed at each of the four corners. "A faire and handsome Church, and storehouses" were built first, and then Dale set his men to constructing lodgings that "were more strongly and more handsome then any formely in Virginia." Within four months, Dale "had made Henrico much better and of more worth than all the worke ever since the Colonie began." Robert Johnson, a contemporary, described Henrico Town as "strong and defensible by nature, a good aire, wholesome and cleere (unlike the marish seat at James towne) with fresh and plentie of water springs, much faire and open grounds freed from woods and wood enough at hand." In addition to housing, each man was allotted sufficient ground "for his orchard and garden to plant at his pleasure and for his own use."[25]

"The spade men fell to digging, the brick men burnt their bricks, the compay cut down wood, the Carpenters fell to squaring out, the Sawyers to sawing, the Souldiers to fortifying, and every man to some what." As a result of his stern authoritarian methods, Dale saw a town rise out of the wilderness. As seen by a contemporary, Henrico consisted of "3 streets of well-framed houses, a hansom Church, and the foundation of a more stately one laid, of Brick, in lenghth, an hundred foote, and fifty foot wide, beside Store houses, watch houses, and such like." The town was defended by five blockhouses along the river and a paled fence two miles inland which stretched two miles across the peninsula from river to river. A ditch was apparently dug on the mainland side of the palisade. Such a defensive excavation was used in the Low Countries where Dale had seen extensive military service. The area got its name, Dale's Dutch Gap, from this ditch. The land between the town and the paled fence was set aside for farming. Writing in 1746, William Stith noted that "there may still be seen upon the River Bank within the Island the Ruins of a great Ditch, now overgrown with large and stately trees."[26]

Once the town was established, the settlement began to grow, and land on the south side of the river was enclosed. About twelve English miles were palisaded, and parts of the area were named Hope in Faith and "Coxen-Dale" (Coxendale). A "retreat or guest house for sick people" was built with "fourscore lodgings" and it was called Mount Malady. Elizabeth Fort, Charity Fort, and Fort Patience were constructed to defend the settlement on the south side. There, also, the Reverend Alexander Whitaker, minister of Henrico Church, built a frame parsonage known as Rock Hall on one hundred acres of land. Five miles downriver, the Appomattoc Indians were driven from their land on the south side of the James at the juncture with the Appomattox River, and a settlement known as Bermuda Hundred was established.[27]

In 1612 John Rolfe imported some tobacco seeds from Trinidad and began to cultivate a new strain of mild tobacco. He shipped part of his crop to the mother country in 1614. The tobacco was mild enough for English tastes and proved to be the marketable product the company needed. The colonists began to plant tobacco, and by 1619 "Virginia went tobacco mad."[28] To insure survival, Dale directed that at least two acres of corn be planted for each man. Hostilities continued with the Indians, and colonists who strayed from the settlements were frequently attacked.

A period of peace followed the marriage of John Rolfe to

Henry Frederick, Prince of Wales, for whom the town of Henrico and later
the county were named. Drawing by Isaac Oliver. (Duke of Buccleuch and
Queensberry, K.T. From a collection at Drumlanrig Castle, Thornhill, Dum-
fries-Shire, Scotland.)

Powhatan's daughter, Pocahontas. Capt. Samuel Argall had captured her along the Potomac River in March 1613, and brought her to Jamestown to be used as a pawn in negotiations for the return of some colonists held by Powhatan. The old chief refused to negotiate, and Pocahontas was entrusted to the Reverend Alexander Whitaker, minister at the church at Henrico Town, which was the first parish church in Henrico. There Pocahontas was converted to Christianity and baptised Rebecca. In April 1614, she married John Rolfe, and this union brought peace between Powhatan's people and the settlers.[29]

The towns of Henrico and Jamestown symbolized the company's policy that towns and town life should be the basic unit of company settlement and thus facilitate company control. Dale did modify the land policy by allowing settlers to work the land in common, and he did allow some to occupy land. The settlers sought more freedom from company rule and began moving beyond the limits of the towns and palisaded lands; as a result, the towns quickly fell into decay. The buildings at Henrico did not "stande above five yeares and that not without continuall reparations." The foundation of the brick church was never finished. When Dale left the colony in 1616, Henrico Town was the "furthest habitacion into the Land," but there were only 38 men and boys living in and around the town. John Rolfe reported in 1616 that the town was under the command of Captain Smalley in the absence of Capt. James Davis. The Reverend William Wickham was reported as minister at Henrico. Twenty-two of the inhabitants were farmers, and the rest were officers, "all which manytayne themselves with food and apparrell." Downriver at Bermuda Hundred, where Captain Yeardley was commander and Alexander Whitaker was minister, Rolfe reported 119 settlers.[30]

When Dale returned to England in 1616, he took John Rolfe, his wife, Pocahontas, and their son, Thomas. She never returned to her native land. After her reception by British royalty, she died at Gravesend, England, while preparing to return to Virginia, in March 1617. That same spring, the Reverend Mr. Whitaker, her teacher, drowned in the James River. Known as the "Apostle of Virginia," Whitaker, the son of the master of Saint John's College, Cam-

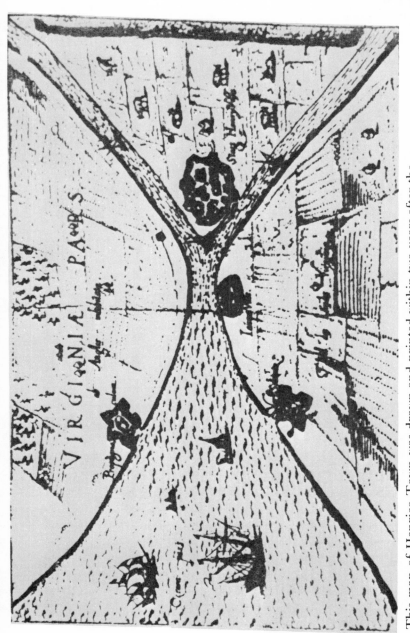

This map of Henrico Town was drawn and printed within two years after the town was built in 1611. The map is not topographically accurate, but to the right of center Henrico Town is identified as "Statt Henry Ville." To the right of Henrico Town, along the right-hand border of the map, is Sir Thomas Dale's fortified ditch. Several buildings and a church appear within the palisade surrounding the town. Across the river from Henrico Town is James-town, identified as "Jacque Ville." (Virginia State Library)

The marriage of Pocahontas and John Rolfe. By Henry Brueckner. (Virginia State Library)

The Sedgeford Hall portrait of Pocahontas and her son, Thomas. Origin unknown. (Virginia State Library)

bridge, and a graduate of that institution, had left a good comfortable living to travel to Virginia with Dale to carry the "True Faith" to the "savages."[31]

One of the principal missions of the London Company was to educate the Indians. Contact with the Indians did not always result in the display of Christian principles, for the struggle to establish a permanent settlement necessitated the use of force to convince the Indians that the colonists were determined to stay. But the belief that the conversion of the Indians was a necessary activity of settlement did not wane. Following Pocahontas's visit, King James I issued a letter to the archbishops urging them to support the London Company's efforts to propagate the Gospel. He authorized two special collections each year for two years and directed that the collections were to be given to the London Company for that purpose.[32]

The leaders of the London Company sought to relax the company's rule and provide for the social, economic, and educational needs of the colony. Lord De La Warr was sent as the new governor in April 1618 with instructions to make changes, but he died in June during the voyage to the colony. Sir George Yeardley was elected governor in November 1618 and arrived in the colony in April 1619, bringing with him instructions calling for a new form of government with a representative assembly. The colony was divided into "four cities or boroughs namely the chief city called James Town, Charles City, Henrico, and the Borough of Kiccotan." The city of Henrico was also referred to as a borough and as a corporation. It included the town of Henrico and the neighboring settlements on both sides of the river and extended from Charles City to the falls on the James River. At Henrico, there were only "two or three old houses, a poor ruinated church with some few poore buildings in the Island; Coxen Dale and the Maine and at arrahatocke one house."[33]

The arrival of new immigrants and the problems of soil depletion became factors in the adoption of new policies toward land use and ownership. Governor Samuel Argall, Yeardley's predecessor, had estimated in 1618 that the soil would only last three years. Land was set aside in each city or borough for company tenants and for support of the settlement. Provisions were also made to provide land to adventurers and to those who paid passage for colonists under the headright system. Three thousand acres in Henrico were designated as company lands to be occupied by the company's tenants for half profits. Ten thousand acres granted for the support of "a University and College" at Henrico were situated on the north side of the river from Henrico to the falls. Another 1,000 acres were set aside for the college for the conversion of infidels.[34]

Under the provisions of his instructions, Governor Yeardley called for elections in each of the eleven settlements. Two delegates were to be elected from each settlement to form a House of Burgesses. On July 30, 1619, the first representative assembly met in the church at Jamestown. The two representatives from Henrico were Thomas Dowse and John Polentine. At this meeting, the burgesses approved the new company regulations, drafted some petitions, debated and passed laws, and adjourned because of the heat. One law called for each settlement to take in and prepare Indian children "so to be fitted for the Colledge intended for them." They petitioned the company "that towards the erecting of the University and Colledge they will sende, when they shall thinke most convenient, workmen of all sorte fit for that purpose."[35]

The company soon notified the colony that it was sending fifty tenants to cultivate the college land under Capt. William Weldon. But when they arrived in November 1619, no preparations had been made to house them. Captain Weldon hired out thirty of the tenants and settled the remainder at Arrohattoc where he found two houses. Dissatisfied with Weldon's action, the company selected George Thorpe to take charge of managing the college land and tenants on April 3, 1620. Thorpe was a gentleman of King James's privy chamber, a member of the council of the Virginia Company, and one of the partners in the Berkeley Hundred settlement. Arriving in the colony in March 1620 to manage the settlement, Thorpe undertook his new responsibility at the college with "a selfless zeal rarely equalled in those early days." He was considered by one of his contemporaries as "an Angell from Heaven." Since the college was to be supported in part from the agricultural labors of the tenants, Thorpe sought to diversify by experimenting with silk culture and setting out grapevines.[36]

The college at Henrico was established to Christianize Indian children and to make the Indians useful members of society. The children of the colonists were to receive their education at the East India School at Charles City Point, and by 1621 it was felt that they would continue their education at the college. The effort to convert the Indians was a direct threat to their own culture. Thorpe approached his task with a sincere desire to improve relations with the Indians, but with a zeal and enthusiasm that required Christian conversion. He felt that the attitude of the colonists toward the Indians should be changed and that the company should proclaim its support of his proselytizing efforts. Seeking to convert Opechancanough, the leader of the Powhatan, Thorpe built him a house with the idea that creature comforts would facilitate conversion. Thorpe believed he detected a response in Opechancanough, but later events proved that Thorpe failed in his efforts.[37]

Across the river at Falling Creek, efforts to establish ironworks had progressed little since the discovery of sufficient deposits of ore in 1619 to warrant construction of a furnace. In 1621 John Berkeley, an experienced ironworks proprietor from Beverstone, Gloucestershire, was transported to the colony to manage the project. He brought his son, Maurice, and twenty skilled workers with him. Funds amounting to £14,000, which had been raised to support the university, were invested in the ironworks. Berkeley established the foundry on the banks of Falling Creek and promised to have it operational by Easter 1622.[38]

When Captain Weldon arrived to settle his men on the college land north of Henrico, he found several prime tracts claimed by others under grants from Governor Argall. These men were directed to "depart and take ground elsewhere." Between 1619 and 1621 some forty-two ships were sent over by the company and brought 3,570 men and women "for Plantation." By 1622 there were some twenty-five settlements in the colony and "neere 80 severall Planations and dividents." South of the James, settlements were clustered in the Bermuda Hundred area, but some land was occupied on Kingsland and Proctor's creeks and in the Coxendale area across the river from the town of Henrico.[39]

The increased numbers and aggressive expansion of settlements caused apprehension among the Indians, and they made plans to expel the settlers. On Good Friday, March 22, 1622, a secretly planned coordinated attack on the numerous settlements was carried out. The Indians gained entrance into the settlements on the pretext of friendly visits and then struck without warning. Their mission was annihilation. Some settlers escaped to warn other settlements, and a friendly Indian warned those at Jamestown. The plantations and outlying settlements suffered the most from the Indians' fury. At Falling Creek, the ironworks were destroyed. John Berkeley and twenty-one men, two women and three children were killed. The ironworks were wrecked, and the tools and machinery were thrown into the creek. Thomas Sheffield, his wife, eight men, one woman, and two boys were killed at his plantation three miles from Falling Creek. Five people were reported killed at Henrico Island, and seventeen men lost their lives at the college. When informed of the attack, George Thorpe, believing that he could reason with the attackers, went out unarmed to talk with them. "They not only wilfully murdered him, but cruelly and [wil]felly, out of devillish malace, did so many barbarous despights and foule scornes after to his dead corpes, as are unbefitting to be heard by any civill eare." Similar acts were carried out on others killed during the attacks. In all, some 347 colonists were reported killed.[40]

The Indians did not succeed in driving the settlers from the colony, but the well-executed plan of coordinated attacks forced the settlers to concentrate and to abandon some of the settlements. On April 20, 1622, Capt. Roger Smyth was ordered to remove "all the said people, and cattell, and goods at Henrico Island and Coxendale." The college, ironworks, and settlements north and south of the James River above its junction with the Appomattox were also evacuated.[41] Jamestown had been saved, but approximately one-third of the settlers in Virginia were slain. The news of the massacre was a terrible blow to the Virginia Company. At great expense it had undertaken efforts to develop the country and produce a return on the investment. The settlers retreated to Jamestown and other fortified settlements, and the territory above the junction of the Appomattox and James rivers was abandoned. The turbulent conditions were compounded by a general scarcity of food. The overcrowded fortified posts also encouraged the rapid spread of sickness.

After the initial shock, the colonists sent out forces to avenge those killed. The hope of conversion had given way to the despair of momentary defeat, engendering the wrath of vengeance by conquest. George Sandys led a punitive force against the Tappahanock opposite Jamestown, while the Chickahominy and Powhatan felt the full fury of expeditions led by Captains William Powell and John West. Few Indians were slain, but their homes were destroyed and their crops were either carried off or destroyed. For the next few years, expeditions against the Indians were conducted to push them away from the settled areas and to maintain pressure to prevent any surprise attacks.

By the end of the summer of 1622, thoughts turned to resettlement of the lands above the Appomattox-James junction. The "replanting" of Henrico and "the Colledg lands" was considered an "absolute necessite; lest the best fire that mantaines the acōon [action] here alive to be putt out." The governing council asked the company to send additional tenants to be settled on the company's land and that orchards and gardens be planted on the college land. The council felt that the brickmakers should be held to their agreement with Thorpe "to the intent that when opportunitie shalbe for the erecting of the fabricke of the Colledge, the materialls be not wanting." New arrivals were integrated with some of the older planters, and by January 1623 preparations were ready to resettle the college lands.[42]

Early in 1623 the colonists were allowed to return to their plantations and settlements to begin rebuilding and planting. Henrico had been "utterlie demolished by the Indians," and in August-September 1623 the fortifications were reported as "now gone to ruyne." Efforts to reestablish the town of Henrico failed. When it was proposed that a town be constructed of brick at Henrico, it was reported that "this must be performed at the publiqs charge for the people that are now there doe onlie worke for them selves & their p[ar]ticular owners and are so miserablie poore that all they can rayse by their private labour is hardlie sufficient to find them Corne to preserve them from starving, and to plant some Tobacco to find them clothes."[43]

Monuments erected on Farrar's Island commemorating the establishment of the town of Henrico and the three-hundredth anniversary of the founding of a church there. The original town site is believed to have been destroyed during excavation work on the Dutch Gap Canal. In 1859 a few scattered bricks along the sides of the Dutch Gap, where stood the nucleus of the settlement, were all that remained. By an act of the General Assembly, Farrar's Island was given to Chesterfield County in the 1920s. (Virginia State Library)

Within the Virginia Company, hostile factions developed and continued with such bitterness that two members of the company challenged each other to a duel. Although the appointment on the field of honor was averted, the situation had degenerated to such a degree that the administration of the company and its colony was affected. The king appointed a commission to go to Virginia on October 24, 1623. When the commission arrived, it was not received with any degree of enthusiasm or cooperation from the General Assembly that met in February 1624. However, the Assembly did "entreat your Lordships that we may retaine the libertie of our Generall Assemblie." The report filed by the commissioners described the efforts of the company and the colonists as failures and put the blame on the leaders in the colony and the company in London. The king brought suit against the company, and on May 24, 1624, the Court of the King's Bench handed down a decision against the company. Based on this decision and the generally poor conditions of the company and its colony, the company was dissolved, and Virginia became a royal colony.[44]

The transition from a company to a royal colony was interrupted by the death of King James I. In May 1625, over three years after the devastating attacks, only twenty-two inhabitants were reported residing in ten "dwelling-houses" in the corporation of Henrico. A total of twenty-three patents, consisting of 2,762 acres, had been issued for land south of the James, but the inhabitants were reported as being on the college lands. The landowners of Henrico, except for Francis Weston (or Wilton) and Edward Hobson, were either dead or living elsewhere. The land within the corporation of Henrico on the north side of the river was still reported as public lands in May 1625, reserved and laid out as follows: 3,000 acres: company land; 1,500 acres: common land; 10,000 acres: university land; and 1,000 acres: college land. No fortifications were reported. The twenty-two inhabitants were armed with "21 snap haunce pieces, 6 swords, 13 armors, 9½ pounds powder, and 52 pounds lead." They had "57 barrels of corn, 6½ bushels of pease and beans, 1,800 fish, wet and dry," and one hog.[45] The Indians had taken the rest of their livestock. The presence of hostile Indians made any efforts to extend the settlements unsafe, and the lack of direction

The Indian massacre of 1622. From Alexander H. Stephens, *A Compendium of the History of the United States from the Earliest Settlements to 1872* (Columbia, S.C., 1872), p. 40.

from the company or crown in London further complicated the development of a settlement policy. For several years the colonists on the frontier in Henrico maintained the outpost by personal willpower. The town site of Henrico was abandoned, and fifteen years after the massacre of 1622, it was included in a 2,000-acre tract patented by William Farrar. Because it was owned by the Farrar family, specifically William Farrar, Sr., Henrico Island became known as Farrar's Island.

CHAPTER II

Frontier County

For the balance of the seventeenth century, conditions in the colony contributed to a gradual resettlement of the previously settled areas of Henrico and the advancement of the frontier beyond the riverbanks and westward above the falls. During this time, Henrico County experienced more active settlement along the Appomattox River and on the south side of the James River than on the north side of that river. After the massacre of 1622 the colonists conducted annual expeditions against the Indians. This practice did not change when the crown assumed control of the colony, and for several years the colonists carried out well-planned attacks against the Indians and pushed them farther into the wilderness. As the Indians were either assimilated or forced back, their lands were taken by the colonists.

The removal of the Indian threat, combined with the arrival of additional settlers, resulted in the advancement of the colonization effort up the rivers. By February 1625 there were 1,209 whites and 23 blacks reported in Virginia. Most of these settlers lived in small farming communities along the rivers. The population more than doubled by March 1628, when there were nearly 3,000 inhabitants in the colony. During this period, 1625-29, the original eastern bounds of the county were extended downriver to include the upper part of Charles City, and some of the older established settlements in that area contributed to the increase in the census figures. The names of the early colonial settlers along the James were the family names of Hereford, Gloucester, and Worcester counties and neighboring districts in England, Wales, and Ireland. By 1634 there were 4,914 inhabitants in the colony. Some 419 of these were in the county of Henrico, scattered on both sides of the river from Arrohattoc down to Shirley Hundred Island.

As the number of settlers increased and additional settlements took root, the institutions of government had to be extended to the regions remote from Jamestown. As early as August 1626 the colony's Council and General Court made provisions for "commissioners for the upper partes" to hold "monthlie Courtes." Sessions of the court were to be held "at the descretione of Mr. William Farrar, one of his Majesties Councell of state either at Jourdans Journey or Sherley hundred." By an act of the General Assembly adopted in February 1632, monthly courts were established in the "upper parts within the precincts of Charles City and Henrico." The members of the monthly court were called commissioners until around 1662 when they became known as justices of the peace. Originally the members of these courts could hear cases involving an amount less than five pounds sterling. They could also investigate petty crimes and take any necessary action to insure the safety of the people and maintain peace.[1]

Recognizing that the borough system was no longer adequate, the Council and General Court addressed the problem of governmental organization in 1634. Drawing on their English roots, they divided the country "into 8 shires which are to be governed as the shires in England." The original shires were James City, Henrico, Charles City, Elizabeth City, Warwick River, Warosquoyacke, Charles River, and Accomack. Henrico's boundaries were not changed. The county was described as lying west of Charles City on both sides of the James River and extending indefinitely westward. The term *shire* soon gave way to *county*. The act establishing the shires called for a county lieutenant of militia "to take care of the wars against the Indians," a sheriff, and a sergeant and/or bailiff "where need requires." One member of the Council was to attend and assist in each court, and the lieutenant was to serve as commissioner. The Assembly thus continued the court system already established and increased its duties and powers. The court not only administered justice but also provided local administration not carried out by the parish.[2]

The parishes were an integral part of the county government, and the governing body of the church was at first appointed by, and reported to, the court. Later the vestry was elected by the parishioners and reported to the court at least twice a year. The vestry consisted of twelve men who served as the governing body of the parish. Their duties also included activities in civil administration. They appointed the minister of the parish, insured the recording of vital statistics, investigated moral offenses, and presented offenders to the court. In addition, they determined the monetary needs of the parish and fixed the amount each parishioner was to pay to the support of the parish. Under the guidance of the court, they provided care for indigents and processioned the boundary lines of all privately owned land every four years.[3]

The date of the founding of Henrico Parish may be traced to 1611 when the city of Henrico was established, although sometimes it is dated from 1634, the year the shire was created. A land patent issued in 1635 refers to the glebe land on the north side of the river just opposite the island on which the 1611 town was built.[4] This land had been set aside for use by the church. The area was referred to as the Varinas in land patents issued in 1632, deriving its name from the resemblance of the tobacco grown there to a variety grown in Varina, Spain.

It was here at Varina that the civil, legal, and ecclesiastical center would be established as the county continued to grow. During the early years, the commissioners had no regular place to meet. They assembled for the monthly court sessions either at the home of one of the commissioners or at a public meeting place such as a tavern. The exact date of the establishment of Varina is not known, but it was the county seat of Henrico County long before the House of Burgesses legally established it as a town in 1680. The act for cohabitation and encouragement of trade and manufacture of 1680 called for laying out fifty acres "for a towne for storehouses, etc. . . . In Henrico county att Verina where the court house is." Under the provisions of the act, the county purchased the fifty acres for 10,000 pounds of tobacco and casks and would sell half-acre lots at 100 pounds of tobacco and casks to anyone who agreed to build a dwelling house and warehouse on the lot. If the dwelling house was not started within three months, the purchaser forfeited the land and the tobacco and casks. All agricultural and manufactured items produced in the county had to be transported to Varina for shipment, and all imports into the county had to come there. Failure to do so would result in loss of the shipment with one-half the value going to the crown and one-half to the informer. To encourage carpenters, sawyers, brickmakers, bricklayers, laborers, and "all other tradesmen whatsoever that will cohabitt, dwell and exercise their trades," they were exempt from paying taxes for five years and immune for the same length of time from arrest for debts previously contracted. Two years later the citizens were levied 540 pounds of tobacco for laying out the town according to these specifications.[5]

Even with the enticements to settle, the courthouse, the parish church, the public storehouse, and the import-export provisions of the act, Varina never developed into a commercial trade center. Situated as it was on the north bank of the James about ten miles below the falls and about ten miles above the junction of the Appomattox, the town was on the northern edge of the area of settlement.

Patents to the land that had been originally set aside as college and university lands on the north bank of the James were issued in 1632. Some land patents issued before 1634 refer to the land above Turkey Island Creek as being in the corporation of Charles City, but this area had been added to Henrico before 1629. Some of these early patents were issued for prior service in the colony, but most of the land was granted under the headright system of fifty acres for every person transported to the colony. The island on which the city of Henrico once stood was granted to William Farrar in 1637. Across the river, the old site of Mount Malady and Coxendale were granted to Thomas Osborne. Thomas Harris received a grant of 750 acres in November 1635, 100 acres of which was due him as "an Ancient planter & adventurer in the time of Sir Thomas Dale." His remaining 650 acres were received for transporting thirteen persons. Many of the early grants were issued to early adventurers or their heirs. Some of the land was never taken up and was declared vacated and granted a second time. The largest early patent was issued to Richard Cocke in 1636 for 3,000 acres. In 1639 only 2,000 acres were issued, "300 acres lying at Bremo" and "1700 acres upon the head of Turkey Island Creek called by the name of Mamburne [Malvern] hills."[6] By 1639 approximately sixty-six patents had been issued for over 30,000 acres on both sides of the James from Turkey Island to the falls.

At Varina approximately two hundred acres had been set

aside as glebe lands. Here a brick parsonage was built near the river and a wooden courthouse was erected inland adjoining the glebe land.[7] The first courthouse was a frame structure built on blocks. In 1688 John Fail, a carpenter, agreed to undertake necessary repairs to the courthouse for seven thousand pounds of tobacco and all materials salvaged. He was to put new girders, new rafters, reshingle, cut two windows in the wall at the gable, relay the floor outside the bar, replace the old blocks under the building, and repair the ground sills, and board the outside down to the ground. Standing near the courthouse was a large oak "with a widespreading limb occasionally used as a gallows." A jail was constructed near the courthouse and also a ducking stool to carry out some of the lighter sentences. In time, a tavern, a racetrack, and "quite a village" surrounded the courthouse. There on May 23, 1689, the accession of "Theire Royall Ma'sies William and Mary" to the throne was proclaimed with "fireing of guns, beat of drum, sound of trumpet and the universal Shouts and Huzzahs of the people assembled."[8]

The interrelationship of the civil and ecclesiastical bodies was accepted as part of the system. When Henry Elfton "sung and published certain libelous writings to the great disparagment of divers in the said county" of Henrico in 1649, he was punished by Capt. Thomas Harris, commander of the county militia. Elfton appealed to the General Court, but the court ruled that he "justly deserved much more" and directed him to "make public acknowledgement of his offense against the said Captain Harris in the Parish church of Henrico at the time of divine service and stand committed until he put in security for his good behavior." That same year Stafford Barlowe, undersheriff of the county, "misbehaved himself towards the commissioners and slandered divers others of good quality" and was "censured by the said commissioners to be whipped."[9]

The monthly courts were plural bodies, consisting of a number of justices, appointed by the governor, who served without pay. The commissioners were not all the same rank, however, for three of them were of the quorum, which meant that one of the three had to be present at each session of the court. In 1642 the Assembly set the number of meetings at six a year and provided a definite court day for each

Nathaniel Bacon leading his army. Sketch by Sidney King. From Charles W. H. Warner, *Road to Revolution: Virginia's Rebels from Bacon to Jefferson (1676–1776)* (Richmond, 1966), opp. p. 36. (Photograph by Thomas L. Williams)

Nathaniel Bacon reading the people's grievances at Middle Plantation (later Williamsburg), August 4, 1676. Sketch by Sidney King. From Charles W. H. Warner, *Road to Revolution: Virginia's Rebels from Bacon to Jefferson (1676–1776)* (Richmond, 1966), opp. p. 20. (Photograph by Thomas L. Williams)

county. Henrico court was set on the first day of every month, and although the law required six meetings, the court could hold extra sessions if necessary. On court day, the people would gather to witness the trials, meet friends, hear the news, and do their trading. The law of 1642 increased the limit for civil cases to sixteen hundred pounds of tobacco, and in 1645 the county courts were given jurisdiction to hear all cases, criminal and civil, in law and equity.[10]

Settlements had grown up on both sides of the Appomattox River, and the distance from the parish church necessitated they be "bounded into a parish by themselves." The new parish, called Bristol Parish, was established in 1643 and extended from the junction of the Appomattox and James rivers and up the Appomattox River to the falls. This area moved toward greater autonomy when its inhabitants were empowered to have "courts to be kept by commissioners residing in Bristoll parish." This court was to be similar to the county courts, "to hear and determine all differences within the said parish . . . and . . . treate with the Indians." Appeals from this parish court could be made to the county court in either Henrico or Charles City.[11]

Relations with the Indians became more relaxed as the settlements expanded. The annual punitive expeditions gave way as trade with the Indians increased, and a treaty of peace and friendship was made with the Indians in 1642. However, the Indians of the Powhatan confederacy, now under Opechancanough, still presented a united front against the encroachments of the English. On April 18, 1644, the Indians struck in surprise attacks and "fell severest on the South-side of James River, and on the Heads of the other Rivers; but chiefly on York River," wherever the vulnerable outlying farms were situated. About five hundred colonists were killed.[12] The survivors retreated to the older, more protected settlements. The two counties of Henrico and Charles City were ordered to "use theire best power against all theire Neighboring Indians, and to march out against the Tancks Weyanokes . . . as farre as theire Ammunition and Abilityes will enable them." Under Governor William Berkeley, the English mounted an offensive and drove the Indians back. Opechancanough was captured and confined at Jamestown where he was shot by one of the soldiers. A fort on the north bank of the James River at the falls had been authorized, and in the latter part of 1644 a stockade fort was built and called Fort Charles in honor of King Charles's son. At the falls of the Appomattox River, a fort to be known as Fort Henry was authorized in March 1645. The fort was located on the present site of the city of Petersburg. The act provided for a levy of forty-five men to defend the fort, with three men to be from Henrico. North of the James, two men from Henrico were part of a sixty-man expedition against the Indians.[13]

The frontier settlers were allowed to return to their homes in October 1644. By treaty, the Indians recognized the king of England as overlord, ceded the peninsula from the falls to the coast, recognized a line from the head of Blackwater River on the south to old Manakin Town on the north as a dividing line, and were allowed to trade only at specified forts. Severe punishment was to be meted out to anyone who ventured into the other's territory. To encourage the establishment of other forts, the Assembly passed an act appropriating land exempt from taxes for three years. The existing forts and all property, boats, and ammunition would be given to anyone who would maintain them. At the falls of the James, the land offered was on the south bank opposite Fort Charles. These forts became trading centers, particularly Fort Henry at the falls of the Appomattox. This fort was under the command of Capt. Abraham Wood, who opened an active trading business with the friendly Indians to the south and west.[14]

The fort on the upper James, Fort Charles, was commanded by Capt. Thomas Harris. It did not develop into a trading center at first because of the hostile Indians to the west. On the ridge of the Chickahominy, south of Fort Charles, was Fort James, under the command of Lt. Thomas Rolfe, the son of John Rolfe and Pocahontas.

In the spring of 1656 a large band of several hundred Indians, known as the Rochahecrean, moved from the mountains to the falls of the James and set up a strong defensive camp. These were either Cherokee or Manahoac and Tutelo Indians.[15] Col. Edward Hill of the Charles City and Henrico militia was assigned to command a combined force of militia and friendly Indians from the Chickahominy tribes to dislodge the Rochahecrean. Chief Totopotomoi led the Pamunkey Indians and was killed, along with many of his followers, in a battle on the north side of the James at the falls. The blood from the casualties so discolored a small stream that it became known as Bloody Run. For his "crimes and weakensses" in leading the ill-fated expedition, Colonel Hill was found guilty by the General Assembly and was suspended from holding public office. He was also ordered to bear the cost for making peace with the Indians. Abraham Wood was then made colonel of the regiment of Charles City and Henrico militia, and Capt. William Harris was made major.[16] No further attempts were made to force the Rochahecrean to leave. They were allowed to remain encamped at the falls, where they stayed without making any advances into the settled tidewater region until they decided to return to the west.

A period of peace followed after the departure of the Rochahecrean. By this time, the Indians that remained in the area below the falls had become assimilated within the social and economic society of the colony, although they were not accepted as equals. By 1669 there were an estimated forty Indian bowmen in the county. Under an act of the Assembly for destroying wolves, they were assessed to bring in eight heads annually. Thirty of these bowmen were Manachee, and ten were of the Powhite tribe. An earlier act had specifically prohibited Indians from coming into Henrico beyond certain bounds under penalty of death. After the bounds were set and "notice thereof given, . . . [It was] lawfull for any Englishman to kill such Indian or Indians soe transgressing." Originally this act was limited to Henrico and was to be applied to other counties if the enforcement proved beneficial, but instead it had an adverse effect and "shewed severall inconveniences and hazard." When it was repealed, "the Indians [were] permitted to come into said county as well as others about their lawfull occasions; provided they be noe way entertayned but by lycense legally obteyned." The last tribes of Indians within the present bounds of Henrico County were on Ivy Creek, near Powhatan's Town, at Arrohattock, and at the mouth of Turkey Island Creek. These Indians were accepted as part of the community and remained peaceable. Some of them maintained their own homes and farms, while some served as servants, laborers, or slaves to the settlers.[17]

Nathaniel Bacon. (Association for the Preservation of Virginia Antiquities, Bacon's Castle)

Before the end of the century, there was one more violent incursion into Henrico by Indian tribes unrelated to those in the county. In 1675–76 hostile Indian activity on the frontier caused reprisals by the settlers. The trouble started in the Potomac River valley in Maryland in July 1675, and after the massacre of several chiefs in September, the Susquehannock Indians began attacking outlying settlements. In January 1676 the Susquehannock moved south and killed thirty-six people near the falls of the Rappahannock. They then moved south to the York and then the James. At the falls of the James, they attacked the settlement at Bacon's Quarter just above the falls on the north bank. Here, "they Slew Mr. Bacon's Overseer whom He much Loved, and One of his servants, whose Bloud Hee Vowed to Revenge if possible." Bacon also lost "a great stock of cattle, which wee had upon it, and a good crop that wee should have made there."[18]

Bacon's Quarter was one of two parcels of land owned by Nathaniel Bacon, Jr. This young, "indifferent, tall but slender, blackhair'd" twenty-nine-year old Englishman had arrived in the colony just two years before. He had been educated at St. Catherine's Hall at Cambridge, from which he was withdrawn by his father because he had "broken into some extravagances." He returned to complete his education after a tour of Europe and then spent time at Gray's Inn. Young Nathanial had trouble holding onto money, and his life-style caused embarrassment for his father. To remedy the situation, his father gave him £1,800 to start a new life in Virginia. When Nathanial Jr. arrived with his wife, he purchased land from Col. Thomas Ballard at Curles Neck. The quarters at the falls on the north side of the James were probably included in the sale. Also on Curles Neck was Bremo, owned by Richard Cocke. To the northeast was Malvern Hill, where Thomas Cocke lived. Henry Randolph resided at Timber Slash just north of Bremo, and James Crewe lived on Turkey Island Creek. Bacon found himself surrounded by very influential neighbors. Members of the Randolph, Cocke, Farrar, and Eppes families held almost every official position in Henrico County between 1670 and 1691.[19]

At the falls, Bacon's neighbor on the south side of the James was William Byrd I, a wealthy planter, landowner, and

William Byrd I, 1652–1704. From Thomas Allen Glenn, *Some Colonial Mansions and Those Who Lived in Them* (Philadelphia, 1899), p. 26.

Indian trader. Byrd had come to Virginia sometime before 1670, the year when, as a youth of eighteen, he inherited from his uncle, Thomas Stegge, Jr., a considerable estate at the falls. Expanding the trade with the Indians, Byrd became the leading Indian trader in Virginia. The volume of trade soon necessitated the establishment of a warehouse at the falls. Using the Indian trading path that ran north-south just west of the falls, Byrd sent trading caravans into present-day western North Carolina and South Carolina to the lands of the Catawba and Cherokee. There his traders bartered cloth and manufactured items for bear and deer skins and beaver and other pelts. Nathaniel Bacon had received a commission to trade with the Indians from his cousin, Governor William Berkeley, and became one of Bryd's partners.[20]

Following the attack by the Susquehannock, in which Byrd lost three of his servants, the outlying settlers concentrated for defense.[21] Thomas Mathews stated that "the most Exposed small families withdrew into our houses of better Numbers, which we fortified with Pallisadoes and redoubts. Neighbours in Bodies Joined their Labours from each Plantation to others Alternately, taking their Arms into the Fields, and Setting Centinels; no Man Stirrd out of Door unarm'd; Indians were (ever and anon) espied, Three, 4, 5, or 6 in a Party Lurking throughout the Whole Land." Mathews "rarely heard of any Houses Burnt, tho abundance was forsaken, nor ever of any Corn or Tobacco cut up, or other Injury done besides Murders, Except the killing a very few Cattle and Swine."[22] Emotions ran high, and as reports came in, they were embellished and the accounts of the encounters between the settlers and Indians were exaggerated. The settlers called on the governor for assistance, but his previous inaction created doubts that he would respond to their needs. Fear led to anger, and uncontrolled anger fed by emotion led to rebellion.

Some of the settlers in Charles City County formed an encampment at Jordan's Point on the south side of the James below the junction of the Appomattox. These men sought authority from the governor to march against the Indians, but Governor Berkeley ordered them to wait for regular troops to come up from Jamestown. While drinking with William Byrd, James Crews, and Henry Isham, Bacon was persuaded to visit the encampment. Bacon had no love for Indians. Not only had he lost his overseer in the Susquehannocks attack; the previous year he had seized some friendly Appomattox Indians and charged them with stealing some corn. He could identify with the fears of the settlers and did so when he began to address them. According to a contemporary historian, "He was young, bold, active, of an inviting Aspect, and powerful Elocution. In a Word, he was every way qualified to head a giddy and unthinking Multitude."[23]

The Assembly had adopted an act declaring war against the Indians who were guilty of murdering the English and called for the establishment of forts at the heads of the principal rivers. These forts were to be garrisoned, and mounted detachments were to patrol the areas between the forts. However, under this act, only the governor could order an attack after he was notified of all particulars of an assault being made by the Indians. The expense of supporting this defensive line was to be borne by a special tax to be levied on the settlers. When this provision was made known, the settlers declared that "the erecting of them [the forts] was a great Grievance, Juggle and cheat, and of no more use or service to them than another plantation with men at it, and that it was merely a Designe of the Grandees to engrosse all their Tobacco into their owne hands."[24] To the men at Jordan's Point, stationary forts were not the answer. They petitioned the governor to commission someone to lead them in an offensive move against the Indians.

The fact that Bacon and his friends happened to visit the encampment appears to have been a contrived plot. The men "shouted and cry'd out, a Bacon! a Bacon! a Bacon! w'ch taking Fire with his ambition and Spirit of Faction and Popularity, easily prevail'd on him to Resolve to head them."[25] Although cautioned by the governor not to act rashly, Bacon assumed command of the militia and asked him for a commission. When Berkeley instead directed him to wait for the regular troops, Bacon moved his men out to attack the Indians as the uncommissioned "General of the Volunteers." His refusal to adhere to the wishes of the governor resulted in his being declared a "Rebel." Berkeley also dismissed him from the Council and revoked his privileges to trade with the Indians. With about three hundred men,

Governor Berkeley set out to inspect some of the forts at the head of the James and York rivers and to seize Bacon. The governor moved his force into Henrico County, but public reaction caused him to retire from the frontier. Before doing so, he informed Mrs. Bacon that he would hang her husband.

After conducting a successful campaign down to the Roanoke River, in the area of present-day Clarksville, Bacon and his men turned on the friendly Occaneechee, who had helped him against the Susquehannock. Bacon returned to Henrico a hero. Believing the governor would try to kill him, he stationed a guard of soldiers about his house at Curles.[26] Rejecting the governor's request that he beg for a pardon, Bacon renewed his demand for a commission and hinted that he would accept the Assembly's distinction between friendly and enemy Indians. At the meeting to elect burgesses, probably at the Varina courthouse, Bacon appeared with some of his men and prevented the reading of the governor's declaration and the Council's proclamation declaring him a rebel. Even though the proclamation called on the people to support the government, the people of Henrico responded by electing Bacon and James Crews, one of Bacon's lieutenants, to the House of Burgesses.

With the people of the frontier behind him, Bacon sailed down the James with fifty men to Jamestown on June 6. He was captured the next day, and on June 9 he confessed to disobedience and presented a request for pardon to the governor before the assembled House. After being pardoned and allowed to take his seat, Bacon left Jamestown and returned to Henrico. A few days later, on June 23, he and his men came downriver again, when he took Jamestown by force and demanded a commission. Three days later Bacon and his men left Jamestown and returned to the falls of the James, the appointed place of rendezvous with his supporters from the frontier settlements. When he heard that Governor Berkeley was in Gloucester County preparing to move against him, he moved his men to Middle Plantation, now Williamsburg. The governor retired across the Chesapeake Bay to Accomack, and on August 3 Bacon issued a "Declaration to the People," justifying the rebellion by setting forth some of the grievances of the people and the reasons for his assumption of authority. He then moved "up again to the Falls of James River, where hee bestirs himself lustily in order to a speedy march against the Indians." From the falls, Bacon marched his men to the head of the York River to attack the Pamunkey Indians. After a lengthy search, he discovered their camp. Meeting little resistance, his men killed and captured the Indians and plundered their camp. Once again friendly Indians felt the wrath of his vengeance.[27]

The Assembly, sympathetic to Bacon's actions, legislated approval of them despite Governor Berkeley's opposition. At the same time, Bacon was appealing his case to the king. Nevertheless, the governor recaptured Jamestown and was prepared to move against Bacon when word came that on October 26, 1676, Nathaniel Bacon, Jr., had died from dysentery in Gloucester County. With Bacon's death, the rebellion disintegrated, and the governor moved to take repressive action against Bacon's supporters.

When news of the rebellion was received in England, the king sent a special commission to the colony with a regiment of troops to settle affairs. The commissioners arrived in February 1677 and sent orders directing the sheriffs of each county to obtain statements of complaints and grievances. These statements were returned sealed. Those who signed them had taken an oath that they were prepared to prove any charges. The primary objective of the commissioners was to insure continuity of government under the crown. Peace was made with the Indians, and a treaty was signed. The General Assembly was called to take the necessary legislative action to change the laws passed under Bacon's rule. The commissioners did not agree with the governor's repressive activities after the rebellion, and the governor left the colony in May.

Upon receipt of the complaints and grievances, the commissioners sought to respond to each grievance presented. Five citizens of Henrico County signed the grievances submitted to the commissioners—Wilton Elam, John Pleasants, Solomon Knibbe, William Hatcher, and John Lowit.[28] Their first grievance complained that the "Indian trade is monolized & it is favour of the monoppolists" and that "the people are betrayed to the perfidians of the mercyless Indians."[29] Many of the other county representatives made the same accusation, and the commissioners conceived "this a reall grievance and a great accation of the warr with the Indians." They further stated that the articles of peace signed with the Indians would allow the next General Assembly to remedy the situation.

The second grievance filed by the Henricoans stated that "noe publique satisfaction or vindecacon hath bin had or Required for the abundance of blood spilt & spoyles of the English people." They also complained of the·defensive system of forts "which wee found not to be of any security either to our lives or estates." Ignoring the complaint about the forts, the commissioners replied that "theis complanants never consider that the breach of the peace has still been made by the English wh[ich] was justified before the Asmebly and denied by none." They stated further that this grievance would come under the articles of peace.

To the third grievance concerning "heavy & unsupportable taxes especially sixty pounds of tobacco for each tithable" the commissioners replied that "none was imposed but by the Asemblies where they had Representatives." However, the citizens were also complaining that they were called on to pay taxes which were not "imployed in any service for the publique benefit." The commissioners did not reply to this but apparently believed it, too, was a problem for the representative assembly.

It appears that the people of Henrico, as represented by the five signers of the "Grievances," wanted to be masters of their own destinies. They opposed what they considered unnecessary taxes and wasteful central government policies. This is clearly revealed in their fourth grievance:

And it is our desire and Request for yor Honors that the Warr against all Indians in Generall be forth wth prossecuted, & that before they are strengthened by ffarther confederasys, and that it may be performed by voluntary aides and contribucons of men and provisions in specie since wee Conceive our selves better able to supply such things then pay Contribucon in tobacco which Commonly is greate part devoured by the greate salarys allowed Sherifs & Collectors &c: and wee allsoe Request that Care be taken to appoynt such men Cumandrs whose merits and intrest in the peoples affecons may incorage & forward their severall aides and assistances.

Malvern Hill, the Cocke family seat, as it looked after it was rebuilt entirely of brick around 1690–1700. This photograph was taken before the house burned in 1905. (Virginia State Library)

To the people of Henrico, the colony's frontier, the threat and fear of Indian raids was still a reality. Even though a peace treaty had been signed, the governor, Council, and House of Burgesses had done little if anything to punish the Indians. Only Bacon and his men had given the people any relief from both sources of irritation. But the commissioners believed this to be "a wild request" and "a mutinous demand" that "is in effect to desire more Bacons." They felt that the commanders desired by the people "are to be such as have interest in the peoples affections" and would seek to do what would please the people and not what would be for the best interest of the crown and colony. To add a final rebuttal to this grievance, the commissioners noted that the people wanted "to have warr with all the Indians of a Continent and the charge to be born by voluntary contribution when thies very Requestors will unwillingly give six pencs a peece towards it."

Henrico local government was in the hands of four well-to-do famlies—the Farrars, Cockes, Randolphs, and Eppeses.[30]— and the citizens saw this as an unjust system, especially in the levying of taxes. They cited this as a grievance and proposed a solution that "at least six of the Comonally" chosen by the people "sit with the Commissioners when the [taxes are] levied." The commissioners believed they should not interfere and that it would be better for the citizens to have the county commissioners of the peace make the decision. They recognized that the "litle chois" of qualified people limited those who could serve and viewed it as one of the evils of the sytem but agreed that "wee knowe not how it can be helped." They also felt that if six of the "comanlty" were added to the county court to discuss the levying of taxes, "the consequence wee believe will be noe Levies wil be laid but the tim spun out in wrangling." However, they did agree that the laying of levies in open court was a reasonable request.

The final grievance concerned the availability of ammunition to defend themselves from "our barborous enemys." This complaint was nullified by the repeal of the law that restricted distribution. The commissioners had taken steps to distribute the powder and ammunition they had brought over and also dispersed the regiment of regular troops to restore order and to defend the colony. A company of regular troops was stationed at the head of the James River by the royal commissioners, and the county commissioners were directed to provide them with provisions and with "so much suffitient for them, to plant corne or other grayne."[31]

After the initial attack by the Susquehannock, there was no large-scale fighting on Henrico soil. A fort was established near the falls of the James with Col. Edward Ramsey as commander, and James City County was ordered to garrison it with fifty men. In February 1676 Colonel Ramsey's command consisted of one lieutenant, an ensign, one sergeant, a drummer, a surgeon, four horsemen, and thirteen foot soldiers. Col. William Farrar and Lt. Col. Francis Eppes, commissioners from Henrico, were authorized to enlist friendly Indians in the war and require and receive hostages from them. Each man was to receive one hundred yards of trading cloth to be used to reward the Indians. Trading of any kind with the Indians was prohibited by act of the General Assembly; if anyone was caught trading powder, shot, or guns, the penalty was death without benefit of clergy and forfeiture of one's estate.[32]

The act establishing the forts was rescinded in June 1676 when Bacon's forces controlled the Assembly. The fort in Henrico commanded by Colonel Ramsey was abandoned, and the soldiers from the fort were ordered to be "quartered and disposed in the fronteere plantations." The same Assembly passed an act for carrying on a war against the Indians and established an army of one thousand men. Henrico's quota was thirty-one men.[33] It is not well known how many men from Henrico joined Bacon's army as he marched back and forth between the falls and Jamestown and Middle Plantation. On one of these marches, Bacon's men plundered Capt. Thomas Chamberlain's house,[34] but generally they contented themselves with venting their anger on the Indians.

The property and estates of those who supported Bacon were seized to provide income to defray the expenses of putting down the rebellion. James Minge was appointed to survey Bacon's land "Lying & being in Henrico County." On March 15, 1676, Governor Berkeley granted 7,351 acres of land on the north side of the James "beginning at the mouth of Shoccoe's Creek, and up the river" to Capt. William Byrd for transporting 122 people to the colony. This grant of land included Bacon's Quarter. Thomas Jarvis, who married Bacon's widow, was appointed to take charge of his estate on November 25, 1679; however, Bacon's land at Curles would remain in the public domain until an inquisition under William Randolph, escheator for Henrico County, on July 21, 1698, started the legal steps necessary to dispose of the property. On December 12, 1699, the county coroner, who had the duty of acting as administrator of deceased persons' estates, was ordered to take the land of Nathaniel Bacon, Jr., to prevent "wasts which are dayly committed upon the same by the Inhabitants of those partes." William Randolph received 480 acres from Bacon's estate on May 7, 1700, for £150 sterling, and John Bolling was granted fifty acres on April 25, 1701, for £30 sterling.[35]

Captain Byrd had managed to survive his early association with Bacon and the active part he took in the rebellion. On one occasion he had led a party of two hundred men to occupy Col. Augustine Warner's house in Gloucester County and had removed goods valued at £1,000. At the General Court held at James City on June 7, 1678, Colonel Warner "obtained that Captain Bird had to pay £1000 with costs." However, Byrd was not among the signers of a resolution to follow Bacon in August 1676 or among those exempted from pardon by Governor Berkeley in February 1677. His willingness to pay Colonel Warner led to a petition to Charles II to except Byrd from the Act of Indemnity for persons involved in the late rebellion.[36]

When the treaty with the Indians was signed, it did not bring an end to confrontations between the settlers and the Indians. Although the general public did not favor the establishment of garrisoned fortified positions, the central government continued to rely on a system of forts to defend the frontier, and the Indians continued to bypass the forts and attack the outlying plantations. On August 23–24, 1678, a band of from 150 to 200 Indians appeared at Col. Rowland Pace's plantation. After destroying the corn and tobacco, they killed some of the cattle and drove some away. Moving to neighboring farms, they drove the inhabitants from their homes, plundered several houses, and destroyed the crops. Colonel Eppes called out the militia, and on August 24, he and Maj. William Harris led a force of 46 mounted men toward Colonel Pace's. Unaware of any danger, Colonel Eppes moved his men toward the house which was occupied by the Indians. As the militia advanced, the Indians attacked and killed Colonel Eppes and Major Harris, wounded two of their men, and then slipped into the forest. Such attacks sent a ripple of fear along the frontier settlements, and some of the inhabitants abandoned their farms and returned to the older, more secure settlements below Henrico. Regular troops were sent out from Williamsburg to present a show of force, but they did more to encourage the settlers than to discourage the Indians.

In 1679 the General Assembly passed an act for the "defence of the country against the incursions of the Indian enemy" calling for the erection of four houses, for stores or garrisons, on four rivers—the Potomac, Rappahannock, Mattaponi, and James. "Att the head of James River on the southside above Capt. William Birds, one storehouse or garrison with a small house for ammunition" was to be built. Byrd was directed "to procure and provide the severall necessaryes . . . for which he shall be paid for by the publique in Henrico county." Every forty tithables were to provide one man for the fort, completely armed. Henrico had 161 tithables available for militia service in 1679. The fort that was erected was called Fort Charles, and it would remain garrisoned until it was ordered abandoned three years later.[37]

The presence of the garrisoned fort did not prevent deadly attacks by both sides. Captain Byrd killed seven Indians and imprisoned their wives and children because he suspected them of having murdered some settlers. In retaliation the Indians attacked one of the outlying settlements and killed one of the inhabitants. To reduce the expense borne by the people, the General Assembly limited the number of men per garrison to twenty in June 1680. Byrd, who had been appointed colonel, was authorized to deliver provisions to the garrison on the south side of the James quarterly, for which he "shall be paid and allowed by the publique after the rate of 200 lbs. of tobacco and caske per annun for each soldier of the said fort." He was also given authority to summon the militia in Henrico and Charles City counties before notifying the governor, if necessary.[38]

In November 1682 the forts were ordered dismantled by December 30. This action was taken because the forts were "very burthensome and chargeable to the country" and because the "apprehentions of danger from the insurrections of certaine Indian enemies . . . are for the most parte removed by peace concluded with those Indians." To provide some protection, the counties of Henrico, New Kent, Rappahannock, and Stafford were to furnish twenty mounted men to patrol the frontier. The Henrico Rangers, under Captain Sands, were alerted once when it was reported that Seneca Indians were prowling on the frontier of Henrico, but the report proved false. To meet the needs of frontier defense, the Assembly increased the number of the troops and enlarged the area for which they were responsible. To gather at monthly musters, each troop of thirty men was to "range and scout every week." The troop raised on the upper James, from Henrico, Charles City, and James City counties, was to be provided with a boat and was to "range and scout from Chickahominy swamp, above the frontier plantations, to the heads of Appomattox River, and in such other places as shall be most likely for the discovery of the enemy." Col. John Farrar and Capt. William Randolph were ordered to provide convenient quarters if none existed. The four troops of thirty men each provided for under this act were in reality a regular army of citizens. By 1686 the Henrico militia was reported as "1 Troop of Horse" of forty-eight men plus officers.[39]

Even with the Indian problems and the turmoil caused by Bacon, life in Henrico County continued without a great deal of interruption. The people moved back to their homes on the frontier not long after each Indian attack, and soon new arrivals came to establish homes, either pushing beyond the westernmost settlements or acquiring land in the older settled areas. When the latter occurred, some of the older settlers pulled up roots and moved westward. By the end of the century, settlements were established beyond the falls of the James. Colonel Byrd expanded his trading operations and exchanged imported articles with his neighbors for tobacco. Every wharf became a point of exchange of manufactured good and supplies from England for tobacco, other farm products, and furs and skins received in trade with the Indians.

The population also increased as white indentured servants and black slaves were brought into the colony. Toward the end of the century, Colonel Byrd became chief owner in a slave ship, and even though he moved his residence from the falls to Westover in Charles City County in 1690, he remained an active landowner in Henrico County. He continued to be directly involved in its economic growth. His trading post on the south bank at the falls was designated a warehouse for the receipt of goods awaiting shipping.[40]

At that time there was greater activity along the Appomattox and on the south side of the James than north of the James. Bermuda Hundred became the commercial center for the upper country, and in 1691 it was designated a port of entry. All imported goods were to be brought up river to Bermuda Hundred, and then they were taken to the buyers who could resell them at stores or at their dwellings. Not all commercial establishments carried just life's necessities. John Foissin, a native of Paris and a storekeeper in Henrico in 1688, carried a variety of fancy French-made wearing apparel from silk-fringed gloves to embroidered waistcoats and lace and velvet caps.[41]

Farming was the chief economic endeavor in colonial Virginia, and agricultural products insured the economic survival of the colony. The rolling land in Henrico insured easy drainage, and the different soils, ranging from sand and gravely loam to clay and river bottom, could support a variety of agricultural and other economic activities. Produce from the land and fish from the river were the chief sources of income for the average citizens. The well-to-do could supplement their income from fees received for public offices they held, but the primary money crop produced in the county was tobacco. Throughout the seventeenth and eighteenth centuries, tobacco was not only the money crop but was also used as money and a means of measuring monetary value. Corn was the main crop produced for consumption. In addition, cotton, rice, and indigo were cultivated in early Henrico. Apple trees and grapevines provided the inhabitants with fruit that could be eaten or used to produce strong libations. Henry Randolph owned eighteen sheep in 1688, but the most common animals were hogs, cattle, and horses. The hogs and cattle were branded and marked by their owners and were then permitted to run wild in the swamps and woods, where they found plentiful food.[42]

Transportation was required for these agricultural products, as well as for the settlers. As early as 1641 ferries and bridges were provided at public expense, but this proved too burdensome. In 1673 the General Assembly established ferries again, and commissioners were appointed to designate the most convenient places. The ferryman was paid by the county, but he had to forfeit whatever was due him if he neglected to keep the ferry and the landing in good order. Two ferries were in operation in Henrico in 1697. The ferry across the James at Varina, operated by Capt. William Soane, ran only on Sundays, court days, and other public days when the justices met. The second ferry was at Bermuda Hundred and was operated by Samuel Kimble. Each ferryman received eighteen hundred pounds of tobacco and was responsible for collecting fees from the passengers. A rider and horse would pay a fee of twelve pence, whereas a foot passenger would be charged only six pence.[43]

Most roads of seventeenth-century Virginia were little more than trails, passable on wagon or horseback and barely wide enough for a wagon or hogshead of tobacco. In some cases, the old Indian paths were adapted and put to use; Powhatan's trail, from the falls east on the north bank of the river, and the trail from Powhatan's village westward to the mountains became principal arteries. Throughout the early colonial period, responsibility for the construction and maintenance of roads was placed on the parish unit of government. Each parishioner was expected to spend six days a year working on the roads without pay. The parish system proved inadequate as the settlement spread farther inland into the wilderness. The responsibility for seeing that "convenient wayes" were constructed was given to the county court by the General Assembly in 1657. The court was responsible for seeing that roads were constructed to churches, the county seat, and Jamestown and from county to county. To supervise the roads, the court appointed surveyors, or overseers, annually. The surveyors requested assistance from the parish vestry, and the vestry assigned individual tithables to work on the roads. The first road financed by a colonywide public levy was ordered in 1691 to connect the forts on the James and Rappahannock rivers. In Henrico, some of the roadways mentioned in the early patents north of the James River were Pamunky Path, Stegg's Path, Kickinoky Road, Powhite Path, and Beauchamp's Path. Whereas many of these have disappeared, the New Kent Road, "the path to the Horse Pen" (now Horse Pen Road), and Three Chopt Road remain.[44]

Although there were individual farms with farmhouses, outbuildings, pasture land, and planted acreage up to the falls, the center of activity was at Varina, where the courthouse and parish church were situated. The activities of the court and church provided an opportunity for the citizenry to come together for social events as well. As a town, Varina also became the center for commerical activity. The need for lodging and refreshment was met when Thomas Cocke was licensed to keep a tavern in 1685. In 1690 William Byrd reported that "for Ordinary's wee have none in our County, Mr. Cocke having left of these two years"; shortly thereafter, in June, Capt. William Soane petitioned the court for a license to keep an ordinary at Varina. The court granted his petition and "Authorized, Lycensed & p'mitted [him] to sell all sorts of Liquors . . . Provisions, horse meat, etc." He also requested the court's permission to use the loft in the courthouse as a lodging room. This, too, was granted with the provision that the loft remained "clear and undisturbed" for use of the several juries during court sessions.[45]

The presence of a tavern encouraged residents of Henrico and adjoining counties to get together for one of the most popular sports of the day—horse racing. Henrico became famous for its races and "seems to have been the 'race-horse region' of the day." There were several regular race paths, courses, or tracks in the county that had starters and judges and established weights for races.[46] The surviving records show that courses were laid off at Bermuda Hundred, Conecock, Ware, Varina, and Malvern Hill. Of course, impromptu races were held in open pastures or along straight stretches of paths or roads. Frequently, disputes over the outcome of races were brought before the county court for resolution. Richard Ligon, Capt. Thomas Chamberlaine, Stephen Cocke, and William Randolph were all ardent supporters of the turf.

In July 1678 a race was run between horses owned by Abram Womack and Richard Ligon at Bermuda Hundred.

Two young boys, Thomas Cocke and Joseph Tanner, were up, and Thomas Chamberlaine signaled when the horses and riders were ready. Abram Childers, acting as the starter, gave a command to "goe." After about four or five lengths, Cocke's horse veered off the track, and Cocke "rained him in and cryed it was not a faire start." Tanner, Chamberlaine's servant, continued the race even though Chamberlaine called for him to stop. When he returned to the starting point, Tanner declared it was a fair start, and Childers upheld his claim. In October 1683 Edward Hatcher and Andrew Martin agreed to race, the loser's horse as the prize. The matter was complicated by the fact that Hatcher intended to ride a horse owned by Richard Ligon, but Ligon refused to let him ride it. The judges for the race directed Martin to run the course. When he got to the end of the course, Martin dismounted and left his knife on the ground. He then remounted and returned to the starting point. The judges declared him the winner of the race and ordered Ligon to give his horse to Martin. When Ligon refused to comply, the dispute was carried to the county court.[47]

During a race at the Varina track where Thomas Batte and Richard Parker waged one hundred pounds of tobacco, Batte claimed that Parker crossed in front of him and forced his horse to a slower stride. When the dispute was submitted to the court, the judges ordered that the race should be run again on the same course. The Varina track was the scene of many other races. In 1687 Christopher Branch witnessed a wager between Hugh Ligon and Stephen Cocke while watching another race there. In 1690 Capt. William Soane filed a suit against Robert Napier for £10, which he claimed to have won by default at Varina. The Reverend James Blair, having acted as endman for Captain Soane, made deposition to the fact that Napier led his horse away before the race was started. The horse that Captain Soane was to ride belonged to Littleberry Eppes, former sheriff of Henrico. William Randolph and Benjamin Harrison were among the other deponents. When the jury ruled in Soane's favor, it upheld the principle that once a race was agreed to, it was to be run. Napier had to pay the £10 he had wagered.[48]

At Malvern Hill in 1689, William Eppes and Stephen Cocke agreed to race for ten shillings. Eppes rode his own

White Oak Swamp. At first this swamp proved to be a natural barrier, but through the years Henricoans found ways to pass through or around it. (Photograph by John S. Salmon)

horse, and Cocke rode a horse belonging to William Sutton. Each horse was to keep its path, but Cocke tried to cross over before he had enough room, and William Randolph, the starter, noted that "they Josselled upon Mr. Epes Horses' path all most part of the race."[49]

Most the races followed the commonly agreed-upon procedures and rules; only those that gave rise to disagreement were settled through the courts. There were straight and circular courses with starters and endsmen to observe the beginning and ending of races. In one reported instance, the riders were not to weigh over 130 pounds. In that race, a mare named Bony, owned by Thomas Jefferson's grandfather, Thomas Jefferson, Jr., raced a horse named Watt, belonging to Thomas Hardiman. The course was one quarter of a mile, and the mare was to start ten yards ahead of the horse. The mare won, but a dispute over the stakes resulted in a court hearing.[50]

Horse racing was only one outlet for the desire to wager. Capt. William Stone and John Broadnax bet five hundred pounds of tobacco on the relative weight of gold and quicksilver. Broadnax lost, and the court ruled for Stone. When Thomas East and Richard Ligon made a wager as to how much quicksilver could be contained in an area one thousand feet square, the court deferred the matter to William Byrd and John Pleasants to arbitrate and declared that their decision was to be final. Even the popular game of nine or ten pins, which was played either in specially built alleys or in large rooms in private homes, could be made a little more exciting with a wager on the side. In 1681 Robert Sharpe and Richard Robine made a wager of four hundred pounds of tobacco on the outcome of a game of pins. Thomas Cocke, Jr., refused to serve as marksman because Robine was under the influence of strong drink. Sharpe won three games and Robine won two before they stopped for a break. When they resumed, Robine won the next two games and a disagreement arose as to the payment of the wager.[51]

Casual bets did not have legal status, but if a formal contract had been agreed to, then it became a legal matter. When Allanson Clerk won £4 from Peter Rowlett in a game of cards, the court refused to rule because no contract to pay had been executed. If no contract was drawn up but the stakes were in the possession of a mutually agreed-to stake-holder, then the court considered it as an agreement or verbal contract executed by the action of depositing the stakes with the stakeholder. As long as the wager did not serve to lower public morality or injure other people's property, the public and the courts accepted it.[52]

There was some laxness in moral conduct in Henrico during the latter part of the seventeenth century. This condition was partly attributable to the proximity of the frontier and the scattered settlements. Although drinking was accepted in all social circles, and quantities of spirits were available at almost all occasions from weddings to funerals, as well as athletic and social gatherings, public drunkenness was not a problem. This may have been because "nowhere was the vice more carefully watched or more promptly punished." When Captain Chamberlaine tried to justify his action of breaking out of jail because he was drunk, the justices rules that drunkenness was no argument "to justify any offence."[53]

One of the responsibilities of the vestry of the parish church was to investigate moral offenses and present the offender to the county court. The General Assembly, not overlooking its control of the parishes, enacted laws directing the election of laymen in every parish as the governing body of the parish in temporal affairs. They were appointed by the county courts at first, but later they were elected by the parishioners. The vestry, through the churchwarden, was required to report twice a year to the county court. The vestry concerned itself with offenses against the laws of God. Bastardy does not appear to have been a common offense in Henrico; only eleven cases were reported between 1682 and 1697. Two of these were women of African decent. When charges were brought against Joane Scot for fornication, it was ruled that the vestry did not have jurisdiction. She was "discharged from the p'sentm'ts of the Grand Jury, It being the opinion of this Court that the Act a'gst ffornication does not touch her [she] being an Egyptian & noe Xtian woman." The vestry also brought charges for other offenses. When Joseph Royall admitted that he had played cards on the Sabbath, he was presented to the grand jury.[54]

Little is known about the administration of Henrico Parish from 1629, when Lazarus Martin was reported as minister, until 1660. From that year to 1720, Henrico Parish was reported as Varina Parish and the principal church in the parish was referred to as Varina Church. In 1680 the Reverend John Ball was reported as the minister of Henrico County serving Varina Parish and the half of Bristol Parish north of the Appomattox. When Samuel Mathews declared publicly that Ball was "fitter to make a hangman than a minister," the vestry presented Mathews to the grand jury on a charge of libel. Ball was followed by the Reverend James Blair in 1685. This well-educated young Scotsman was serving as a clerk in the Rolls Office in London, England, when he was assigned to the parish. He arrived in the colony late in 1685 to assume his duties. As minister in Henrico, Blair found that his services were required in surrounding parishes where the pulpits were vacant. Two years after his arrival, he purchased one hundred acres of land from William Byrd. On December 15, 1689, the bishop of London appointed Blair as his commissary, or deputy, to the colony. As commissary, he fostered the idea of a college for Virginia and spent three years in England from 1691 to 1693 petitioning the crown to charter one. He remained the minister of Henrico, or Varina, Parish until he was appointed president of the proposed College of William and Mary in 1694. As parish minister, Blair served settlers on the land that had been set aside for the first English college established in the New World.[55]

Blair's successor, George Robinson, became embroiled in "a little controversy between our Vestry men & me about our church Glebe." When Robinson laid claim to the glebe, the vestry informed him that "only an inducted minister has just title thereto." The governor and Council refused to give an opinion on the matter, and it was reported that "it is carefully buzzed into the people's ears that they must not encourage the coveteousness of the Clergy, nor be priest ridden, otherwise they shall soon have a Bishop with a salary to be raised by the County and tythes, which the church Government will allow." This attitude toward the church was not so much directed against ecclesiastical rule of the Church of England as much as it was toward defending the right of the individual vestry.[56]

Life on the frontier was hard, and it did not lend itself to following all the rules of the established church. The distances between houses as well as the distance between the colony and the Church of England contributed to an inability to staff the local parishes properly, and they did not function as efficiently as did the parishes in England. Nevertheless, the established church was united against dissenters, and the government supported its efforts against them. Chief among the dissenter groups were the Quakers, who opposed the parish levy, refused to bear arms or pay tithes to support military actions, and held secret religious meetings of their own.

The first Quaker missionary appeared in the colony in 1656, and the next year the Council ordered that the master of any ship bringing Quakers into the colony would be fined and would have to carry them back to England. Despite this order and repressive measures taken by the General Assembly and governor, the sect continued to grow and won many converts. In 1658 the General Assembly passed an act banishing Quakers from the colony. This act carried a fine of £100 for anyone who received a Quaker into his home. By another act passed in 1661, anyone who failed to attend services of the established church for a period of one month would be subject to a fine. In 1666 an act was passed imposing fines on "refractory persons" for failure to comply with the militia laws and regulations.[57]

Henry Watkins received a patent for 170 acres in Henrico in 1679 and became "a small but apparently energetic farmer." As a member of the Quaker sect, he suffered under the repressive acts. In 1684 his petition for remission of fines was refused because he was "continuing still in his Quakerism." When his wife was assaulted, he refused to prosecute the criminal because the law required actions contrary to the Quaker doctrine. His sixteen-year-old daughter, Elizabeth, refused to take the oath of allegiance to the king before the county court. Her willingness to affirm her statements did not satisfy the court, and she was placed in confinement. Two months later, in June 1685, she was ordered to appear before the judges. Still "persisting in the same obstinancy as she pretends out of conscience sake and therefore desiring to be excused and her father also humbly seconding her request the court have out of their clemency in consideration of her young years remitted her offence and release her of her confinement."[58]

The most prominent Quaker in the county was John Pleasants, a planter of means and a respected member of the community. He allowed his house to be used as a meeting place for Quakers and was warned repeatedly. The enforcement of the anti-Quaker acts came when he and his wife were indicted for living together unlawfully according to the rules of the established church, which did not recognize their marriage under the Quaker doctrine. He and his wife were fined £240 each for illicit cohabitation and £20 each for every month they failed to attend services of the parish church. Additional fines were imposed of two thousand pounds of tobacco for not having their children baptized and five hundred pounds of tobacco for allowing Quaker meetings in their house. The adoption in England of the Declaration for Liberty of Conscience and Indulgence in Religious Matters of 1687 and the Toleration Act of 1688 allowed dissenting religious groups to hold religious services openly without having to conform to the doctrines of the established church. The governor was directed to proclaim the declarations in every county, and it was to be done with the beating of drums, the firing of cannons, and expressions of popular enthusiasm. The proclamation was spread on the Henrico County Minute Book in 1690. The passage of the act relieved Pleasants and his wife of the charges and nullified the fines. That same year, Pleasants set aside a parcel of land for a meetinghouse and graveyard. This meetinghouse was registered with the county court in 1692.[59]

The recognition of dissenting religious groups did not relieve them of having to conform to requirements of the law that may have been contrary to their beliefs. In 1692 John Pleasants was elected to the House of Burgesses, but because he refused to take the oath prescribed by act of Parliament and the oath of a burgess, he "made himself incapable of serving as a Burgess for Henrico County." Military training and preparations for military action were contrary to Quaker beliefs. By payment of a fee, a Quaker could avoid attending militia muster. Alexander Makenney refused to attend the muster in 1691 because "his conscience did not permit him to bear arms." The sheriff took his featherbed, rug, and blanket, and Makenney appealed to the General Court. The court ruled that if he wanted his property, he would either have to pay the fine or attend the muster. John Pleasants, John Woodson, and other Quakers from Henrico petitioned the General Assembly in 1692 for "a new bill concerning the militia and repeal of the severall acts relateing thereto." Although the committee considering the petition reported a proposed bill, the House did not agree to the report and ordered that it be laid aside. When John Pleasants petitioned "in the behalfe of himselfe and Severall other Quakers in Henrico County" in October 1696, "complaineing of the Rigour of Several Lawes against them for not beareing & providing Armes & for not appeareing at musters, and of the severity of severall of the Militia," the House agreed to the committee's report and ordered that a bill be brought "imposeing less fines then in the said Acts" of 1666 and 1684.[60]

Quakerism continued to grow in Henrico during the 1690s. In 1696 a report was filed showing that they assembled in three different places, the "public meetinghouse," the residence of Mary Maddox, and John Pleasant's home. In 1699 a new meetinghouse was under construction; in that year, Henry Watkins subscribed five hundred pounds of tobacco toward the building of the Friends Meetinghouse at Curles, and in 1703 he paid £50 for furnishings. By the end of the seventeenth century the number of congregations had diminished because the "sect derived more nourishment from persecution than it did from toleration." Even so, Quakers continued to play a part in the county's history.[61]

The established church, as in England, took most of the responsibility for the development of common schools. Although Governor William Berkeley was correct to a degree that Virginians followed "the same course that is taken in England out of towns; every man according to his ability instructing his children," one historian reported that "in most Parishes are Schools (little houses being built on Purpose) where are taught English and Writing; but to prevent the sowing the Seeds of Dissension and Faction, it is to be wished that the Masters or Mistresses should be such as are approved or licensed by the Minister and Vestry of the Parishes, or Justices of the Colony; the Clerks of the Parishes being generally most proper for this Purpose; or, (in Case of their Incapacity or Refusal) such others as can be procured."[62]

Public education by the parishes was confined to an attempt to provide for the instruction and training of the poor. Vestries were allowed to establish "parsons' schools" and "workhouses," but the primary means was the apprenticeship system whereby trade training and schooling was provided to the poor. Except for certain statutes governing the College of William and Mary, there was no demand from the people for the development of a system of education. Most of the action of the General Assembly relating to education was in approval of free school foundations or in the regulation of apprenticeship. There was no free school foundation in Henrico, but the vestry and county court did provide for public instruction and did supervise the apprenticeship agreements. It is known that Thomas Dalby served as a schoolmaster under hire to Robert Bullington before 1688. In one case, Alice Alvis charged that Richard Ligon failed to "educate and maintain" her son in conformity with their agreement. The court found the evidence insufficient to support her claim. To encourage the immigration of teachers, special exemptions were made. When Nathaniel Hill moved from Gloucester County to Henrico, the county court exempted him from payment of taxes for one year "for the encouragement of learning and instruction of youth in this county by inviting able tutors here to reside."[63]

The wealthy planters hired tutors for their children, and some arranged for the children of their servants and employees to receive basic instruction. Books and individual libraries were recognized as prized possessions. Mrs. Ann Bevill divided her library equally between her two sons by deed of gift, and Henry Kent bequeathed forty-five books to his heirs. On the frontier, books were a major link with the culture of the old world and a principal vehicle for passing that knowledge on.[64]

Frontier life required a degree of self-reliance and self-sufficiency. As each family had to assume the responsibility of educating its children as best it could, it also had to develop means of producing personal and community necessities. Mills were constructed by local citizens at their own expense, and they in turn allowed their neighbors to use them on a fee basis. Henry Randolph, John Pleansants, and Richard Kennon constructed mills. William Cocke owned a loom, and Thomas Cocke received a reward from the county court for linen he made.[65]

For services they could not obtain locally, planters entered into an indenture with a craftsman for his services for a specified time in return for certain benefits. Peter Wyke acquired the services of Robert Cate, a shoemaker, for four years. Cate was exempt from planting and tending tobacco, but not other agricultural work, and was to receive food, clothing, and lodging during the four-year period. At the end of four years, Cate received a new suit and three barrels of Indian corn. Contracting for specific services was also common. When James Gates, a carpenter residing in Henrico, agreed to construct a house for Maj. Thomas Chamberlaine in 1679, he contracted to frame out a two-story house, forty feet by twenty feet, and add siding, the roof, and a chimney on each end, within seven months. The absence of a cellar necessitated the construction of sills on the ground to support the house. Each floor was divided into two rooms by a wooden partition. Chamberlaine agreed to pay Gates twelve hundred pounds of tobacco in cask for the work.[66]

The agreement between Robert Sharpe and John Hundley for the construction of a house was slightly different. For a framed house, thirty feet by twenty feet, with a chimney at each end, Sharpe agreed to supply the boards and shingles and pay Hundley twenty-two hundred pounds of tobacco when the work was completed. Hundley agreed to supply the nails and timbers and his own food.[67] The types of houses constructed by Gates and Hundley were typical of the period. The clay for the bricks used in the chimneys probably came from the red clay along the north bank of the James. This clay had been used for the bricks at the town of Henrico in 1611 and would be utilized to support a large brick manufacturing industry in the future.

By the end of the century, Henrico was still a frontier county. Settlements had progressed little beyond the fall line, and although the economic growth of the county was hampered by the open frontier, it was steadily developing as the colony continued to prosper and grow economically. The personal estates appraised at the end of the century were comparatively small, and land was selling for about one tenth of a pound sterling per acre.[68]

That Henrico was becoming more of a settled community is reflected in the interest of its citizens in colonial policy and the petitions they submitted to the General Assembly in 1699. Their grievance to lessen millers' tolls was rejected, but their petition for a bill to prevent exportation of "Old Iron" was agreed to and a bill was ordered to be prepared. Reversing their previous stand on Indians, a proposition from Henrico asked for a law "for the paying of Levyes for Such Tuscarora Indians as make Tobacco and Corne amongst the English for their Use and that they may be listed as Tythables."[69] This petition was rejected by the burgesses. The clerk of the House of Burgesses at this time was William Randolph of Henrico, who had been elected as a burgess along with James Cocke. The position was not unknown to the Randolphs because Henry Randolph of Henrico, the revisor of the laws of the colony, had served as clerk in 1661, when Theoderick Bland of Henrico was the Speaker. William Randolph also served as county coroner and lieutenant colonel of the county militia. In the latter position, he served under William Byrd, Esq., "Colonel and Commander in Chief."[70] Another sign of stability was that Sheriff Thomas Cocke could rely on the service of a constable in each of the county's five districts. These individuals served the quarterly court in the administration of the law that was gradually transforming the area from a frontier to a settled community.

CHAPTER III

Expansion and Contraction

From 1700 to 1752, as the population moved westward, the county underwent changes. Its geographical boundaries were contracted, and its governmental and religious center shifted. These changes were brought about by the movement of the frontier westward and the growth of a more permanent farming community within the county. The western lands of Henrico were cut off in 1727 when the inhabitants of the county petitioned the General Assembly to divide it into two distinct counties "by a line beginning on the bounds of Hanover County to run down the East branch of Tuckahoe Creek called the deep Run and down the said Creek to the mouth thereof and a straight line crossing James River to the mouth of Skin quarter Creek on Appomattox River."[1] The land west of the line became Goochland County. In 1747 Henrico County was divided again when the area south of the James River became Chesterfield County. The boundaries between Henrico and New Kent and Hanover counties were also defined during this period. The Chickahominy River was the dividing line between Henrico and Hanover, but the main channel shifted over the years and this boundary remained in constant dispute. Except for some minor changes and the expansion of the city of Richmond, Henrico's boundaries have remained unchanged since 1747.

The governmental and religious center of the county and parish shifted as a result of expansion and growth of economic activity at the falls of the James, first visited by Captain Newport in 1607. At this site developed the first new town in the county since the establishment of Varina. Richmond began as a small town east of Shockoe Creek semiautonomous within the county; the citizens of the town were subject to county administration rule, but they retained the right to petition the General Assembly if necessary. Later, farther up the river, the town of Westham was established. Varina and Westham were destined to fade and to leave only their names to the geographic areas they occupied, but the city of Richmond grew to become the capital of the Commonwealth.

As early as 1691 the General Assembly established a western boundary line beyond which land was not to be granted.[2] A boundary line road ran from Manakin Town, some twenty miles above the falls on the south bank of the James, north to the Rappahannock River above the settlements on that river. Manakin Town, which had been deserted by the Monocan Indians as the colonists advanced westward, was to become the site of a new settlement. During the summer of 1700 more than eight hundred Huguenots, fleeing persecution in France after the repeal of the Edict of Nantes in 1685, sought refuge in Virginia. The first of four groups arrived under the leadership of the marquis de la Muce and Charles de Sailly with the expectation of settling in Norfolk County, but except for some land in dispute with North Carolina, there was no vacant land in that region. For this reason and because the climate in the area was considered unhealthy, they were offered land at the old Indian village known as Manakin Town.[3]

The first group of 207 refugees journeyed up the James to the falls. There Col. William Byrd II gave them shelter "upon his own Plantations" and allowed them "to furnish themselves from thence with Corn, and other Necessities."[4] Byrd had preceded the group to the falls and had made arrangements to quarter them there. He then led the marquis and Sailly to Manakin Town to show them the land. After they moved up the river beyond the falls, the refugees laid plans for a village and divided the land around the village site into small farms. In the spring of 1701 Byrd went to visit the settlement and reported that their "Hutts" were "very mean." He was encouraged by the fact that they had cleared a great deal of the land and had planted gardens and corn, but he was apprehensive because they had not started to break up the ground. He felt that continued support would have to be provided until their crops came in.[5] Acting under orders to lay out 10,000 acres for the French refugees in 1704, Byrd reported that 77 acres had been laid out before he set the bounds encompassing 10,033 acres for the settlement. While setting the bounds he reserved a parcel of 344 acres within the 10,033 acres for himself.[6]

About this time, or soon after, the refugees began developing a town. The small town, called King William's Town, had a square in the center intersected by two streets. A main building was to be built at each corner of the square—a church, rectory, hospital, and schoolhouse—and connected to either gardens or houses along the sides of the square. The central square was to be called Nicholson Square in honor of then Governor Francis Nicholson, and the street running through the square, parallel to the river, was Byrd Street. As the other groups of French refugees arrived in the colony, they were sent up to Manakin Town, "but afterwards upon some Disagreement, several dispers'd themselves up and down the Country." A major split occurred in 1710, and the Reverend Phillipe de Richebourge left the town with a large following and moved to South Carolina. By special act of the General Assembly, the Huguenot community was designated a separate parish within Henrico Parish, to be called King William Parish. The act exempted the Huguenots from paying any taxes for seven years so that they could support their own ministers.[7] Their first ministers were Huguenots, and Benjamin de Joux of Lyons was ordained as their pastor by the bishop of London.

The settlement at Manakin Town increased to about five hundred inhabitants, and they eventually built a church, a parish house, and a schoolhouse. After some difficult times during which the Huguenot settlers received assistance from the General Assembly, the governor, and the general populace, the settlement prospered. Byrd was particularly helpful during the hard times. He not only ordered his people to assist them but allowed the Huguenots to grind their corn at his gristmill without charge. In 1708 the sum of £8 13s. 6d. was levied against each parishioner of King William Parish "to be employed in the building of a church for the said parish." Two years later, the vestry paid Daniel Maubain for having made the chimneys for the church. That same year they entered into a "contract with a joiner for . . . the decoration of the interior of our church." Land was set aside as glebe land, and a parish house with two chimneys was constructed. Because they did not always have a resident minister, the vestry frequently agreed to rent out the glebe land in return for maintenance of the parish house.[8]

Even though they had been designated a separate parish within Henrico Parish, the settlers came under the jurisdiction of the Henrico County Court. When they first moved to Manakin Town, they requested that someone be designated to govern their settlement, and the governor and Council empowered two of their number "to Rule & Govern them . . . in all Causes both Civill & Military . . . Consonant & Agreeable to the Lawes of England & of this his Majesties Colony & Dominion of Virginia." Later, the gentlemen justices of Henrico were "authorized to administer oaths and test appointed by law to the French Refugees at Manakin town and the parts adjacent in order to their naturalization." In November 1705 Abraham Salle was added to the Henrico County Court "as resident magistrate for French Refugees at Manakintown." At the same time, the governor announced his intention to form a "foot company from Refugees" and requested that Col. William Randolph meet with the leaders of the settlement to obtain recommendations for officers. Governor Nicholson had expressed reservations about allowing the Huguenots to settle as a community. He did not believe that they should be allowed to retain their own language and customs, but he acceded to the crown's wish in the matter. Through the years, as the settlement prospered, it was assimilated. As the frontier moved westward, the threat of Indian attacks diminished, and the refugees moved from the town to their farms. The difficulty of obtaining ministers, intermarriage with the English, and the abundance of land eventually led to the dispersal of the Huguenot community.[9]

When Byrd visited the Huguenot settlement on the south side of the James in 1701, he reported that he returned on a new road that he had caused to be marked, an "extraordinary Levell and dry way" and "a very good well beaten path for carts." This road, which led to Byrd's mill at the falls, also served to transport coal from the newly discovered outcrop about a mile and a half upriver from the settlement. The deposit was "on the great upper Creek, w'ch, riseing very high in great Raines, hath washed away the Banke that the Coal lyes bare, otherwise it's very deep in the Earth, the land being very high and near the surface is plenty of slate." According to tradition, the coal was uncovered when a hunter pulled out a small tree on a steep bank near the stream.[10] The quality of the coal outcrop was not particularly good, but efforts were made to mine it until higher-quality coal was discovered. The first coal mined in the United States by the white settlers was in the Richmond Coal Basin in Henrico County. In May 1702 David Menestrier, one of the French refugees and a blacksmith by trade, requested permission to use the "lately discovered" coal mines. The governor and Council granted him permission to do so. Recognizing the value of the discovery, Colonel Byrd acquired 344 unclaimed acres "within the limits of the land laid out for the French refugees" that included the coal lands. On the same date, October 20, 1704, he acquired 3,664 acres on both sides of the road to the French settlement. In November 1705 he acquired the patent to Sabot Island in the James just above Manakin Town.[11]

Byrd hoped to find a good grade of coal to use in his iron furnace on Falling Creek. His expectations were not realized until 1711 when coal was discovered on his land farther up Falling Creek. In that same year, he noted in his diary that he went to Manakin Town "and from thence to the coalpit where he found all well and George [Smith] told me they had pressed through the rock and found very good coal." Unfortunately the quality of the coal from the Manakin Town area was poor and would not produce the heat needed for his ironworks. The discovery on Falling Creek negated any further efforts at Manakin Town.[12]

Unknown to those who settled on the land and to Byrd, the outcrop at Manakin Town was only a small part of what became known as the Richmond Coal Basin. This rather large area extends 33 miles north and south and about 9½ miles east and west at is widest point. Its geological position is considered remarkable, for it reposes within an extensive depression or trough of granite, with large feldspar crystals. About one-fifty of the basin lies north of the James. The coal area is of the Triassic age and of bituminous rank. There are five principal beds of coal and two beds of coke, but the geologic structure is complex. The coal, sandstone, granite, and rock strata are folded and faulted. An estimated one

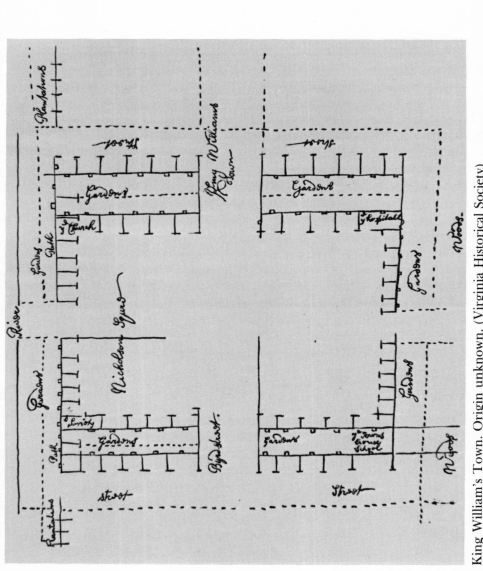

King William's Town. Origin unknown. (Virginia Historical Society)

billion tons of coal exist in the basin, but the quality of the coal varies. Benjamin Latrobe visited the coal region in 1796 and left the following description.

The coal country, which begins eleven miles above the City [of Richmond], . . . reaches to the distance of about 23. This range of country has many singularities. Its materials fill an immense hollow, formed between the last range of the lower strata of the Granite Rocks of Virginia, and the edge of the Second. . . . the coal is jumbled into the hollow [on the north side of the river, west of the city], & is in many places covered with sand-stone, which from the Wood that is found in it seems once to have been in a loose state, & to have been deposited by Water. It would appear as if the whole Mixture has been brought from some other part of the Continent, and had been left here by accident, having been in its fall broken into large distinct Masses. They lie very irregularly, but their General arrangement suits the hollow into which they appear to have tumbled."[13]

At the time of the initial discovery of the coal outcrop, the entire basin was in Henrico County. After the county was divided and Goochland and Chesterfield counties were created, only the area around Tuckahoe Creek in western Henrico and a smaller field about three miles east of the main coal basin remained in Henrico. The smaller field is about two miles long and a quarter of a mile wide and is known as the Deep Run Basin. Mining operations did not begin in these areas until after the second half of the eighteenth century.

The early mining techniques were rather simple. The coal was dug where it was exposed at ground level, creating a hole, or coalpit. Once the area was excavated at the outcrop, the miners could follow the seam until it played out or became too deep. During the colonial period, the excavation of outcrops and mining of seams were the principal techniques. When mines followed the seam, then the coal was removed by small cars on wooden tracks. Later, as mining techniques improved, vertical shafts would be used to reach deeper parts of the seams and to ventilate the gases and stale air. When shafts were put down, the coal was hoisted by buckets on a cable, or rope, attached to a revolving drum or windlass.[14]

There were at least two pits or mines operating in the

Richmond Coal Basin in 1745. There is no record of how
much coal was mined in the basin before 1758, but one authority estimated that fifty tons were produced annually
from 1748 to 1751. The quantity produced depended on
demand as well as the difficult conditions of operating a
mine in the wilderness. Robert Beverley noted in 1705 that
"they have very good Pit-Coal . . . , but no Man has yet
thought it worth his while to make use of them, having Wood
in Plenty, and lying more convenient for him." He predicted
that "as for Coals, it is not likely they should ever be used
there in any thing, but Forges and great Townes, if ever they
happen to have any; for, in their Country Plantations, the
Wood grows at every Man's Door." As Beverley rightly suggested, the demands of "great Townes" would be needed to
encourage increased mining activity. The town of Richmond
was still in the future, but as it grew into a great city, the
mining industry grew and became a vital part of the economic life of Henrico and the other counties in the Richmond Coal Basin.[15]

Life in Henrico began to accelerate as the vacant lands
were patented and the county ceased to be the frontier.
Growth required more regulations and government, and as
the colony grew, the General Assembly had to become more
involved in some local matters. Henricoans were not reluc-
tant to request relief or legislation through the right of petition. Sometimes their efforts to legislate by petition did not
meet with success. When they appealed to the General Assembly "that no Imposicons or taxes may be laid contrary to
the Charter granted by his late Majesty King Charles the
Second," their petition was rejected. The General Assembly
felt that "there are no Such impositions to their knowledge
intended." On the other hand, when they petitioned against
the attorney general's opinion that "the buildings and improvements made upon Land which Escheat to his Majesty
Should be valued by the Jury finding the Escheat and that
the Grantee Should pay So much Per Cent composition for
the Same," the Assembly resolved that the attorney General's
report was "Erroneous" and therefore "Contrary to Law."[16]

The petitions filed by the citizens of Henrico reflect their
thoughts and attitudes. Though few of the original manuscripts survive, we do know from the Assembly's records that

Henricoans were concerned about "Regulation and Settlement
. . . of Rights for the takeing up on Land"; that "ministers
may not be allowed forty pounds of Tobacco per pole for
their Annuall maintenance"; "for erecting a work house";
"that the law declaring Negroes & Slaves be real estate be
repealed"; "that money debts be paid in tobacco at the rate of
ten shillings per hundred"; and that "Ministers &c. Register
births and burials *Ex Officio*." All of these petitions were
either tabled or rejected outright by the House of Burgesses
or Council. Only the petition asking for a workhouse evoked
a responsive note when the committee to which it was assigned reported that it was "impracticable at this time &
therefore Rejected." Even when several Henrico citizens petitioned for the establishment of a bounty for killing crows and
squirrels similar to the one hundred pounds of tobacco they
received for killing each wolf, their petition was rejected.[17]
Petitions for internal improvement projects were submitted
also. A request from the inhabitants of New Kent and Henrico submitted in December 1700 that a bridge be built over
Chickahominy Swamp was agreed to.[18]

By an act passed in 1705, the General Assembly empowered
the county court to divide the county into road precincts and
to appoint annually "surveyors of the highways" in each precinct responsible "for making, clearing and repairing the
highways . . . for the convenient travelling and carriage by
land, of tobaccos, merchandises, or other things within this
dominion," and for constructing roads "to and from the city
of Williamsburg, the court house of every county, the parish
churches . . . public mills and ferries . . . and from one county
to another." The surveyors of the highways were empowered
to contract for construction of bridges and causeways to be
paid for by county levy. This system provided for some control over construction and maintenance, and a system of roads
evolved as the land was granted, especially after Goochland
and Chesterfield counties were formed.[19]

The control of the county court and the vestry of the parish church remained in the hands of the well-to-do families
in the county. This was not an uncommon situation in colonial Virginia. The consolidation of the county and parish
leadership was further strengthened by the appointments
these bodies made. Even militia appointments were made by

the governor upon recommendations made by the gentlemen justices. The militia of Henrico County throughout the
seventeenth century had never been numerically strong and
had to be combined with militia from other counties. William
Byrd I had been colonel of the combined militia of Henrico
and Charles City, and he continued in that capacity when the
new century began.

The militia consisted of all freemen between the ages of
sixteen and sixty, and in Henrico there were 345 militiamen
in 1703. By law the militia was to be mustered once a year,
while individual troops and companies were to drill three or
four times a year. In 1705 four barrels of powder and arms
and shot for twenty horse and fifty foot were sent to Henrico. Two years later the militia was called out to patrol the
frontier and to seize Tuscarora Indians who had taken part
in the murder of Jeremiah Pate of New Kent. In 1710 William Byrd II was appointed commander in chief of the militia of Henrico and Charles City, and he left an account of
the annual muster of that year, held on September 22.

About 10 o'clock we got on our horses and rode towards Henrico
to see the militia. Colonel Randolph with a troop met us at Pleasant's mill and conducted us to his plantation, where all the men
were drawn up in good order. The Governor was pleased with
them and exercised them for two or three hours together. He
presented me likewise to them to be their commander-in-chief [and
they] received me with an huzzah. About 3 o'clock we went to
Colonel Randolph's house and my hogshead of punch entertained
all the people and made them drunk and fighting all the evening,
but without much mischief.[20]

The next year there was increased hostile Indian activity to
the north and in North Carolina, where the situation was
aggravated by the tension over the boundary between Virginia and its southern neighbor. In August an erroneous
report of possible invasion supported by fourteen French
men-of-war resulted in the calling out of the militia. On August 15, Col. Frank Eppes was ordered to muster the Henrico militia, and on August 27 Colonel Byrd met with Colonel Eppes and his officers and "assigned troops." The next
day, word came that the six ships in the James were English,
so the militia were discharged and sent home. On September

William Byrd II (1674–1744). Copy by George Vaughan Curtis of original by Sir Godfrey Kneller. (Virginia State Library)

4 Colonel Eppes conferred with Colonel Byrd about Indian activity and conditions on the frontier. Colonel Byrd "ordered that every week two troops should range at the head of the river and if they found any Indians on patented land to take away their guns." On September 22 the Tuscarora Indians attacked the Carolina settlements on the upper Neuse and Pamlico rivers. Governor Spotswood sent detachments of militia to the border area to prevent Virginia Indians from joining the Tuscarora. He assembled a force of militia at Nottoway Town and warned the Indians that trade would be cut if they did not agree to a treaty.[21]

The situation was tense, and settlers on the frontier were fearful of sudden attacks from roving Indian bands. Colonel Byrd reported that he went to Henrico to inspect the militia in October. After the troops "exercised," they held games such as run-for-the-prize, cudgels, and wrestling. At a militia court all the Quakers were fined, and he warned them "they would certainly be fined five times in a year if they did not do as their fellow subjects did." The number of Quakers in Henrico caused apprehension as to their loyalty. Governor Spotswood charged them with disloyalty when they refused to sell any pork for use by the militia engaged in a campaign against the French in Canada. He was furious when he heard they had openly declared that they would "feed their enemies" if the French sailed up the James for supplies.[22]

In December 1711 Governor Spotswood concluded a treaty with several tributary tribes of Tuscarora which called for them to support the Carolinians in their efforts against the rebellious Tuscarora in that colony. Some thirty-nine men from Colonel Byrd's contingent of militia volunteered to go to North Carolina on an expedition against the Indians, but Spotswood was apprehensive of news that the Five Nations from New York would give assistance to the Tuscarora in Carolina. At the request of the settlers in the southern district of Henrico, between the James and Appomattox rivers (now Chesterfield County), Thomas Turpin was appointed lieutenant and directed to enlist "a party of Rangers" to patrol the frontier. The Tuscaroras in Carolina were defeated and driven into the Virginia mountains near the source of the Roanoke River in March 1713. Governor Spotswood then proposed to lead an expedition of two hundred men made up of militia from Surry, Prince George, and Henrico together with all the force of the tributary Indians against them, but he was unable to raise enough men and instead sent Capt. Robert Hix with a band of Indians to locate them and to arrange a treaty. The Tuscarora requested that they be allowed to remain in Virginia as peaceful tributaries, and a treaty was signed in 1714, but they eventually made peace with the Carolinians and returned to that colony.[23]

The inhabitants of western Henrico from the Appomattox to the James requested that they be allowed to muster the militia in their neighborhoods so that they would not have to travel to the annual muster. Their request was rejected, but they were still apprehensive. Governor Spotswood sought to establish outposts of friendly Indians along the western edge of the frontier, but this did not allay their fears. The inhabitants of Henrico north of the James asked that a force of rangers "be appointed for the Security of the said Frontier against the Indians," but their plea was rejected by the House of Burgesses. They petitioned Council for relief in 1719, "representing the great and eminent danger they apprehended themselves exposed to by the frequent marches of the Northern Indians through their Plantations, their Insolent behavior towards the said inhabitants and threatening to come in great numbers to fall upon the English of this Colony and so cutt off and destroy the Sappone Indians," a friendly tribe on the frontier.[24]

The threat of Indian attacks would be reduced through the efforts of Governor Spotswood. In 1720 he created the counties of Spotsylvania to the northwest and Brunswick to the Southwest, and these counties extended the frontier westward and served as buffers against the Indians from the north and south. Two years later, he concluded a treaty with the Iroquois Nations at Albany, New York, in which they agreed to remain west of the Blue Ridge. The decade of the 1720s marked the irresistible urge for western migration that was to characterize the century, and before long the Blue Ridge would cease to be a barrier to advancing civilization. Evidence of the advancing frontier was the division of Henrico County and the establishment of Goochland County along its western boundary in 1728. A side benefit of this was the removal of the Indian problem and the opportunity for the county to develop in peace.

Earlier efforts to Christianize the Indians had given way to conversion by military force, but the established church as a social and reigious center for the settlers continued to flourish. This growth of the population necessitated the building of chapels in outlying areas and eventually the movement of the Varina Parish church. In 1702 Jacob Ware was the minister in Varina (Henrico) Parish. George Robinson had become minister in Bristol Parish, south of the James; and de Joux was minister to the Huguenots in King William Parish.[25]

Little is known of the activities of the Hernico vestry except what survives in the court records. The vestry books before October 30, 1730, are not extant. A chapel was approved by the General Assembly in 1715 "for the ease of the said inhabitants at or near the Stooping Hickory about a mile below the Lower Westham in the Said Parish of Henrico and that the minister be appointed to preach therein every fourth Sunday." This chapel was to be built by March 31, 1717, on a half-acre parcel, and a reader was provided by the vestry. Services continued to be held in the chapel until December 1741. The chapel was apparently abandoned at that time, and John Eals, its reader, and Eleanor Williams, its sexton, were transferred to the newly constructed church in the town of Richmond.[26]

The parish of Henrico was divided in 1720 when the General Assembly assumed the authority to establish and fix the boundaries of parishes because the Church of England did not have diocesan government in the colony. The new parish was called St. James's Parish, and it ran west from a line "on the North side of James River . . . from the Mouth of the Little Westham Creek and up that Creek to the main road and from thence a North Course to New Kent County, and . . . on the South Side James River . . . from the River along the Upper line of the Land appropriated for the French Refugees & from that line a South Course to Apamatok River." When Henrico County was divided in 1728 and Goochland County was formed, St. James's Parish became coterminous with Goochland County. All of Henrico Parish west of the dividing line became part of St. James's Parish and all of St. James's Parish east of the line became part of

Henrico Parish. The greater part of King William Parish was in the area that became Goochland, but a portion of it remained in Henrico and was included in the area that became Chesterfield County in 1749.[27]

The Reverend Mr. Ware was one of the victims of an epidemic in 1709, and he was succeeded by the Reverend William Finnie.[28] At the end of his fourteenth year of service in Henrico Parish, Finnie reported that his parish "is, I believe, about 25 miles in length and about 18 in breadth in some places, having in it 2 churches and a Chappel the number of families I cannot tell, but there are 1100 tythables in it, that is slaves male and female about 16 years old, and all males of that age that are free, I believe, there may be 400 families."[29]

One of the churches he mentioned was the new parish church at Curles. This church had been constructed in 1720 or 1721 and was the successor to the parish church at Varina. Located on land donated by Richard Randolph on his plantation known as Curles, which included the land area known as Curles Neck, this church had been built by Richard Randolph. It was situated approximately four miles down river from the old Varina church site and was sometimes called Four Mile Creek Church and Curles Church because it lay between those geographic features. The second church mentioned was probably the one constructed by Thomas Jefferson, Jr. (the grandfather of the president), in 1723 near Rock Hall on the site of Mount Malady, the tract on which Dale had established a hospital across the river from Henrico Town. The chapel mentioned was the one "near the Stooping Hickory about a mile below the Lower Westham."[30]

The Reverend Mr. Finnie noted that divine services were held once every Sunday and on Good Friday, Christmas, and other holidays. One hundred to two hundred parishioners attended the services. The sacrament of the Lord's Supper was administered six times a year at each church and twice a year at the chapel with not more than twenty communicants at one time. On the matter of "Infidels, bond or free," and their conversion, he remarked: "There are that are bond, but their Masters, do no more than let some of them now and then go to Church for their Conversion." The distance of families from the church and the difficulty of travel were reasons given as to why he did not "Catechise the Youth."

This was done "by the Schoolmasters or parents and when they grow to any bigness they care not to abide the public catechising of a Minister." Even though the church was there to provide divine services and to minister to the people of Henrico, Finnie commented that "the people [are] not so observant of Devout postures as could be wished."[31]

The minister of any parish had to rely on his parishioners for his salary and living quarters. The minister in Henrico Parish received 16,000 pounds of tobacco, which was levied on the tithables in the parish. Out of this amount, he had to pay 1,280 pounds for each cask. Finnie lamented that the tobacco he received "has never, one time with another been worth one penny per lb." He occupied a house on the glebe, which he farmed himself rather than leasing it out. The house was in good shape, but he had discovered the parish was "generally too backward" when asked to tend to repairs. As minister of Henrico Parish, he was responsible for only that parish, but "in my vicinity the parishes so vacant employ me for an occasional week day's forenoon." In 1727 Finnie also served the refugees at Manakin Town while they were without a minister.[32]

In May 1730 some inhabitants of the county petitioned "for Erecting a Chappel on the deep run of Tuckahoe Creek." Their petition was rejected. In that year, the Reverend James Keith was reported as the minister, and he served until October 12, 1733. Because the inhabitants of Henrico Parish south of the James "do lie under divers inconveniences," the General Assembly passed an act in August 1734 establishing a separate parish between the Appomattox and the James. This act stipulated that after May 31, 1735, that part of the Henrico Parish south of the James would be combined with that part of Bristol Parish north of the Appomattox to form "into one other district parish, and be called and known by the name of Dale parish."[33]

Between the date of passage of the act and its implementation, the vestry of Bristol Parish decided to build a new church south of the Appomattox and assessed and levied a tax of twelve pounds of tobacco per tithable for construction of the new church. Those members in the area north of the Appomattox that was to become part of Dale Parish petitioned the General Assembly for relief, and an act was passed

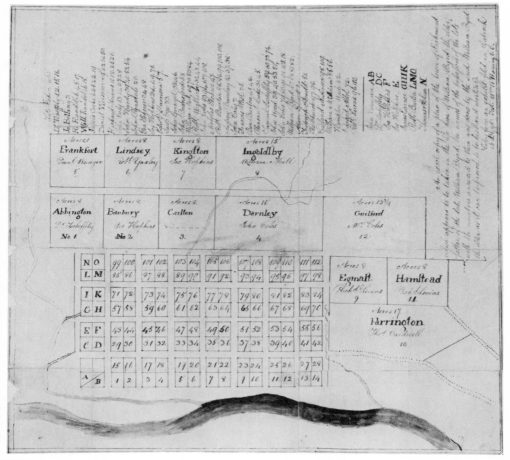

William Byrd's 1736 map of Richmond. (Virginia State Library)

Varina Parish Church, later called St. John's Church, as it looked before the nave was increased and the tower was added. By F. E. Gretter. From J. Staunton Moore's *The Annals and History of Henrico Parish* (Richmond, 1904), opp. p. 2 of Vestry Book.

requiring repayment to those north of the Appomattox. The separation of that part of Henrico Parish south of the James left only that part of the original parish which would be coterminous with the county of Henrico after the division and establishment of Chesterfield County in 1749. The Reverend Zachariah Brooke, who had served as temporary supply at the chapel, became the first rector of Dale Parish. After a year, he was succeeded by George Frayser, who served the parish for twenty years.[34]

After Keith left in 1733, the Reverend David Mossom, rector of St. Peter's Parish, New Kent County, conducted services at the Henrico Parish church every fifth Sunday. This arrangement continued until September 1735 when the Reverend Anthony Gavin became rector of Henrico Parish. He came with letters of recommendation from Lieutenant Governor William Gooch and the Reverend James Blair, commissary, former rector of Henrico Parish. After he had performed "his office both in reading and preaching . . . the Vestry . . . unanimously agreed that he be received and entertained as minister of this parish." Gavin served the members of the parish for nine months before he left under rather mysterious circumstances. Whether his antislavery feelings led to his departure is not known, for the Vestry Book is silent. Bishop William Meade considered him a zealous and laborious man, but very plain of speech.[35]

The position of rector did not remain vacant long. After a trial sermon, the Reverend William Stith became minister on July 18, 1736. A native of Charles City, born in 1689, he married his cousin Judith, daughter of Thomas Randolph of Tuckahoe. After theological studies in England and ordination, he returned to Virginia in 1731. At Williamsburg, he served as master of the Grammar School and chaplain to the House of Burgesses. During his fifteen years as rector of Henrico Parish, he wrote a *History of Virginia,* published in 1747. He resigned on December 3, 1751, and was elected president of the College of William and Mary in August 1752, in which position he was serving when he died three years later.

Soon after Reverend Stith came to Henrico, the vestry began discussing the possibility of moving the parish church

from the Varina area. When they met to set the parish levy
on October 8, 1737, they did "agree to build a Church on the
most Convenient place at or near Thomas Williamson's in
this parish to be Sixty feet in Length and Twenty-five in
Breadth and fourteen foot pitch to be finished in a plain
Manner After the Moddle of Curls Church." The clerk was
ordered to advertise "the particular parts of the Said Building and of the time and place of undertaking the Same," and
every tithable was to give five pounds of tobacco "to be apply'd towards building the New Church at Williamson's" on
the Brook Road.[36]

It was in the year 1737 that Maj. William Mayo surveyed
and laid out the town of Richmond for William Byrd II; and
for whatever reason, the construction of a new church was
delayed. On December 20, 1739, the vestry "agreed that a
Church be Built on the most Convenient Spot of Ground
near the Spring on Richardson's Road, on the South Side of
Bacon's Branch, on the Land of the Honourable William
Byrd, Esq." Richard Randolph contracted to build a structure the same as described in the 1737 minutes for £317 10s.,
to be completed by June 10, 1741. This site was northwest of
the town. Apparently work had not started by October 12,
1740, when Byrd wrote Randolph: "I should with great pleasure, oblige the Vestry, and particularly your Self, in granting them an acre, to build their Church upon; but there are
so many roads already thro that Land, that the Damage to
me would be too great to have another of a mile long cut
thro it." However, Byrd went on, "I should be very glad if
you sou'd please to think Richmond a proper place, and
considering the great number of people that live below it,
and would pay their Devotions there, that wou'd not care to
go so much higher I can't but think it wou'd be Agreeable to
most of the people, and if they will agree to have it there, I
will give them two of the best Lots that are not taken up, and
besides give them any pine Timber they can find on that side
Shockoe Creek, and Wood for burning of Bricks into the
Bargain." The two lots offered by Byrd were numbers 97
and 98 fronting on what is now Grace Street, on the high
ground on the northeast edge of town overlooking the town
and surrounding the countryside. The vestry then considered this offer:

Whereupon the Question is put whither the said Church should be Built on the Hill caled Indian Town at Richmond, or at Thomas Williamson's plantation on the Brook Road, and is caryed by a Majority of Voices for the former.

It is thereupon Ordered that the Church formerly Agreed on to be Build by Richard Randolph, Gen: on the South side of Bacon's Branch, be Built on Indian Town at Richmond, after the Same Manner as in the said Former Agreement was mentioned.[37]

The church, which was variously called the New Church, the Town Church, the Upper Church, and the Richmond Church, was completed by Randolph in 1741. The church was not called St. John's Church until 1829. By that time the building had been modified by the construction of a forty-foot by forty-foot addition onto the north side of the original building. The churchyard and cemetary had been expanded when the city government purchased the other two lots in the square in 1799. The city enclosed the square with a brick wall, and the churchyard was opened as a burying ground for the city at large. Until the opening of Shockoe Cemetery in 1826, this was the only public cemetery in Richmond. In the first half of the 1830s, a tower was added to the northern entrance; since then, except for minor modifications, the church's exterior has remained unaltered.

In 1742 the vestry agreed and ordered "that a Chappel be built on a hill above Deep Run on the main road, on the land of John Shoemaker, to be in length, forty eight; and Breadth, Twenty-four—to be weatherboarded with Fether-edge planck and covered with hart shingles, nailed on—to have three Pews, Reading-Desks, Pulpit and Gallery, to be finished workmanlike in a plain strong manner." William Street was reported as the reader at Deep Run Chapel in 1744, when Peter Randolph and John Coles were appointed to "agree with the cheapest workman" to finish the chapel. The church acquired title to the land in 1750.[38]

Between 1724 and 1750 improvements had been made to the church at Curles and the buildings on the glebe lands. This church served as a model for the Richmond Church that became St. John's. Even after the construction of the Richmond Church, the Curles Church remained the principal church of the parish for a number of years. On the glebe lands at Varina the vestry built a 24-foot by 16-foot kitchen in 1735 which was "under-pined with Brick" and had "an inside Brick Chimney." In 1743 the vestry contracted with Beverley Randolph to construct a 40-foot by 20-foot "Tobacco House" on the glebe land, and in 1748 the church wardens contracted with workmen to construct a new glebe house "48 by 20, two outside Chimneys, a cellar 20 by 20, to be finished Strong, Neat, and Plain."[39]

The number of tithables in the parish dropped from 1,754 to 973 when the parish divided in 1735, but it increased to 1,470 by midcentury. The vestry processioned, or walked the boundaries of, each individual parcel of land as required, and each year they set the parish levy based on the projected needs for the coming year. A partial list of the projected needs for the year 1748 included:

To the Reverend William Stith, Minister, Salary and cask,	16,640
To John Bryand, reader,	1,789
To Mark Clarke, do.,	1,789
To William Street, do.,	1,789
To Solomon Cary, Clerk Vestry,	450
To John Hobson, Sexton,	536
To Elenor Williams, do.,	536
To John Shoemaker, for Cleaning the Arbour,	536
To the Church Wardens, for Bread and Wine,	344
To do., for keeping Mary Burnett,	1,000
To the Church Wardens, for Jane Jennings,	600
To Colo, Richard Randolph, for the use of Benja. Goode,	896
To the Church Wardens, for Elizabeth Bailey,	850
To Edmond Allen, for his son, an Idiot,	1,000
To Colo. Richard Randolph, for Wm. Ford,	600
To do., for Lame Childers,	500
To the Church Wardens, for James Jennett,	800
To William Lawless, for keeping Mary Burnet's bastard child, she being an Idiot, and upon the Parish,	600
To Robert Morris, for buying Rebecca Pruitt,	200
To Daniel Baker,	600
To John Liptrott,	400
To Anne Smith,	300

To Peter Randolph, for keeping Eliz'a Bailey the
   remaining part of her life,   300
To John Jones, for keeping his Daughter, being a
   Fool,   300
To Humphrey Smith, for keep'g Thomas Bethel,   500[40]

The Quakers continued to be a strong dissenter group in eastern Henrico. The first Quaker meetinghouse had been given by John Pleasants to "Friends in these parts called Quakers." It was replaced with a new structure in 1700. The interior, finished in 1704, contained a circular row of seats and a double seat at one end. The latter was ten feet long, and a "bar of banisters" was constructed before it "for the easement of Friends of the Ministry." A small burying ground was contained on the same plot of ground on which the meetinghouse stood. The building on Curles Neck was the only Quaker house of worship until the construction of the White Oak Swamp Meetinghouse in 1723 at Edward Mosby's. This small building measured twenty-four by seventeen feet and was built of pine boards. A movable partition in the center divided the men and women during part of the service, and two doors on one side provided access for each sex. A third door at one end led to "a small galery for ministring friends." Both the Curles Meeting and the White Oak Swamp Meeting were very active and conducted monthly meetings. The road connecting the two areas was frequently traveled by members of each meetinghouse, and it became known as the Quaker Road. In 1772 John Pleasants's grandson, John Pleasants, deeded both sites to the Quakers.[41]

After 1747, a new religious group made its appearance in Henrico. In 1741 a split in the Presbyterian Synod of Philadelphia had led to the establishment of two groups—New Light, also Known as New-Side, and Old-Side Presbyterians. New Lights believed the individual could experience conviction of sin and conversion and receive a new light. They also believed that a minister could preach as the Spirit led him and that earthly authority in church and state was subordinate to the leading of the Spirit. The Old-Side Presbyterians maintained the traditional Presbyterian form of worship and church structure. The split lasted from 1741 to 1758. In 1747 Samuel Davies, licensed and ordained as an evangelist by the Presbytery of New Castle, Delaware, came to Virginia.

Within a decade after its beginning in Hanover County, Pres-
byterianism was established in Henrico, Hanover, Goochland, Caroline, and Louisa counties. Under the preaching
and teaching of New Light Presbyterian ministers, the denomination grew and spread into Henrico and the other
counties.

The Reverend John Roan served in Hanover and Henrico
during the winter of 1744–45, but it was not until 1747 when
Samuel Davies petitioned for a license to preach that a Presbyterian meetinghouse was reported in Henrico on the land
of Thomas Watkins. As a preacher, Davies was capable of
delivering a forceful message that kept people under the
spell of his eloquence without evoking enthusiastic uncon-
trollable outbursts of emotionalism. Operating within the
constraints of government control by the crown and the established church, he succeeded in establishing meetinghouses
in Louisa, Goochland, and Caroline, but his effort to have
one set up in New Kent in 1750 was rejected by the General
Court.

The number of dissenters grew at the expense of the established church, both in people and tax base. Their presence
represented a threat to the established order. Their method
of worship, the emotional exhortations of their ministers,
and their credentials were frequently criticized. A message to
the House of Burgesses in 1751 complained:

That there have been frequently held in the counties of Hanover, Henrico, Goochland & some others, for several years past,
numerous Assemblies, especially of the common People, upon a
pretended religious account; convened sometime merely by Lay
Enthusiasts who, in those meetings read sundry fanatical Books &
used long extempore prayers, and Discourses; sometimes by
strolling pretended Ministers; and at present by one Mr. Samuel
Davies, who has fixed himself in Hanover; . . .

That tho' these Teachers, and their adherents . . . , assume the
Denominations of Presbyterians, yet, we think, they have not just
claim to that character; as the Ringleaders of the Party were, for
their erroneous Doctrines, and Practises, excluded the Presbyterian
Synod of Philadelphia, in May 1741.[42]

Although not directly affected, Henrico citizens would experience changes in governmental policies brought on by the

St. John's Church as it looks today. (Photograph by John S. Salmon)

influx of Scotch-Irish and German immigrants in the Shenandoah Valley, Rappahannock River, and northern Virginia areas. Blocked in the Piedmont area, Davies went to the Southside frontier to continue his work.

Education remained under the jurisdiction of the church and the individual families. When asked about "public Schools," the Reverend Mr. Finnie, minister of Henrico Parish, reported to the bishop of London in 1724: "We have none. I wish we had, and that some Charity by your Lordship's means were found to promote it." The Reverend George Robinson replied that there were no public schools in Bristol Parish, "but there are several private ones to teach children to read, write and cipher, and the children's fathers hire those Schools and pay you [the minister] out of their own pockets.[43]

Some wealthy planters assumed the expense of employing a tutor or would transport someone under an indenture agreement to serve as a teacher. Some planters assigned an indentured servant who had received some education the responsibility of teaching their children. Whenever classes of instruction were set, children from neighboring farms would be invited to attend the "school." A traveler in the colony observed that a clever servant often was indentured as a schoolmaster. Some wealthy planters sent their children to England to receive an education, and some sent them to the College of William and Mary. However, the private tutor seemed to be preferred. An example of this can be found in the will of William Randolph of Tuckahoe. He left instructions that his son Thomas Mann Randolph receive his education from a private tutor and not be sent to either England or the College of William and Mary.[44]

The chief agricultural crops in Henrico, as in the rest of the colony, continued to be tobacco, corn, and wheat. The first was the money crop and was generally used as money. Corn and wheat were necessities, and they required mills to grind them into meal and flour. As the trade product, tobacco had to be carried or rolled in casks to shipping points. A warehouse had been established at Varina to store tobacco and other goods while awaiting shipment. As the frontier advanced westward, the need for a warehouse and a mill closer to the producers was met when William Byrd I established them on his land at the falls. In 1730, the General Assembly authorized a public warehouse at Shockoe on William Byrd II's land, the same area where his father's uncle, Thomas Stegge, Jr., had established the family's trading post. On the south side of the river, opposite Shockoe, Byrd had two mills.[45]

In 1732, while on a journey up the James, Byrd stopped to inspect his land at the falls. Crossing the river at Shockoe, he "visited three of his quarters, where besides finding all the people well, I had the pleasure to see better crops than usual both of corn and tobacco." Due to the lack of rain upriver, both of the mills were standing still. Taking advantage of the low water, Byrd blasted a channel through the rocks to the mills. The next year, while on a journey to his land in the vicinity of present-day Danville, Virginia, and Eden, North Carolina, Byrd and his companions "laid the foundation of two large cities: one at Shacco's to be called Richmond, and the other at the point of the Appomattox River, to be named Petersburg." Maj. William Mayo agreed to lay out the cities into lots "without fee or reward." Byrd had concluded that the two sites were naturally intended for marts because they were the uppermost landings before navigation was interrupted by the falls. The colonists relied on water transportation to move their goods and Byrd realized that up-country planters needed a marketplace and depot on each river.[46]

Although he commented about the plans for the two cities as not only building "castles only, but also cities in the air," Byrd faced reality. The area at the falls of the James, once referred to as "world's End," was ordained by nature as a market center. Evidence indicates that Byrd opposed an act of the General Assembly that would have established a town at the falls of the James in 1727. In return, other entrepreneurs tried to have the act setting up the public warehouse at Shockoe repealed and to establish a town on the south bank of the James. The threat of competition and the growth of commercial activities weighed in Byrd's decision to lay out Richmond. If he waited too long, the General Assembly would establish a town and he would have to surrender fifty acres for the town site, losing not only a portion of what the land was worth but control over the development of the town as well. Another thought that must have crossed his mind was that the inspectors at the public warehouse would remain under his influence if he was involved in the establishment of the town.[47]

It was four years before Major Mayo surveyed the site for the town and laid out the lots. Byrd named his new town Richmond because the terrain and surroundings reminded him of Richmond on the Thames. The town site was just east of the Shockoe Creek and included the southern face of present-day Church Hill. The town was divided into thirty-two squares in a grid of four squares deep and eight squares long. Each square was divided into four lots, and all but two of the western flank of squares were designated by letters. The lots in the remaining squares, 112 in all, were numbered west to east. Lots 97 and 98 were later donated to the parish for its church. Lot 18 would be the site of the Henrico courthouse. The cross streets, numbered First through Ninth streets, are present-day Seventeenth through Twenty-fifth streets. The east and west streets were given letters of the alphabet, D through H. Present-day Cary Street was D Street, Main was E, Franklin was F, Grace was G, and Broad was H. Thus, Byrd's original town was encompassed by the present streets of Cary on the south, Twenty-fifth on the east, Broad on the north, and Seventeenth on the west. North and east of the boundaries of the town, twelve large plots varying from eight to seventeen acres in size were laid out. Each plot was given a name— Abbington, Banbury, Charlton, Guilford, Frankfort, etc.— and perhaps they were to be country estates.

The town lots were offered for sale for £7 each. In April 1737 the *Virginia Gazette* ran the following advertisement.

This is to give Notice, That on the North Side of James River, near the Uppermost Landing, and a little below the Falls, is lately laid off by Major Mayo, a Town, called Richmond, with Streets 65 Feet wide, in a pleasant and healthy Situation, and well supply'd with Springs of good Water. It lies near the Publick Warehouse at Shoccoe's, and in the midst of great Quantities of Grain, and all kind of Provisions. The lots will be granted in Fee Simple, on Condition only of building a House in Three Years Time, of 24 by 16 Feet, fronting within 5 feet of the Street, The Lots to be rated according to the Convenience of their Situation, and to be sold after this April General Court by me,

William Byrd.[48]

A number of longtime residents of Henrico purchased lots in the town, and William Byrd retained one square of four lots himself. John Bolling, Richard Randolph, William Randolph, and John Pleasants were among those who purchased lots. Dr. Tscheffely, "Chemist and Practitioner of Physick," purchased six lots. Fifteen of the lots were acquired by John Coles, who presented a petition to the county court requesting that the town be established by an act of the General Assembly. The petition was presented to the court and certified on May 1, 1742. Because the town had not been established by an act of the General Assembly, the freeholders and inhabitants were not entitled to any privileges given to freeholders and inhabitants of towns so established. This was rectified by passage of an act of incorporation entitled "An Act, for establishing the Town of Richmond, in the county of Henrico; and allowing fairs to be kept therein" on June 19, 1742.[49]

Recognizing that Byrd had "made sale of most of the said lots to divers persons, who have since settled and built thereon," and that he "intends speedily to lay out other part of his adjacent lands into lots, and streets, to be added to and made part of the said town, and is willing that part of his lands, situate between the said town, and Shoccoe's Creek, and the river, shall remain and be, as and for a common for the use of the inhabitants of the said town, for ever," the Assembly "constituted, appointed, erected, and established, a town, in the manner it is already laid out, . . . to be called by and retain the name of Richmond." Fairs were authorized, one in May and one in November, each to last two days for the "sale and vending of all manner of cattle, victuals, provisions, Goods, wares and merchandises whatsoever." All those attending the fairs would be "exempt and privileged from all arrests, attachments, and executions, whatsoever, except for capital offences, breaches of the peace, or for any controversies, suits, and quarrels, that may arise and happen" for the two days of the fair and for the two days before and after the same.[50]

The act of the Assembly gave the town legal standing under the law and constituted legislative recognition and approval of Byrd's town. There were no provisions for independent government for Richmond. The town was a part of

Chesterfield County Courthouse. This building was built in 1750 on the design of the Henrico County Courthouse at Varina, of which there are no known extant drawings or pictures. (Valentine Museum)

the county, and county and parish officials had the same authority there as anywhere else in the county. Citizens of Richmond and the county could petition the Assembly equally. The county court heard legal disputes and administered justice, but specific regulations were set down by act of Assembly upon petition from the inhabitants of the town. In 1744, when a petition called attention to the fact that the citizens of Richmond were "often in great and imminent danger of having their houses and effects burnt and consumed by reason of many wooden chimneys in the said town," the Assembly passed the necessary act ordering the sheriff to demolish any wooden chimney still standing three years after the passage of the act. A companion petition was a request to prevent hogs from running at large. The Assembly did not act on the petition or similar petitions submitted later until March 1773, when an act prohibiting hogs and goats from running at large was passed.[51]

William Byrd II died in 1744, but by that time the town of Richmond had taken hold, and even though his son would prove a poor financial manager, the town survived. The rate of settlement and development of western lands influenced the settlements at the falls. In May 1748 the General Assembly approved an act to establish the town of Warwick on the south bank of the James below Richmond, just above Falling Creek. A warehouse and mills had been built on the site earlier, and tobacco inspection had been authorized at the warehouse in 1730. The town later served as a supply point for the state navy during the Revolutionary War, and when the British occupied it in 1781, they burned it. In 1748, additional inspectors were requested for the warehouses at Shockoe and Warwick, and the citizens of Henrico and Amelia petitioned for a warehouse on the land of John Osborne on the south side of the James below Warwick. This petition was approved, and the House of Burgesses also recognized the need for the warehouse at Rocky Ridge "on the land of the late William Byrd" across the river from the town of Richmond.[52]

It was at this time in 1749, that the inhabitants of Henrico petitioned for a division of the county north and south of the James River. Usually the distance from the courthouse, difficulty of travel, and density of settlement were used as reasons for establishing new counties from older ones. The petitions do not survive, but the Assembly records make it clear that Henricoans were not united on the question. A petition from inhabitants north of the river and petitions from inhabitants south of the James supported the division, but one petition opposed the move. However, the latter petition was rejected by the House of Burgesses, and a bill was prepared dividing the county "for the Ease and convenience of the Inhabitants . . . in attending Courts and other public meetings." The Council concurred and the governor gave his approval on May 11, 1749. The act stipulated that the division would take effect "immediately after the twenty fifth day of May next ensuing" but gave the sheriff authority to collect "any Levies Fees or Dues which shall be due." The area of Henrico south of the James became Chesterfield County.[53]

From a population of about 250 in 1742, Richmond had grown in population and activity by 1750. Both the county court and the sheriff, who served as the court's law enforcement officer, found it too cumbersome to use the courthouse at Varina as the county's population and commercial center shifted to Richmond. As a result, the "Justices and other Inhabitants of the County" petitioned to have Richmond made the county seat, and this was approved April 24, 1750. The old wooden courthouse at Varina had been replaced by a brick rectangular structure, a story and a half high, with a steeply pitched roof. It served as a model for the Chesterfield County Courthouse in 1749, which was built "of the same dimensions and materials," except it was to have a plank floor. The courthouse at Varina, still standing as late as 1853, apparently had a masonry floor. The site in Richmond selected for the new courthouse was lot 18, on the southwest corner of present Twenty-second Street, but the structure was constructed in the middle of the street and not on the lot. The courthouse at Varina continued in use until the new structure was completed. In April 1752, Lieutenant Governor Robert Dinwiddie issued a proclamation ordering the removal of the Henrico court to Richmond.[54]

In 1752, the Assembly responded to a petition in which the inhabitants of Richmond "represented . . . that they labour under great inconvenience for want of trustees to lay off and regulate the streets, and to settle the bounds of the lots." The

Assembly authorized trustees, who were "to settle and establish such rules and orders, for the more regular and orderly building of the houses in the said town, as to them shall seem best and most convenient." The appointment of trustees for the town relieved part of the burden on the county court and proved to be the first step toward a separate governing body and eventual independent status for the city. The trustees appointed in the act were Peter Randolph, William Byrd, William Randolph, Bowler Cocke, the younger, Richard Randolph, Thomas Atchison, Samuel DuVal, and John Pleasants. Any five or more of them could rule in disputes, and the entire group could elect a successor to fill any vacancy caused by death, removal out of the county, or other legal disability.[55] Although this could be considered a step toward local control, the composition of the board represented the politically strong and well-to-do families who were members of the county court and served on the parish vestry. The trustees were appointed by, and responsible to, the General Assembly, and the Assembly continued to regulate some town affairs, especially in response to petitions received from the town's inhabitants.[56]

West of Richmond, above the falls on the north bank of the James, a public storehouse had been authorized "at Westham on the land of William Byrd," in 1745. Seven years later, after laying off a town of "one hundred and fifty lots, with streets . . . at Westham in the county of Henrico, on the land lately belonging to Beverley Randolph, esq., deceased," William Randolph requested that his land between the town and the river be included in the town. In "An Act for establishing the town of Westham, in the county of Henrico" passed in February 1752, the General Assembly, reasoning that "whereas the said town is seated near the lower landing of an extensive navigation, above the falls of James River, and is likely to become the chief place of trade for all the upper inhabitants of that river, and its several branches," enacted "that the said one hundred and fifty lots, and streets, already laid out, together with the land between those lots and the river, be, and are hereby appointed, erected and established, a town, to be called by the name of Beverley."[57] Thomas Jefferson's father, Peter Jefferson, surveyed the town site in 1756 and prepared a "Plan of the Town of Bev-

Wilton. Built by William Randolph of Turkey Island for his son William Randolph III about 1750, this is perhaps the best-known Henrico eighteenth-century river plantation. During the 1930s the mansion was moved to Richmond's West End. (Virginia State Library)

erley." A number of names are entered on numerous lots
indicating purchase, but the town was never developed. Apparently it failed to attract permanent settlers because of the
close proximity of Richmond. Beverley was only a stopping
point where goods were transferred from boat to wagon or
stored awaiting land transportation around the falls to Richmond. The town and name Beverley have vanished, but the
name Westham has survived, and the area became important
during the Revolutionary War because of the military supplies manufactured there.

The first half of the eighteenth century witnessed a growth
in population in Henrico County despite the shrinking of the
county's borders. In 1702 there were 863 tithables in the
original county, and this number was increased by 52 in
1703. The census of 1703 reported 2,413 souls in the county
excluding the French refugees. Of this figure 915 were tithables and 1,498 were women and children. A total of 148,757
acres of land had been patented in the county, and 98 horses
were reported. In 1714 there were 1,335 tithables on
196,683 acres. In 1722 and 1723 the numbers of tithables
reported in Henrico County were 1,842 and 1,922 and in
1726 there were 2,453 tithables and 7,359 souls, or 14.4 persons per square mile of owned acreage. After the establishment of Goochland County, the vestry reported 1,574 tithables in Henrico Parish. This dropped to 973 tithables when
the area south of the James was cut off as a separate parish.
After that, the number of tithables increased each year, and
in 1750 there were 1,470 in the parish, which by that time
had the same boundaries as the county.[58]

The total number of acres taxed in 1751 was 115,117.
There were a number of large farms along the north bank of
the James as well as throughout the county. Those along the
river were held by politically influential and wealthy families,
and it was there that many large homes were built. Chief
among the landowners were the Randolphs. William Randolph had built his manor house at Turkey Island around
1680. His oldest son, William Jr., built a stately house nearby
early in the eighteenth century. His second son, Thomas,
built above the falls in 1710 and called his home and plantation Tuckahoe. His fifth son, Richard, built his home, a two-
story frame structure measuring ninety-five by twenty-six

feet, at Curles. A sixty-foot colonnade connected the main house with a brick dairy, a laundry, an icehouse, and a stable. Farther up the river, William Randolph, Jr., built a brick mansion known as Wilton for his son William III around 1750. This two-storied Georgian residence was fully paneled in pine. When William III died in 1761, the house passed to his son Peyton Randolph. Later it passed out of the Randolph family, and in the 1930s the vacant house was purchased by the Colonial Dames and moved to Richmond's West End. Above Wilton was Chatsworth, home of Peter Randolph, grandson of William Randolph of Turkey Island. This two-story framed dwelling was built before 1750.[59]

The Randolphs were actively involved in local and colonial government. William Randolph had served in the House of Burgesses and was appointed Speaker in 1698. Richard Randolph of Curles served as a burgess between 1736 and 1748 and was treasurer of the colony from 1736 to 1738. Peter Randolph of Chatsworth served as clerk of the House of Burgesses and attorney general of the colony. Peyton Randolph of Wilton served as Speaker of the House of Burgesses and as president of the First Continental Congress. The Randolphs continued to move up the river. William's third son, Isham, built Dungeness, the site of Goochland Courthouse. Isham's son-in-law Peter Jefferson, father of Thomas Jefferson, moved from below Richmond on the south bank to the north bank above Richmond and then up the James near the Rivanna River.

Below Wilton was Lilly Valley. Except for references in deeds and on maps, little is known about the structure. Above Wilton was Powhatan, the seat of the Mayo family. Joseph Mayo, a merchant, came to the colony around 1727. His brother, William, was a surveyor and prepared the survey for Richmond. The Mayo family was active in both the county's and the city's history. Their two-story brick mansion was sixty feet long, and a later wing gave it a T-shape.

As the frontier moved westward, the younger Randolphs and other Henricoans moved with it. For the next half century a great deal of land would begin to change hands, and as the town of Richmond began to develop, it would begin to affect commercial activity in the county.

CHAPTER IV

Unrest and Revolution

The Revolutionary War years brought changes that culminated in the separation of the mother (Henrico) and her child (Richmond). As the town grew and the Assembly increased the authority of its trustees, there remained but one step to be taken—the establishment of the independent city of Richmond. Old ties would remain, and for many years afterward, the city was the dominant partner in the relationship. It was not to be until the twentieth century that the county reasserted itself.

The significance of moving the courthouse to the town of Richmond in 1752 was more than a logistical one. The courthouse was the center of governmental, political, and social activity in that day. The power base of the wealthy landowners in Henrico began to gravitate to Richmond where trade and industry began to develop. The presence of the church and the increased trade and commercial activities naturally stimulated greater interaction between members of the populace in the area, which began to grow commercially.

As the colonies began to move toward separation from the mother country, the people of Henrico tended to mirror the general attitudes and actions of the colonists. This was especially true with the first significant problem—the pistole fee. When Lieutenant Governor Robert Dinwiddie arrived in the colony to assume his duties, he found waiting for his signature more than seventeen hundred patents for land and over one thousand surveyor's certificates upon which patents would be issued. On April 22, 1752, a few months after his arrival in Virginia, Governor Dinwiddie requested the opinion of the Council on the propriety of his charging a fee for putting his seal on the patents. The Council agreed that the requirement of a fee would be reasonable and advised that the amount for each patent be one pistole, a small Spanish coin. The amount of the fee was not excessive, but in a country where hard money was scarce, it was considered a hardship.

Dinwiddie's proposal did not meet with favor. One of the leaders in opposition was the Reverend William Stith of Henrico Parish, who was involved in a three-way contest for one of the three offices of councilor, commissary, and president of the College of William and Mary. All three offices could be combined or filled separately, and even though he opposed the governor on the pistole fee issue, Stith won the presidency of the college. As early as May 1752, Stith voiced opposition to the fee. He believed that it was wrong to levy any taxes without a law and doubly wrong if he did not speak out against such an oppressive tax. He felt that Governor Dinwiddie had demanded the fee for his own private use and advantage. For Stith, the attempt to lay taxes without a law of the Assembly was an illegal invasion of property. When called to give a toast during a debate over the fee, Stith proposed: "Liberty and property and no pistole." He attacked the proposition with fanatical zeal and led Dinwiddie to write that an evil spirit had entered into Stith. The Randolphs supported Stith in his opposition and were accused by Dinwiddie of stirring up the House of Burgesses. A family connection existed between Stith and the Randolphs; Stith's mother, Mary, was the daughter of William Randolph of Turkey Island, and his wife was his first cousin Judith Randolph.[1]

Stith's parishioners followed the lead of their minister and became as vocal as he. On November 14, 1753, two weeks after the General Assembly convened, a petition from "sundry freeholders and inhabitants of the counties of Henrico, Chesterfield, Cumberland, Albemarle, and Amelia" was received and read. The petitioners set forth "the many hardships they labour[ed] under, by being obliged to pay one pistole . . . over and above the Fees formerly demanded and allowed." They prayed for relief and asked the House of Burgesses to appoint an agent to go to London "to sollicit the Affairs of this Government, in Support of the Rights and Privileges of the People." The House tabled the petition received from the freeholders and inhabitants but went so far as to pass a resolution "that whoever shall hereafter pay a Pistole, as a Fee to the Governor for the Use of the Seal to

Patents for Lands, shall be deemed a Betrayer of the Rights and Privileges of the People." Advising Dinwiddie that they had "the undoubted right" to "enquire into the grievances of the people," the burgesses informed him that "the rights of the subject are so secured by law, that they cannot be deprived of the least part of their property, but by their own consent: Upon this excellent principle is our constitution founded, and ever since this Colony has had the happiness of being under the immediate protection of the Crown, the royal declarations have been, 'That no man's life, member, freehold, or goods, be taken away or harmed but by established and known laws.' "[2]

Dinwiddie contended that the fee only covered land owned by the crown and did not come under the jurisdiction of the Burgesses. The Assembly responded by appointing an agent and appropriating money for his passage to England to present the colony's case to the crown. Dinwiddie prorogued the Assembly and refused to rescind the fee. The Privy Council ruled in Dinwiddie's favor, but it also set down detailed regulations that did not give the governor a complete victory. Henricoans and their fellow Virginians did not agree with Dinwiddie's actions and showed that they were willing to debate for their rights, although they were not ready to break with England. The pistole fee controversy was the first of a series of governmental actions that led to polarization over constitutional issues and eventual separation from the mother country.

The French and Indian War was the second major event to affect Henrico citizens immediately before the Revolution. Although the roots of that war could be traced back to Europe, Virginians were fighting for their religious liberty as well as for their political institutions within the empire. The brunt of the war was felt on the frontier, which had progressed beyond the Blue Ridge, but the economy of the entire colony was directly affected. When the governor requested funds to prosecute the war effort in October 1754, the Assembly granted £20,000 for military purposes and levied a poll tax on all tithables to raise the money. At the August 1755 session, the Assembly passed an act for raising £40,000 for the protection of the frontiers. An additional poll tax on all tithables of one shilling a year for four years and a tax of fifteen pence a year for four years on each one hundred acres of land was levied to cover the authorization. Treasury notes were authorized payable in one year to be redeemed with anticipated revenues from the taxes levied. This was only the beginning, as each session of the Assembly was called on for additional funds. During the war, Virginia issued £539,962 10s. in treasury notes, all guaranteed by direct and indirect tax levies in the form of land, poll, license, import, and export taxes.

As the war continued, money became increasingly hard to find. During the October 1755 session, the Assembly passed a bill authorizing the issuance of £200,000 in paper money for the purpose of setting up a loan office. The money was not to be backed by future tax levies as security, but it was to be good for eight years from date of issue. The governor and Council rejected the measure as inflationary. The circulation of unsecured paper currency was seen as a means of providing relief to the local economy where the barter system remained the primary means of evaluating and paying for goods and services. The governor's rejection caused the people to voice their concern and to back the Assembly's proposal. The citizens of Henrico joined with those of surrounding counties to petition the House of Burgesses. Setting forth "that great Inconveniences have arisen to most of the Inhabitants of the Colony, and are like to continue, for Want of a proper Circulation of Credit, inasmuch that Business is obstructed and many Families are likely to be ruined, by having their Goods sold for less than half the Value, thro' the great Scarcity of Cash," the petitioners prayed "that a Loan Office may be established, and Paper Currency may issue, to the amount of £300,000 or any greater Sum that may answer the present Exigencies." Under the heavy expense of war, Virginia was compelled to abandon the policy of avoiding the use of paper money. In June 1757 the governor agreed to the issuance of £20,000 in treasury notes secured by taxes. By March 1762 there were eight issues totaling over £40,000. Notes were issued that by enactment of the General Assembly were made legal tender, and funds were provided for their redemption at maturity. The tight-money situation brought on the companion ills of tight credit and high interest. Already burdened by the increase in taxes and sluggish economy, many colonists

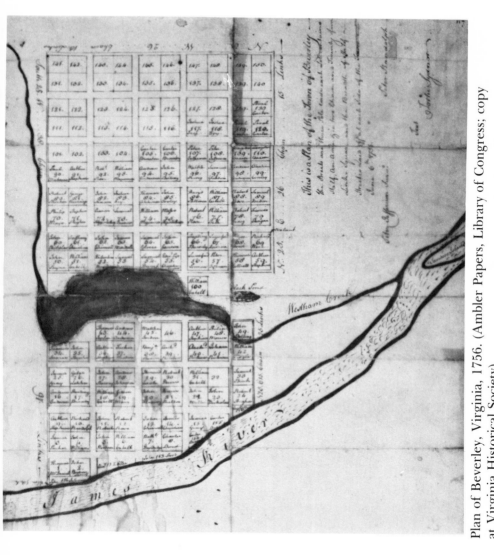

Plan of Beverley, Virginia, 1756. (Ambler Papers, Library of Congress; copy at Virginia Historical Society)

found themselves in dire financial straits. One of the victims of the economic downturn was William Byrd III.[3]

When William Byrd II, known as the "Black Swan," died in 1744, the town of Richmond was a settlement with signs of stability and promise of growth. His son's lack of business acumen, combined with his insatiable gambling habits and the general economic climate, was further complicated by problems over a fradulent loan. William Byrd III had received a loan of £14,921 from John Robinson, Speaker of the House of Burgesses and treasurer. As treasurer, Robinson was authorized to destroy the paper currency issued during the French and Indian War when he received it in payment of taxes. Instead of burning the money, he made it available to his friends. Before his death on May 10, 1766, he took more than £100,000 illegally from the treasury and lent it to those in desperate need. When the Robinson scandal became know, Byrd and others who had received similar loans were directed to pay them back. To do so, Byrd executed a deed of trust conveying his property on both sides of the James at the falls to seven trustees "for the purpose of paying his . . . debts."

Between 1755 and 1759 Byrd built Belvidere on what is now Oregon Hill near the street that bears its name. Surrounded by seventeen acres, the main house had wings on either side and measured 128 feet long, including the wings. It was built of wood on a brick foundation, and various dependencies such as kitchen, smokehouse, and slave quarters were built on the grounds behind the mansion. Byrd lived at Belvidere until 1776 when he moved to Westover in Charles City County. The construction of Belvidere could only have added to Byrd's financial problems. In April 1767 he advertised his properties for sale, including Belvidere and some thirty thousand acres of land on both sides of the James at the falls. In August of that year, he advertised "A Scheme, for disposing of by way of Lottery, the Land and Tenements under mentioned, being the entire towns of Rocky Ridge and Shockoe, lying at the Fall of James river, and the land thereunto adjoining." The lottery was to be conducted under the management and direction of five of the original trustees to whom Byrd had issued the deed of trust. The town of Rocky Ridge was on the south side of the James opposite Shockoe

(Richmond), and it would become the incorporated town of Manchester by act of the General Assembly in 1769.[4]

The advertisement in the *Gazette* stipulated that ten thousand tickets would be sold at £5 each for a total of £50,000 and that 839 prizes, valued at £56,796, would be offered. South of the James, there were 312 lots or prizes; 300 unimproved lots, "each an acre, to be laid off in a town convenient to the river," and twelve "unimproved" lots including eight tenements, a twenty-year lease on the ferry and a half acre of land, a similar time lease on a fishery, a twelve-year lease on the inspection at the Rocky Ridge warehouse, and "a double forge, a mill, with two acres and a half of land adjoining, the use of the landing, the canal, with ten feet on each side, and 2000 acres of back land, the furthest part of which is not more than five miles from the forge." The latter lot was valued at £8,000.[5]

North of the James in Henrico County, Byrd listed 527 lots, which included twelve-year leases on the inspections at the Shockoe and Byrd warehouses, twelve-year leases on thirteen tenements, twenty-year leases on the ferry and fishery, "10,000 acres of land, to be laid off in lots of 100 acres each," ten islands "on some of which are very valuable fisheries," and 400 unimproved lots.

The lottery drawing was to be at Shockoe in June 1768, but it did not take place until November of that year, and then the drawing was conducted at Williamsburg. The delay was apparently the result of lagging ticket sales. Even the promise to remove "the obstructions through the Falls, and in other parts of the river above" to make the river navigable to the western frontier "so that the immense treasure of that valuable country must necessarily be brought to market . . . which will occasionally raise the rents, and enhance the value, of the lands and tenements . . . beyond the powers of conception" did not create a great deal of enthusiasm for the lottery. When the drawing was held, one of the winners was George Washington. Although he won seven parcels consisting of 568½ acres, there is no evidence that he retained his prize. Daniel L. Hylton, a Richmond merchant, won Belvidere, but he did not occupy it until after Byrd moved to Westover in 1776. Some of the winning tickets were turned in and deeds were issued, and others were sold or retained for future filing. In 1781 a special act of the General Assembly authorized Charles Carter, the only surviving trustee, to make the necessary deeds of conveyance.[6]

William Byrd III remained at Belvidere in Henrico until 1776, but he was not a force in Henrico's history after his financial downfall. The town that his father established as a part of his economic empire would continue to grow. The act that established the towns of Manchester and Gloucester Courthouse in November 1769 added an additional 0.54 of a square mile to the western part of the town of Richmond, bringing into the town the land that would become Capitol Square and the area westward to present-day Foushee Street. This was the first annexation act whereby a "piece or parcel of land . . . of Henrico" was "added to and made part of the said town of Richmond." In doing so, the General Assembly recognized a separate status for the citizens of the town when it stipulated that the freeholders and inhabitants in the annexed area "shall be intitled to and enjoy all the rights and privileges granted to and enjoyed by the freeholders and inhabitants of the said town of Richmond, and be subjected to the same rules and restrictions."[7]

The total number of inhabitants in the town in 1769 was 574, up from 250 in 1742, the year of incorporation. As the population and economic activity increased, it became apparent that the town needed more local autonomy. This came in 1773 when the General Assembly provided for the succession of the trustees and enlarged their powers. Only three of the original trustees were living, so the Assembly appointed William Byrd III, Richard Randolph, Samuel DuVal, Richard Adams, Robert Brown, George Donald, Turner Southall, Patrick Coutts, Archibald Bryce, George Donald, William Randolph, and James Buchanan "directors and trustees for building, carrying on, maintaining said town." All legal matters continued to be brought before the Henrico court and the right to petition remained, but the town trustees did not receive more administrative responsibility over the life of the town. The act spoke to their responsibility in the areas of establishing quays, public landings, wharves, and rules for placing houses. Under this form of government, the town would enter the Revolution.[8]

Farming was still the primary occupation in Henrico

County in the 1750s. Tobacco warehouses were located at Four Mile Creek, Richmond, and Westham. The public warehouse at Turkey Island was discontinued in 1752, and two warehouses on Four Mile Creek were designated public warehouses; John Pleasants and Charles Woodson, the proprietors, rented them for £5 a year. In 1753 the General Assembly authorized a ferry "from Four Mile Creek Warehouse Landing on the Land of Charles Woodson in Henrico County, across James River, to the Neck of Land belonging to Tarlton Woodson, in the County of Chesterfield, . . . also a Ferry from the Land of Charles Ellis in Henrico County to the land of Daniel Weldon in Chesterfield." Upriver the ferry at Osborne's was still in operation, and Thomas Mann Randolph's efforts to establish a ferry in the same area were rejected by the General Assembly. At Richmond several ferries were in operation connecting the town with the settlement of Rocky Ridge, later Manchester, and Byrd's mills on the south bank of the James.[9]

At Westham, William Byrd III encountered an interesting problem. Up-country farmers transported their tobacco and grain downriver on flatboats and landed at Westham for the overland trip to Richmond. Instead of placing their tobacco in Byrd's warehouse and paying a fee, they unloaded their boats and stacked the tobacco in the open on Byrd's land. When wagons or hogsheads became available, they transported the tobacco to Richmond and did not pay Byrd for any use of his land. Byrd petitioned the House of Burgesses for relief, and a resolution was passed requiring payment for storage from everyone who left their tobacco on his land for twenty-four hours.[10]

Above Westham, in the Tuckahoe Creek valley, a chain of events unfolded, dramatically changing the economic future of the county. An Englishman by the name of Durst discovered that the clay in the region was a good-quality fireclay that could be used in the manufacture of pottery. The clay on the north bank of the James south of the town of Richmond had been used in the making of bricks ever since the early settlers moved up the river, but the clay in the Tuckahoe Creek valley could be fired. Durst set up a pottery at Tuckahoe which he operated until the close of the Revolution when he emigrated west. As he fired the clay, Durst discovered that it could not only be used in the making of pottery but also in firebricks for use in furnaces, fireplaces, and chimneys. Benjamin DuVal worked with Durst and continued the pottery business at Tuckahoe for a brief time. He then moved to Richmond and transported the clay by wagon to his pottery at Richmond where his business survived for two or three years.

In his *Travels through the Middle Settlements in North America, 1759-1760,* the Reverend Andrew Burnaby noted that "some coal mines have been opened upon James River near the falls which are likely to answer very well."[11] Six miles north of the clay deposits and some twelve miles northwest of Richmond, coalpits were opened at the head of Deep Run, a large stream that emptied into the James. This Deep Run Basin, isolated from the main coal basin some three miles west of it, is two miles long and one fourth of a mile wide. As early as 1760, Samuel DuVal of Mount Comfort in Henrico opened a coal mine or pit next to the Three Chopt Road, which at that time formed a junction with the Richmond-to-Charlottesville road west of Richmond. Utilizing ten laborers, DuVal excavated coal by the pit method of digging into the coal outcrop. Once the coal was dug, it was piled by the roadside and carried in wagons to Richmond where it was sold for domestic and industrial use. Although it was advertised as "not inferior to the New Castle coal," it was soft and did not produce intense heat unless used in quantity in a restricted area. In 1766 DuVal advertised his coal "to be sold at Rocket's landing about a mile below the falls of the James River, any quantity of *coal* for 12d a bushel."[12]

The Deep Run pits continued in operation throughout the Revolution under DuVal's management and supplied the coal used at the Westham Foundry from 1777 to 1780. The foundry records are not complete, but they show that 5,998½ bushels were delivered for the years 1777 and 1777–1778 from the Deep Run pits. In addition, 2,781 bushels of "good pit coal" were sent to the Pennsylvania Committee of Safety at ¼d. a bushel. DuVal offered his coal pits "containing 1400 acres" for sale for "Cash or Tobacco" on September 20, 1780. The sale was to be made on November 6, and he noted that "the vein of coal extends 2 miles in length, and as to its width and depth, the labor of 10 hands ever since the year 1760 has proved sufficient for a discovery. . . . it lies well and commands many advantages unmentioned." The Deep Run pits continued in operation for the next century. Additional pits had been opened after the war, and other individual pits were opened later. One group of pits east of DuVal's original excavations was called the Springfield pits; thus the basin is sometimes referred to as the Springfield Basin.[13]

Samuel DuVal was deeply involved in Henrico's economic and political life, and his wealth allowed him the opportunity nity to raise and race Thoroughbred horses. He had imported Silver Eye from England in 1750. About this time, horses of the English racing stock were imported for breeding and racing. Many wealthy planters in Virginia owned "more or less 'blooded' stock, used either for the saddle, harness, or racing." A number of jockey clubs were formed by planters involved in breeding and racing, and annual races were held at Williamsburg. Thomas N. Randolph of Tuckahoe and William Byrd III raced their horses against those owned by Col. John Tayloe of Mount Airy, Richmond County, William Fitzhugh of Chatham, Stafford County, and others.[14]

Members of the Randolph and the Cocke-Adams families almost monopolized the county's representation in the House of Burgesses from 1750 to 1771. With the exception of Philip Mayo's election in January 1762 to succeed William Randolph III after his death, the Randolph dominance was interrupted for only four years between 1750 and 1771. Richard Randolph won the seat back in 1765. The second seat was held by Cocke-Adams families during that time period. Bowler Cocke served from 1752 to 1765, Bowler Cocke, Jr., from 1766 to 1768, and Richard Adams from 1769 through the Revolution.

The Randolphs dominance was ended by Samuel DuVal in 1772 when he contested the election of 1771 after Richard Randolph and Richard Adams were declared the winners. On behalf of himself and the freeholders of Henrico County, DuVal petitioned the General Assembly "Setting forth, that at the last Election of Burgesses to serve in this Present General Assembly, for the said County, a great Number of Freeholders voted for the Petitioner, who was one of the Candidates, than for Mr. Richard Randolph, who was, with Mr.

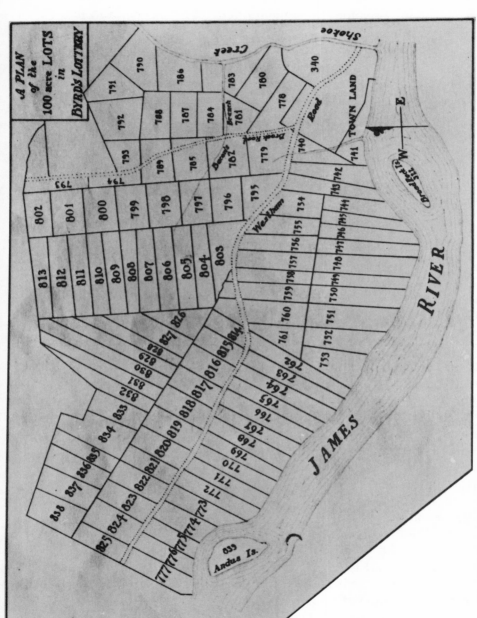

In 1768 William Byrd III disposed of 10,000 acres of land, ten islands, and various leases to his business enterprises in and around Richmond by lottery. (Virginia State Library)

Richard Adams, returned duly elected, and therefore praying that the Poll taken at the said Election may be examined, and that the Petitioner may be declared duly elected a Burgess for the said County." The petition was referred to the Committee of Privileges and Elections, which found that there had been some irregularities in the election process and that because the date of the election had been changed, "many Freeholders were absent on the Day of Election, but that it was more probably occasioned by the Badness of the Weather than the Want of Notice of the Day last appointed." The committee ruled that "Mr. Adams, and Mr. Randolph, are not duly elected to serve as Burgesses in this present General Assembly for the said County of Henrico" and declared the election illegal. At a special election on March 10, 1772, Samuel DuVal and Richard Adams were elected.[15]

The citizens of Henrico were no strangers to "the Badness of the Weather." On May 27, 1771, a wall of water came roaring down the James River valley engulfing everything in its path. The warehouses at Westham, together with some three hundred hogsheads of tobacco, were swept down the river, which reached a flood stage of forty to forty-five feet above normal. As it swept through Richmond and on down the James, the force of the water took entire buildings and their unfortunate occupants, together with boats, animals, vegetation, and general debris, with it. The public warehouses at Shockoe's, Byrd's, and Rocky Ridge were heavily hit, and many hogsheads of tobacco were swept down river.

The inhabitants in the Richmond area were not unaware that the river had overflowed its banks before, for they had heard of the floods of 1667 and 1685. Rather, the lack of rain in the Richmond area had left them unprepared when the floodwaters hit. It had been raining heavily for ten to twelve days in the Blue Ridge area, and as the water ran off, the James, Rappahannock, and Occoquan rivers were inundated. The public warehouses at Falmouth, Dixon's in King George County, and Quantico were heavily damaged, and much of the tobacco was swept away. Along the James, the inhabitants of Amherst, Buckingham, Goochland, and Henrico counties petitioned the General Assembly for relief. A special session of the Assembly was called, and a committee was appointed to examine the accounts of the inspectors of

the warehouses at Shockoe's, Byrd's, Rocky Ridge, and Warwick. Efforts were set in motion to retrieve as much of the
tobacco as possible, and citizens were paid for hogsheads
they recovered. The tobacco was carried back to temporary
warehouses where it was inspected and evaluated. The committee reported a total loss of 2,375,541 pounds and noted
that the expense of "examining, sorting and reprizing" the
tobacco was £244. 8s. 6d. Some of those who helped recover
the tobacco did not submit their expenses before the final
report. In one case, Thomas Watkins of Henrico waited until
1783 to petition the Assembly for £26. 10s "for riding in
public service and finding 45 hogsheads of tobacco" after
"the great May Fresh" of 1771. Although submitted twelve
years after the event, his petition was allowed.[16]

The river area was heavily damaged, and petitions were
sent to request moving the warehouses to higher ground. A
petition to move them to the land of Charles Lewis was rejected in favor of moving Byrd's and Shockoe's to "the lots
commonly known by the names of James Buckanan's and
Housling's tenements, in the town of Richmond." The Assembly also levied additional taxes on vehicles, court papers,
and tobacco marked for export to pay off an issue of £30,000
of notes to "relieve the unhappy sufferers on the present
occasion."[17]

About one hundred and fifty people lost their life as they
were swept away in the swirling waters of the James. When
the waters subsided, the destructive force of the "freshet"
became apparent when walls of debris twelve to twenty feet
high could not be approached because of the stench of de-
caying carcasses. Downstream at Turkey Island, the water
was reported forty-five feet above normal. A monument to
the flood was erected by Ryland Randolph of Curles in
1771–72. The foundation of the eighteen-foot-high granite
obelisk was laid in 1771 to commemorate his parents. It car-
ries the inscription that it was started "in the calamitous year
1771 When all the great Rivers of this Country were swept by
Inundations Never before experienced Which changed the
face of Nature and left traces of Violence that will remain for
Ages."[18]

A storm of another type was brewing between the colonies
and the mother country. The year after the Treaty of Paris

ended the French and Indian War in 1763, Prime Minister George Grenville proposed the imposition of stamp duties on American colonies to assist in the payment of all war debts. The Virginia General Assembly protested against the proposed stamp duties, and many colonists ignored or openly opposed the Stamp Act. Throughout the colonies the courts either declined to act on matters requiring stamps or ignored the requirement for the stamps. The actions of the colonies caused repeal of the Stamp Act, not on principle, but on the grounds of expediency.

On May 31, 1767, Charles Townshend, chancellor of the exchequer, introduced in the House of Commons his program to tax the colonies. Virginia joined with other colonies in protesting the passage and implementation of the Townsend duties. The people of Massachusetts were directly affected by the acts and actions of Parliament. Troops were sent to Boston, and protestors were ordered to be transported to Great Britain for trial. Again the Virginia General Assembly responded, asserting the principle of taxation by consent of the colonists and the right of concerted action and appeal to the crown. Sundry freeholders of the counties of Henrico, Chesterfield, Dinwiddie, and Amelia petitioned the General Assembly to speak out against Parliament's action. Addressing Parliament's decision to suspend the legislative power of the colony of New York, they termed it a "fatal Tendency," so "destructive of the Liberty of a free People," that the Petitioners are impressed with the deepest Sense of the Danger of Lossing their antient Rights and Privileges as Freemen, dependent on and Subjects to the Crown of Great Britain." Recognizing their position as Englishmen, the colonists prayed that the House of Burgesses would "implore his Majesty, in the most humble Manner, for a Repeal of the said Act of Parliament."[19]

Virginians wanted their rights and freedoms protected under the crown; they felt that neither they nor any other colonist should be subjected to unjust acts of Parliament. They agreed not to import British goods until colonial grievances were adjusted. With the exception of the tax on tea, the Townshend duties were repealed on April 12, 1770. In protest against the continuation of the tea tax, the burgesses and merchants signed a nonimportation association on June

22, 1770. Several Henrico citizens signed this agreement, and each county established a committee of overseers to monitor adherence to the agreement.

On March 12, 1773, the Assembly unanimously adopted a resolution to create a committee of correspondence to keep in touch with similar committees in the other colonies. Three days later, Lord Botetourt dissolved the Assembly. When they were allowed to reconvene again, they reacted to the Intolerable Acts and the closing of the port of Boston by declaring June 7, 1774, as a day of prayer and fasting. Again the Assembly was dissolved.

The members of the Assembly gathered unofficially at the Raleigh Tavern and voted to make the cause of Massachusetts their own. Virginia, considering the need for united action, took a step in advance and proposed that a congress of all the colonies be called to meet annually. The same gathering also issued a call for a Virginia convention, and the counties of Virginia responded, holding meetings, passing resolutions, and electing representatives. Richard Adams and Samuel DuVal were elected from Henrico. The citizens of the county addressed a lengthy resolution to them on July 28, 1774.

We the Subscribers, Freeholders of the County of Henrico, assembled for the Purpose of deliberating on the present Posture of publick Affairs, return you our Thanks for the Part you acted in the late Assembly, as our Burgesses.

When we reflect on the alarming and critical Situation of Things respecting the Mother Country, our Minds are filled with the most anxious Concern. The Acts of the British Parliament made for punishing the Inhabitants of Massachusetts Bay are repugnant to the first Principles of Justices, and if they are suffered to have a full Operation will not only crush our Sister Colony, and involve the Guilty and Innocent in one common Ruin, but will stand as a fatal Precedent to future Times for adopting the same fatal Measures towards this and every other British Colony. We therefore have passed this Determination, and shall conduct ourselves conformably, that the Cause of the Colony of Massachusettes Bay in general, and of the Town of Boston in particular, is the Cause of this and every other Colony in North America.

We hope, Gentlemen, that the exceeding great Importance of the present Crisis will plead our Excuse for giving you our Senti-

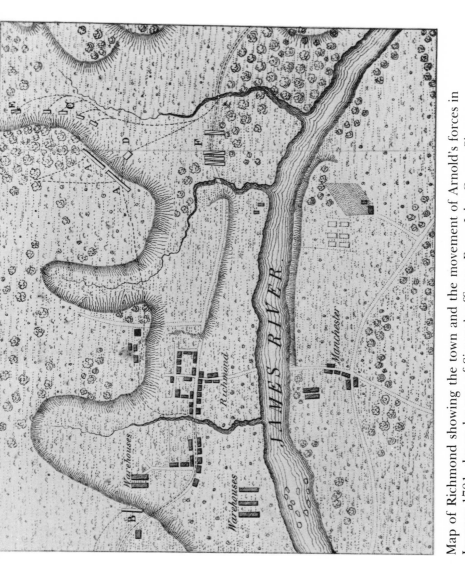

Map of Richmond showing the town and the movement of Arnold's forces in January 1781, drawn by one of Simcoe's officers. From John Graves Simcoe, *Simcoe's Military Journal* (New York, 1844), opp. p. 162.

ments touching that Conduct which we wish you to observe in the
ensuing Congress, on the first Day of August next, at Williamsburg, to which we depute you to act on our Behalf.

With Grief and Astonishment, we behold Great Britain adopting
a Mode of Government towards her Colonies totally incompatible
with our Safety and Happiness. We cannot submit to be taxed by
her Parliament; we cannot sit still and see the Harbour of Boston
blocked up by an armed Force; we cannot behold, without Indigna-
tion, the Charter Rights of a Sister Colony violated, or the Form of
its Government changed, by an Act of Parliament as derogatory to
the Honour of the Mother Country as it is repugnant to Justice;
and lastly, we will not suffer our Fellow Subjects to be seized and
transported beyond Sea to be tried for supposed Offences committed here. If these things are suffered to be reduced to Practice, we
shall account ourselves the most miserable of Men, unworthy the
Name of Freemen; we shall not wonder if in future we are treated
as Slaves.

We therefore most solemnly charge and conjure you to use your
best Endeavours to save us from these Calamities. We earnestly
entreat you for your utmost Exertion to procure, by all possible
Ways and Means, a total Repeal of the late oppressive and detest-
able Acts of Parliament. We trust you will heartily concur in such
Measures as the said Congress, shall judge most efficacious to preserve our ancient Rights; for be assured, Gentlemen, that nothing
shall ever induce from us a Submission to Tyranny,, and that we
resolve, once for all, to live and die Freemen.

In order to effect those desirable Ends, we give it as our Opinion
that the most effectual Method for opposing the said several Acts
of Parliament will be that a General Association between all the
American Colonies ought immediately to be entered into, not to
import from Great Britain any Commodity whatsoever, except
such Articles as the General Congress shall judge necessary, until
the just Rights of the Colonies are restored to them, and the cruel
Acts of the British Parliament against the Colony of Massachusetts
Bay, and Town of Boston, are repealed.

A love of Justice, and the tender Regard we have for our
Friends, the Merchants and Manufacturers of Great Britain, to
whom we are indebted, and who must of Course suffer in the
common Cause, prevents our recommending the stopping our Exports at this Time; but, at a future Day, we will heartily concur with
the other Counties of this Colony to stop all Exports, as well as
imports, to and from Great Britain, unless what we have already
recommended to you shall be found effectual.

We most cordially recommend that no Time be lost in administering every Comfort and Aid to our distressed Brethren of Boston that their unhappy State may require, and may comport with our Situation to afford.

We further recommend to you, that you will, in Conjunction with the Deputies from the different Counties of this Colony, choose fit and proper Persons, on the part of this Colony, to meet the Deputies from the other Colonies in a General Congress, at such convenient Time and Place as shall be agreed on, then and there to advise and consult upon such Measures as, (under the Circumstances of Things at that Time) they shall deem expedient.

We strictly charge and enjoin, that at all Times, and on all Occasions which may present, you testify our Zeal for his Majesty's Person and Government; and that we are ready and willing, with our Lives and Fortunes, to support his Right to the Crown of Great Britain, and all its Dependencies.[20]

The first Virginia Convention assembled in Williamsburg on August 1, 1774, with Adams and DuVal representing Henrico County. The convention elected delegates to the Continental Congress and agreed to a nonimportation association. Before adjourning, the convention agreed that its president, Peyton Randolph, would have authority to call the next meeting.

At Philadelphia, the Continental Congress met in September and on October 18 approved a Continental Association designed to bring a halt to British-colonial commerce until there was a redress of colonial grievances. The eleventh article of the Continental Association called for the election of a committee in every county, city, and town "to observe the conduct of all persons touching this association." Each committee was charged with publishing information about anyone who violated the association so "that all such foes to the rights of British-America may be publicly known, and universally condemned as the enemies of American liberty and thenceforth we respectively will break off all dealings with him or her." On Thursday, November 17, the freeholders of Henrico gathered at the courthouse in Richmond "for the purpose of choosing a committee, agreeable to the 11th article of the resolves of the General Congress, to see that the association is duly carried into execution within said county." Those elected were Richard Adams, Samuel DuVal, Richard Randolph, Nathaniel Wilkinson, Turner

Southall, Joseph Lewis, Peter Winston, Joshua Storrs, James
Buchanan, Isaac Younghusband, Daniel Price, John Hales,
Martin Burton, the Reverend Miles Selden, and Samuel
Price. At the same time it was "*Resolved*, that they be appointed a committee for this county, that they, or the majority of them, do meet from time to time, as occasion requires, for the purposes aforesaid."[21]

The committee then "formed themselves into a meeting"
and appointed John Beckley as clerk. This young man served
as clerk and keeper of records for most of his life. He came
to the colony at the age of eleven from England as an indentured servant to the clerk of the Gloucester County Court.
He served as clerk to the Henrico committee and later as
clerk of the Henrico County Court. By occupation he was an
attorney, and in 1782 he was elected to the Common Hall of
the city of Richmond and served as Richmond's second
mayor. Later he served as clerk of the United States House
of Representatives and the Librarian of Congress.[22]

When the committee met again on Monday, December 12,
the Reverend Miles Selden was appointed chairman. The
members present agreed that any three members could request that the chairman call a meeting of the committee and
that he was authorized to do so. A "corresponding committee" was appointed, and Richard Adams, Samuel DuVal,
Richard Randolph, Turner Southall, Joshua Storrs, James
Buchanan, Issac Younghusband, John Hales, and Samuel
Price, "or any three of them," were authorized "on behalf of
this county . . . to inform the respective committees of the
several counties within this colony, of any breach of violation
of the general association by any person whatsoever." The
entire committee agreed unanimously "that the resolutions
of the General Congress should be . . . considered, by the
committee, as the sole rule of their conduct, respecting their
present political engagements" and "that, for the most effectual carrying into execution the association of the General
Congress, and obtaining a speedy redress of American grievances, we will, as an immediate step thereto, enter into a
subscription for the encouragement of all kinds of husbandry and manufacturs within this county."[23]

Under the tenth article of the Continental Association, any
items imported between December 1, 1774, and February 1,

1775, were to be either returned, turned over to the local committee for storage, or sold under the direction of the committee. One item that passed through the Henrico Committee was salt. In January 1775 at least three shipments were turned over to the committee for sale. In each case a subcommittee was appointed to advertise and manage the sale at public auction. Capt. Thomas Fisher of the ship *Peggy* brought in 3,636 bushels of salt valued at £425 5s. 5d.; Thomas Bowen imported 3,596 bushels valued at £332 13s. 7d. All three shipments, plus two packages of goods received by Robert Pleasants and Company, valued at £55 5s. 10½d., and "sundry packages of goods amounting to £790 7s. 9¼d. current money" imported by Captain Fisher, were sold at public auction at the invoiced value, except for Captain Fisher's "sundry packages of goods," which fell short of the invoiced value by 7s. 11¼ d. A confused "Friend of Liberty" from Charles City County questioned the committee's handling of the sale of Captain Fisher's "goods" in an open letter to Peyton Randolph published in the *Virginia Gazette* on February 2, 1775. Captain Fisher had delivered some goods in Charles City County also, and the unidentified correspondent apparently jumped to an unwarranted decision that the committee did not handle the sales properly.[24]

In January 1775 a call went out for the Second Virginia Convention to meet at Richmond, Henrico County, on March 20. Meeting at the Town Church, later called St. John's, the convention made some modifications to the interior to transform it for use by the legislative body. The Reverend Miles Selden, of Henrico Parish, was appointed chaplain and was called on to open the daily sessions with the reading of prayers. Henrico was again represented by Richard Adams and Samuel DuVal. It was at this convention that Patrick Henry delivered his famous "Liberty or Death" speech and called for the convention to put the colony "into a posture of Defence." A defense committee was established, and a plan for embodying, arming, and disciplining the militia was adopted. Under this plan, Henrico was one of the counties encouraged to form "one or more troops of Horse" out of the volunteer militia. After the convention elected delegates to the Continental Congress, it adjourned on March 27 with the recommendation that delegates be chosen for another convention. Following the convention, the county committees and the House of Burgesses approved its proceedings.

Relations between the colonists and the representatives of the crown did not become tense until April 21 when the governor's order to seize the gunpowder stored in the public magazine at Williamsburg was carried out between three and four o'clock in the morning. The Henrico committee met on April 26 and added its voice of protest to the colony's reaction, declaring "that the removing of the said gunpowder . . . is an insult to every freeman in this country." By resolution the committee "consider[ed] the act itself as a determined step, tending towards establishing that tyranny we so much dread, and which the British Ministry, with unrelenting fury, have so long and are still endeavouring to effect: And farther, . . . we consider it as injurious to the same, and tending to destroy the pleasing idea, we had entertained, of his Excellency's regard for the happiness and true interest of this colony." Committing itself to "use our best endeavours to procure an immediate restitution of the said powder," the committee directed its "committee of correspondence to write to the committee of the city of Williamsburg, or to the committee of York or James City counties, and procure the most authentick intelligence respecting the same, and report to this committee at their next meeting." The texts of the communications sent and received do not survive and any further action taken by the committee is not known, but an independent militia company was formed in the county.[25]

To the northest, in Hanover County, Patrick Henry collected a detachment of about five hundred men and prepared to move on Williamsburg. Governor Dunmore fortified the Palace. As the situation became more strained, he moved his family to the *Fowey,* a British man-of-war. When negotiations resulted in payment for the powder, Henry was persuaded to stop his advance. The governor's family returned from the *Fowey,* and he issued a proclamation calling for the General Assembly to meet on June 1, 1775, to dispatch public business. On June 8, fearing for his personal safety, Lord Dunmore and his family left Williamsburg and thus abandoned the seat of the government.

Without the governor, the assembly could not conduct public business. A Third Virginia Convention was called for on

June 26, and it convened in Richmond on July 17. Richard Adams and Richard Randolph represented Henrico at the convention, which met at the Town Church as did its predecessor, and the Reverend Mr. Selden again served as chaplain. This convention provided for a Committee of Safety with emergency executive powers to carry out the rules and regulations adopted by the convention. One area of prime responsibility delegated to the Committee of Safety was the protection and defense of the colony. An ordinance for the "raising and embodying a sufficient force for the defense and protection of this colony" placed Henrico, Hanover, Goochland, and Louisa in the District of Henrico. Each district was to provide a battalion of 500 men between the ages of sixteen and fifty to be divided into ten companies of 50 men each. The local committees were charged with preparing an inventory of arms and gunpowder, collecting money for the purchase of same, and reporting to the Committee of Safety, which held its first meeting in Richmond on August 26. When the convention adjourned on August 26, it issued a declaration stating the need for "putting the country into a posture [of] defence, for the better protection of their lives, liberties, and properties."[26]

The convention had provided for annual elections of twenty-one men in each county to serve as a committee to continue the association and to carry out the measures adopted by the Continental Congress, Virginia Convention, and Committee of Safety. The elections were held on court day in November. The Henrico freeholders gathered at the courthouse on November 6 and elected Peter Winston, Nathaniel Wilkinson, Turner Southall, Martin Burton, Samuel Price, Richard Adams, Joshua Storrs, Joseph Lewis, Daniel Price, John Hales, Samuel DuVal, Thomas Prosser, Abraham Cowley, David Bowles, Julius Allen, Richard Randolph, Dr. John Powell, and Isaac Younghusband. Fifteen members being present, a meting was held. The Reverend Mr. Selden continued as chairman, and John Beckley was unanimously appointed clerk. The committee then addressed the central issue of supplies and "resolved unanimously, that no provision, fuel, or naval stores, be allowed to be water-born, from this county, without the permission of the Hon. Committee of Safety first had and obtained for that purpose."[27]

The Fourth Virginia Convention met in Richmond on December 1, 1775, and moved to Williamsburg where it met from December 5, 1775, to January 20, 1776. Again, Henrico was represented by Richard Adams and Richard Randolph. This convention voted to raise seven new regiments to add to the two regiments previously authorized by the earlier convention. The Committee of Safety activated one company from the Henrico Battalion between December 1 and 10, and on December 11 the committee authorized payment of £ 122 10s. for a month's pay to Capt. William DuVal for his company of militiamen of the Henrico Battalion. They also authorized payment of £9 3s. 2d. to Captain DuVal "for necess. to his Comp." Captain DuVal's company was ordered to Williamsburg where troops were gathering. While there, Ens. William Mosby and Pvt. Daniel DuVal were discharged on January 30. Mosby later served as a captain in the Fifth Virginia Regiment of Foot and with the rank of major at Camden, South Carolina. DuVal became a lieutenant in the Second Georgia Battalion of Foot. Captain DuVal's company remained at Williamsburg until it was ordered discharged March 6, 1776. Two days later, DuVal received £115 19s. 6d. for the pay of his company through March 11.[28]

The Henrico committee was directed to nominate a captain, two lieutenants, and an ensign for a company of regulars authorized by an act of the Fourth Virginia Convention on January 11, 1776. John Pleasants, Jr., was appointed captain of this company. The state Committee of Safety directed that the regular companies from Hanover, Henrico, Chesterfield, Caroline, Louisa, King William, King and Queen, and Spotsylvania counties be ordered to Williamsburg as soon as reviewed. Captain Pleasants's company was reviewed on February 24, but the orders to march to Williamsburg were countermanded on March 8 when the company was allowed a fortnight before marching to the courthouse in Richmond County.[29]

The Fifth Virginia Regiment of Foot (also known as the Fifth Virginia Battalion of Foot in the Service of the United States and Fifth Virginia Regiment on Continental Establishment) was organized in Richmond County, and Captain Pleasants's company was assigned to the regiment as the Third Company. The regiment moved to Williamsburg for

Lieutenant Colonel John Graves Simcoe commanded the Queen's Rangers when the British under Gen. Benedict Arnold occupied Richmond in January 1781. Under orders from Arnold, Simcoe destroyed the Westham Foundry. From *Harper's New Monthly Magazine*, August 1887.

training, and there the men suffered from severe illness in September 1776. In December, when the regiment joined Adam Stephen's brigade, only fourteen commissioned officers and 115 enlisted men were fit for service. The regiment was transferred to Gen. P. G. Muhlenberg's brigade in 1777 and served in the New Jersey campaigns. At White Plains, New York, the remnants of the regiment were transferred to the Third Virginia Regiment of Foot on September 14, 1778. A second consolidation occurred in late 1779 when the regiment was combined with the Second Virginia Regiment of Foot and the Fourth Virginia Regiment of Foot. These three regiments formed a new Second Virginia Regiment of Foot and joined Gen. William Woodford's brigade at Charleston, South Carolina. There the regiment was captured along with the garrison at that place, and the survivers remained in captivity for the balance of the war.[30]

After the battle at Great Bridge in December 1775 and the burning of the Borough of Norfolk, January 1–3, 1776, troops from the up-country moved through Richmond and Fredericksburg to Williamsburg where the Virginia forces were headquartered. Prisoners captured at Great Bridge were transported to Richmond where they were quartered under the guard of Henrico militiamen. Col. Turner Southall, commander of the Henrico militia, reported to the Committee of Safety in April 1776 that the prisoners had attempted to escape and that one had succeeded. The committee ordered that the prisoners be removed to Charlottesville and directed Colonel Southall to see to it.

Except for the movement of the Virginia troops through the county, there was little military activity in Henrico during the early years of the war. The training of the local militia continued, and detachments were stationed in Richmond and at strategic points in the country, but they saw little, if any, action. Thomas Prosser had secured a drum and "Colours" for the county militia in February 1776, and he was reimbursed £5 by the Committee of Safety. A census of men of military age taken in 1776 revealed that there were 500 eligible men in Henrico. No contemporary record was kept of all those who served in Henrico, but a later compilation recorded the names of 646 Henricoans. In addition to the companies already mentioned, two companies of militia,

Capt. Miles Selden's and Capt. David Bowles's were paid for active field service in September 1777. The Henrico militia did not experience combat until Benedict Arnold's expeditionary force marched into Richmond in January 1781.[31]

The citizens of the colony encountered many shortages early in the war, but they were able to make do or do without. However, salt was a commodity for which there was no substitute, and the English policy of seizing all shipments compounded the problem. Captured supplies of salt were inventoried and parceled out. When salt taken at Hampton was divided, the Henrico committee was sent 500 bushels to distribute. Only 82 bushels were designated for Henrico; the balance was to be distributed by the committee to Goochland (63 bushels), Albemarle (144 bushels), Amherst (96 bushels), and East Augusta (214 bushels). One unidentified "gentleman" in Henrico wrote to his friends in Williamsburg of a "truly alarming" situation caused by the fact that "the uplanders do not, or will not, understand that more salt is necessary in the families of the poor and middling sort of people, in this part of the country, than in the upper part; for they not having it in their power to raise pork and beef, are obliged to live upon salted fish." He reported: "We that live on the river, and have fisheries, are in daily aprehension of being visited by the upland people, and have our houses searched for salt, as it seems they are in extreme want of that article, and imagine we have laid up a super-abundance. Several companies of armed men have already come down, and taken it from merchants. One company, on Monday last, came by my house, and went over to Four Mile Creek, where they took from one gentleman 50 bushels, being part of 200 which he had laid up for his own use." The gentleman feared the situation "may be productive of the most fatal consequences" and "may produce civil discord, and other bad consequences." Some relief came with the shipment sent to the committee, and no further incursions of "upland people" are known to have occurred. The Fifth Virginia Convention received a number of "proposals for the making of salt." Its members "were of the opinion that large quantities might be made by the operation of the sun" and appointed commissioners to supervise the efforts in a number of tidewater counties. But the success of these and other efforts was marginal, and salt continued to be in short supply throughout the war.[32]

Salt was not the only scarce commodity. As before the war, the average citizen had little hard currency, and even paper money was not plentiful. The increased business activity in Richmond and other parts of the colony did not increase the supply or circulation of money for the citizenry at large. When the Fifth Virginia Convention met in May 1776, a petition from the freeholders of Henrico expressed concern "that in their private transactions they had experienced great inconveniences from the unequal circulation of paper money," the only currency available. Their inability to sell their agricultural and manufactured items abroad because of "the necessary supression of our trade" left them without a cash flow. They expressed "their apprehensions of the ill consequences that may attend an immediate demand of their taxes." The petitioners acknowledged that "the army supply, though rendered as diffusive as possible, has hitherto been inadequate to the purpose of circulating generally our paper emissions." To relieve the burdens of having to pay taxes with hard or paper money, the petitioners felt that they should be allowed to supply "their quota of whatever may be requisite for the army, whether of arms, ammunition, clothing or field equipage," in lieu of paying their taxes with money. The convention was willing to listen, but it was not sympathetic. The petition was referred to the Committee of Propositions and Grievances for study.[33]

This convention, at which Henrico was represented by Richard Adams and Nathaniel Wilkinson, took several significant steps that gave direction to the colonial effort. On May 15, 1776, the convention voted to instruct the Virginia delegates in the Continental Congress to propose separation from Britain. On June 7 Richard Henry Lee presented a resolution to the congress proposing that the "United Colonies are and of right ought to be, free and independent States," and his resolution was adopted. The Virginia convention then proceeded to adopt a constitution for Virginia on June 29 and elected Patrick Henry the state's first governor. The Continental Congress adopted Lee's resolution on July 2 and directed that a formal document be prepared.

On July 4, 1776, the Declaration of Independence was approved. When news of the action reached Virginia, the sheriff of each county was ordered to proclaim it at the door of the courthouse on the first court day after he received the copy. Court day in Henrico was the first Monday. On August 5, 1776, the sheriff carried out his orders. The *Virginia Gazette* reported:

> On Monday last, being Court day, the Declaration of independence was publicly proclaimed to the town of Richmond, before a large concourse of respectable freeholders of Henrico County, and upwards of 200 militia, assembled on that great occasion. It was received with the universal shouts of joy, and re-echoed by three volleys of small arms. The same evening the town was illuminated, and the members of the committee held a club, where many toasts were drunk. Although there were nearly 1,000 people present, the whole was conducted with the utmost decorum, and the satisfaction visible on every countenance officially evidences their determination to support it with their lives and fortunes.
> Now will America's sons her fame increase
> In arms and science, with glory, honour, and peace.[34]

Steps had been taken to encourage the development of private manufacturing to produce the necessary military supplies, but the convention also established state-owned facilities. Richmond became a center for military stores, and even the Henrico courthouse was used to store gunpowder until a magazine and a laboratory were constructed in 1777 and 1779 respectively. Muskets were repaired and cartridges were made at the laboratory. In 1777, two rope yards and one tannery were established by private citizens. Across the river at Warwick, the public ropewalk produced ship riggings and other rope products. A tannery was built at the public ropewalk installation in 1777.

Lacking heavy industry, the colony was faced with the necessity of either procuring ordnance and shot from an outside source or establishing its own means of production. The Committee of Safety recognized that any external source could be cut off by the enemy, so it decided to begin to develop the means of production. The scarcity of trained artisans and artificers and the lack of abundant supplies of necessary raw materials did not deter them. Up the river from Richmond, the committee took steps to establish a foundry. They had appointed John Reveley on March 29, 1776, to "examine the Lands in the Neighborhood of the Coal Pitts on James River & make experiments of any Clay he might suppose to be of the Sturbridge kine & fit for making Fire Bricks." The clay at Tuckahoe Creek was suitable, and Reveley found a ready source of coal at the DuVal pits. The one missing ingredient was the iron ore. The Buckingham Furnace, Buckingham County, operated by Reveley and John Ballendine, provided a sufficient supply to experiment with and begin production. Additional ore was received from other furnaces throughout the state.

John Ballendine had a natural proclivity for getting involved in a potentially prosperous venture and turning it sour. Earlier, he had purchased fifty acres below Westham with the intention of excavating a canal on the north bank around the falls in the James. A canal had been approved by the General Assembly in 1772, but failure to get sufficient subscriptions aborted that effort. Ballendine obtained backing and started work in 1774.[35]

After Reveley's report, the Committee of Safety purchased 3 ½ acres of Ballendine's land below Westham and contracted with Reveley to built "a Foundry with four double Stacks & eight Air Furnaces, for the purpose of melting Pig Metal for Casting Cannon &ct &ct." Under the trusteeship of Richard Adams, Nathaniel Wilkinson, and Turner Southall, Reveley began work on what became known as Westham Foundry on June 6, 1776. After a two-month search for artisans and craftsmen, Reveley began to construct the foundry he was to manage. He entered into an agreement with Ballendine to furnish water for the mills from his canal, which was still under construction. Using government-owned slaves, slaves leased to him by their owners, and white laborers, he took two and a half years to construct the foundry. Delays and frequent requests for additional funds for the canal construction, which was behind schedule, caused Governor Thomas Jefferson to consider contracting with a French firm.[36]

When production of ordnance and ordnance supplies and ammunition started in February 1779, the Westham Foundry consisted of a foundry with four double stacks, eight air furnaces, a boring mill, storage sheds, a magazine, the manager's house, and cabins and huts for the artisans and slaves.

Lieutenant Colonel Banastre Tarleton commanded part of Cornwallis's cavalry in 1781 and took part in the occupation of Richmond in June of that year. From John Fiske, *The American Revolution* (New York, 1896), 2:265.

Reveley trained the slaves in the various operations and hired technicians to work at the foundry and boring mill. The surviving records reveal that fifty-five to sixty hands were employed at the foundry, including eleven white men and one free Negro by the name of Abram, who served as a furnace fireman from May 1779 to January 1781. The balance of the work force was slave labor. Tradesmen such as bricklayers and carpenters were hired and brought in to make major repairs when necessary.[37]

Because of the distance from the city and surrounding settlements, the work force at the foundry constituted a community. The government provided some articles of clothing, including shoes, and material and thread for the production of needed garments. Beef, bacon, wheat flour, corn, beer, and rum were provided. Negro women and children were part of the community also, and they were called on to wash clothes, cook, sew clothing, and perform other domestic chores.

Active operations at the foundry began in March 1779, and the first items to be produced were iron boxes, grates, flatirons, bake irons, utensils, nails, spikes, and similar items including one 27½-pound sledgehammer. In April, Reveley began to manufacture cannonballs and grape and canister shot, and these items remained in production until January 1781. It was not until September 1779 that any cannon tubes were cast at the foundry and transported to the boring mill where they were bored in December. The first cannon produced and delivered from Westham were six fourpounders and two sixpounders, weighing between eight and nine hundred pounds each. These were delivered in May 1780. Between May and December of that year, thirty-three cannons were cast and bored, and an unknown quantity were cast but not bored. Reveley estimated that with sufficient supplies of ore and the work force he had on hand, he could produce three hundred canons and one hundred tons of solid shot, grape, and canister a year. Given this actual rate of production, however, he could have realistically produced about two hundred cannon if adequate supplies of iron ore had been received. Reveley was plagued by his partnership with Ballendine, and to add to his problems of insufficient production of ore from the Buckingham Furnace, he found it necessary to detail some of his slaves to assist Ballendine on the canal so that sufficient water could be supplied to the foundry.

In 1780 the State Laboratory was moved from Richmond and erected on land adjacent to the foundry. Three acres of land were taken from Thomas Booth for "erecting publick buildings," and he petitioned the General Assembly for relief because "his Farm will be rendered almost useless, it being impossible to prevent the persons who are generally employed in those Publick works from trespassing & plundering their neighbours." The Assembly referred Booth's petition to its next session, but there is no evidence that it reached a decision. Booth's loss of land affected his livelihood, but it was not as severe a loss as his neighbor John Kelly suffered. In the year 1780 a certain Nathaniel Henderson, with a party of Virginia soldiers, took Kelly's dwelling house "into the public service in order to lodge in it the aforementioned party of men who were at work on the laboratory at Westham." Kelly petitioned the General Assembly for relief because "while they were in possession of the said house they burnt it down," but his petition was denied. The confiscation of land was not uncommon for other reasons as well. Not all the colonists supported the war effort, while some remained openly sympathetic to the crown. The latter group became known as the Loyalists, and even those who did not act enthusiastially enough were suspected of being Loyalists. In Henrico, one such case stands out. Robert Baine had left Virginia in 1775 to go to the West Indies on business, and when he returned in 1780, he found that his six-hundred-acre "plantation" in Henrico with "stock of all kinds, Plantation Utensels &c; and a Tenement in the Town of Richmond, Household & Kitchen Furniture and 4 Negro slaves [had been] . . . sold by Virtue of an inquisition of Escheators & purchased for and now possessed by the State." He petitioned for the restoration of his property in 1781, and the General Assembly granted his request.[38]

Henrico County enjoyed relative quiet during the first three years after the war. Although the town of Richmond had been considered as a possible site for the capital, no decision was made until June 12, 1779. On that day the Assembly voted to move the capital to a central location on a navigable river far enough inland so it would not be exposed to enemy attack. The seat of the government was moved to Richmond because it was "more safe and central than any other town situated on navigable water." The government's records had already been moved to Richmond in 1777, and Miles Selden had been appointed keeper of the public record. He rented a house in Richmond to store them in. The act that established Richmond as the new capital also provided for setting up the seat of government. Under the act, five persons were appointed directors of the public buildings and instructed to acquire six squares for the construction of public buildings. The act also provided for the enlargement of the town by adding two hundred half-acre lots "to be laid off adjacent to such parts of the said town as to them [the directors] shall seem most convenient." One hundred acres adjacent to the eastern boundry of the town were annexed, and three acres on the western edge on Shockoe Hill were acquired for the construction of public buildings. The directors were also given responsibility for erecting or acquiring buildings for the General Assembly, the courts, various boards, and the governor. In addition, the act required that a public market was to be built and that the Henrico jail be enlarged to serve as the public jail "until a more commodious one can be built."[39]

Early in 1780 the public was notified that "the business of government, in the executive department will cease to be transacted at Williamsburg from the 7th of April next, and will commence at Richmond, on the 24th of the same month." Richmond was not ready for the influx of government officials and their families. One observer noted that "accommodations cannot be found for one half of the people who are necessarily brought here. It is indeed a lovely situation, and may at some future period be a great city, but at present it will scarce afford one comfort in life."[40]

The General Assembly began its first session in Richmond on May 1, 1780. The members resolved that the public buildings (Capitol, halls of justice, statehouse, and governor's mansion) would be located on Shockoe Hill and the public market was to be located at the base of the hill west of Shockoe Creek. Thomas Jefferson, Richard Adams, Edmund Randolph, and Samuel DuVal were added to the directors of the public buildings, and the body was instructed to lay out the streets and the rest of the town in squares. Even though the town had a board of trustees and the state directors of public buildings, Richmond was still a part of Henrico County, and the county court and county officials had jurisdiction in the town. It would be two more years before the town would become a city with its own form of government.

The war came to Henrico in January 1781. In addition to the regular company of infantry and those men who had volunteered, the county had been called on to supply 219 men for regular service. Many of the local citizens provided "rugs," guns, and provisions for the men from the company. The county had also been directed to supply the army with fifty-five suits of linen or cotton and to supply each man with one pair of overalls, two pairs of stockings, one pair of shoes, and one wool, fur, or felt hat or leather cap. Various acts of the General Assembly also called on the counties to provide provisions, wagons, and other vehicles to transport them. Throughout the war, approximately one-fourth of the county's milita was called out to remain on active service for specific intervals.[41]

When Benedict Arnold's force of 1,200 light infantry grenadiers, and rangers sailed up the James in early January 1781, they caught the state off guard. Early on January 4, Arnold disembarked his force at Westover and marched his men toward Richmond. Governor Jefferson had issued a call for 4,650 men from the counties southwest and west of Chesterfield and Henrico and for one-half of the militia from Henrico, Hanover, Goochland, Chesterfield, Dinwiddie, and Amelia. On the morning of the fourth, Jefferson, hearing that the enemy was advancing up the James, called out every man able to bear arms from Henrico, Goochland, Powhatan, Chesterfield, and Dinwiddie. While the troops gathered, Jefferson directed the removal of public stores and documents from Richmond and Westham to the south side of the river.[42]

Advancing on Richmond by the Darbytown Road during the afternoon of the fourth, Arnold halted at Four Mile Creek. He sent a proposal to Jefferson calling for the surrender of the town without resistance. If he was allowed to enter the town and remove tobacco and other stores, he promised that he would not allow his men to commit any depredations. Jefferson refused the offer. The state's militia responded to Jefferson's call and marched for Richmond as Baron von Steuben, military commander in Virginia, was busy preparing defenses around the town to resist Arnold's advance. A small force under Col. John Nicholas was sent out from Richmond to reconnoiter Arnold's position with instructions to fire one volley and then retire. After an un- successful effort to locate the enemy, the force retired to the high ground on Church Hill. When Arnold's force ad- vanced, Col. John Graves Simcoe, commanding the Queen's Rangers, dismounted his men and led them up the hill. On Simcoe's right, Capt. Johann Ewald deployed his men in two ranks and and ordered them to advance up the hill. After firing one volley and wounding one of Ewald's men, the milita retired to the crest of the hill and moved off to the northeast. As they retired, they captured three of Cap- tain Ewald's jaegers, German mercenaries fighting in the crown service, who had gone too far to the right. A second force of Virginia militia gathered on Shockoe Hill in the area of what was to become Capitol Square, but this force failed to make a stand. As Colonel Simcoe's command crossed Shockoe Creek valley from Church Hill, a British force under Col. Thomas Dundas advanced around the southern base of Church Hill and up Shockoe Hill. A foot- race resulted in the capture of a few of the "defenders," as the rest of the militia faded into the woods.[43]

After his troops began to occupy the town, Arnold ordered Colonel Simcoe to take command of a detachment of 400 men and move on Westham to destroy the foundry and laboratory some seven miles west of Richmond. Again a body of militia assembled to block Simcoe's advance, and again they retired in all directions without great pressure from Simcoe's men. However, some fifteen tons of gun- powder and a large quantity of ammunition, arms, and stores were removed across the river before the enemy ar- rived at the foundry. Three hundred stand of arms had to be dumped into the river when the British came up, but after they retired, the Virginians recovered the sunken arms. With orders to destroy the installation, Simcoe removed the re- maining powder. His men carried it down to the river and poured the explosive material into the water. The torch was then put to the foundry, mill, warehouse, magazine, laboratory, and other buildings, including the Reveley's dwelling. As Simcoe assembled his men late in the evening of January 5 to return to Richmond, the sky was aglow with the fires raging through the foundry.

When orders came to assemble his men for the return march to Richmond, Captain Ewald discovered that "two thirds were drunk because large stores of wine and beer had been found in the houses." He noted that "they were now so noisy that one could hear us two hours away." That night Arnold's men occupied Richmond, and on the next day, January 6, the British retired downriver and returned to their ships. During the British occupation, several public buildings, the ropewalk, and several warehouses and workshops were put to the torch, and before the fires burned out, they had destroyed several houses. At Westham the boring mill and magazine and the outbuildings and dwellings had been destroyed. But the roof of the foundry had burned, and because the chimneys and furnaces remained intact, consideration was given to rebuilding it. A contract was let by the commissioners of war for a new boring mill and molding house, but the project was dropped. The Westham Foundry was never rebuilt, and the labor force was detailed to make cartridges at the Continental Laboratory.[44]

The attack on Richmond was no hit-and-run tactic. Arnold withdrew down the James to Portsmouth, and that town became the base for this operations. A British force under Lord Cornwallis was operating in the southern theater and was moving north toward Virginia. Virginians had to come to grips with the reality of the situation: the state was to become the theater of operations. The local militia had been trained to maintain order in Richmond, but they could not be counted on to stand in defensive positions against the British regulars. Their failure to make a determined stand against Arnold's men was evidence of this. The art of warfare had not progressed beyond the fortification concept followed by the crown a hundred years earlier. The local military commanders established defensive posts along the rivers and at strategic points along avenues of approach by land to deter any British advance while warnings were sent to the main force. The effectiveness of such positions was questionable since they were generally poorly manned and could be bypassed if necessary. Maj. George Lee Turberville reported on February 12 that he was holding the post at Sandy Point with "seventy effectives" from the counties of Hanover and Henrico. Requesting additional reinforcements, he reported that sixty of the men had deserted because they feared they would have to cross the river and go into action.[45]

After receiving reports of the British forces converging on Virginia, Gen. George Washington decided to send support in the form of a Continental force of approximately 1,200 men to confront Arnold. The young marquis de Lafayette was ordered to assume command of this force of three battalions on February 20. Arriving at Yorktown on March 14, Lafayette examined the defensive measures taken to contain Arnold and retired with his force northward into Maryland.

The British force to Portsmouth was reinforced to about 4,500 effectives by Gen. William Phillips, and he then assumed command and led an expedition up the south side of the James. Lafayette returned to Virginia with his force and arrived in Richmond on April 29. Before his arrival, all the militia in Henrico, Hanover, Goochland, Dinwiddie, and Prince George and half the militia of Cumberland and Amelia had been ordered to concentrate at Richmond by Governor Jefferson. The Powhatan County militia had been directed to rendezvous at Petersburg and Manchester across the river from Richmond. General Phillips moved his force to Petersburg and then turned north toward Manchester. General von Steuben retired before the British force to Richmond. When he reached Manchester, Phillips ravaged the town and prepared to cross the river to take Richmond. His initial wave of assault troops crossed the river and disembarked only to be driven back to their boats by a force of militia. Phillips realized he would be denied. The large American force occupying Richmond held a strong defensive position, reinforced with artillery. From the high ground, the artillery could rain shot and shell down on the British troops as they crossed the river and moved up the banks. Lafayette's Continentals had been reinforced by about 3,000 militia, and the combined force, occupying a formidable position, forced Phillips to decide to withdraw.

He did so, but took out his frustration on the countryside as he retired.

While Phillips's command moved down the south bank of the James, Lafayette remained at Richmond and prepared his army for field service. On May 3, 1781, Lafayette moved his army to Bottoms Bridge. General Phillips was aware of Lafayette's move and decided to discontinue his march east; instead he moved to Petersburg where he awaited the arrival of Cornwallis's troops moving up from North Carolina. Lafayette then moved his command to Wilton where he encamped. While there, he continued training his troops and put them through battle maneuvers. While waiting for the British to move, Lafayette received word that General Phillips had died on May 16. Four days later, Cornwallis arrived at Petersburg and united his command with Phillips's, now commanded by Arnold. On the same day, May 20, Lafayette withdrew his command to Richmond and quartered his men at the ropewalk. A detachment of Henrico and Goochland militia were stationed at Mrs. Coxes's to observe the river crossing.[46]

Outnumbered, Lafayette abandoned Richmond and retired northward to await the arrival of a brigade of Continentals under Gen. Anthony Wayne. After leaving Petersburg, Cornwallis crossed the James below the junction of the Appomattox and encamped near White Oak Swamp. After advancing to Bottoms Bridge, he moved his army up the southern edge of the Chickahominy Swamp in an effort to intercept Lafayette. Even though he did not move directly on Richmond, many of the town's inhabitants feared that he would, so they evacuated their families and removed their valuables. The government officials moved some of their records and government supplies, while the members of the Assembly adjourned to Charlottesville. Later, the Assembly would move to Stauton to escape one of Cornwallis's raiding parties. For two weeks the armies maneuvered and Cornwallis sent detachments to Point of Forks and Charlottesville to destroy stores of supplies and military installations. Wayne's command reinforced Lafayette on June 10, and the combined American force moved south. Cornwallis retired to Richmond and occupied the town on June 15. Col. Banastre Tarleton's cavalry force, returning from Charlottesville over the Three Chopt Road, united with Cornwallis's troops from Point of Fork on the River Road. For five days, the town was under British military rule. All military stores and a great deal of private property were either destroyed or requisitioned. When Cornwallis's troops retired from Richmond on June 20 to continue their march to Williamsburg, they left the town in shambles. Several houses had been burned along with some two thousand hogsheads of tobacco, and the military stores that the British did not want were destroyed along with large quantities of salt and flour. They also left the smallpox. When Lafayette entered on June 21, he moved through the town in pursuit of the British force and encamped two miles beyond the town on the night of June 21–22. He then continued the pursuit; when his troops crossed Bottoms Bridge, the scene of active military manuevers passed from Henrico County to the lower peninsula where Cornwallis was forced to surrender at Yorktown on October 19, 1781.

The impact of the war went beyond the destruction of military supplies, equipment, produce, and buildings. The coming of the British had "throw'd all into Confution." Those who were captured were released on parole and could not take part in any activity that might contribute to the war effort. When ordered to collect supplies, they refused to break their parole. Capt. Isaac Younghusband replied to such a request by stating that "I am now parol'd by the Brittish, to be call'd on at pleasure, and tho' I have acted as a magistrate, as to people proveing property, commiting Theifs & Keeping the peace, that may be wrong. My Excuse is that in the worst of times, there ought to be such Officers—if it is not law, it is Justice and Equity; but my now taking on me to do more is like an Officer in the Army going to the field after being taken and Paroled."[47]

The greatest loss suffered by the county during Arnold's and Cornwallis's occupations of Richmond was the destruction of most of the county court records. Arnold's men applied the torch to "all the magazines and workshops." When the British retired from Richmond on January 6, "half of the place was in flames." Except for some order books beginning in 1677, some loose deeds and wills beginning in 1650, and some miscellaneous books, all the records were destroyed.

Marquis de Lafayette. This young Frenchman commanded the American
forces sent to drive Cornwallis out of Henrico. From J. T. Headley, *Washington and His Generals* (New York, 1847), opp. p. 271.

The records that survived had been removed to a place of safety at Powhatan Furnace. The clerk of the court, William White, was suspended because "of neglect of duty and other misconduct whereby a great part of the Records and papers of this Court fell into the Enemy's hands and were destroyed; and . . . other proofs of incapacity in the discharge of his duty as Clerk." John Beckley was appointed clerk pro tempore on October 1, 1781, but resigned on November 5 of that year. White's resignation was accepted on November 4, 1782, and Adam Craig was appointed. By act of the General Assembly, a special commission was established to review all records submitted for rerecording to examine witnesses, and to order the clerk to rerecord the same.[48]

Although the theater of war had changed, one-fourth of the Henrico militia had to serve on regular duty every three months, as did the militia in other counties. Not all of the men of military age responded to the orders, and on occasion, the names of some Henricoans appeared in the *Virginia Gazette* as "wanted." When Turner Southall issued the call for muster in July 1781, he found that "several of those whose tour it now is, had Engaged with Samuel Williamson for the purpose of collecting horses &c. left by the Enemy for which service . . . they are to be Exempt from Militia duty for twelve months. Others under the Like circumstances . . . are engaging with the Qr. Masters as Express riders." He observed that "they make a shew of Imploy in public service until the men march, they then rest at home in quiet." Writing to Governor Thomas Nelson, he complained that "this kind of manuvering has never as yet been countenanced in this County" and "unless some regular system is laid down I never shall know how to proceed regularly in ordering out the militia." He suggest that the invalid and physically unfit be employed in auxiliary services but that those so employed be enrolled for twelve months service and credited as part of the county's quota. The Henrico militia also saw service on the boats that plied the James. These sailors seemed to be as anxious to do their duty and go home as did the express rider. One contingent assigned to the boats made one five-day trip and refused to stay on board, claiming they were discharged after one trip. Both Colonel Southall and Maj. Richard Claiborne of the Henrico militia examined the orders but could not find "one tittle to warrant" the action taken by their men, so it was determined that they be apprehended and sent to camp to be tried according to martial law. The record is silent as to their fate. Governor Nelson advised the commissioner of war, Col. William Davies: "Whatever method you shall find best to answer this purpose will be approved by me." Davies later reported to the governor that he "had brought the boat party in order" and that he "hope[d] they will continue so."[49]

Because Richmond was a center for supplies, doubtless many Henrico militiamen were employed in the public service as guards, mechanics, artificers, etc. At one point, Colonel Davies informed Governor Nelson that the coats and jackets being made could not be completed because of the lack of buttons; however, "one Humphries in the militia of Henrico, now at Camp," has agreed to make buttons if he could do so at home. Davies urged the governor grant Humphries's request because buttons were in short supply and "this Article, tho' it may seem a trifle, is yet a matter of real importance, as the clothing will be retarded for want of them."[50]

The issue of separation from Great Britain and the colony's right of self-government went beyond the halls of the legislature or the battlefield. The status of the established church was questioned also, and steps were taken toward disestablishment. As early as December 1775 the Henrico Parish vestry had petitioned the delegates about their uncertainty as to the manner in which the minister's salary should be levied and collected. By law, citizens were no longer required to contribute to the minister's salary. The Town church had become the parish church, but services were also still being held at Deep Run Church, Curles Church, and Boar Swamp Church in early 1775. The latter was abandoned in 1775 and became the meeting place of the first Baptist congregation. The Reverend Elijah Baker, a Baptist minister from Lunenburg County, arrived in Henrico in 1773, and two years later he organized the Boar Swamp Baptist Church. Baker's efforts contributed to the establishment of the Baptist Church of Christ on the Four Mile Creek at Clayton Springs in August 1781. The denomination continued to grow, and other churches were established, including the Chickahominy Baptist Church. Out of this church grew the Hungary Baptist Church, which occupied the old Deep Run Chapel of the established church in 1792.[51]

The era of the Revolutionary War witnessed the completion of the shift of the focal point of social, political, economic, and religious lfe and the center of county administration from Curles to the north bank of the James at the falls. As a town, Richmond grew and prospered in spite of the two occupations by the British. As the city developed and the citizens of the county contributed to its growth by taking advantage of the markets and services it offered, the relationship between the city and the county would prove to be interesting and, at times, trying.

CHAPTER V

Mirror of a New Nation

The era after the Revolutionary War witnessed significant changes in Henrico County. The presence of an abundant supply of clay and coal played a more signficant role, and the county began to develop a diversified economy. Unlike many other counties in the state, Henrico had a ready market for its goods and services. The town of Richmond had grown in population and economic activity as a result of becoming the capital and a manufacturing center and military supply point. From a small-town center for trading raw materials, the city and the area around it became involved in manufacturing pursuits. Trade in raw materials and agricultural products increased, and manufacturing, coal mining, construction trades, and supporting services and crafts became a more active part of the economic picture.[1]

As part of Henrico, the town of Richmond and its citizens came under the jurisdiction of the Henrico County Court; the county courthouse was even within the city limits. As one historian noted: "The remarkable thing about the effect of the Revolution on the Virginia county is that little or nothing resulted from it. . . . In the field of local government, . . . the innate conservatism of the Virginian succeeded very well in keeping things as they were."[2] The justices of the county court continued to serve on appointment by the governor for life without pay, and vacancies were often filled from those recommended by the sitting justices. The county court remained the one body vested with the local legislative, executive, and judicial powers. It could levy taxes, appoint county officials and try cases all at one session. The officers of the court, the sheriff, the clerk, and the attorney for the Commonwealth, functioned for Richmond as well as for the county.

It soon became evident that the county court system was not capable of meeting the demands placed on it by the urban growth experienced in the town of Richmond. On May 28, 1782, sixty-five citizens from the town and county petitioned the General Assembly:

To the Hon'ble the Speaker and the Gentlemen of the House of Delegates this Petition of the Inhabitants of the Town of Richmond Humbly sheweth

That your Petitioners, actuated by a Love of Order & good Government, are desireous the Town of Richmond should be incorporated and therefore Pray your Hon'ble House that the same be incorporated under the name of the City of Richmond & with jurisdiction to extend two miles all round the present extremeties of the Town and under such other Establishment as may be most conducive to the Peace, Happiness, and good Government of the Inhabitants, and your Petitioners, &c., &c.

The General Assembly responded with the passage of "An act for incorporating the town of Richmond, and for other purposes." The act did not extend the jurisdiction of the city two miles as requested in the petition, but it did set the jurisdiction of the newly established city court of hustings "one mile on the north side of James River, without and round the said city and every part thereof, including so much of the said river to low water mark on the shore of the county of Chesterfield" across the river. On July 2, 1782, the citizens of Richmond gathered at the Henrico courthouse to elect twelve men to serve three years as the Common Hall. The twelve then publicly elected a mayor, a recorder, and four aldermen from their ranks. The six remaining men became known as councilmen. After the first election, the members of the Common Hall were sworn in by the clerk of the Henrico court; but all succeeding elections were to be held where the Common Hall determined, and all those elected were to be sworn in before either the city's court of hustings or the common council.[3]

The incorporating act defined the powers of the city and transferred all property, real and personal, formerly vested in the trustees of the town of Richmond "to and vested in the corporation for the benefit of the said city." The Common Hall could acquire and dispose of property, levy taxes, and adopt all bylaws, rules, and ordinances necessary to manage the city within the framework of the state's constitution and laws. The city's court of hustings was composed of the mayor, recorder, and four or more of the aldermen. Under the act of incorporation, the hustings court of the city of Richmond could only hear cases arising from violations of city laws and ordinances, provided the fine did not exceed forty shillings or two hundred pounds of tobacco. Only civil cases under £100 or ten thousand pounds of tobacco could be heard. All other civil cases and all criminal cases had to be taken to the Henrico County Court. However, the hustings court could examine all criminals who committed offenses within the limits of the corporation. Even though the county courthouse was within the city's limits, it remained under the county's jurisdiction and the land on which it stood remained part of Henrico.

When the Common Hall election was held on July 2, Isaac Younghusband, a member of the Henrico court, received the highest number of votes—60. William Hay, James Hunter, Robert Mitchell, Dr. William Foushee (another member of the Henrico court), Richard Adams, James Buchanan, Samuel Sherer, Robert Boyd, Jaquelin Ambler, John Beckley, and John McKeand were elected also. These twelve men met on July 3 and chose Dr. Foushee as mayor. Hay was selected recorder, and Ambler, Beckley, Mitchell, and Hunter were designated aldermen. The remaining members served as common councilmen. Turner Southall, another member of the Henrico court, administered the oaths of office, and he was elected city chamberlain (treasurer) at the first meeting of the Common Hall. This dual officeholding in separate political jurisdictions would continue until 1788 when the General Assembly passed an act prohibiting the practice. However, for a number of years the county and city had overlapping administrative and judicial jurisdictions in a number of administrative areas.[4]

Relations between the county and the city were amicable. This was partly because the same people were active directly or indirectly in both political entities, and because the city was not totally independent of the county. As relatively young units of local government in a newly formed independent nation, they shared leadership and common facilities. For many years, the Common Hall and husting court held their meetings and court sessions in the Henrico County

Courthouse. At first the city paid its share of the cost to maintain the building. However, in later years, when the city's Common Hall failed to make payment, as it did in 1815, the county's governing body suggested that the sheriff keep the key and not allow anyone to enter the building except the county magistrates. The two jurisdictions also shared the use of the county jail, and again the city paid a portion of all repair costs. The county paid the initial costs, and when a whipping post with the necessary stocks and a pillory were needed, the county court ordered Dr. Foushee and James Buchanan to have them built. The treasurer of the county was ordered to pay Reuben Blakey "the sum of three pounds, ten shillings for erecting a pillory and stocks" and "eleven shillings and six pence" to Thomas Prosser "for one large Stock Lock." The area of several blocks around the jail was under city control; but as was common during the early years of the Republic, it was designated the prison bounds, and the prison rules that applied to prisoners within the area were drawn up under the direction of the Henrico court. Those convicted of failure to pay debts and other non-violent crimes were allowed to move freely within the prison bounds. Those city residents who lived and operated stores, taverns, and shops in the area were not affected by the rules and sold food and goods to the prisoners. When the jail was taken over to house state prisoners, the sheriff complained to the county court, and Nathaniel Wilkinson and Miles Selden were appointed to meet with the governor "in order that the difficulties attending the same may be removed."[5]

The Henrico County Court also agreed to allow the city officials to use the county's weights and measures to check the scales throughout the city. Despite the air of cooperation these instances represent, it must be realized that the two jurisdictions were moving toward separation. After 1782, Henrico County began to deal with the city of Richmond the same way it did with the counties adjacent to it. Following the annexation of one hundred acres for the public buildings in 1780, a portion of Shockoe Creek remained a common boundary between the city and county. By law, two jurisdictions sharing a common water boundary had to appoint commissioners to meet and determine the best method of bridging the watercourse, and the two jurisdictions had to share the expenses. On February 2, 1784, Nathaniel Wilkinson, Turner Southall, David Lawrence Hylton, and Miles Selden, Jr., "or any two of them" were appointed by the county court to meet commissioners appointed by the Common Hall "to make an estimate of the probable expense which will attend the building [of] a Bridge over Shockoe Creek." On December 6, 1784, Beverley Randolph, George Webb, and Bolling Starke, "or any two of them" were appointed commissioners to meet with commissioners appointed by the Common Hall "to proportionate the expense [between] this County and the said City in erecting a bridge over Shockoe Creek." These men reported back to the court on January 2, 1785, and the court agreed to appoint commissioners to meet with commissioners from the city to plan the construction of the bridge. After an extensive period of negotiation, the treasurer of Henrico County was directed to make funds available to the commissioners, and a partial payment was made to William Burton "for building the bridge over Shockoe Creek" on October 3, 1785. In all, he was paid £200 8s. 5d. by the county. An additional £82 18s., the balance of £160, was paid to Dr. Foushee "for erecting the abuttment to the Bridge across Shockoe Creek." When the Common Hall failed to keep the Shockoe bridge in good order, the county grand jury brought presentments against it in 1788. On July 6, 1789, the treasurer of the county was directed to pay the chamberlain of the city of Richmond one-half of the expense of repairing the bridge across Shockoe Creek. It is understandable why a petition to erect a stone bridge over Shockoe Creek with funds raised by lottery or appropriated from state funds was rejected by the General Assembly in 1792.[6]

Similar county commissions were appointed to meet with their counterparts from Goochland to "let the repairing or rebuilding to Tuckahoe Bridge" while other commissions were appointed to meet with commissioners from New Kent "to let the repairing or rebuilding Bottoms Bridge." Still other commissioners were appointed to rebuild "Turkey Island Bridge in conjunction with the County Court of Charles City."[7]

The most troublesome county boundary was that portion of the dividing line between Henrico and Hanover counties along the Chickahominy River. Unlike the James, the Chick-

ahominy was shallow and swampy. The boundary, as established by legislative action, was the main channel, but the
channel changed with the volume of water flowing down the
river. Since land had been granted and later sold with refer-
ence to the main channel, the subject of the exact position of
the line was disputed in court. Because of the legal problems,
the matter became the subject of petitions to the General Assembly. In 1774 a petition from "sundry of the inhabitants of
Hanover & Henrico Counties . . . who live on each side of the
said Swamp [and] hold their lands to the Main Run of the
same" pointed out that they wanted to have the main run
"unalterably established" because "the low Grounds are very
Wide & the Banks of the Main Run very low." The petitioners
pointed out that "by Beavers & other means, the run in many
places is turned from its Antient Course which is a means of
our property becoming precarious, as well as the County line."
A second petition submitted at the same time requested that
commissioners be chosen from Chesterfield, King William,
"or some distant County; who are no ways in affinity or connected with any of the Proprietors of Lands, on the said
Swamp." A third petition from "sundry freeholders and inhabitants of the County of Henrico" questioned the need to
ascertain the main run since it had not "been drawn in Question" and since "no inhabitants reside in the said Swamp."
Their real reason for opposing the request to draw the line
was that "runing the Line aforesaid will be attended with
a considerable expence. That your Petitioners have been
heavily Taxed for sundry new Bridges across Chichahominy
Swamp forced on them by Hanover County. That a great
number of the inhabitants of the County of Henrico are Poor
& barely able to pay their Publick and Parish Levies." The
petitions were referred to committee, and no action was taken.

Whether or not it had been forced on them by the citizens of
Hanover, the county of Henrico had taken part in the construction of a number of causeways and bridges over the Chickahominy. Because of its low banks and shallow water, causeways
were built to the main runs and bridges were built over the
deeper channels. This type of construction had been undertaken at Meadow Bridge and New Bridge. At Meachums Ford,
a bridge was built over the ford, and bridges were built at
William Lewis's, Nathaniel Wilkinson's, and Peter Winston's.

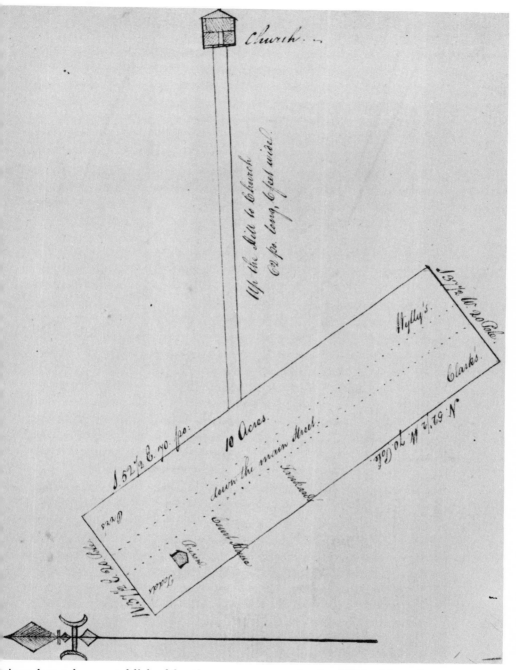

Church ...

Up the Hill to Church
62 po. long, 6 feet wide.

137½ W. 20 Pole.

Hylly's

Clarks

S 52½ E 70 po:

10 Acres.

down the main street

N 52½ W 70 Pole

Davis

court house

Goal

N 37½ E 20 Pole

-rison bounds as established by the county court in the 1780s. Note the ex-
-nsion of the bounds to the parish church. (Virginia State Library)

Commissioners had to be appointed by both counties for each of these bridges when they were built and every time they needed to be repaired or rebuilt.[8]

The boundary line question was brought before the county court in 1785 when Julius Allen and others petitioned it to appoint commissioners to meet with commissioners from Hanover County to prepare a memorial to be laid before the General Assembly for establishing a boundary line "for the Sole purpose of ascertaining the Jurisdiction of the Courts of the said Counties." Noting that the Chickahominy "is divided into many Small Streams, leaving the Boundary & the Juris- diction of the said County's Vague & Uncertain," the com- missioners petitioned the General Assembly "to Appoint dis- interested, Good men no ways connected with, or related to the land Holders on the said Swamp as Commissioners to Examine & fix on the Runs which Ought to be deemed the Main Run & mark the Same as the Boundary line of the said Counties." Counterpetitions were filed questioning the con- stitutionality of the court's levying taxes to defray expenses, especially "the unnecessary expense in running the line . . . to gratify a small party of men." The General Assembly re- jected the counterpetition and did not act on the original petition for two years. In the meantime, the Assembly re- ceived a petition to defer any action and to let the court decide. This too was set aside.[9]

Finally, the General Assembly passed "An act for estab- lishing a new boundary line between the counties of Hen- rico and Hanover" on December 18, 1787, calling for each county court to appoint "two commissioners, respectable freeholders, not inhabitants of either of the said counties, who shall act upon oath, and . . . [shall be] empowered and required to proceed to chop a line of marked trees, to begin at the place where the New Kent line corners on the swamp, and run up the said swamp to the place where a bridge formerly stood, commonly called and known by the name of Winston's bridge, opposite the land late the prop- erty of Peter Winston, deceased." The commissioners were to follow the main run when it could be ascertained "except where there are disputes existing respecting the main run, or suits already commenced by persons owning lands adja- cent to the said main run, they shall in every such instance chop a line in such manner as may appear most convenient, without having regard to any run whatsoever." One major case concerning the boundary question was before the court at the time; Nathaniel Wilkinson owned extensive lands along the river in Henrico, and his title to some parcels was challenged by Thomas Austin and William Ellis. Numerous depositions concerning the water flow, inlets, bogs, and crossings were recorded in the court records. In response to the Assembly's action, the court appointed Robert Goode and George Woodson "Commissioners for chopping a dividing line" on June 2, 1788, but their report was not recorded in the court records as required by the act of Assembly. The matter continued in the courts, and when the General Assembly was petitioned again to ascertain and clear the main run "at the expense of the Landholders adjacent thereto," Wilkinson petitioned for relief, pointing out that he owned about three miles along the swamp and that the boundary "has been Ascertained by divers Heavy, oppressive (and almost ruinous) Lawsuits in the General Court." The Assembly found his petition "reasonable."[10]

The question was not just one of possession of land. Schemes were proposed to open the waterway for commercial traffic. As early as 1786 the Assembly was sent a memorial from sundry landholders on the Chickahominy calling for the appointment of trustees with authority to raise money by subscription "for the opening, improvement, and extension of navigation of the said river as far up the same as the Meadow Bridges." Again in 1818, landowners along the Chickahominy from Henrico, New Kent, Hanover, and Charles City petitioned for the establishment of a company to make the river navigable from the Mechanicsville Turnpike to Holly Landing. The state Board of Public Works was requested to direct its engineer to examine the river from its mouth to the highest point navigable by boats and to report the best practicable plan of opening and improving the navigation of the river. After extensive examinations and surveys, it was determined that the project would be too difficult and costly to warrant the undertaking.[11]

Fortunately, the county's other boundaries were relatively quiet. The problem over the construction of the Shockoe Creek bridge was minor in comparison, but it necessitated communication and cooperation between two separate units of government when, at the same time, the county had jurisdiction over other areas of city life. The representatives from Henrico County represented Richmond in the House of Delegates until 1789, when in accordance with an act passed on December 22, 1788, the freeholders of the city were authorized to elect "one discreet and proper person, being a freeholder, and who shall have bona fide resided within the said city for twelve months, last preceding, as a delegate to represent the said city in the house of delegates." The election was to be conducted in April 1789, and "no freeholder of the said city shall be entitled to vote in right of such freehold, at any county election of delegates to the general assembly."[12] Henrico continued to elect two delegates. It was in a senatorial district with Goochland and Louisa from 1776 until 1818 when the county was redistricted into a middle peninsula district with James City, Charles City, New Kent, Elizabeth City, York, and Warwick counties, Williamsburg, and the city of Richmond.

The jurisdiction of the city's hustings court was extended to the trial of slaves and to summoning grand juries by act of the General Assembly passed December 20, 1790. The Henrico County Court continued to handle criminal cases from the city as well as all cases from the county. It was not until 1822 that an effort was made to extend the session time of the court because of the heavy case load. Pointing out the inconveniences to the parties involved and the added expense as a result of the delays, the justices of the peace of Henrico petitioned the General Assembly to extend the quarterly session of the court. Five years later, the justices and officers of the court petitioned the Assembly again. Noting that the criminal business of the court was still increasing because of "the increase of population and the situation of a large Town in the centre of the County," they asked that the court be allowed to hear criminal matters at the monthly terms as well as the quarterly terms. The Assembly found the request "reasonable," and a bill was drawn.[13]

Even though the county court had jurisdiction over criminal matters and the overseers of the poor in the city, the city did exert its independence where it had authority to act. The same act that extended the jurisdiction of the hustings court in 1790 authorized the formation of a separate regiment of militia within the city. The city regiment was not "obliged to attend company or regimental musters except in or near the said city," but it was to "remain under the lieutenant or commanding officer of the militia of the county of Henrico, and be subject to and governed by the several laws respecting the militia, in like manner as the militia of the county of Henrico." The militia officers continued to be appointed by the governor upon recommendation of the county court. Two years earlier, the militia of Henrico, including the men from the city, had numbered 1,198 men in one regiment under Col. William Lewis. With the establishment of the city regiment, the county regiment averaged between 500 and 600 men and officers. Although the militia did patrol the county on a regular basis just before and after Gabriel's insurrection in 1800 and saw limited local service during the War of 1812, it remained primarily a reserve force of citizen soldiers. As the state population shifted to the west and additional counties were organized, the state militia was reorganized, and the regimental designations were changed. Henrico's Seventy-fourth Regiment of Militia was redesignated the Thirty-third Regiment Militia, and in 1820 the adjutant general reported 25 officers and 575 noncommissioned officers, musicians, and privates in the regiment.[14]

Jurisdiction over the warehouses along the James within the city limits and navigation on the river were other areas where the county's governing body had responsibility for regulating activities that affected the city and its citizens. By act of the General Assembly, warehouses for storage of agricultural products were established "in the county of Henrico, at Byrd's, at Shockoe, and at Rockett's," and these warehouses came under the jurisdiction of the county court. With the jurisdiction over Rockett's Warehouse, the court's authority extended to Rockett's Landing, the city's port. Although the authority of the city's hustings court extended to Rockett's in civil and certain criminal matters, the land was outside of the city limits, and the Common Hall was not given the same jurisdiction as the hustings court. The Henrico court appointed John Hague as "Harbour Master within the jurisdiction of this Court" and recommended John Haynes, Ingram Thompson, Anthony

Bellamy, and Thomas Goodwin for commissions as branch
pilots in the upper district of the James. Hague was also commissioned as searcher for the district of Richmond in 1787
with responsibility for securing the revenue arising from customs. The county also paid for the construction of wharfs at
Rockett's and at Rock Landing for the use of Shockoe and
Byrd's warehouses. When necessary, the county court appointed commissioners to acquire additional land and to supervise construction of additional warehouse space, inspection rooms, or buildings as needed at Rockett's. In addition to
a warehouse for tobacco there, a separate lot was set aside and
a building was constructed for the receipt of hemp. The court
contracted for the construction of additional warehouses and
a picking house at Shockoe Warehouse, and for enclosing
"Shockoe Warehouses" with "Gates to the same."[15]

At Byrd's Warehouse the court ordered that the shed adjoining Trueheart's "Lumber House" be added to the warehouse for the storing of tobacco in June 1785. Two years
later, in January 1787, the warehouse was engulfed in
flames. It burned to the ground along with between forty
and fifty houses and business establishments during a three-
hour fire. Only the demolition of two dwellings in the path
of the fire prevented further destruction. The General Assembly authorized the rebuilding of Byrd's Warehouse, and
the county court appointed commissioners to view and examine the new structure. On November 3, 1788, they reported:

We the subscribers have viewed and examined the Warehouses
lately rebuilt at Byrd's and report to the Court as follows: That the
Warehouses are rebuilt of brick; That they are not covered with
slate or tile as the law requires, but are covered with brick and
coated with pitch and sand; That there is an Iron Gate which opens
in to the Square and four doors opening into the inspection room
which are made of wood; That the floor of the Warehouses are
unfinished and the drain which is necessary to carry off the Water
that falls within the square remains to be opened.

Despite the problems, the court then ruled that the warehouses "are fit for the reception of Tobacco & are built
agreeable to law" and "ordered that the same be certified
accordingly." The General Assembly authorized a warehouse
at Seabrook's within the city, but it was not until the annexa-

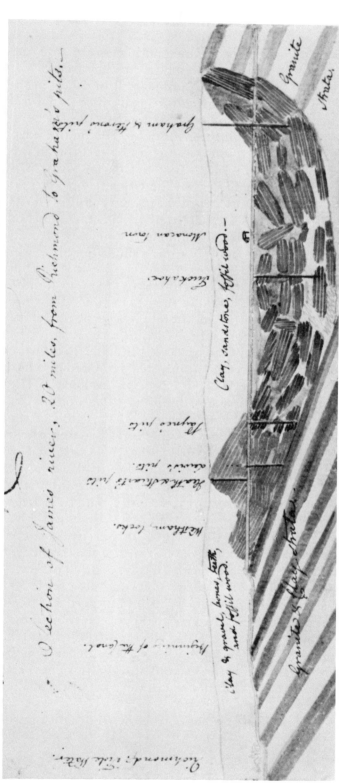

Benjamin Latrobe's sketch of the coalfield in western Henrico. From "An Essay on Landscape." (Virginia State Library)

tion of Rockett's early in the nineteenth century that the Common Hall's jurisdiction was extended to that area.[16]

Life in Henrico County was not unlike that in other localities in the Commonwealth. Agriculture continued to be the principal industry, but the soil was not kind to the farmers. One traveler passed through the county in 1795 on the stage from Williamsburg to Richmond and, after a brief stay in the city, departed by way of the River Road to Charlottesville. His ride though the countryside east of the city left him with an uninspired opinion of the county's primary industry, its people, and their houses. He reported that "a few fields of Indian corn occasionally met my sight, and some new cleared grounds of considerable extent, but not a single field that was tolerably well cultivated, whereas I am assured, that, within four miles on each side of the road, the lands are good and the plantations are numerous." West of the city he noted that "the soil is poor, and partly cultivated, though in a very indifferent manner." The houses along the Williamsburg Road were "mean and wretched," while those along the River Road were "small, bad, and not numerous" and were "inhabited by white people, who do not seem to be in easy circumstances." The land between these two roads north and northeast of the city was also under cultivation, and it was in that region of the county that the soil was rich and productive. Corn and wheat continued to be the primary crops, and slaves continued to supply the necessary labor. The exact number of slaves in the county before the Revolutionary War is not known, but the first personal property returns for the county, dated 1783, list a total of 3,925 slaves in the county and city combined. Five hundred and thirty-one of them were in the city, and the balance, 3,394, were in the county. The largest slaveowner in the county was Peter Randolph with 106 slaves. Richard Randolph was second with 74, George Cox was next with 58, Thomas Prosser had 55, and Peter Winston reported 51. Most of the politically prominent citizens held between twenty and fifty slaves. Among these were the Reverend Miles Selden with 32, Thomas Mann Randolph with 37, Joseph Mayo with 37, Nathaniel Wilkinson with 39, and the estate of Robert Carter Nicholas with 41. Twenty slaves were reported at the Richmond Ropewalk.[17]

The number of blacks, slave and free, in Henrico County

was a little over a half of the total population. In 1790, out of a total population of 8,239, there were 3,583 whites, 4,340 slaves, and 316 "free persons, except Indians." Between 1790 and 1830, the last figure would increase by 300 percent whereas the other two figures would increase less than 50 percent.

	Total	Whites	Slaves	Free persons, except Indians
1790	8,239	3,583	4,340	316
1800	9,149	3,999	4,608	542
1810	9,945	4,384	4,846	715
1820	11,600	5,318	5,417	865
1830	12,737	5,716	5,932	1,089

By contrast, the city of Richmond's population grew from 3,761 in 1790 to 16,060 in 1830. A portion of its growth was at the expense of Henrico County when in 1793 "the lots laid off by the Reverend William Coutts, and adjoining the town of Richmond," and "all that part of the tenement commonly called and known by the name of Watson's tenement, or so much thereof as has been laid off into lots and improved, or which shall hereafter be laid off into lots and improved," were "thenceforth considered as comprising a part of the said city of Richmond." By 1810 the city's boundaries had been extended to include Rockett's and to straighten the western, northern, and part of the eastern boundaries. This annexation of land brought the total area of the city to 2.40 square miles. But the acquisition of land from Henrico was not the main reason for Richmond's population growth. It provided the city with land and some people, but the economic and political life of the city caused people to immigrate to it. By comparison, the figures for the city are:

	Total	Whites	Slaves	Free persons, except Indians
1790	3,761	2,017	1,479	265
1800	5,737	2,837	2,293	607
1810	9,735	4,798	3,748	1,189
1820	12,067	6,445	4,387	1,235
1830	16,060	7,755	6,345	1,960[18]

The presence of a large number of free blacks caused apprehension among the slaveowners. Even though the state had strict laws regulating their activities, the feeling among the white inhabitants was that they should not be allowed to remain in the community. Many blacks found themselves in the precarious position of losing their freedom. A number of Henrico's larger slaveowners petitioned the General Assembly in 1782 to pass an act to put a stop to what they termed "pernicious practices," complaining that

many Persons have suffered their Slaves to go about to hire themselves and pay their masters for their hire and others under pretence of putting them free set them out to live for themselves and allow their Masters such hire as they can agree on by which means the said Slaves live in a very Idle and disorderly Manner and in order to pay their Masters their due hire are frequently stealing in the Neighborhood in which they reside or which tends to a worse Consequence encourage the Neighboring Slaves to steal from their Masters and others, and they become the receivers and Traders of those Goods, having time to go at large, and allso gives great discontent to other Slaves who are not allow'd such Indulgencies, it being generally believ'd that those Slaves do not labour effecient to pay their Masters their hire and clothe themselves in an Honest Manner.

A similar petition was filed in 1784 pointing out the probability that some of the free blacks had been unlawfully freed by the British army and requesting that they be required to register with the courts and prohibited from trading with or for slaves. The county court Order Books reveal some cases in which whites were tried for "Letting Negroes go at large as freemen," "for dealing with Negroes," and "for keeping unlawful assemblies of Negroes and allowing them to Game." Blacks were tried before commissioners of the peace and of oyer and terminer who were generally slaveowners. The records are sketchy before Gabriel's Insurrection, but severe punishment was handed out to blacks in the name of justice. One such instance concerned a slave named Jeffrey, Dr. John K. Read's slave, who denied that he had passed on a bottle of "crude mercury" to another slave while working in Dr. Read's Apothecary Hall. The bottle was intended for a slave named Harry, owned by Joseph Kay. Both Harry and the unnamed go-between testified to Jeffrey's participation, and when Dr. Read affirmed that the bottle and some mercury were missing, Jeffrey was convicted of perjury. Harry admitted that he obtained the mercury and confessed that he "intended to have poisoned the whole family of Mr. Kay, consisting of sixteen whites; & for that purpose had actually put the said mercury into some Hash which was prepared for supper." For perjury, Jeffrey was sentenced to be "pillored agreeably to law . . . have both his Ears cut off, and receive on his back thirty-nine lashes well laid on; which being done by the Sheriff, it is further ordered that he be discharged out of custody."[19]

The slave was considered a piece of property, and under the laws of the state, he or she was denied basic rights, and the rights of free blacks were severely restricted. A slave could not own property, receive a trial by jury, assemble freely, or bear arms. Although slaves could marry, the owner did not have to recognize the marriage. To maintain order, laws directed that each county militia unit conduct monthly patrols throughout its county. On a normal patrol, the men would check the slave quarters and observe any social or religious gatherings of slaves or free blacks. This requirement was relaxed to quarterly patrols in 1779, but it is doubtful that the patrols were conducted with any degree of thoroughness. Toward the end of the century, the whites in Henrico displayed a disdain for the letter of the law regulating the activities of slaves; and that disdain indicated that they either did not fear or could not conceive of their slaves rebelling.[20] There appears to have been a wave of antislavery feeling in the county beginning in the late 1780s and extending to the late 1790s. During that time, a number of county citizens petitioned the court for deeds of manumission so that they could free their slaves. Also, restrictions on travel and assembly were relaxed. The blacks were allowed to assemble at Brook Run where they would meet on Sunday afternoons and on holidays for barbecues and religious services. Also, many slaves were allowed to travel freely throughout the community. The system of control through fear had given way to a mixture of trust and unconcern as the century ended.

The fear of any attempt on the part of the slaves to obtain their freedom by force was always present, but it appears that belief in the strict laws governing the movement of slaves led to a false sense of security. Except for two factors that tended to complicate matters in the political realm, things appeared calm in 1800. The whites focused their attention on the political issues between the Federalists and Republicans. Although Richmond was considered a Federalist stronghold, there was strong support for Thomas Jefferson and the Republicans, and a Republican committee was active in Henrico.[21] During the campaign, southerners were reminded of the successful slave revolt in Santo Domingo in 1791. Some of the refugees from that island had settled in Virginia, and their stories of atrocities were used in the campaign to rally an emotional defense of the institution of slavery in the southern states.

Although many whites found themselves caught up in the rhetoric of the campaign, they tended to accept the belief that the slaves were content in their role as property. This feeling was shattered one night in August 1800 when word was received that some slaves and free blacks planned to kill their white owners and their families. After killing the whites, they planned to assemble at the Brook Bridge and march on Richmond where they would set fire to the buildings at Rockett's and pillage the city. The complete plans of the proposed insurrection were never fully revealed, but a large number of blacks in Henrico, Hanover, Caroline, and Chesterfield counties and the cities of Richmond and Petersburg were party to it. The exact number of slaves who were to take part in the insurrection was never accurately reported, but the evidence indicates that the revolt was to extend well beyond the Richmond-Henrico area. One free black preacher in Gloucester County was implicated, as were other blacks in Charlottesville and Albemarle and Louisa counties.

Information about the planned insurrection was circulated throughout the slave quarters on the farms in the county and in the houses in Richmond. The prime leader of the insurrection was Gabriel, a young powerfully built man of twenty-four who was described as "a fellow of courage and intellect above his rank in life."[22] Gabriel was owned by Thomas H. Prosser, whose plantation, Brookfield, was located on the eastern side of the Brook Road just beyond

Benjamin Latrobe's drawing of a bateau on the James River above the city of Richmond. From "An Essay on Landscape." (Virginia State Library)

Brook Run. Gabriel's two brothers, Solomon and Martin, were also implicated in the plot, and they too were owned by Thomas Prosser. Just up the road, at Meadow Farm, the home of Mosby Sheppard, the slaves planned to take part in the revolt by killing Sheppard before moving to join the other slaves at Brook Run. Gilbert, the slave of William Young, agreed that his master should be killed along with his wife, but he refused to take part in the act because they had raised him as a child. The center of the plot appears to have been in what is now the Chamberlayne Farms–Glen Allen area of the county. North in Caroline County a slave by the name of Ben Woolfolk had recruited between 250 and 600 men to take part in the revolt.

Gabriel's right-hand man was Jack Bowler, a twenty-eight-year-old who was described as about six feet four or five inches tall, stout, strong, with long hair tied behind and twisted at the sides and a scar over one eye. Jack was a ditcher by trade. When he tried to assume leadership of the revolt, the other participants chose Gabriel as their "General." Investigations after the abortive effort revealed that Gabriel was "clearly proven to be the main spring and chief mover in the contemplated rebellion." He planned that the movement would be carried out in the middle of the night. After killing their masters and their families, the slaves were to assemble at Brook Bridge with whatever weapons they had managed to manufacture or take. They would then march to Rockett's and set fire to the buildings at the landing. While the citizens of the city concentrated on putting out the fire, the slaves would occupy Richmond, take over the buildings, and kill the white inhabitants and any blacks who refused to take part. Later testimony was conflicting, but some of the citizens were to be spared. Once the city was occupied, Gabriel planned to either defend it or to retreat down the peninsula, depending on the force brought against him.[23]

The night of August 30, 1800, was picked, and "nothing less than revolution was envisioned."[24] Fortunately for the white inhabitants, heavy rains caused the creeks to rise and turned the roads into mud. After taking counsel with his brother Solomon, Gabriel concluded that the bad weather would prevent his people from meeting that night, so he changed the time to the next night, Sunday, August 31. At that time Gabriel did not know that his plans had been revealed. Late on the morning of August 30, two of Mosby Sheppard's slaves, Pharoah and Tom, informed Sheppard of an impending insurrection. He was told that the whites near Thomas Prosser's land would be killed. After warning his neighbor William Mosby, Sheppard rode to Richmond to inform Governor James Monroe. The governor ordered the commander of the militia to post troops at the powder magazine, penitentiary, and Capitol. Mounted units were mustered and sent out to patrol the roads and to scour the countryside. They did so in the midst of the heavy rainstorm during the night of August 30 and reported that they did not see any signs of insurrection.

After spending all night on patrol, William Mosby returned home on the morning of August 31. One of his slaves informed him that the planned insurrection had been postponed because of the rainstorm and that another attempt would be made that night. Upon receipt of this information, Governor Monroe continued the militia patrols and directed the mayor of Richmond to take all steps necessary for the defense of the city. Orders were sent out to arrest any slaves suspected of having taken part in the plot, and an immediate investigation was undertaken by officials in the county. The exact number of slaves taken into custody is not known, but fifty-four slaves belonging to thirty-three different masters and one free black appeared before the bar.[25]

Most of the slaves who had taken part in planning the insurrection were arrested within a few days, but Gabriel and Jack Bowler managed to elude the patrols for weeks. Gabriel took to the swamp and made his way to the James where he hailed the three-masted schooner *Mary*, which had left Richmond on September 11. Capt. Richard Taylor, an antislavery Methodist, took Gabriel on board. When he was told by two slaves serving in the crew that they thought Gabriel was a fugitive with a reward on his head, the captain answered that he thought he was a free man. Soon after the ship reached Norfolk, one of the slaves from the crew told a free man about Gabriel, and he informed the authorities. Several constables were sent on board to apprehend Gabriel, and after his arrest, he was returned to Richmond. On September 27, he was brought before Governor Monroe, who hoped

that Gabriel would tell him the details of the plot. Even
though his only chance to escape the gallows was a pardon
from the governor, Gabriel refused to tell him anything of
importance. Gabriel was then sent to the penitentiary where
he was placed in solitary confinement. He maintained his
silence. Jack Bowler surrendered to Gervas Storrs, one of the
Henrico constables, on October 10. Peter, or Peter Smith, a
free black, had persuaded Jack to surrender. He too, refused
to reveal any of the details of the plot. By mid-November a
total of thirty-eight slaves had been found guilty in Henrico
County Court. Of these, five were pardoned by the governor. The remainder were sent to the gallows along with at
least three others who had been convicted in Caroline
County. The sentences of the courts were carried out in various parts of Henrico and Caroline, but most of the public
hangings were carried out at the usual place in Shockoe
Valley. Blacks were allowed to witness the hangings, and
many of them did so with the singing of hymns and tears of
sorrow.[26]

There are no records to explain the organizational details
of Gabriel's plot or the development and planned execution
of the insurrection, but it is significant that he could develop
such a plan and that he found support from such a large
area. Local conditions may have stimulated Gabriel and his
followers to conceive the idea of striking out for their freedom. The planning of a coordinated action indicates that
they could act in concert. The abortive effort rekindled the
fears of the whites about the possibility of other attempts.
More stringent laws were passed, and a public guard was
established at Richmond. One of the laws authorized the governor to purchase Pharoah and Tom as a reward for disclos-
ing the plot; after doing so, Governor Monroe presented
them with their emancipation papers. A number of separate
instances of slave plots were reported during 1800-1802, including another one in Henrico planned by Arthur, a slave
of William Farrar, but it was not so extensively organized and
was quickly suppressed.

Surveillance of blacks continued as Virginians sought to
control the slave population by stricter laws. There was also a
feeling that harsh laws were not the answer, and a bill to
prohibit all emancipation of slaves unless they then left the

state failed in 1801. Five years later the measure passed. Henricoans continued to petition the court to grant deeds of manumission, and in 1810 a special petition was sent to the General Assembly requesting the passage of a law for the immediate emancipation of Walter Spurloch. This petition throws some light on conditions of slavery in Henrico.

Your petitioners humbly pray that your Honors will take into consideration the Emancipation of Walter Spurloch (or by some called Walt) a black Man about forty-five years old, & late the Property of William Winston of Henrico County. This Man has been raised in the lower end of this said County of Henrico, & has behaved so well ever since he has arrived to Manhood, as to gain the good opinion of not only his Neighbours, but of all who know him. For the last five years that he belonged to Mr. Winston he paid him considerable hire & not withstanding that, made Money sufficient to pay his last Master the sum of £110 the price he asked for his future services; true it is that Bowler Cocke, Bowler F. Cocke, & William Dandridge assisted him in making the first payment of $200, but they were soon reimbursed by said Walter Spurloch; and Bowler Cocke fearing that some ill disposed Person or Persons might disturb him the said Walter Spurloch in his honest pursuitts has listed him as his Slave & acted as Master for him in every respect since. As no person can possibly be injured by the Emancipation of this Man, & the County much benefitted by having so good a Wheel[w]right, we hope your Honors will think our Prayer reasonable & pass a Law for the immediate Emancipation of him the said Walter Spurloch.[27]

The petition was agreed to, but not all other petitions received the Assembly's favor. Capt. Izard Bacon freed his slaves in his will, but the law prohibited their staying in the state once they were free. A trust was set up to insure that the slaves could live off the income of the estate while they remained in the state as slaves. Two years later the trustees petitioned the General Assembly to authorize the court to allow them to remove the slaves from the state to carry out the provisions of the will. The Assembly found the request reasonable.

Two years later, in 1820, John Winston, a free man of color emancipated by Captain Bacon's will, petitioned the General Assembly for permission to return to Henrico. He stated that he had been forced to leave the state or give up his freedom, and now he wanted to return to be with his wife and two children. His request was rejected. Frequently, when a will called for the slaves to be given their freedom, there was not enough money to cover the owner's debts and the slaves had to be hired out. A trust could be set up to insure that all debts were paid from the income received from the slaves hired out by those administering the estate. A different twist was encountered when Bartholemew Dandridge died. He was a free man of color, and his children petitioned the Assembly to allow them to sell his estate so they would not be sold into slavery to pay the debts.

The condition of the blacks in Henrico was no different from conditions in other localities in the Commonwealth, but the proximity of the capital provided opportunities for employment for the free blacks who settled in the city's suburbs and for slaves who were hired out by their masters. The slave population continued to grow, as did the number of free blacks, and the combined black population outnumbered the white population, but no attempt to revive Gabriel's plan occurred. Many blacks had taken a wait-and-see attitude, while others had taken a stand against his plans. After the initial shock, both whites and blacks appear to have welcomed a return to the status quo.[28]

Before Gabriel's Insurrection, the economic life of the county had prospered with the institution of slavery, and this may have allowed the relaxation of controls on the part of the whites, which fostered a boldness on the part of some slaves to strike for their freedom. Slaves were used primarily on the farms and in the coal mines in the county, and their labor contributed to the development of local economic activity. The increases in agricultural and mineral production had a direct effect on the establishment and growth of local business in the county. However, the presence of the city, with its numerous commercial enterprises, had an adverse impact on the commercial establishments in Henrico. Because citizens could travel to Richmond for many items, the county's local business ventures tended to serve only those who lived nearby. They were individually owned, and except for mills, the establishments were either part of or attached to each owner's dwelling.

Milling was the type of enterprise that prospered in the county, because it was directly tied to agriculture. Many farmers or large landowners with a good stream of water on their land would build a mill to grind the grain produced in their own fields. The mills were owner-operated, and the ground grain was for the owner's needs and for sale to neighbors or in the city markets. Some millowners would grind their neighbors' grain for a fee, but the mills were built for personal and local use and not purely as a commercial business venture. Smyth Blakey and Charles Davis received permission to build a water gristmill on Gilley's Creek, and Joseph DuVal had built one on Stoney Run. John Crenshaw obtained land to build a mill on Chickahominy Swamp near Winston's Bridge. Philip Turpin was given permission to build a gristmill on Shockoe Creek below the mill of Richard Adams. The year 1790 saw three new gristmills; Tarpley White's on Little Boar Swamp, Robert Pleasants, Jr.'s on Four Mile Creek, and Edward Cox's on Ware Creek. On Horse Pen Run, William Booker had petitioned the court for one acre of Robert Price's land for the purpose of erecting a gristmill.

Although there were a number of ordinaries in the city of Richmond, Isham Freeman and Ann Whitlock had ordinaries in the county in 1783. As was usual at that time, an individual maintained an ordinary in his or her home and was required by law to renew the ordinary license every twelve months. All rates for meals, lodging, and care of animals were set by the county court, and failure to post the court-approved rates could result in a fine. Failure to obtain a license and failure to report the establishment on the personal property return were violations of the law also. However, even with court regulation and strict enforcement of laws relating to sale of spirituous liquors, gaming, trading with blacks, and running "disorderly" houses, the number of taverns and ordinaries increased. By 1785 James Freeman had opened a tavern at his house near Seven Pines, and Thomas Johnson obtained a license to "keep" a tavern at his house on Adams's Hill. That same year Thomas Gennet, Jr., was operating a tavern at the house of John Price at Deep Run Church. A license was granted for keeping a retail store in the county in 1787, and the next year Elizabeth Castlin was granted a licence to keep an ordinary at Prosser's Old Store. Other licenses were issued, including one to Richard Sharpe, Jr., for a tavern at his dwelling near Four Mile Creek. Travel by foot and horse was slow and tiring; consequently, the taverns and ordinaries in Henrico tended to be about one day's journey from Richmond on all the main roads leading to and from the city.[29]

Along the James, there were also signs of economic activity and growth. Col. John Mayo had been granted authority to erect a bridge over the James to connect Richmond with Manchester. Once it was completed, Mayo charged a toll to anyone wishing to cross the river over his bridge. James Rumsey had been granted exclusive rights to operate a fleet of steamboats on the James, and the merchants held high hopes that he would be successful. Along the north bank of the James, the canal started by John Ballendine was given new life when George Washington urged the construction of a canal to reach from Richmond to the Ohio River. The James River Company was launched after a visit by Washington to Richmond in 1784, the same year that Lafayette visited the city. The company was operated as a private corporation, and books for subscriptions were opened in 1785. Under its charter, the company was authorized to purchase and condemn lands and to cut a canal, erect locks, and construct dams in the James when necessary for the completion of the task. On December 29, 1789, the members of the General Assembly were invited to take a trip from Westham to Broad Rock, a short distance west of the city. By 1794 the seven-mile-long canal around the falls was completed. This opened the way for direct transport of goods to and from Richmond to the west by water. Samuel Mordecai noted that "the canal as originally constructed was navigated by open batteaux, carrying ten or twelve hogsheads of tobacco, and the river was rendered navigable by dams and sluices as far as Lynchburg." This was the beginning of what was to become the James River and Kanawha Canal. While the canal was under construction, some citizens of Henrico and Chesterfield petitioned the Assembly for protection against "speculators, who ransack earth, air, and water for their private emolument." Protesting that the "speculators" had "entered and actually surveyed the stream, the rocks, & the fishing stands in the falls of James River, which always has been

James River and Kanawha Canal. This canal was built along the northern bank of the James River in Henrico to bypass the falls in the river. (Photograph by John S. Salmon)

and Ought to be considered as a Common, for the Good Citizens at large," the petitioners pointed out that they were divesting "a large part of the Community of their Natural rights & privileges."[30]

Downriver from Richmond, the river was still being crossed by means of ferries. On petition of sundry merchants from Richmond and several inhabitants of the county, a ferry was established from the landing at the glebe lands at Varina to Battes's ferry on the opposite side of the James in 1791. The Varina ferry was also in operation, and farther downriver George Woodson operated a ferry at Four Mile Run. The fees charged by these enterprises were strictly regulated, and George Woodson commented about the general economic conditions of the times when he petitioned the General Assembly in 1798 to allow him to increase his rates to meet his rising costs. Observing "that when the law compels any person to perform a service for the benefit of another an adequate compensation should be allowed," Woodson pointed out that "when that said Ferry was first established the primary necessaries of Life, and Labour was cheap, to wit: Corn is now about double the price it was then, Beef & Pork more than double, and a good Ferry-boat, which at that time might have been bought for £10, will now Cost about 100 Dollars." His request to raise the fee to three-sixteenths of a dollar for the ferriage of a man and a horse and proportionate increases for other freight was not considered necessary by the Assembly.[31]

Between the James and Chickahominy a network of roads had evolved, and as Richmond continued to grow as a marketplace and political center, several main roads radiated out from the city through the county like spokes from the hub of a wheel. Most travel was by foot, on horseback, or in horse-drawn wagons and carts. A new conveyance to the county scene came when John Hoomes received exclusive rights to establish stage lines to and from Richmond, Petersburg, Hampton, Norfolk, and Portsmouth in 1784. Hoomes also stood security for Nathaniel Twining's bond when he appeared in Henrico County Court to record his intention to "run Stage Coaches from Richmond to Alexandria and from Alexandria to Richmond for a certain term," in accordance with an act of the General Assembly. The visitor who traveled by stage from Williamsburg to Richmond in 1795 reported that he was "crowded in the stage by ten passengers and their baggage" and that the trip took from eight in the morning until eleven o'clock at night. He attributed the length of his journey to "the rain, which has been abundant during the last two days, having rendered the roads very bad."[32]

Control of the public roads remained under the jurisdiction of the county court. The court appointed an individual as surveyor and made him responsible for seeing that a specified portion of a road was kept in repair. A typical order was recorded in Order Book 1 on November 3, 1783: "Ordered that William Fauss (son of William Fauss, Sr.) be appointed Surveyor of the Road from White Oak Swamp bridge to Bottom's Bridge in the room of William Gathright." Frequently the court designated other citizens who lived along the road or their slaves to assist in keeping the road in repair. One order directed that "the hands of his Excellency Patrick Henry, Esq., at his plantation on the Brooke" be "assigned to keep the road in repair from the Brooke to Winston's Bridge." Another directed the hands of the James River Company to maintain the road from Westham to William Cocke's. Failure to maintain the road or to put up signposts resulted in a fine after a grand jury investigation. James Valentine was fined 250 pounds of tobacco for failing to keep the road from the fork of the Reverend Miles Selden's to the New Bridges in satisfactory repair. At the same grand jury sitting, Thomas Prosser was charged with failure to note that Brook Bridge was in need of repair; unlike road maintenance, the county paid for all construction or repair work on bridges. Whenever a landowner wished to open a new road, he would have to petition the court, as Prosser did on July 8, 1783, when he requested permission to open a new road leading from his mill to the main road. Similarly, if a landowner wanted to "turn" or change the direction of the roadbed, he had to petition the court; any attempt to do so without the court's approval brought a heavy fine. When Isham Truman wanted to "stop up the Old road leading by his House and open a new road at the distance of about twenty-five yards therefrom" on his own land, he had to obtain the court's permission.[33]

The general road law was revised in 1785 in an attempt to bring greater uniformity of action throughout the state. County courts were ordered to appoint investigating commissions of three members to study and report to the court on petitions to have new roads opened or old ones altered within the county's boundaries. The next year the Assembly authorized a turnpike from Chester Gap in Culpeper County to Richmond through Culpeper, Orange, Louisa, Spotsylvania, Hanover, and Henrico counties and a road from Fredericksburg to Richmond. Commissioners were appointed to determine the routes, and the county courts were directed to appoint county commissioners and hands to see that the work was accomplished. The road from Chester Gap to Richmond was made a turnpike because of heavy wagon traffic. Private turnpikes were not authorized or established until 1795, and no private turnpikes were incorporated in Henrico until after the turn of the century. Between 1785 and 1800, the principal area of road construction lay between Meadow Bridges on the east and Westham on the west. A number of investigating commissions were appointed to study existing public and private roads connecting the Deep Run Coal Pits with the Brook Road and the River Road through Westham and leading from William DuVal's village at the Deep Run Coal Pits to Richmond. All three roads were approved, but not without a great deal of negotiation and in some instances the condemnation of property for a right-of-way. Good roads were needed to transport the coal to Richmond, for the absence of a water route necessitated transporting the coal in wagons and carts.[34]

In addition to setting rates for taverns and administering the roads, the court ordered the sheriff to summon grand juries of twenty freeholders to inquire into any breach of the laws. Most of the hearings dealt with failure of surveyors to maintain roads and bridges, but the court did hear a variety of other cases. Keeping a gaming house, maintaining a disorderly house, retailing liquor contrary to law, and failure to report all personal property for tax purposes were common offenses. Several cases of assault and charges of trading with blacks were reported, but there were some unusual cases such as failing to vote in national and state elections, profane swearing, being a disorderly person and a cheat, waggoning tobacco from Westham on the Sabbath, and assaulting a minister of the Gospel at his divine worship. One case that caused a stir in the county was that of Agnes Smith, who was convicted of murder. She was sentenced to be hanged by the sheriff on May 8, 1789, between 10:00 A.M. and 2:00 P.M. "at the usual place of execution," in Shockoe Valley.[35]

The court also was responsible for protecting the community from contageous diseases and seeing that the poor and infirm received protection under the law. When cases of smallpox began to appear in February 1782, the court ordered that the house on John Cocke's plantation be established as "a pest House for this County, until the fifteenth of November next." Dr. William Foushee was appointed physician, with permission "to inoculate any person for the smallpox at the said Pest House, that may apply to him for that purpose." James Buchanan, Gabriel Galt, Thomas Prosser, and Miles Selden, Jr. were appointed commissioners to superintend the facility. In order to receive pensions, all wounded veterans of the Revolutionary War had to be examined by a surgeon, and the surgeon's report had to be filed with the court. In 1785 the courts in the Commonwealth were assigned several functions previously administered by the established church. Supervising the care of orphans, the activities of the newly established overseers of the poor, and the processioning of land thus came under the courts' jurisdiction.[36]

Although the formal disestablishment of the Church of England did not take place until October 1784, the authority of the parish and the vestry began to disappear after the Revolutionary War. The problem of ministers' salaries was settled when the law fixing the salaries was repealed in 1779, and the formal disestablishment of the church ended its career as a branch of government. All laws concerning the church were repealed, and all vestries were dissolved. The Episcopal church became a private incorporated body, and the new vestries were elected by the members of the individual churches. Under the law, the vestries were required to report to the county court every three years on the administration of church property and the glebe lands. The vestry in service at the time of disestablishment was allowed to make one last levy if any legal obligations were outstanding. This part of the act was not well received by a number of Henrico citizens, and they let the members of Assembly know that when they adopted such a provision to "tax the Inhabitants of this State for the Support of the Teachers of the Christian Religion, they have departed from the spirit of the Gospel and the Bill of Rights." Another Henrico group expressed opposition to the Assembly's passage of an act for incorporating the Protestant Episcopal Church and considered it an "invasion of the Divine Perogative." They were not pleased with the decision to let the church retain the glebe lands because they believed that the lands had been "procured at the Expense of the whole Community" and "Belong to the Publick" and should not be taken from them and given to any "particular society." They invoked the Virginia Bill of Rights and prayed that the members of the Assembly would be "Directed by the Supreme Wisdom" in their "Deliberations and Decisions for the promotion of the Publick good."[37]

The idea of equality before the law applied to all religious acts. After 1780 any minister of any lawful sect could perform a marriage provided he was licensed by the court. Under this law John Lindry, an Anabaptist preacher, was the first minister licensed by the Henrico Court. In 1784 Joshua Morris, "a dissenting Minister of the Gospel and of the Baptist Association," produced a certificate signed by four elders of the association and was licensed to perform marriages. In that same year a new rector, John Buchanan from Lexington Parish, Amherst County, assumed responsibility for Henrico Parish. He encountered a church that was suffering from declining attendance; with a resulting decline in financial support. He was described as a frugal bachelor, but his pay from the parish was not enough for him to subsist on. For some ten years, he tutored the children of Jaquelin Ambler, a vestryman and the treasurer of the Commonwealth. According to Bishop Meade, the Reverend Mr. Buchanan continued his duties without compensation. Later he inherited some property from his brother, James, who had been a prosperous merchant in the city, and the income from the land helped relieve his poor financial situation.[38]

The Episcopal church in Henrico was not the only denomination to suffer a decline after the Revolutionary War. The Presbyterian congregations in Hanover, Henrico, and Goochland lost members, and some of the congregations disbanded. Those Presbyterians who remained in Henrico assembled together and obtained the services of the Reverend John D. Blair as minister. His situation was little better than Buchanan's, and he found it necessary to open a school in Richmond to supplement the financial assistance he received from the church. He and Buchanan became close friends, and because of this friendship, the Reverend Mr. Buchanan and the vestry of the Episcopal church allowed the Reverend Mr. Blair and his Presbyterian congregation to worship in the parish church on Richmond Hill on the Sundays when the rector was holding services at other churches in the parish. This arrangement continued for some twenty-five years. Other denominations were allowed to use the parish churches in the county whenever they were not being used by the parish minister, but later the parish church on Richmond Hill was all but abandoned when regular services were held on alternate weeks in the Capitol.[39]

Efforts to collect subscriptions for the support of the church met with little success when members failed to contribute what they had pledged. The parish still had a glebe of 196 acres with some buildings that were in need of repair. The real property was valued at £1,000 in 1791. At that time it was being rented for £40 per year.[40] The Town Church, on Richmond Hill, later named St. John's, was opened for special services on Christmas, Easter, and Whitsunday when the Holy Communion was administered and confirmations were held. The center of activity for the Episcopal and Presbyterian churches had shifted to Richmond, and it is of interest to note that in a state where the philosophy of separation of church and state was so strong, that the congregations of the two denominations were allowed to meet in the Capitol on alternate Sundays for a number of years. Throughout the county smaller congregations continued to meet and eventually established their own places of worship. Another denomination, the Methodists, made their appearance in the county before 1803. Under the inspiration of Bishop Francis Asbury, Willis Methodist Church South (now Willis Methodist Church) was organized. In 1803 the congregation received title to a parcel of land near Glendale, where it constructed a church. As the denomination grew, other congregations and churches were established.

Early in the nineteenth century, the glebe lands became a center of controversy between the vestry and the overseers of the poor for the county. Under the law, the overseers of the poor had been given authority to levy a tax to care for the poor and to assume those responsibilities for the poor previously held by the vestry. Gradually, by administrative action and legal direction from the General Assembly, the overseers of the poor assumed all responsibility for care of the poor and orphans. The act of processioning, or walking the bounds, of all land parcels had been the responsibility of the vestry also. As late as 1784, the county court ordered the vestry of Henrico Parish to divide the parish into precincts and to appoint "at least two intelligent honest Freeholders of every particular Precinct to see such processioning performed." After walking the parcels of land in each precinct, the processioners were to report to the vestry, and the vestry was to inform the court of any problems encountered. This activity was taken over by the overseers of the poor, and they were directed to divide the parish into as many precincts as they thought necessary and to appoint processioners. After the passage of the act of 1785, the county court divided Henrico into five districts and directed that the election of overseers of the poor be held in each district on March 23. At this time, the jurisdiction of the county court in matters of the poor extended to the city of Richmond, so the authority of the overseers of the poor did also. When the county was redivided in 1788, it was divided into two districts, upper and lower. The road leading from "the Church on Richmond Hill to the Meadow Bridges" was the dividing line. In 1798 the city was made responsible for the poor within its limits, but the county overseers of the poor continued to act in both the county and city in matters concerning the binding out of orphans, executing indentures, etc. In doing so, the county overseers acted on orders handed down by the hustings court of the city. It was not until 1817 that the city court was given authority to appoint its own overseers of the poor.[41]

The county court retained control over all actions taken with regard to orphans, the apprenticeship of orphans, the poor, and the maintenance of bastard children. Just as the

Sketch of Col. John Mayo's house at the Hermitage near Richmond, Virginia, July 10th 1797.

Benjamin Latrobe's sketch of Col. John Mayo's house, the Hermitage, July 10, 1797. (Maryland Historical Society, Baltimore)

churchwardens of the parish had been ordered to bind out
orphans, the overseers did so under court order. It was their
responsibility to carry out the court order and to maintain
contact with the parties. When John Woodfin, one of the
overseers of the poor in the fourth district, presented the
court with the arrangements made for Moses Morris, a poor
orphan, he was ordered to bind him out to John Scott. At
that same session of court, Turner Southall, an overseer
from the third district, was directed to bind out John Sharpe,
orphan of Francis Sharpe, deceased, to the same John Woodfin as a blacksmith apprentice.[42]

The matter of the ownership of the glebe lands did not
come into question until 1817 when the overseers of the poor
petitioned the General Assembly for permission to sell the
Varina glebe and to use the proceeds for the erection of a
poorhouse and the establishment of a free school. They
pointed out that the glebe land had been given by the government for the support of the parish minister and that the
General Assembly had passed an act in 1802 authorizing the
sale of vacant glebe lands by the overseers of the poor in the
counties in the Commonwealth. At the time John Buchanan
was rector, but on May 1, 1815, William H. Hart was elected
assistant minister with the right of succession to the rector-
ship by the vestry. Buchanan assumed full-time duties at the
new Monumental Church in Richmond, and Hart was given
responsibility for the older parish church on Richmond Hill.
With these responsibilities, he also received "the Profits, rents
and emoluments" of the glebe. Writing for the overseers,
Edward C. Mayo advised the General Assembly that the
transfer from Buchanan to Hart was "a virtual relinquish-
ment of the Glebe and that the same has become vacant" in
the manner defined in the act of 1802.[43]

The vestry did not waste time in preparing a reply to the
petition. It met the same day the petition was drafted, December 16, 1817, the day before it was admitted to record on
the House of Delegates journal. The vestry was of the opinion that the glebe lands were received as a private donation.
After adopting a resolution protesting sale of the lands on
the grounds that the incumbent minister at the time of the
passage of the 1802 act was still living and that they were a
private donation and not subject to the general provisions of

the act, the vestry agreed that it might consider sale of the lands provided the incumbent minister, the Reverend Mr. Buchanan, approved, and further provided "that the proceeds of such sale be ordered to be immediately invested in some productive stock, and that the interest or profit thereon earning be annually paid to the present incumbent during his life and for his benefit, and provided further that at the death of the present incumbent, it shall be decided by the Chancery Court to whom the proceeds of the sale of the glebe thus invested in stock shall belong."[44] Buchanan endorsed the vestry minutes and thus acknowledged his consent to the resolution. A committee of three, Thomas Buchannon, B. A. Carrington, and William Shephard, was appointed to meet with any committee of the legislature and to employ counsel if necessary. The matter was fraught with problems, and the petition was ordered to lie on the table December 29, 1817.

This apparently successful defense of the vestry's right to the glebe land did not end the dispute. After the death of the Reverend Mr. Buchanan on December 9, 1822, the overseers of the poor renewed their efforts to acquire the glebe lands. After offering the glebe for sale, the overseers were advised by a decree of the Chancery Court that their claims were not valid. They appealed the ruling, and the litigation prevented the vestry from selling the land to a potential buyer. Attempts to negotiate failed, as did an attempt by the vestry to lease the land. "Prefering rather to suffer loss than promote strife, and thereby injure the cause of religion," the vestry ceased to contend for the land. The overseers of the poor erected a poorhouse west of the Charles City Road on part of the glebe land in 1822, and there they provided assistance to the poor of the county. Between 1822 and 1828 an average of sixty paupers annually received assistance there. The average annual expense to the county was $2,015, and the average annual expense of each pauper was $34. Less than two each year were "free colored paupers." On July 2, 1831, the overseers of the poor sold the balance of the glebe lands to the highest bidder. Pleasant Akin acquired 163 acres of the old glebe lands for the sum of $1,600. The money was used to support the poor and to open a road from the poorhouse to the Charles City Road.[45]

The administration of government was financed through the local tax levy, and the law stipulated that only the amount required to administer the government was to be levied. Under the 1782 act authorizing the levy, Henrico was classified in the first district, or class, along with those counties whose "soil and situation are nearly similar." The tax act of 1782 was the first to place a tax on the value, not the quantity, of land and personal property. To implement the law, the county court divided the county into precincts and appointed collectors to take the list of tithables and their personal property in each precinct. The amount to be levied was then determined by the court, and the sheriff was made responsible for collecting the taxes after giving bond with security. The levy for the overseers of the poor was separate, and again the sheriff had to make the necessary collections. Payment of taxes was made either in tobacco or money, but scarcity of the latter made collection difficult in many areas of the state. The rate in Henrico in 1783 was sixteen pounds of tobacco or twenty shillings per hundred dollars of value. The value of tobacco doubled, and in 1784 the rate was eight pounds of tobacco or twenty shillings per hundred dollars of value. The scarcity of money resulted in hardships for some, and Henrico citizens petitioned for a change in the credit laws. Because of the tight-money situation, in some cases when property was seized for taxes to be sold, either there were no bidders or the amount received from the sale did not cover the taxes. The value of tobacco dropped in 1785, and the rate was set at twenty-five pounds of tobacco or twenty shillings. Conditions improved after 1786, and the rate fluctuated between three and six pounds of tobacco or twenty shillings. When one of John Pleasant's undersheriffs mismanaged the collection of the taxes, the sheriff had to assume responsibility. The undersheriff was dismissed, but Pleasants, and later the administrator of his estate, had to pay the taxes due.[46]

Economic activity would increase in 1786 with the discovery of the Tuckahoe Valley coal deposits on the northern bank of the James River in the western end of the county. The clay in this area was being used for the manufacture of pottery and firebrick, and even though Benjamin DuVal had moved his pottery works to Richmond, he still had the clay transported to the city by wagon. While excavating for some clay, his men discovered a crawfish hole with some dark coal-like substance around its sides. After notifying DuVal, they started an excavation of the site and discovered the Tucka-hoe Creek coalfield. This field consists of a series of strata comprising sandstone, shale, fireclay, and four seams of coal. The uppermost seam of coal had been subjected to such heat as to convert it into a bed of natural coke, or carbonite. Pits were opened in the same fashion as the excavations at the Deep Run pits. To remove the coal, a crude lock was built at the mouth of Tuckahoe Creek and a dam was built to main-tain the water level. The coal was loaded on bateaux, which floated downstream to the locks where they were lowered to the river level and then proceeded down the James to Richmond.[47] These boats were sixty to seventy-five feet long and from five to six feet wide; each was manned by three men and could carry a load of twelve hogshead of tobacco or from 200 to 300 bushels of coal. The coal was mined by Col. Thomas Randolph, the owner of the land. He used the coal in his blacksmith shop and sold it to the citizens of Rich-mond. The original mines were worked periodically until 1812 when they were abandoned. Other pits were opened by William Cottrell, John Wickham, and John Ellis.

Across the James in Chesterfield County, several small pits were opened, and farther south the Black Heath Pits began operations in 1788. The Deep Run Coal Pits had changed hands, but they continued in operation. In 1789 Francis Hy-land advertised that he would supply coal from the Deep Run pits from his "large and commodious yard . . . which was always full" and that he had a good wharf for the conve-nience of loading vessels and would allow its use without charge. A number of pits were opened in the Deep Run area by other proprietors, and it was estimated that 500,000 bush-els could be raised from the pits in the area in a year. The combined production of the Henrico and Chesterfield mines in 1786 was estimated at 400 tons, and this figure held for the period 1787-92. Approximately 589 tons of the 700 tons excavated in 1793 were exported. The local market con-sumed great quantities of the coal to heat homes. The soft coal gave off heavy smoke when burned, and the presence of the coal smoke hovering over the city lead some to conclude that the citizens were healthier because of its febrifuge side effects. As fuel for household grates, the coal was enjoyed because it burned with a bright flame and made a warm, cheerful fire. The discovery of coal in the Tuckahoe Valley and the increased mining activity reduced the quantity of clay excavated there for pottery and bricks. Small quantities were used for firebrick at the Virginia Armory and at the foundry on Belle Isle between 1805 and 1820.[48]

The period from 1800 to 1830 was one of growth in Henrico, and the citizens of the county witnessed the undertaking of a number of internal improvements that bettered communication and transportation in the county. Except for occasional militia musters and a false alarm about a British fleet sailing up the James, the War of 1812 had little impact on the county or its citizens. The British fleet operating off the coast and in the Norfolk and Hampton areas frequently caused alarm at the seat of government. Governor James Barbour issued an executive order on April 19, 1812, detailing Virginia's quota of 12,000 men to be ready for instant mobilization. One light infantry company of fifty men from the Second Battalion, Thirty-third Regiment from Henrico was attached to the Second Brigade, Fourth Division of this force. A series of camps were established around Richmond as militia from other counties mobilized. The Thirty-third Regiment of Militia from Henrico was mobilized by executive order on March 18, 1813, for an eleven-day period from March 19 to March 29. Eleven companies assembled at Camp Carter, south of the Williamsburg Stage Road just west of Deep Bottom. Two other companies from Henrico saw active duty for brief periods of time. Capt. Thomas H. Prosser's troop of cavalry was mustered into active service from August 27 to September 18, 1814, and Capt. William Byrd Chamberlayne's company of infantry was stationed at Deep Bottom Bridge from August 28 to December 1, 1814. The eastern end of the county along the James was examined for the establishment of defensive fortifications early in the war, but the governor decided not to order any construction because the area was "covered with forests in their original state, or such as have grown up since industry declined and the country has been abandoned," making the county easy to defend. A detachment of militia under Maj.

William Armistead of Amherst County established an encampment known as Camp Randolph in the eastern part of the county on Richard Randolph's land in April 1813. Instead of accepting the flat, humid area offered at no expense, Major Armistead chose a field in cultivation, and the soldiers were "let loose" on the "flourishing crop of wheat, clover, &c." Randolph allowed the officers to use his house, and they occupied the first floor and turned the second floor into a hospital for the sick. To recover his damages, Randolph petitioned the Assembly for $250 in damages for his crops and additional sums for the "injured" furniture and windows.[49]

Before and after the War of 1812, a new wave of road building occurred in the county and in other areas of the Commonwealth. Except for a few short roads constructed through the passes of certain mountains and a road started from Fredericksburg toward the Blue Ridge, early turnpike construction was confined principally to the northern Virginia area and the counties around the seat of government. These undertakings were regulated by the General Assembly, and each act that authorized a particular turnpike prescribed the organization, financing, construction, and fees that could be charged. Pointing out the potential benefits if the coal from the Deep Run pits could be transported over a turnpike road direct to Richmond, citizens of the county petitioned the General Assembly in December 1803. They noted that the existing roads were almost impassable at some seasons and even when they were in good condition the wagons could only carry 40 to 45 bushels of coal. They requested that a turnpike be constructed from Richmond to Deep Run, about ten miles, and then west to the Three Chopt Road. Predicting that a wagon could carry up to 100 bushels of coal on a turnpike, the petitioners believed that an increase in supply of coal would reduce the cost per bushel to the inhabitants of Richmond and would also increase the supply available for export. The proposed route of the turnpike road followed some existing roads, and a number of citizens who used the roads to transport wood to Richmond requested that their needs also be considered. On January 5, 1804 a bill passed establishing the Richmond Turnpike Company. The managers were authorized to open books in the city of Richmond for the purpose of taking subscriptions from those who wished to obtain stock in the company. They were given two years to start the project, which had to be completed seven years after it was started. The road was to be constructed at least forty feet wide with ditches on each side, and its surface was to be covered with gravel or stone "so as to render the passage of waggons thereon as convenient as possible."[50]

Tollhouses were to be built at each end and at specified intersections with other roads, and the tolls were to be paid in proportion to the distance traveled. The toll for a loaded wagon and team was twenty-five cents for every cart (except those carrying wood to Richmond, which were exempt) and six cents per wheel. The same charge was set for every riding carriage. All horses, mules, or horned cattle not attached to a carriage were charged a fee of three cents each. The Assembly reserved the right to increase the tolls if necessary and did so in 1814 by increasing the toll for coal wagons carrying over sixty bushels by six cents and by adding a toll of two cents for carts carrying wood. This turnpike was built in stages and continued in operation for a number of years and was extended to John J. Dickenson's tavern in Goochland County in 1816. The present Broad Street follows the general roadbed.[51]

The turnpike provided a means of transporting the coal from the Deep Run pits, and work in the field expanded. When the pits were advertised for sale in 1815 by W. M. Hancock, the tract contained 1,750 acres. A number of shafts had been opened during the War of 1812, and Hancock presumed that they would yield at least one million bushels of coal. In addition to the pits, the purchaser would acquire "a considerable quantity of coal already raised" and "mules, machinery, tools, etc., sufficient to commence immediate operations." Daniel Burton, who lived within a mile of the Deep Run pits, had been engaged in wagoning coal from them for a number of years. He noted that there were usually large banks of coal available, and he was of the opinion that there was considerably more than 180,000 bushels of coal left. The estimated production of all the coal pits on the north side of the James in 1825 was 400,000 bushels. Within the Richmond Coal Basin, there were an estimated twenty-five differ-

Walkerton Tavern. This structure on Mountain Road was built by John Walker sometime between 1815 and 1830. (Virginia State Library)

ent pits in operation, and their total production was 66,720 tons in 1825 and 102,799 tons in 1830.[52]

Turnpikes became a means of investing with the opportunity of good returns, but the maintenance costs tended to cut into the income. If the road was closed for repairs, tolls could not be charged. Twenty days after the passage of the Richmond Turnpike Company bill, the Assembly passed an act incorporating two companies for opening a turnpike road from Richmond to Staunton. The Richmond and Columbia Turnpike Company was given responsibility for the eastern end of the road, which ran through Henrico. The Brook Turnpike Company was established in February 1812 to construct a turnpike from the city of Richmond to Dabney Williamson's tavern (in the area of present Solomon's Store on U.S. 1). A survey of the proposed road was to be filed with the Henrico County Court, and the managers were authorized to construct a road thirty feet wide. They were also given permission to take timber, gravel, earth, or stone from property along the route to make necessary repairs provided they reimbursed the landowners. Again, the Assembly set the fees, but it added a provision that anyone driving a wagon, cart, or carriage was to drive to the right when they meet a vehicle coming in the opposite direction. Failure to do so carried a $2 fine for a free person and ten lashes for a slave unless the slave was acting on the order of his master. If such was the case, the master had to pay the fine. Within the next four years, separate turnpike companies were established to connect the terminus of the Brook Turnpike with Ground Squirrel Bridge, Merry Oaks, and William D. Taylor's mill in Hanover County. In 1819 the Shockoe Turnpike Company was incorporated to connect the Brook Tavern on the Brook Turnpike by the most convenient road to Hanover Courthouse.[53]

The Meadow Bridge Turnpike Company was established on December 16, 1814, and the next year several citizens petitioned to open a turnpike to the New Bridges. The Chickahominy Turnpike Company was established by the Assembly in response to the petition, but the managers were not able to lure enough subscribers. They returned two years later with a petition to establish a turnpike to Freeman's Tavern on the New Bridges Road. An act to incorporate the Richmond Hill Turnpike Company to run from the termination of Twenty-fifth Street to the house of Walter Shelton, commonly called Freeman's Tavern, was passed on February 9, 1818. Three additional turnpike companies were established in Henrico during the time: Westham Turnpike Company, February 12, 1816; Mechanicsville Turnpike Company, February 21, 1817; Richmond and Osborne Turnpike Company, January 17, 1818. The general road laws of the state were revised in 1819, and the county courts were authorized to establish toll roads where necessary. One sign of increased traffic on these roads was the provision that horse racing on the public highways was unlawful. The turnpikes, the Stage Road from Richmond to Williamsburg, and the Stage Road from Richmond to Charlottesville, a portion of which became the Westham Turnpike, all radiated out from Richmond and passed through the county. They are all recorded on John Wood's map of the county prepared by direction of the Assembly and presented to the governor on October 25, 1819.[54]

Around this time, in the western end of the county, work had started on a more permanent canal on Tuckahoe Creek. The Tuckahoe Creek Company had been chartered in 1813 to open the creek from the James River to the highest part practicable on its main branch. The Randolphs had opened a part of the creek for navigation by the construction of a lock, and they had built a millpond at Tuckahoe Mill on the creek. In carrying out its venture, the Tuckahoe Creek Company had to build locks to cut the canal around the milldam. A second Tuckahoe Creek Company was established in 1820 with authority either to negotiate with Thomas Mann Randolph for land to cut a new canal from the creek to the James or to negotiate with McRae, Dorrington and Company for the uncompleted canal they had been cutting through Randolph's land. The same conditions relative to the millpond were enumerated. Construction of the canal consisted of deepening the existing creek bed, building dams across the mouths of feeder branches, and erecting locks. Work on the James River and Kanawha Canal had been progressing, and in December 1821 the principal engineer, Claudius Crozet, reported that the Tuckahoe aqueduct was completed with the exception of the parapet walls. He also reported that next to the aqueduct were three lift locks by which a boat was lowered into the bed of Tuckahoe Creek. A contract was let with William Hetherton to excavate the bed of the eastern branch of the creek for four miles. John G. Gamble, engineer for the James River and Kanawha Company, advised against making the Tuckahoe Creek canal a part of the main canal because the drainage into the creek could cause it to be filled with sandbars and other deposits and because there was no provision for controlling the freshets on Tuckahoe Creek after heavy rains. Gamble pointed out that the volume of water in the creek could cause a flood forty feet wide and ten feet deep.

In 1827 the Tuckahoe Canal Company was incorporated with Thomas Mann Randolph as one of the managers. The purpose of this company was to construct a canal "from some point on the James River canal, the western side of Tuckahoe creek, to some point on said creek, in the county of Goochland, near Crouch's coal pits." The next year the company was given approval to "construct a railroad upon so much of the ground intended for the location of Tuckahoe canal," provided the roadbed was constructed to allow foot and horse traffic free passage whenever the tracks crossed a public road. By 1829 the canal was opened to Cottrell's Coal Pits above the junction of Deep Run Creek with Tuckahoe Creek. In that year a petition was filed requesting that the canal be extended to the junction of Big and Little Tuckahoe creeks so that the landowners could transport coal, wood, and timber from the area.[55]

The total number of acres in Henrico in 1820 was 155,235, and the total value of the land and buildings was $7,393,818.83. The average price of land per acre, including buildings, was $47.63. The total number of inhabitants was 11,600, and of these 2,469 were engaged in agriculture, 27 in commerce, and 455 in manufacturing. The average revenue from taxes for 1820-30 was approximately $13,500 per year. Looking back from 1830, it is possible to observe that Henrico had grown in population since the Revolutionary War and that Henricoans had utilized the resources of the county in their efforts to develop the county's economic potential. Also included in this growth were other diverse local businesses that served the farmers and miners. New demands had been placed on local government, and changes had occurred to meet them. But, as in other counties in the state and in other southern states, any prosperity that existed was tainted by the presence of the institution of slavery.

CHAPTER VI

Coming of Age

The years from 1830 to the Civil War witnessed dramatic change in some aspects of life in Henrico County. It was the time when spikes were driven into Henrico soil for the tracks of the Richmond, Fredericksburg and Potomac Railroad (1834), Virginia Central Railroad (1851), and Richmond and York River Railroad (1853). The advent of the railroads contributed to the decline and eventual demise of the turnpike companies. The operational and maintenance costs drained the resources of many of the private turnpike companies and their charters were withdrawn, making it necessary for the local government to assume responsibility for the maintenance of the roadbeds again. The thirty-year period 1830-60 was a time of growth in the county's population, and the economic picture frequently reflected conditions on the national scene. Strides were made in scientific farming, leading to the formation of an agricultural society and the beginning of the annual agricultural fair. In the field of education, Henrico began the development of free schools for the education of many of the white children in the county.

The population of Henrico in 1830 was 5,716 whites, 5,932 slaves, and 1,089 free blacks, for a total of 12,737. Only white males over twenty-one who owned property had the right to vote, and few Henricoans exercised their vote to adopt the state constitution of 1830. Out of a total of 326 votes cast, 280 voted for and 46 voted against adopting the constitution. The depression in the mid-1830s slowed down economic growth, and there was a corresponding slowdown in the population growth during the decade. Between 1830 and 1840 Henrico's population increased by only 186 souls, and only the number of whites showed an increase. In 1840 there were 6,182 whites, 5,728 slaves, and 1,013 free blacks in the county for an aggregate of 12,923. Of the freeborn, white and blacks, the number employed was reported as 2,801, and of this sum the breakdown was: mining, 250; agriculture, 2,256; commerce, 1; manufactures and trades, 267; learned professions and engineers, 27. There was a dramatic increase of 3,166 from 1840 to 1850 when the total population was reported at 16,089. The 1850 figure included 8,493 whites, 6,202 slaves, and 1,394 free blacks. This was the first time since 1790 that the number of whites was greater than the number of slaves and free blacks combined. An interesting statistic in the 1840 census noted that of the 2,960 whites over twenty years of age, 612 could not read and write. At that time, there were four academies and grammar schools in the county with 181 scholars and twenty-three primary and common schools with 425 scholars. Ninety-five of these were being educated at public charge.[1]

Before the development of an educational system, individual families had to see to the education of their children as many families had done during the colonial period. One such effort in the post–Revolutionary War period was the acquisition of one-half acre of land from Robert Price, owner of Westbrook plantation, on January 1, 1787. Five men, Samuel Williamson, William Burton, Barret Price, Allen Williamson, and John Williamson, purchased the lot for £3 for the purpose of erecting a schoolhouse. The date of construction of the Brook Schoolhouse on the Brook Turnpike, just south of Brook Run, is not known, but it was apparently administered by members of the families who enrolled their children in the school. Funds for construction and the salary of the teacher were paid for by the families. Later, in 1859, this schoolhouse served as the first meeting place of Emmanuel Church. During the Civil War the schoolhouse served as a hospital, and in July 1864 the building became a casualty of the war when it was burned by Confederate wagoners.[2]

The initial step in the development of an educational system in the Commonwealth occurred in 1810 with the establishment of the state Literary Fund. This fund was set up to receive funds from specified sources, and the income was to be used for providing schools. When the income of the fund reached $45,000 a year, it was to be distributed among the counties of the state on the basis of white population for the instruction of poor white children. Locally appointed county commissioners were to supervise the use of the funds. At first the income could only be used to pay teachers, but in 1820 the law was amended to allow 10 percent of the county allotment to be used for buildings, provided the parents paid three-fifths of the cost, 5 percent for the purchase of books, and $100 for paying the teacher if a matching amount was paid by the parents. For each poor child sent to the school by the county commissioners, the teacher received four cents per day. The amount received from the parents of children not sent by the commissioners had to be negotiated between the parents and the teacher. If the parents built the school building and turned it over to the commissioners, they were entitled to a rebate of 10 percent of the yearly fee. In addition, glebe lands and church property in the possession of the overseers of the poor could be used for educational purposes.

There were several drawbacks to the school program under the Literary Fund, not the least of which was the stigma of pauperism. There were no state regulations pertaining to schoolhouses, teachers, pupils, or instruction. The schools were subsidized by the state through the payments to the teachers for each poor child placed in the school by the county school commissioners. In 1845 an act was passed that provided for the education of any white child between the ages of six and twenty-one provided a certain percentage of voters in a county elected commissioners to manage the school system. Before the Civil War, Virginia evolved a common school system through the growth and popularization of a system of state subsidies.[3]

Two other factors that contributed to the acceptance and development of the common school system were the existence of charity schools and the Sunday School movement. Charity schools were usually set up in large cities expressly for the purpose of taking care of orphans and poor children. Although there is no evidence of a charity school in Henrico, there were some in Richmond. The Sunday School movement began in the state as early as 1812 and emphasized reading, spelling, and Bible study. Churches provided this opportunity to learn as a religious experience, and although it had nothing to do with any state-supported school system, it served to encourage the development of the common school program. Several churches in Henrico conducted such

Tuckahoe Creek, looking south, about a half mile from the James River. The bank of earth on the right may conceal the site of an old lock on the Tuckahoe Canal. (Photograph by John S. Salmon)

schools as a regular part of their worship services. The proponents of the Sunday School movement saw the school as a
mission venture to provide an educational opportunity to
those in need and to provide the church with an opportunity
to encourage the children and their parents to attend divine
services. In one recorded incident, a gentleman was traveling
past "the smokey cabins" along the Mountain Road. "Seeing
the children engaged in mischief and growing up in vice,
[he] was led seriously to consider their situation." He began
discussing the need to establish Sunday Schools "in order to
reform, if possible, the evils he witnessed." The people in the
area responded, and a Sunday School was established at
Hungary Meetinghouse with "thirty scholars." The number
in attendance grew to fifty, and some parents even attended
to learn the basics of reading and writing. A total of sixteen
teachers, four of them rotating every week, gave instructions
in reading, writing, and spelling. The school grew in spite of
efforts on the part of some members of the community to
"prejudice the minds of ignorant parents, and to hinder the
progress of the children." Because of the efforts at Hungary
Meetinghouse, the Hungary Sunday School Society was established "to disseminate learning and moral improvement
among the poor inhabitants." This group adopted rules for
the internal government of the school. The idea spread, and
three other schools were established. One near Brook Tavern enrolled twenty-five "learners." The second school, at
Deep Run Church, had eighty-four "learners," and the third
one, at Ground Squirrel Church, had "fifty or sixty" pupils.
The effort in northern Henrico was so successful that a
meeting was held at Winar's Meetinghouse in Hanover
County to encourage the development of a school in that
community. Although the Sunday School was not a substitute
for the common school, it helped create an atmosphere of
acceptance for the development of the free school system.[4]

In 1818 the first significant step was taken on the state
level when provision was made for a system of private
schools to which indigent children were sent at state expense.
Under this act, school commissioners were appointed by the
court and each commissioner was responsible for determining the indigent children in his district and designating those
assigned to a school. The first meeting of the Henrico school

Tuckahoe Creek, looking north, about one mile from the James River. (Photograph by John S. Salmon)

commissioners was held in 1819, and their report covered the school year in 1818-19. There were sixteen schools in the county at that time, and only 25 of the 131 poor children were sent to schools at a tuition expense of $146.34. The commissioners estimated that it would take $1,946.66 per year to send all of the indigent children within the county to school. The number of schools varied each year, depending on availability of teachers, the response of parents who paid to send their children, and general economic conditions. Schools were made up partly of students who were able to pay the tuition and partly of those children who were paid for out of funds received from the Literary Fund. A teacher could go into a neighborhood and arrange with the parents to conduct a school for a specified amount per student. If he or she was not able to obtain a sufficient number of students, then the school commissioner would agree to send enough poor children to make up the difference. Usually the minimum number of pupils was twenty. If the teacher or parents could only register fifteen, then the other five would be sent by the commissioner. Sometimes the parents agreed to establish a school and then contracted with a teacher, and if necessary, the commissioner supplied the necessary number of indigent children to complete the quota. As one observer of the Henrico system noted in 1823, the number of poor children sent at state expense made it possible for other families to send their children to school. "They all go without distinction, are treated alike, and the school commissioners draw on their treasurer from time to time, as the tuition fees become due."[5]

The schools were conducted as one activity in a building constructed for another purpose, or they were held in a building built expressly as a school. However housed, the school was established in a location convenient to each household with students in attendance. The schoolhouses for the most part were log cabins. They were furnished with slab seats, and the fuel for heating was "gathered by the boys from the surrounding forests." Reading, writing, and ciphering were stressed, but arithmetic, geography, history, grammar, and literature were included. The Henrico commissioners were not pleased with having to rely on individual effort on the part of the teacher or parents to establish the

Possible canal cut on the east bank of Tuckahoe Creek, about one mile from the James River. (Photograph by John S. Salmon)

schools. As early as 1823 they recommended the division of the county into school districts with the establishment of schoolhouses with suitable endowments in each district. They also estimated that it would require $3,000 to pay the expense of tuition for all the poor children in the county. Although they were not successful in establishing the district schoolhouse concept or in obtaining sufficient funds, eventually they managed to get a special act passed allowing the payment of a higher per day tuition of up to eight cents in 1853.[6]

The number of schools in 1830-60 varied, and seldom were the same numbers reported for more than two years in a row. The number of poor children sent changed from year to year, and the total number of pupils in attendence at all the schools was never reported. The commissioners encountered a number of difficulties, and even though they had money left over, they could not always persuade parents to send their children to school. Many parents did not have sufficient food and clothing and did not want to reveal their poverty to others by accepting what they considered charity. In an agricultural economy the services of every member of the household were needed, and many parents felt that the children could learn to do the work from their parents and in doing so would procure their daily subsistence. Another hindrance was the lack of a sufficient number of schools conveniently located to serve all areas of the county. In areas where the economic situation was such that the majority of the citizens were poor, a school could not be started. Thus the commissioners found themselves with money to spend, but no school in an area of need.

The commissioners negotiated with the schoolmasters or teachers for a child to be educated in the manner outlined in the law during the "common scholastic year" and "in the course of two scholastic terms." The majority of the schools were in operation for nine months. The commissioners always considered the term *indigent* "as strictly applicable to such children only, whose parents are unable to defray the charges of education, without depriving themselves of the means of supplying their families with the common necessaries of life." No preference was given as to sex, and those between the ages of eight and eighteen were considered eligi-

Bridge abutment near Tuckahoe Creek. The James River and Kanawha Canal is on the right. (Photograph by John S. Salmon)

ble. As the schools began to grow, the teachers admitted fewer students paid for by the commissioners. This situation led commissioners to report that they found it more difficult to get the teachers to admit the scholars into their schools than in finding children to send. Part of the problem was the small compensation allowed by law of four cents per day per student. As early as 1840 the Henrico commissioners wanted to raise the fee to six cents and pointed out that "the fund allowed has been sufficient thus far to educate all who will go to school, where the teachers will take them for the small compensation allowed by law. The teachers, for the most part, are those patronized by the commissioners as individuals, and by the neighbors."[7]

The educational program in Henrico County before the Civil War was not different from that found in most localities in the state. Some, a very few, had adopted the modifications authorized in 1845. Henrico did not adopt the free public school system, but the act allowed for those who maintained the old system of court-appointed commissioners to have a superintendent of schools to manage the school program. Henrico's first superintendent was Jesse F. Keesee. Basically, the teachers were independent contractors who could accept or reject indigent children farmed out by the commissioners, and the commissioners were citizens who were interested in education, the poor, or both. Some teachers refused to accept children because of the low tuition fee allowed, and there were those who "taught the children a large number of days more than they were entered for, and when they knew they would not be paid therefor." When teachers refused to take the children, the commissioners did not seem to express any desire in placing the children that they should have. Superintendent Keesee put much of the blame at the feet of the commissioners. He believed that if the commissioners would take the interest that the importance of the subject of education demanded, then the parents "might be induced to send and the teachers to teach." The statistics are not complete for the period before the Civil War because the commissioners failed to file reports for a number of years, but from the reports that were filed and printed, it appears that there were never fewer than eleven or more than twenty-five schools in the county. The number of indigent children sent varied from a low of 27 in 1828 to a high of 283 in 1843. In that year, a total of 283 of the 600 known indigent children were sent to the twenty-five schools in the county. The commissioners summed up the state's effort to provide educational opportunities through the Literary Fund in 1843 when they reported: "The progress made by the children is respectable, and the advantages derived from the fund considerable, both to teachers and children, for in some neighbourhoods the schools could not be sustained without its aid." The schools did have an impact on the community and did contribute to the development of the basic communicating skills—reading and writing. Frequently the statistics for Henrico County and the city of Richmond were combined in annual reports, but occasionally relevant figures for the county alone were reported. Of the 116 people who applied for marriage licenses in Henrico in 1817, 22, or 18.97 percent, could not write their names. In 1827, when 98 people applied, 20, or 20.41 percent, could not write their names, and in 1837 only 15, or 17.05 percent, of the 88 who applied could not write their names. However, it is important to note that in 1840, 612 white persons over twenty years of age could not read and write.[8]

As strides were being made in the field of public education, significant activity was occurring in the farming community. New techniques were being explored, and new scientific discoveries were affecting the farm family. These involved not only the tilling of the soil but also animal husbandry and a variety of other branches of farming. The improved methods of farming were developed by individuals who were seeking better ways to improve the product and the amount produced. The learning process was a combination of trial and error and the dissemination of information on proven techniques. Agricultural activities had depended on the quality of the soil and the repeated planting of any crop that proved profitable regardless of the consequences to the soil and future production. Crop rotation was not practiced intentionally, and the ruinous tobacco culture was leaching the soil. A combination of scarce capital and the institution of slavery had helped to perpetuate this practice. During 1830-60, there was an agricultural revival. The period witnessed the practice of scientific farming, greater production, more diversified agriculture, and improved land values. The organization of agricultural societies and farmers' clubs, the publication of farm journals, and the establishment of agricultural fairs were evidences of a general acceptance of the concept of scientific farming, which contributed to the relief of the agricultural dilemma.

One of the local groups formed during this period was the Henrico Agricultural and Horticultural Society. Organized in December 1840, the society included citizens from the city as well as the county. The Reverend Jesse Turner served as its first president. Although it did not survive the Civil War, the Henrico organization was instrumental in the creation of a board that became the Commonwealth's Department of Agriculture. During its first year of existence, the society sent a memorial to the House of Delegates through Sherwin McRae, the Henrico delegate, asking for the establishment of a board of agriculture, and the Assembly acted on the suggestion. The eight-member board was charged with the responsibility of reviewing the general situation of agriculture in the state and of reporting its findings to the legislature. The Henrico Agricultural and Horticultural Society was also one of the chief supporters of a similar statewide organization and petitioned the legislature on numerous occasions for aid to agriculture.[9]

William Harvie Richardson, a Richmonder by birth, was a resident of Henrico County and an active member of the Henrico society. He was serving as clerk to the Council of State and as secretary of the Commonwealth while living on his farm west of Richmond near Westham. There he practiced scientific farming techniques in raising grain, fruit, and livestock. Not only was he instrumental in organizing the Henrico society, serving on its executive committee from its founding until 1844 and as president in 1845, but he was also the driving force behind the formation of a state agricultural society. He served as a member of the executive committee of the state society and as its president in the 1850s. "The General," as he was popularly known after his appointment as adjutant general of Virginia in 1841, urged the necessity of deep plowing, the use of fertilizers and lime, the proper care of livestock, the use of corn crops, and scientific management in all phases of farm life and was active in the organization of annual fairs for the local and state societies.

Meeting at Goddin's Spring on Bacon Quarter Branch, the Henrico society held an exhibition and fair in May or June of each year and an annual meeting in October or November at the Exchange Hotel in Richmond. Generally, at the exhibition and fair the activities started with a plowing competition, and committees of the society were called on to judge livestock, agricultural produce, and handiwork placed on exhibit. While the general membership listened to an address, other activities were held for families and friends. One committee had the task of traveling throughout the county and into the city to judge cultivated fields, farming operations, and gardens. The principal speakers would hold forth on the great benefits of education to improve farming and "the importance, not to say necessity, of Agriculture to the support of Republican institutions." When James M. Wickham addressed the society, he acknowledged that the agricultural progess of the county had been retarded and prevented by the "poor quality of the soil and the employment of slave labor" but asserted that the situation had improved with new farming techniques and "the influx of means" from Richmond.[10]

To foster the study of scientific farming, the society considered the purchase of a small tract of land near the city on which to construct a place for the society's exhibitions and to establish a garden and model farm for society members. To encourage competition, monetary prizes and silver medals were given to those who participated in the exhibits. The proceedings of the society list all winners in a variety of categories such as flowers, vegetables, poultry, market gardens, orchards, fruits, wines, domestic manufactures, butter, agricultural implements, and plowing. The "Wilmot Super Strawberry" was an annual winner. One interesting match-up in the market garden competition was Charles Marx of the county and Mrs. Elizabeth Van Lew, who lived on Church Hill in the city. Although she was very active in agricultural pursuits and was frequently mentioned in the society's annual reports, Mrs. Van Lew was to receive greater recognition for her services as a spy for the Union during the Civil War. Marx's twenty-acre garden contained "much the greatest variety . . . [of] the ordinary staple vegetables in great abundance, but many rare varieties." Mrs. Van Lew's garden was always in a "high state of cultivation" and "beyond anything" the committee could "say in its praise." However, Marx received the $20 prize and Mrs. Van Lew the $15 prize. Occasionally a special award would be given, and in one case the society gave $1 each to the "Head men" on the farms of several members "as manifestations of their industry and fidelity in their several employments, and of their remarkable devotion to their masters' interests." General Richardson's headman, Lunsford, was one of the recipients.[11]

To encourage local industry, the society restricted all entries to local farms, and all manufactured items had to be produced in Virginia. Efforts were made to paint a glowing picture of agriculture in Henrico, and frequent references were made at the annual meetings as to the beauty of the countryside in comparison to the run-down condition it had been in. However, the committees appointed to review the farms in the county reported many instances where citizens failed to take advantage of new techniques or new equipment. They did see "a general spirit of improvement in the agriculture of the county," which they considered "necessarily gradual," but "progressive and permanent." Just under half of the farmland in the county was considered improved land in 1850 (53,617 acres) and the balance (53,804 acres) unimproved. The total cash value of the farms in 1850 was $2,601,202, and the value of farming implements and machinery was $72,786. The value of livestock was placed at $2,568, and the value of animals slaughtered at $132,605. During the same year, only 400 pounds of tobacco were produced as compared with 113,044 bushels of wheat, 266,011 bushels of Indian corn, 83,832 bushels of oats, and 1,150 bushels of rye. Three hundred and thirty-eight bales of ginned cotton at 400 pounds per bale and 3,615 pounds of wool were produced. Gardens throughout the county produced a variety of vegetables, but only the quantities for peas and beans (2,909 bushels), Irish potatoes (24,435 bushels), and sweet potatoes (10,285 bushels) were reported. The value of the market gardens was put at $39,976, and the value of orchard products at $1,965. A total of 207 gallons of wine, 66,615 pounds of butter, and 750 pounds of beeswax and honey were produced. For local consump-

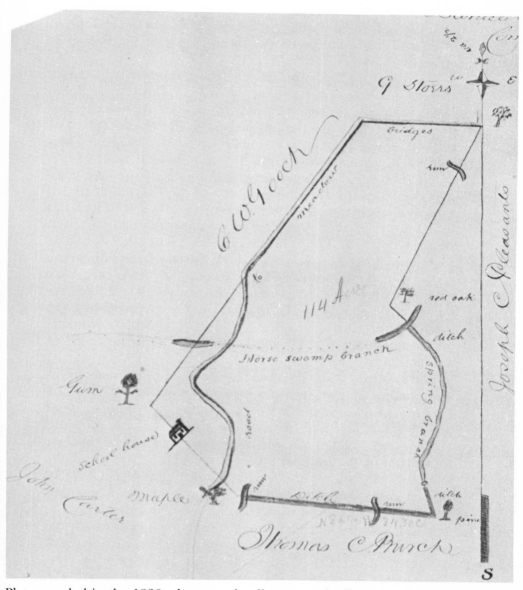

Plat recorded in the 1830s shows a schoolhouse on the line near the gum tree. (Virginia State Library)

tion and sale, 2,196 tons of hay were cut in the fields of
Henrico. Henricoans had produced more and a greater variety than before, and one must attribute this to the institution
of scientific farming methods and to the marketing demands
of Richmonders.[12]

The farm of William Roane, the grandson of Patrick
Henry, just east of the city on the Williamsburg Stage Road,
exhibited signs of neatness and improvement. The application of lime had contributed largely to the improvement of
the soil. It was here at Tree Hill, formerly the home of Miles
Selden, which had passed into his son-in-law's hands in 1837,
that Henricoans, Richmonders, and lovers of the turf from
many parts of the Commonwealth and the East Cost came to
witness trials of speed. The racecourse at Tree Hill farm was
well known in racing circles, and visiting dignitaries often
were escorted to Tree Hill to view the races. On his trip to
Richmond in 1824, Lafayette visited the course to witness the
races. The events were well organized, and the Jockey Club
at Tree Hill established rules to govern races and even required that horses entered in the races have names not given
to any other American horses. They also considered requiring a statement of the horse's age, color, and the name of
dam and sire.

The stables at Tree Hill could house up to fifty horses, and a
like number of people could be accommodated at Tree Hill
house. The track was exactly a mile in length, but because of
the nature of the soil, the track was plowed to "save the limbs
of the racers." The loose dirt caused the races to be three or
four seconds longer per mile. The entire area around the
Tree Hill course was enclosed by a ditch eleven feet wide by
six feet deep. The inner side of the ditch was perpendicular,
and the entire bank was guarded to keep out intruders. The
only entrance to the course was through one gate, and spectators had to pay a fee to enter. Anyone on foot or horseback
had to pay 25¢. If they were riding in a gig, the fee was 50¢.
The owners of all other carriages, except those belonging to
members of the club, were charged $1. After paying the fee
and proceeding to the track area, spectators found extensive
buildings for public use. Members of the club had their own
dining facility large enough to house several hundred people.
After the races were over, club members and their guests

would "unite around the social board with excellent cheer and the kindest feelings."[13]

Races were usually held for one week in the spring and fall, and it was a time of social activity. The week of the races was a perfect carnival, and one of the events of the week was the Race Ball. Taverns and boardinghouses were fillled to capacity, and many private homes were opened to visiting friends and relatives. Races were run in two-, three-, and four-mile heats, and special sweepstake races were run for colts. The Jockey Club purse of $1,000 was awarded for four-mile heats, and each heat was timed separately. Odds were posted and betting was accepted as part of the sport. In later years, a race course was constructed just beyond the city's limits on the Mechanicsville Turnpike. Fairfield Racetrack had a number of stables and a large building for public use. One observer lamented in 1856 that "the sports of the turf have so degenerated of late years" that "exclusive of the racing, the field presents a scene of the lowest gambling and dissipation; but there is now a prospect of the sport being more respectably patronized and conducted."[14]

During this same period, places of amusement and entertainment for county and city dwellers abounded in Henrico just a short ride from the city limits. Buchanan's Spring, just west of the city limits on the Richmond Turnpike (Broad Street) was a favorite gathering place for the Quoit Club. This group was also called the Barbecue Club. It met on Saturdays, and although quoits was the game played, toddy, punch, and mint juleps were consumed while most of the members held forth on the issues of the day. Jasper Crouch, the club's rotund mulatto cook, officiated at all public dinners. The members made wagers on the outcome of the games, and all bets were forfeited to the club to defray expenses. Amid the relaxed atmosphere, the excitement of the game, the forensic exercises, and the jokes and jesting, the members consumed a plain but substantial dinner and washed it down with more beverages. A similar club met at Clark's Spring near the present site of Hollywood Cemetery, and these two clubs frequently met together in a spirit of fraternity under the cool shade of the stately trees that surrounded the cool waters of the spring.

At Goddin's Spring on Bacon Quarter Branch (near the

present Chamberlayne Avenue overpass), the public could find a place of rest and amusement. The tavern provided a traveler with entertainment, and shuffleboard and other similar games were played at the cool and shaded spring. At Jackson's Garden and the French Garden, citizens and visitors could sip lemonade as they enjoyed the terraced hillside. Northwest of the City Poorhouse at Mitchell's Spring, an attempt was made to provide a variety of recreational activities, but it did not prove to be a profitable venture. Before too long the fields around the spring were cultivated. Visitors could still enjoy the sweet water from the spring, but the absence of recreational facilities resulted in the eventual abandonment of the springs as a meeting place.

As the city grew in population from 16,060 in 1830 to 37,968 in 1860, these recreational areas provided an escape for the city dwellers. A natural result of the increase in population was the development of the county land around the city. Streets were extended into the cornfields and pastures as lots were marked off for potential buyers, and suburbs began to spring up. Eventually, the subdivisions became part of the city. East of the city, the suburb of Marion Hill boasted an academy and several residences. Unfortunately, the academy burned. On the river below was Port Mayo, where a large warehouse was constructed. The town of Fulton was built at the foot of the hill. From east to west around the city, the areas that developed into suburban clusters were Darby Town, Butcher Town, Bacon Quarter, Sydney, Scuffle Town, and Oregon Hill. Farther out, the communities of Westhampton, Bankstown, and Mechanicsville were started. Many of these settlements derived their names from the geographic feature on which they were built or from the individual who was the prime mover in developing the area. Some of the names describe the activity or character of the inhabitants or the architecture of the particular subdivision. Except for Mechanicsville, the main part of which was and is just over the Chickahominy River in Hanover County, these towns either were absorbed by the city as it spread out into the county or went out of existence.

The growth of subdivisions and the modest growth in the county's population did not result in any improvement of the county's road system. The roads throughout the county were

William H. Richardson (1795–1876). (Virginia State Library)

in tolerable condition when the weather was good. During a long dry hot spell, a traveler would have to contend with the dust. The least amount of moisture made the surface soft, and any heavy rain turned them into lanes of mud. Even the turnpikes were difficult to negotiate during and after a rainstorm. Only the tollgates and tollhouses distinguished them from the other county roads, and weary travelers found these irritating when they had to pay to use poor roads. The roads were crude and ill-kept and were generally referred to as mud roads. When the turnpike companies failed to complete or maintain a road, the road fell back under the jurisdiction of the county court. A new public roads act in 1835 brought two major innovations: control of county roads by a commission and a direct county road levy. The stockholders of the Westham Turnpike Company, chartered in 1816, spent large sums on grading and building culverts, but they were not able to complete the road within the seven years prescribed in the act. In 1835, when the surviving stockholders petitioned the General Assembly to revive the turnpike company, they pointed out the need to turnpike the road because "during the whole winter season and at all other times when the weather is very wet said road is almost impassable." A counterpetition presented by wood haulers pointed out the added expense to them and the fact that the county court had just spent $250 to repair the road. Although the Westham Turnpike Company was not revived, the Richmond and Tuckahoe Turnpike Company was authorized by an act of the legislature incorporating sundry companies to construct turnpike roads from Richmond to Big Bird Bridge in Goochland County. No new turnpike companies were incorporated in Henrico County to construct new roads, but the Richmond and Henrico Turnpike Company was authorized on March 12, 1850, to construct a turnpike road "on the track of the old Richmond turnpike from the city of Richmond to the short Pump in the county of Henrico." Whenever necessary, the company was authorized to substitute plank, not less than sixteen feet in width, for stone or gravel as a cover for the road. Planking provided the necessary hard surface and was considered a cheaper means of construction. The planking method became very popular, and a number of companies thought they could make road building profitable by using planks. In 1852 the House of Delegates received a request to pass legislation to plank or macadamize the Richmond and Henrico Turnpike. During the 1853-54 session of the General Assembly petitions were received to incorporate the Henrico and Goochland Plank Road Company, Richmond and New Market Plank Road Company, and Richmond and New Bridges Plank Road Company. None of these were legislated, but a bill to incorporate the Richmond and Bottoms Bridge Plank Road Company did pass the House.[15]

Except for the roads that radiated out from Richmond, there were no major roads connecting the county from east to west. There were a number of connector links from the main roads to farms, mills, ferries, and to the other roads, but these were country lanes. Macadam and planned road networking were things of the future. Roads continued to develop as a result of need and convenience. It was on this type of road system that the citizens of the county would witness the movements of the armies of North and South as they maneuvered to prevent each other from accomplishing their objectives.

The turnpike and plank road companies never produced enough revenue to keep the roads in good sound condition and to provide a profit for those who purchased stock in the companies. The natural tendency was for investors to seek more profitable ventures. One reason for the decline in the investment money for turnpike development was the rise of the railroad. Cost of construction was greater, but increased speed and passenger and freight capacity provided an opportunity for greater profit and return on investment than the turnpikes. Rivers, canals, and roads were not enough to meet the needs for transportation of staples, livestock, raw materials, and manufactured goods. Like the roads, various railroads eventually would link into systems running north and south and east and west, but no central system or network was planned at the time. Initially, all railroads were local projects undertaken to benefit the towns they connected. State financial assistance was provided through the purchase of a percentage of the stock. The acquisition of stock also gave the state a voice in the operation. Even with state involvement in the individual lines, consolidation came slowly.

The first railroad constructed through Henrico County was the Richmond, Fredericksburg and Potomac, chartered in 1834. An act had been passed to incorporate the Richmond and Turkey Isle Railroad, but the line failed to get the necessary subscribers. The Richmond, Fredericksburg and Potomac was the sixth railroad to be chartered in Virginia, and the third to operate in the state by steam. This company had a unique provision in its charter which stated that for thirty years no other railroad was to be chartered to run between Richmond and Washington. When the Louisa Railroad Company, chartered in 1836, attempted to continue its line from Taylorsville (where it formed a junction with the Richmond, Fredericksburg and Potomac) to Richmond, the dispute was taken to court. Eventually the Supreme Court declared the charter exclusion illegal, and the Louisa Railroad Company, which became the Virginia Central Railroad, was allowed to build a line to Richmond in 1851. It would be the second steam railroad to cut through Henrico.

The Richmond, Fredericksburg and Potomac was to be a part of the north-south line stretching from the Potomac River below Washington to Weldon, North Carolina. The preliminary surveys were made between October 1833 and January 1834 under the direction of a native Richmonder, Moncure Robinson. The road from Richmond to the North Anna River, about twenty-seven miles, was put under contract on December 27, 1834. The company purchased a lot at Eighth and H (present Broad) streets where the necessary shops, warehouses, turntable and depot were constructed. The track was laid in the roadbed from Eighth and H streets down H Street to the western boundary of the city where H Street became the Richmond Turnpike. The track continued in the roadbed of the Richmond Turnpike to present-day Harrison Street, where it angled to the north. Under agreement with the stage line from Richmond to Potomac Creek, operated by Edwin Porter and Company, passengers would be interchanged at the terminus of the railhead. The line was completed and opened to the South Anna River on February 13, 1836, and a fare of $1.25 was charged for adults and half fare for children under twelve. The first company experienced little difficulty in acquiring its right-of-way through the county. This part of the line was free from curvature.

Fairground in Henrico in 1854. (Valentine Museum)

The rails of white oak were keyed into notches in the ties, and an iron plate two inches wide by half an inch thick was fastened on the top of the rail by spikes every foot. The width of the track was 'four feet eight and a half inches. By January 23, 1837, the railroad line reached Fredericksburg. The company acquired a tract of timberland for fuel in Henrico, and a water station was built at Hungary Station (present-day Laurel), Henrico.[16]

After the line was opened to Fredericksburg in 1837, a fare of $4 was charged for passage one way. Leaving Richmond, the train could reach a speed of ten miles per hour. The first stop was 4 miles from the depot at Sinton's for a fare of 25¢. One mile farther the train would stop at Gregory's Mill (fare of 37½¢). The Hungary Station stop was 8 miles from Richmond (fare 50¢), and the Mountain Road stop was 9½ miles (fare 75¢). The last stop in Henrico was at the Chickahominy River crossing, 12 miles from the city (fare 87½¢). The principal engineer of the Board of Public Works, Charles B. Shaw, examined the road in 1836 and reported that "the attempt to economize in the construction has resulted in the production of inferior and, as I fear, a perishable work." The next year the president of the company reported to the stockholders that "the heavy business on the first eight miles of the road between Richmond and the Hungary water station, has led to an early renewal of this portion of the line." New iron was put down for the first three miles in 1837, and additional iron rails were ordered for the remaining five miles. The new iron rail was thicker and wider than the original rails. After removing the older rails, the company used them for repairs on other parts of the line. The first T-rail on the RF&P was purchased from Tredegar Iron Works of Richmond and was laid on fourteen miles of track out of the city in the spring of 1854.[17]

At its annual meeting in 1837, the stockholders of the RF&P voted to construct a branch line from Hungary Water Station to the Springfield and Deep run coalpits. On December 16, 1837, DuVal, Burton & Company and John Barr, owners of the pits in operation, made a proposition to the company that was accepted. The colliers agreed to advance the money to construct the branch line. In return, they were to be repaid with 6 percent interest out of the tolls placed on the coal transported from their pits. Also included in the five-year agreement between the colliers and the railroad was the establishment of a fixed freight rate of 4½¢ per five-peck bushel of coal. At the end of the five years, the debt would be either paid off by toll charges or canceled, and the branch line would become the property of the railroad. Work on the 3½-mile branch line began early in 1838, and it was completed and opened for service on August 28, 1838. Each of the coal-mining firms had advanced $13,500, and the railroad company had started giving the credit for toll fees as early as May 1838. By the end of October 1838 John Barr had received credit for $4,874.63 and DuVal, Burton & Company, $4,128.01. The total cost of the branch line was reported as $32,612.72. Over two-thirds of the cost was liquidated by tolls the first year the branch line was in operation, and the entire cost was credited to the coal operators in less than two years after the line was opened. In less than two years the line became the property of the railroad and the mine operators had to pay the toll charges in cash.[18]

The railroad owned sixty coal cars in 1841, and the peak period during which coal was moved over the branch line appears to have been between 1838 and 1847. The number of coal cars dropped to forty in 1846 and to thirty-two in 1850. The freight rate for shipping coal was reduced several times, and in 1847 it was down to three cents per bushel. After 1846, the opening of the coalfields in western Virginia reduced the demand for the soft coal from the pits, and this resulted in a drop in production which made the operation of the branch line unprofitable and contributed to the abandonment of the operation.[19] To find new uses for the Henrico coal, test studies were conducted using the coal in the locomotives, but the results were not conclusive enough to warrant conversion from wood-burning engines. The branch line continued in operation at least through 1847, when tonnage and equipment figures were reported in the company's annual report. The exact date the line was closed down is not reported, but it is known that the line was dismantled before 1856. Between 1837 and 1847 an estimated 180,000 tons of coal were transported on the RF&P from the Deep Run pits. The shipping records are silent for the period 1848-57 when 4,000 tons were mined. Activity at the mines increased in

1858-59 and 4,000 tons of coal were excavated. This coal was shipped by wagon, either by road to Richmond or to Hungary Station where it was loaded into coal cars for transport to the city. In 1860, 3,569 tons of coal were shipped over the RF&P line to Richmond. During the war years, 1861-65, only 500 tons were reported excavated and transported by rail. The war brought a halt to the active mining operations at the pits, and shipments of coal did not resume until 1867.

The Richmond, Fredericksburg and Potomac Railroad was not the only railroad route proposed for construction through Henrico. The fact that the RF&P was able to lay track and to establish its route helped it to stave off competition during the early years of railroading in Virginia. The General Assembly gave its consent to a second railroad through the county when it authorized a survey and estimate of a route from Richmond to the South Anna River and from some point on the James River Canal to the South Anna River in February 1834. The survey was conducted and a route was proposed running just west of the Deep Run pits. This line was to intersect the RF&P tracks at the Hermitage plantation, and from there the line was to proceed down Bacon Quarter Branch to Shockoe Creek and then to Rockett's. The cost of the construction through a layer of rock was estimated at more than the expected revenue on either line, and since the coal on Tuckahoe Creek was moving down the canal, the principal engineer of the Board of Public Works suggested that instead a line be constructed from the South Anna River to connect with the RF&P. Engineer Shaw also reported on a survey for a possible railroad route from Richmond to Yorktown which was designated on paper as the Richmond and Yorktown Railroad. Recognizing that the final decision would be a political one, he reported on a proposed route in 1835. As surveyed, the line crossed the Chickahominy River near the Quaker Meetinghouse and then cut through White Oak Swamp and extended to Rockett's. He doubted that the road would be "productive as a mere travelling road" and pointed out the competition that any road would have with the existing Fredericksburg route and the water route up the James River. The RF&P took advantage of its exclusive right to the route between Richmond and Washington; but when the General Assembly au-

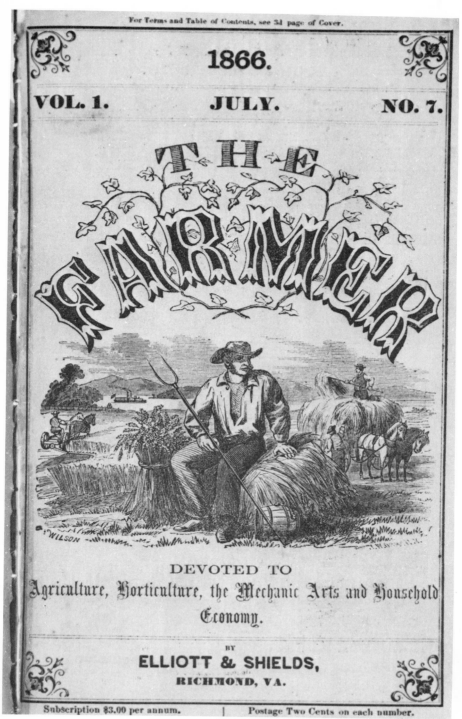

1866.

VOL. 1.   **JULY.**   **NO. 7.**

THE FARMER

DEVOTED TO

Agriculture, Horticulture, the Mechanic Arts and Household Economy.

BY

ELLIOTT & SHIELDS,
RICHMOND, VA.

Subscription $3.00 per annum. | Postage Two Cents on each number.

Farming was the backbone of Henrico's economy. This front cover of an 1866 almanac depicts several farming activities. (Virginia State Library)

thorized the railroads from Washington to Weldon to put up a
telegraph line in 1847, the president and directors of the
RF&P agreed with a provision that the Commonwealth subscribe to some of the stock and demanded free telegraph service. When the commonwealth did not subscribe, the Washington and Petersburg Telegraph Line was built along the old
stage road north of Richmond, and this road became known
as the Telegraph Road. On July 24, 1846, telegraph service
was initiated between Washington and Richmond.[20]

While the coal from the Deep Run pits was moving by coal
car and by wagon, the coal mined along Tuckahoe Creek was
transported to Richmond by boat. Like the railroad company, the canal company fixed the freight rate. The colliers
along the Tuckahoe Creek Canal complained of the high
tolls and petitioned the Board of Public Works to regulate
them. Jesse Snead, John Barr, William Frith, George M.
Harding, and other owners and operators of coalpits in the
Tuckahoe Valley registered their complaints. However, when
the board sought legal advice as to whether it had jurisdiction, the attorney general advised the board that it had no
control over the canal tolls since the canal was not established
by law as an internal improvement like a turnpike company.
The entire canal was 6½ miles long, 22 feet wide at the surface waterline, and 3 feet deep, with three locks, a dam, two
bridges, a guard and flood gate, and two aqueducts, one 320
feet long and the other 150. The canal, which had been
started in 1828, was constructed in a temporary manner, and
the locks and bridges were built of wood. Very little stone or
masonry work was employed. The entire cost of construction
and maintenance from 1828 to 1832 ran to $14,022.62. Dur-
ing that same time, the income from tolls amounted to
$14,493.28⅝. The income from tolls remained steady, and in
1834 the coal traffic on the canal produced tolls amounting
to $3,189.23. Of this amount, $2,638 was used to make necessary repairs to the canal and locks. The materials used in
the construction of the canal were wearing out and deteriorating, leading the president of the company, Stephen Du-
Val, to report on February 6, 1835, that "the present condition of the canal is unfavourable," and "the Locks having
been originally constructed of perishable materials will require . . . a thorough reconstruction."[21]

Rather than continue rebuilding the deteriorating canal and the locks and bridges or connect portions of the canal by short rail lines as provided under the 1828 act, the directors of the Tuckahoe Canal Company sought approval to construct a railroad along the edge of the creek. At the same time, five of the colliers along Tuckahoe Creek, John G., Thomas, and Richard Crouch, John Barr, and Jesse Snead, petitioned the General Assembly in December 1835 for authority to incorporate a company to build a railroad along Tuckahoe Creek. They complained about the condition of the canal, the tolls, and its poor management. They concluded that "unless they can procure a cheaper transportation for their coal than they now have they must soon abandon the coal business or be crushed in their efforts to carry it on." Each group sought the passage of the necessary legislation, and after two years of maneuvering, the directors of the canal company succeeded in obtaining it. By an act of the General Assembly passed March 27, 1837, the directors of the Tuckahoe Canal Company, rather than the colliers, were given authority to construct a railroad from Martha Ellis's to a point on the James River Canal and from Martha Ellis's northward to William A. Dietrick's. The entire line was to be in Henrico County, and the directors were given two months from the passage of the act to open books, to receive subscriptions, and to begin work. The act stipulated that failure to do so would result in the forfeiture of the right to construct the railroad and the awarding of the right to construct a railroad to the Tuckahoe and James River Railroad Company, under the direction of Edward Anderson, John Barr, Richard Crouch, Joseph Mosby, William A. Dietrick, and Jesse Snead, all colliers. The act relating to the Tuckahoe Canal Company was amended in April 1838 to allow the construction of lateral railroads from any point on the canal to any of the coalpits in the Tuckahoe Valley. When the directors of the canal company failed to begin construction of a railroad, the directors of the Tuckahoe and James River Railroad Company decided to proceed with their venture to provide a more rapid means of transporting their coal. The canal would remain in operation, but the railroad would carry the bulk of the trade.[22]

The Tuckahoe and James River Railroad Company was

incorporated with a capital stock of $59,000, and this amount
was raised to $68,600 in May 1841. The track was laid from
the James River and Kanawha Canal, about three-fourths of
a mile below the Tuckahoe aqueduct. A very short stretch of
the line was opened and used on March 19, 1839. The entire
length of the railroad was 4⅝ miles in length and cost
$55,539.85. It was opened along its entire length on July 2,
1840. The cars on the road, which was constructed "in the
usual manner," were hauled by mules, and the necessary
outlay in cars, mules, depots, etc., amounted to $13,782.63.
The railroad was described as "a tram road laid with strap
iron" and was reported as still in operation in 1866. Between
March 19, 1839, and June 30, 1842, a total of 1,567,713
bushels of coal were carried over the railroad to the James
River and Kanawha Canal for transport to Richmond. Tolls
on the coal amounted to $21,026.31. To pay off the accrued
debts, no dividend was declared in July 1841. A net profit of
$5,944.16 was earned during the period July 1841–June
1842. The entire revenue of the company was derived from
the transportation of coal; consequently, a depression in the
marketplace affected the income received.[23]

The coal industry in Henrico received a death-dealing
blow after the Baltimore and Ohio Railroad track reached
Cumberland, Maryland, and that railroad began to tap the
rich coalfields in the western regions of Virginia and Pennsylvania. About this same time, the age of independent operations was coming to an end along the Tuckahoe Creek.
Although a number of independent pits continued to function, there was a move toward consolidation of previously
independent operations. Several of the colliers who were
served by the railroad, John S. Crouch, Jesse Snead, William
Cottrell, Richard Crouch, and Temple Redd, received authority from the General Assembly to incorporate as the
Runnymead Coal Mining Company. As such, the company
could "have the right to purchase and hold land, not exceeding five hundred acres in the said county of Henrico." The
same year, 1837, Thomas Mann Randolph and John Brock-
enbrough were given authority to incorporate the Tuckahoe
Coal Mining Company "for digging, mining, raising and
transporting coal in and from the counties of Goochland and
Henrico." The act limited the number of acres the company

Henrico County Courthouse as it appeared on Robert P. Smith's map of 1853. (Virginia State Library)

could own to no more than two hundred. The coal from the Randolph mines was transported on the Tuckahoe Creek Canal, and it was not long before the competition of the other mines and the railroad caused the Randolphs to divest themselves of interest in the coal mines. After they did so, the canal fell into disuse, and it was allowed to deteriorate.[24]

The period from 1840 to 1842 was one of relative inactivity in the coal-mining regions of Henrico. A total of 1,012,200 bushels, or 40,488 net tons, of coal were raised by 223 hands in the mines and pits in Henrico in 1840, and this rate of production was greater than that in Chesterfield, Goochland, or Powhatan. A. S. Wooldridge, president of the Midlothian Mining Company, described the activity in the coalfields in a report dated September 1, 1841.

On the Goochland and Henrico side of James River, are several mines, some of them now in operation, and some not. The largest operators in that neighborhood, are the Messrs. Crouches & Snead, the owners of extensive mines in good working condition, employing about one hundred and fifty hands, and raising four hundred thousand bushels of coal the present year. Near these mines, on James River, are those of the Tuckahoe Coal Company. The old mines are out of work, but a shaft is sinking, employing from fifteen to twenty hands, &c.

Near these are Woodward's and Cottrell's Mines, both now unwrought. Northeast of Crouches & Snead's mines, lie the Edge Hill pits, now worked but not extensively, by Richardson, probably employing some thirty hands, and producing about eighty thousand bushels. On the north part of Crouches & Snead's property, Towne & Powell are engaged in hoisting coal, but not working more than some twenty hands, producing the present year about one hundred thousand bushels. There may be some other mines in this vicinity not remembered. There is a railroad connecting these mines with the James River canal, down which the coal passes to Richmond. The coal on the north side of James River sells for a less price than that on the south side, being considered not as good.

Some four or five miles north of these mines, lie those called the Deep Run Pits, worked by John Barr, who at present employs some forty hands, and raises some two hundred and fifty thousand bushels of coal; he uses steam power. This coal is a fair quality, as is also that from Burton's pits, now mined by Grub & Co., who will probably raise about the same quantity as Barr, and employ many hands. The coal from these mines is transported to Richmond by the

Fredericksburg and Richmond Railroad Company, a branch of their road having been extended to the pits. The charge for coal on this road is four cents per bushel from the mines to Richmond. The charge for boating coal down the James River canal, including tolls, is about three cents from the mines.[25]

Wooldridge appended a note to his report that the miners had found "a substance formerly called deal coal, recently called natural coke, that has lately been used and very much approved as grate fuel." The state's geologist, William Barton Rogers, noted that the coke in the Tuckahoe Creek area "retains only a minute fraction of the volatile ingredients of the unaltered bituminous coal of this region, but it ignites readily, and burns like the compacter kinds of ordinary coke." The mineowners found a ready market for the coke in the homes in Richmond as well as at the Richmond Gas Works and private industry in and around the city. In an effort to find a market for the vast amounts of clay removed in the mining process, Jesse Snead sought to interest local industry. The clay covered the coalfield and was "coextensive with the coal" in seams from twenty to twenty-four inches in thickness. There were "millions of tons" of clay in and around the pits. Snead sent samples off for analysis and encouraged the owners of the Tredegar Iron Works and the Belle Isle Manufacturing Company to test it. The Tredegar purchased fourteen tons to line a furnace, and the manager of the Belle Isle works found it "superior fire-clay." However, except for local use, Snead did not find wide acceptance of the clay for use in firebricks because a better clay was available to northern industrialists from the Pennsylvania fields.[26]

Jesse Snead was a major in the county militia and a justice of the peace. He had been engaged in the coal-mining business for many years, and he had encountered the peculiarities of the geological formations. In describing the mining operations, he noted:

The usual, or what we colliers term the regular, dip of the coal is 30°. The coal seams are frequently interrupted by what we term *roles*, troubles, and dikes. The roles and troubles are frequently driven or mined through; they are composed of rock and slates, and approximate together, or within a few inches of the roof and pavement of the coal seams. The dikes are not mined through. These interruptions of the coal seams in our coal field, and I believe generally throughout Eastern Virginia, all have the same bearings, which is from the surface across the coal seam in a southwest direction. All the accompanying formations, *earth, rocks* of various kinds, *clays,* and *shales* or slates, have the same *bearings* and *dip* with the coal seams in the coal fields.[27]

The mine operators along Tuckahoe Creek employed slave labor and hired slaves from the farmers in the vicinity. To support the large number of hands, vegetables, meat, and poultry were purchased from the farming community. The entire area from the James River and Kanawha Canal up the Tuckahoe Valley extended for about five miles and resembled a small village. In 1843 Major Snead took over the Tuckahoe Pits, formerly operated by Thomas M. Randolph, and the Tuckahoe Coal Mining Company, where work had stopped after sinking a 412-foot shaft. By 1846 Snead had turned the operation into a profitable venture. Using fifty hands, he raised 300,000 bushels a year. The mining activity along the creek during 1846 was extensive. A mile and a half north of the Tuckahoe Pits, William Cottrell employed thirty hands at his pits and raised 400 to 500 bushels per day. Thomas and Robert Crouch's pits, a hundred yards north of Cottrell's, employed eighty to ninety hands and raised 800 to 900 bushels per day. North of these pits was a pit owned by Perry, Farris and Company that had been allowed to fill with 300 feet of water during a dispute between the partners. The Edge Hill Mine, operated by J. C. Deaton and Company, was half a mile northeast of the vacant pit. Both coal and coke were mined there by thirty hands, and 150,000 bushels were raised each year. A little beyond this mine, the Locust Hill Mines, worked by R. W. Jordan, employed thirty hands to raise 90,000 bushels a year. This mine had been opened in 1843 and produced only coke. The next and last mine on the Henrico side of Tuckahoe Creek consisted of a series of coke pits operated by Towne and Powell. These pits were at the end of the railroad, and a total of thirty hands were used to raise 500 to 600 bushels of coke per day. The pits along the creek continued in production during the Civil War, after which

Wichello's Tavern before it was restored. This tavern, located on River Road, was owned and operated by Richard Wichello and was known locally as "Tall House." Built before 1835, the house was converted into a wayside inn soon after that date. (Virginia State Library)

mining in the area lapsed into a period of inactivity. During the war, the Tredegar Iron Works received large amounts of coal from this region. The Richmond Basin mines supplied the bulk of the coal used by that firm for smith's work, puddling and heating in the rolling mills, and melting gun iron. In 1863 the company leased some 250 acres in the Tuckahoe Coal Basin for five years. In 1864 Tredegar employed 250 workers, mostly slaves, at the Dover mines in Goochland County and in the Tuckahoe mines in Henrico. These two mines supplied the company with coal for the duration of the war. The production was severely reduced, however, in January 1865 when an enrolling officer conscripted the black hands at the Tuckahoe pits.[28]

The people of Henrico County were very industrious and independent by nature. They worked hard at their agricultural pursuits and enjoyed community gatherings and church socials. Politics was a very serious issue. It was never treated lightly whether it was a local, state, or national election. This was particularly true of the presidential race of 1860. The institution of slavery had become an accepted practice, and many Henricoans who did not own slaves considered it a personal right for those who did. Henrico citizens joined the Richmond and Henrico Society for the Protection of Slave Property in order to prevent the absconding and abduction of slaves. As the year 1860 opened, it was evident that a pending struggle between and within the parties was inevitable. Sectionalism and the issue of slavery were beginning to prove stronger than party loyalty. The Republican party was emerging as a sectional party, while the Democratic party was being threatened with disruption over the issues of slavery and sectionalism. The John Brown raid and the Kansas struggle had caused many Southerners to rally in defense of southern institutions.

When the Democratic party met at Charleston, South Carolina, a factional struggle developed over the wording of the platform. The adoption of a platform plank evading a strong defense of slavery resulted in a split in the convention. Southern delegates walked out, and the convention adjourned to meet in Baltimore to choose a candidate. When the delegates reassembled at Baltimore to choose a presidential and vice-presidential slate, a dispute over the seating of rival delegates resulted in the secession of southern members. While the remaining Democrats nominated Stephen A. Douglas of Illinois for the presidency and Herschel V. Johnson of Georgia for the vice-presidency, rival conventions of southern delegates were being held in Baltimore and Richmond. At both meetings the Southern Democratic groups nominated John C. Breckinridge of Kentucky for president and Joseph Lane of Oregon for vice-president. A fourth party, the Constitutional Union party, held its convention in Baltimore after the Democrats and nominated John Bell of Tennessee for the presidency and Edward Everett of Massachusetts for the vice-presidency. At Chicago, the Republicans nominated Abraham Lincoln of Illinois for president and Hannibal Hamlin of Maine for vice-president.

The division within the Democratic party on the national level was mirrored on the state and local levels. Henricoans were strong Democrats, but they were Southerners first. At a meeting in the courthouse on July 2, 1860, Robert A. Mayo was elected chairman of the Democratic party of Henrico. After enthusiastic endorsement of Breckinridge and Lane, the meeting adopted a resolution declaring the right of Southerners to be equal to the rights of Northerners. The resolution also included statements declaring that southern property was protected under the Constitution, that slaves were property under the law, and that the slave laws were constitutional.

Within the state, the southern wing of the Democratic party was referred to as the Democratic party while the national party of that name was referred to as the Douglas wing and called the National Democratic party. In Henrico, those citizens who supported the Douglas platform gathered at the courthouse on August 6 and elected Anthony Robinson chairman of the National Democrats of Henrico. After endorsing Douglas and Johnson, the party authorized the chairman to appoint a committee of ten to represent the county at the state convention in Staunton.

In another room in the courthouse, the members of the Constitutional party, referred to locally as the "Opposition Party," met on the same day. George M. Savage was elected party chairman. The citizens at the meeting called for all "Union-loving conservative men" to support the Bell-Everett ticket "in order that the rights of the citizens of every section of our country may be protected, sectionalism destroyed, and peace and harmony restored to the distracted country." After adopting the party platform of "Union, the Constitution, and the Enforcement of the laws," an executive committee was appointed, and each magisterial district was called on to appoint "Business Committees."'

Support for Lincoln in Virginia was centered mainly in the northern border counties. The citizens of Henrico, like those in most of the counties in the state, failed to organize a local Republican party committee.

The campaign in Henrico and Richmond was primarily between the Breckinridge Democrats and the Bell Constitutional Unionists. Nightly meetings were held at Metropolitan Hall in the city where Democrats gathered to hear local and national speakers. The Bell supporters rallied at the Bell and Everett Club House to listen to their speakers and to discuss and debate the party platforms. Even during the frenzied campaign, Henricoans took time to enjoy the Agricultural Fair, to attend the October races at Fairfield Race Course, and to welcome the Prince of Wales on his visit to the city. When it was all over and Henricoans went to the polls early in November 1860, they gave their support to the Constitutional Union candidates, Bell and Everett, by more than two to one over the Southern Democratic candidates, Breckinridge and Lane, 1,403 to 641. Douglas and Johnson came in third with 189 votes, and the Republican candidate, Lincoln, failed to receive even one vote. The vote reflected a desire on the part of an overwhelming majority of Henricoans to seek a peaceful settlement of the slavery and sectionalism issues within the union of states. It was hoped that some sort of a compromise could be worked out through the existing governmental system. The story was the same in the city, where Bell received 2,402, Breckinridge 1,167, Douglas 753, and Lincoln 0. Bell carried the state by less than a thousand votes over Breckinridge. Virginia, Tennessee, and Kentucky went for Bell, while Breckinridge carried the entire lower South. Only two states, Missouri and New Jersey, went for Douglas. The disunity of the Democratic party fragmented its efforts and allowed what they feared most to happen, a Republican victory. Lincoln's opponents received more popular votes

Varina. This brick mansion was built by Albert Aiken in 1855. In 1864 Gen. Benjamin F. Butler moved his headquarters to Varina and remained there until after the war was over. The house, with some structural changes, still stands today. (Virginia State Library)

combined than he did, but he had the necessary electoral votes. His election brought despair to many Southerners. Their only relief from what they believed would be an oppressive situation was to leave the Union. Henricoans would be caught up in this emotional wave, and when Virginia made its decision, they would follow willingly.

CHAPTER VII

A Field of Honor

Although many Henricoans felt the urge to prepare for war, there was still a majority of voting citizens who felt that peace could be preserved within the Union. The court appointed a committee early in January 1861 to prepare a plan for raising a sufficient amount of money to put the county in a state of defense for arming a portion of the Thirty-third Regiment Militia, the county's own. J. Lucius Davis, a prominent farmer with military training and the commander of a local volunteer company, chaired the committee and urged that the county mobilize one squadron of cavalry and four companies of infantry. Sufficient arms were available from the state to arm the infantry companies, but $2,500 was needed to purchase pistols for the cavalry. The court deferred the decision on how to raise the money to a public meeting. At a meeting in the courthouse on January 17, several "patriotic Southern speeches" were made before the attendees addressed the issue of raising the needed sum of $2,500.

Unwilling to grant the court blanket authority, the citizens voted down by 100 to 87 a resolution to give it the power "to levy on the people such amount as may be necessary to put the county in an efficient state of defence." Instead, those citizens present agreed that a bill should be submitted to the General Assembly authorizing the court to raise $2,500 by issuing bonds on the county. By separate resolution, the meeting appointed a committee to raise $1,500 for the volunteers of the militia regiment. A total of $500 was collected at the meeting.

The General Assembly was in session at the time, and similar requests for legislation and funds were submitted from other localities. While debating the momentous national issues, Henricoans found that they had to rally to protect their lands from an internal threat. Through its delegates, the Richmond City Council introduced legislation calling for the annexation of a portion of the county on the eastern edge of the city. Petitions for and against the proposal were sent to members of the legislature, while City Council refused to extend gas lines into the area. However, even though this local matter was critical to the citizens of the county and the city, it was lost in the great tide of debate over legislation dealing with the peace efforts and the secession issue. The House committee considering the annexation bill asked to be discharged on the grounds that there was not sufficient time to consider it properly before the end of the session. On the secession issue, the Assembly authorized a special election of delegates to a state convention to consider the matter. In doing so, the Assembly provided Virginians with the opportunity to vote for or against requiring a popular referendum on the convention's actions.

Throughout the state, citizens rallied around Union and Secessionist candidates for the state convention. The desire to maintain peace within the Union and the violation of southern rights in the Union were debated in printed word, in the lecture halls, on the courthouse steps, and on the stump. William C. Wickham, the Union candidate in Henrico, ran against John R. Garnett, the Secessionist candidate. On election day, February 4, there was "great excitement" at the courthouse where some arrests were made for "turbulent demonstrations." Wickham received 578 votes to Garnett's 470 at the courthouse. When all the votes were in, the citizens had voted to send Wickham, the Unionist candidate, by 200 votes over Garnett. The totals were 917 for Wickham and 717 for Garnett. On the referendum issue, a majority of 447 voters approved referral of any convention action on secession back to the people for a vote.

Even though the mood of the county appeared to be for restraint, many citizens continued to agitate for defense and for southern rights. On February 19, while the Henrico Troop conducted a shoot at Westham house for two saddles presented by William F. Mitchell and Samuel S. Cottrell of Richmond, two new volunteer companies, the Oregon Hill and Sidney Home Guard and the Sidney Guard, were organized. On that same day, the Varina Troop mustered at Tree Hill Farm for drill. A few days later a number of Henricoans

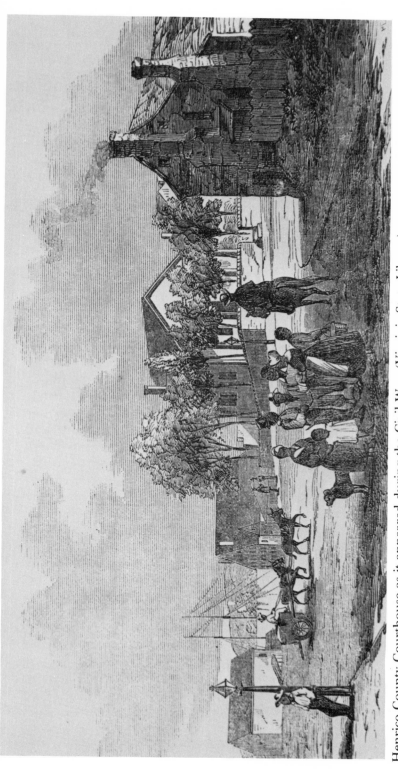

Henrico County Courthouse as it appeared during the Civil War. (Virginia State Library)

for "Prompt Action" raised a large flag three miles from the city on the Virginia Central Railroad. On an eighty-foot pole, this flag of blue bunting with fifteen stars in one corner proclaimed to all the inscription, "the South." When Mrs. J. A. Pilcher of Sidney raised a flag of the Southern Confederacy, she was ordered to take it down by a band of "Union boys from Oregon Hill." A brief note of their action in the *Richmond Dispatch* brought responses from about one hundred "gentlemen" who came to her aid and defended her right to put up the flag.

At a meeting on March 16, about one hundred citizens gathered at the courthouse to consider the political condition of the country. Dr. Zachariah S. McGruder, the county's representative in the House of Delegates, was asked to define his position. He replied that although he had voted for the Peace Conference, the last major effort to get the North and South together to discuss their differences, he saw no hope for success given the condition of the country. Perhaps he represented the majority of Henricoans who had changed from Unionists to Secessionists when he stated "that he would lay down his life cheerfully to preserve the Union as handed down to us by the patriots of the Revolution; but whenever it was ascertained that Virginia could not get her rights in the Union, he would be in favor of her resuming all power delegated to the Federal Government, not to go *North or South,* but to stand under the flag of Virginia." As in other such public meetings, a committee was appointed to draft resolutions. The committee reported back with a preamble and a series of strong secession resolutions narrating the grievances of the South. A minority report favoring secession and calling for the state convention to adopt an ordinance of secession immediately was also introduced. A substitute for the minority report was also introduced "in favor of obtaining our rights in the Union." Both the minority and the substitute reports were defeated, and the majority report was adopted "almost unanimously, the Union men refusing to vote on the ground that they had instructed their delegate [William C. Wickham] at the polls."

Events moved rapidly after the failure of the Peace Conference as the actions of both the southern states and the federal government were caught in the winds of hysteria.

People began to show their support for the Southern Confederacy. When a Confederate flag was raised near Yellow Tavern, citizens gathered to hear several speeches against moderation and for secession. When the flag was raised, "three cheers and a 'tiger' were given with a hearty good will." At another flag raising at Camp Hill where troops had encamped during the War of 1812, Lucy W. Childrey, accompanied by several other young ladies, appeared on the platform and hoisted the Confederate flag after prayer. The flag was "greeted with loud and enthusiastic cheers," and "the band played *Dixie,* and the military fired a salute." Units of the local militia regiment began to assemble at Hermitage Fair Grounds, which became known as Hermitage Camp of Instruction and later as Camp Lee.

The firing on Fort Sumter and Lincoln's call for troops forced Virginians to make a decision. The state convention adopted an ordinance calling for secession, and on May 24, when the vote was taken in Henrico, 1,417 Henricoans voted unanimously for secession. Little did they realize that their county would be the scene of some of the bloodiest fighting during the war that was to follow. It would be a war that put an end to the institution of slavery and one that left a scene of desolation on both sides of the fortifications that would be cut deep into Henrico's soil. Nature would quickly heal the sharp gashes cut during a fierce struggle between the two armies, but it would take years to heal the scars of desolation where the two armies sat down on the defensive behind their fortifications and devoured the land and its produce like locusts. Henricoans numbered some 23,706 souls in 1861 when the war clouds gathered. Of this total, 14,350 were white, 1,014 were free blacks, 8,342 were slaves, and 19 were Indians. The white population had increased three times greater than the slave population between 1850 and 1860. There were approximately 6,000 more whites in 1860 than in 1850, while the number of slaves increased by 2,000 and the free black population decreased by 380 during the same time. The quantity of improved acres in farms increased from 53,617 to 96,220, and the number of unimproved acres brought under cultivation rose from 53,804 to 66,490 during the same decade. The cash value of farms rose from $2,601,202 to $5,128,610, and the value of livestock rose from $256,800 to $423,672. The number of bushels of wheat produced in 1860 was just about twice the amount produced in 1850, while the bushels of Indian corn increased by 50 percent during the same period. A marked increase was reported in the pounds of tobacco, and increases were seen in the production of peas, beans, Irish potatoes, and sweet potatoes as well as other produce. Although the value of orchard products rose only slightly, the gallons of wine showed a marked increase from 207 in 1850 to 1,524 in 1860. The value of market garden products increased from $39,976 to $80,280, while the value of animals slaughtered dropped from $132,605 to $115,479. Generally, economic conditions were good, and Henricoans found a ready market in Richmond where the population had also shown a marked increase.

Henrico County entered the decade of the 1860s with a combination of prosperity, political rhetoric, and an underlying martial spirit. The war clouds that gathered were welcomed by some and feared by others. Henricoans entered the period with the same elation and exuberance that many other people on both sides of the impending conflict felt. The men of military age in Henrico were assigned to the Thirty-third Regiment Militia before the war, and as members of that regiment, they received what little military training they had. Before the war some of the young men had joined independent military companies, while others activated their militia companies and conducted drills on a more regular and frequent basis. The Henrico Troop was one of these companies. It had been organized in May 1854, the successor of an earlier troop that had disbanded before 1850. The first captain of the Henrico Troop, J. Lucius Davis, was elected at the organizational meeting at Goddin's Tavern. Captain Davis was a graduate of the United States Military Academy and the author of *Light Artillery for Frontier Service,* published in 1839. He resigned from active military service that same year and settled in Henrico County in 1847. During the Civil War he served as colonel of the First Regiment of Cavalry, Wise Legion, from 1861 to 1862, and as colonel of the Tenth Regiment Virginia Cavalry from 1862 until the end of the war. The members of the unit took pride in their organization, and as early as 1858 the Henrico Troop were commended for their zeal in maintaining a unit equal in

Defensive line established during the battle of French's Field, also called the battle of Oak Grove, King's Schoolhouse, or the Orchard. This line is now on the grounds of Byrd Airport. (Photograph by John S. Salmon)

efficiency, if not in show, "to any that have flourished under a favourable system of militia laws."[1]

Virginia withdrew from the Union in April 1861, and soon afterward Governor John Letcher issued a call for troops to defend the Old Dominion. Those militia and independent companies which had been organized in the county tendered their services as county units. Other citizens of the county joined units organized in the city of Richmond. The Henrico Troop changed its name to the Henrico Light Dragoons, and Dr. Zachariah S. McGruder, the delegate from Henrico in the General Assembly, was serving as captain when the company enrolled into state service at the courthouse on May 9, 1861. The company marched to the cavalry camp of instruction at Ashland, and there the raw recruits and their companies were molded into fighting units. The Henrico Light Dragoons petitioned to be assigned to the First Regiment of Cavalry, Wise Legion, commanded by their old captain, J. Lucius Davis. As part of the Wise Legion, the company saw active service in the Kanawha Valley in western Virginia until December 1861, when the legion returned to Richmond. The company was detached and ordered to Petersburg and later to Murfreesboro, North Carolina, where it remained until recalled to Richmond in May 1862. At that time, the regiment was removed from the Wise Legion and designated the Tenth Regiment Virginia Cavalry. As an independent regiment, it was assigned to Gen. J. E. B. Stuart's brigade, and it remained with the cavalry arm of the Army of Northern Virginia for the balance of the war.

The Henrico Light Dragoons was not the only all-Henrico unit to serve from the county. Many of the young men, particularly those from the suburbs around the city, enlisted in units that were credited to the city of Richmond. However, there were units from the suburbs credited to the county. The Henrico Grays, first called the Henrico Rifles, were recruited from the Church Hill area and enlisted under their captain, John Wilder Atkinson. The company became Company A, Fifteenth Regiment Virginia Infantry and saw active field service at the battle of Big Bethel, June 10, 1861, the first major battle of what was to be a long and bloody war. Another Henrico company with the Fifteenth Regiment Virginia Infantry was the Henrico Guards. This company was originally called the Sidney Guard and was composed of men from Oregon Hill and Sidney on the western edge of the city. Under Capt. Lawson H. Dance, the company enrolled and became Company D, Fifteenth Regiment Viriginia Infantry. Although on the field at Big Bethel, this company was not ordered to advance when the Henrico Grays, Company A, was moved forward to reinforce the front line.

Another Henrico company, composed of men from the city and the county, took part in the second major engagement of the war—Blackburn's Ford on the Manassas front. The Henrico Southern Guard, which had been organized in July 1859 at Springfield Hall, was composed of men from Church Hill and Union Hill. Under Capt. William H. Gordon, the company enrolled for active service on April 21 and was mustered into state service on April 27 as Company G, First Regiment Virginia Infantry. This regiment entrained at Richmond on May 25 for the Manassas front. The company served on outpost duty at Fairfax Courthouse, June 2-21, and was engaged in the battle at Blackburn's Ford on July 18 where it lost three killed and five wounded. When Gen. Joseph E. Johnston moved his army to the peninsula early in 1862 to reinforce Gen. John B. Magruder, the regiment was in Richard S. Ewell's brigade.

In late July 1861 one of the field batteries dispatched to reinforce the troops under General Magruder was the Henrico Artillery. This company had been Company B, Thirty-third Regiment Virginia Militia. Under Capt. Johnson H. Sands, the company served at Lee's Mill on the defensive line below Williamsburg. These four Henrico companies, the Henrico Rifles, Henrico Guards, Henrico Southern Guards, and Henrico Artillery, remained with their parent units, retired up the peninsula with General Johnston's command in May 1862, and took part in the Seven Days' Battle around Richmond, June-July 1862. The men of the Henrico Artillery served with the Army of Northern Viriginia as a unit until the company was disbanded in October 1862. The companies in the First and Fifteenth Regiments remained with the Army of Northern Virginia until the flags were furled at Appomattox Courthouse in April 1865.

One of the units to organize early in 1861 was the Henrico Mounted Rangers, formed on January 31, 1861, at the home of Ronald Mills near Varina. After changing its name to the Varina Troop, the company encamped near Rockett's. It created quite a stir whenever it went on parade, but it failed to muster in as a cavalry company. After reorganizing, the company joined the artillery arm of service and became known as the Varina Artillery. Under Capt. John P. Harrison, the company moved to Fort Powhatan on the south side of the James River where it served as heavy artillery. When Johnston's army retired up the peninsula in 1862, the units on the south side withdrew to Petersburg. There the Varina Artillery was combined with other independent companies to form an infantry battalion, the Fifth Battalion Virginia Infantry. The Varina Artillery became Company D and served with the battalion during the Seven Days' Battle. When the battalion was disbanded in September 1862, the men between the ages of eighteen and thirty-five were assigned to the Fifty-third Regiment Virginia Infantry. Thus, throughout its brief career, this unit had the distinction of having served in all three arms of the service—first as cavalry, then as artillery, and finally as infantry.

When the young men marched off in 1861, little did they know that they would return to fight on their home soil, or that the city of Richmond would become the capital of the confederacy of southern states and the principal objective of federal military movements. As this became evident, those who remained found it necessary to organized local defense units. The Marion Artillery, another Henrico company, was organized in December 1861 to man the fortifications on Marion Hill. The Henrico Mounted Guard was organized on March 17, 1862, under Capt. John F. Wren at Westham house in Sidney. The company was accepted into service as a local defense company for exclusive use on local service in and around the city of Richmond. In September 1862 the company was divided into two companies, and they became the Thirty-first Battalion Virginia Cavalry. This battalion was consolidated with the Thirty-second Battalion Virginia Cavalry to form the Forty-second Battalion Virginia Cavalry, and this battalion was later redesignated the Twenty-fourth Regiment Virginia Cavalry. The companies remained on duty in Henrico County until February 1865 when the regiment was transferred to the Petersburg line.[2]

Kusi's Lancers.   Capt. Porter's First Massachusetts Battery.   Hexamer's Battery.   Old Flat's Regular Battery.   Sixteenth New York lying down behind the Batteries.

Battle of the Charles City Road, June 30, 1862. (Virginia State Library)

After the transfer of the Confederate capital to Richmond, troops from other southern states were concentrated at or passed through the city on their way to the front in northern Virginia. Camps of instruction were established all around the city in Henrico. The buildings and campus of Richmond College, west of the city, became the artillery camp of instruction, and the old fairgrounds at what is now Monroe Park, then on the western edge of the city, became a camp of instruction for infantry known as Camp Lee. Later, the area occupied by the Hermitage Fair Grounds, more recently the old Broad Street Station that is presently the Science Museum of Virginia, was designated as the infantry camp of instruction and renamed Camp Lee. This camp became the training camp for all conscripts before they were assigned to field units and also served as the duty station for all exchanged prisoners of war before they were reassigned or returned to their units. At first, tents were pitched in just about any vacant field near the city along the major roads and on either side of the railroad tracks of the Virginia Central and the Richmond, Fredericksburg and Potomac.

The Henrico County Court continued to perform some of the same routine administrative and judicial functions as it had before the declaration of war. Surveyors of roads were appointed, and reports were received and filed, as were those received from the overseers of the poor. The requirement that all free blacks had to register each year was more strictly enforced, and those white residents who were not citizens had to appear before the court to be naturalized after swearing allegiance to the constitution of the Confederate States of America. Ordinary licenses were granted, as were licenses to perform marriages. Administratively, the court set the amount of the county levy and the tax rate needed to meet the projected cost of government. Every quarter the court appointed citizen patrols that were responsible for visiting slave quarters and places frequented by free blacks and slaves. Five patrols, consisting of a captain and four or five men, were appointed each quarter, and they served without charge to the county. These patrols continued to be appointed throughout the war; however, the older citizens of the county were called to serve on them with greater frequency after the first year of the war.

To meet the demands of mobilization, the court authorized a bond issue in the name of the county in the amount of $10,000 to be used for the purchase of firearms, accoutrements, and clothing for the volunteer and militia companies from the county. Relief committees were established in each district to solicit subscriptions to be used for the benefit of those persons or families who were suffering because of the absence of the principal provider who had volunteered for military service. An additional $6,000 in bonds of the county were authorized, and $5,000 of the amount was set aside for maintenance of families of volunteers. The remaining $1,000 was set aside to purchase equipment for Capt. William H. Gordon's company, the Henrico Southern Guard. To discover the needs of those units already in the field, the court set up a committee to communicate with the captains of companies from the county about their need for uniforms and shoes. This committee was also authorized to locate a source of the needed supplies.[3]

As if preparations for defense and mobilization were not enough, the court found it necessary to pay $200 to Maj. John B. Young and Sherwin McRae for services rendered the county in opposing the extension of the city of Richmond in October 1861. Once again the city's representatives had introduced a resolution of the City Council in the General Assembly for the expansion of the corporate limits. The delegate from Henrico, Dr. McGruder, presented eight petitions from more than four hundred citizens of the county opposing the measure. David J. Saunders, a city delegate, replied with "certain memorials of citizens of Henrico, asking that the corporate limits . . . be extended," but the resolutions died in committee. Successful in its defense, the county court divided the county into ten school districts in November 1861 and appointed one school commissioner to each district. The court and the surveyors of the roads also had to reroute roads around fortifications. This became a problem as early as December 1861 and required the construction of turnouts and new roads across private land. Access roads had to be built to fortified positions, also, and these added expenses taxed the county's resources.[4]

In the spring of 1862, with the approach of the Army of the Potomac under Gen. George B. McClellan, greater effort was exerted to strengthen the fortifications east of the city in Henrico. As the Federal army approached and the Confederate army under Gen. Joseph E. Johnston retired, the court found itself busy with a number of cases dealing with slaves and slavery. Several whites were charged with "maintaining that owners have no right of property in their slaves," with "permitting an unlawful assembly of slaves," and for "selling ardent spirits to a slave without the consent of his master." The members of the court handed out justice without fear of the enemy's presence, but when the Union army was encamped on Henrico soil in June 1862, the court did not meet.[5]

On May 15, 1862, the war was brought home to Henricoans. On that day, the Federal gunboats tried to force their way past the guns at Fort Darling on Drewry's Bluff on the south bank of the James about eight miles below Richmond. After a 3½-hour engagement, the commanders of the Federal gunboats decided to break off the attack and retired downriver. The attempt to approach the Confederate capital by the water route had failed. However, as the Federal sailors tried unsuccessfully to elevate their guns to counter the direct fire from the Confederate gunners at Fort Darling, the Confederate forces under General Johnston retired across the Chickahominy into Henrico. Abandoning the middle and lower stretches of the Chickahominy, Johnston withdrew all his forces back to a line about seven miles east of Richmond. On May 17, finding his line of defenses too weak and the supply of water inadequate, Johnston ordered his army to fall back again. The new line was in front of the earthworks that had been thrown up in 1861 within three miles of Richmond. The newly plowed fields in Henrico became campsites, and some of them were destined to be fought over in some of the bloodiest fighting in the war.

The Federal army under General McClellan approached the Chickahominy with caution. On May 20 McClellan crossed troops over the river at Bottom's Bridge. Units of the Federal IV Corps commanded by Gen. Erasmus Keyes crossed the river unopposed. Three days later Keyes's entire corps was across the Chickahominy. With one corps across the river, McClellan began moving other units of his army up the north bank of the Chickahominy. By May 24 Federal cavalry occu-

After darkness halted the fighting, those who survived began the search for their wounded comrades. This print is an artist's sketch drawn in Henrico during the Seven Days' Battle. From *Harper's Weekly,* October 29, 1864.

pied the town of Mechanicsville and a Federal force under Gen. Irvin McDowell at Fredericksburg began showing signs of moving south. At Atlee's Station, Gen. L. O'Bryan Branch's brigade encountered Gen. Fitz-John Porter's Federal command on May 27, and the engagement known as the battle of Hanover Courthouse ended with Porter's men firmly established at the courthouse and Branch's men retiring to Ashland. North of McClellan's right wing, under Porter, the Federal command under McDowell began retiring to Fredericksburg on orders from President Lincoln to move toward the Shenandoah Valley to engage the Confederate force under Stonewall Jackson.

Meanwhile, in the Bottom's Bridge area, General Keyes's troops had advanced as far as Seven Pines by May 25. On that day, Gen. Samuel Heintzelman's III Corps crossed the Chickahominy into Henrico to support Keyes's corps. The Federals established a defensive line a mile and a half west of Seven Pines on May 27, extending from Fair Oaks Station on the York River Railroad south across the Williamsburg Road to White Oak Creek. A strong artillery redoubt was started near the left of the line consisting of a line of rifle pits with trees felled in the direction of the Confederates, just west of the line. The branches of the felled trees, entangled with thick vines, would serve to slow any attacking force. Gen. Silas Casey's division was moved forward to occupy the defensive line, and a battery of six guns was placed in the earthen redoubt, which became known as Casey's Redoubt. Casey's line extended from White Oak Creek north across the Williamsburg Road to Fair Oaks Station, where elements of Gen. Darius Couch's division extended the line toward the marshy waters of the Chickahominy. The balance of Couch's division was held at Seven Pines in a second line of defensive works. Behind this position, a third line extending from Savage Station south across the Williamsburg Road was under construction. The two Federal corps numbered about 35,000 men. The balance of McClellan's army extended up the left or north bank of the Chickahominy.

General Johnston believed that an attack on McClellan's left at Seven Pines would prevent any junction with McDowell moving south from Fredericksburg. Upon receipt of word from Gen. J. E. B. Stuart that McDowell was returning to

Fredericksburg, Johnston decided to take advantage of the
fact that McLellan's army was divided by attacking the two
Union corps in the Seven Pines area. After issuing a call for
Gen. Benjamin Huger's division to move up from Petersburg,
he ordered reconnaissance in brigade force down both the
Charles City and the Williamsburg roads. This reconnaissance
revealed that the enemy strongly defended the Williamsburg
Road but that the Charles City Road, just south of it, was not
defended. Huger's division, which consisted of units evacuated from Norfolk and from the defensive positions along the
south of the James, included the Varina Artillery, serving as
Company D, Fifth Battalion Virginia Infantry. When the division arrived in Richmond, Johnston ordered Huger to move
his men to the Charles City Road on the Confederate right.

   On May 30 Johnston decided to make the attack on the
next day. Without a clear plan of action, he issued some
verbal and some written orders to his divisional commanders
to concentrate the major portion of his army for the attack.
From his headquarters on the Nine Mile Road, Johnston
directed Huger's division to move down the Charles City
Road to flank the enemy position while D. H. Hill's division
was ordered to move down the Williamsburg Road to assault
the works in front of Seven Pines. James Longstreet's division was directed to advance down the Nine Mile Road to
attack the Federal position at Fair Oaks Station. After successfully accomplishing this task, Longstreet was to continue
the advance by moving on Seven Pines to converge with
Hill's troops while Huger turned the Federal left flank. Gen.
Gustavus W. Smith's division was ordered to take up a position behind and to the left of Longstreet on the Nine Mile
Road to protect the Confederate left flank from attack from
across the Chickahominy. Unfortunately, Johnston failed to
communicate his plan of attack to his superiors, and none of
his subordinates knew all of his attack plan.

   The battle was to commence on the morning of May 31
after Huger signaled that he was in position on the Federal
left flank. A very heavy rain the night of May 30-31 caused
the roads to turn to mud. As the water ran off, it filled the
streams, and several bridges were washed out. A great deal
of confusion occurred as the troops moved to their attack
positions. Longstreet failed to move down the Nine Mile

Road. He assumed from the verbal orders he had received from Johnston that he was in command of the right wing, and he moved his men to the Williamsburg Road to join Hill's division. Late in the day, Longstreet formed his and Hill's divisions in two lines perpendicular to the Williamsburg Road. Gen. G. W. Smith moved his division up to Old Tavern of the Nine Mile Road as ordered to be in position to support Longstreet, but Longstreet was on the Williamsburg Road. When Johnston learned of Longstreet's whereabouts, he ordered Smith's division down the Nine Mile Road to be ready to carry out the attack as planned.

Longstreet sent his and Hill's divisions forward, and the attack succeeded in cutting off that part of Casey's division at Fair Oaks Station. After heavy fighting through the vine-covered felled trees, Longstreet's and Hill's men succeeded in capturing Casey's Redoubt. Smith's division moved forward on the Nine Mile Road toward Fair Oaks Station when he heard the sound of battle on the Williamsburg Road. Unfortunately, Johnston did not hear the musketry fire. He did not know that Longstreet was heavily engaged until he received a message from Longstreet calling for support on his left. The Confederates on the Williamsburg Road succeeded in turning the captured artillery pieces on the flank of the Federals still holding the first line and then drove them back to the second defensive line. Units from Heintzelman's corps were sent to support the second line as the Confederates succeeded in pushing the center of that line back a mile. Johnston rode forward to direct the movement of Smith's division toward Fair Oaks as President Davis rode up. When he reached Smith's men, Johnston sent one brigade south to connect with Longstreet's left and ordered the others forward at Fair Oaks. The Federal commander on this part of the line began retiring toward the Chickahominy. As he did so, he encountered reinforcements from Gen. Edwin Sumner's corps, which had been sent over the swollen river when the sounds of battle were heard. The reinforcements blunted the Confederate advance at Fair Oaks and thwarted any effort to link up with Longstreet.

During this action General Johnston was gravely wounded, and Gen. G. W. Smith assumed command as the battle subsided. Any prospect of success had been lost because of a

This home was used as a hospital during and after the battle of Seven Pines, May 31–June 1, 1862. (Virginia State Library)

number of factors. The failure of the various Confederate divisions to get into position on time, their lack of coordinated action, and the arrival of Federal reinforcements all contributed to a lost opportunity. Further action being fruitless, the Confederate forces were ordered to disengage and to fall back to the original line from which the attack had been launched. A heavy price was paid on both sides during what turned out to be two separate battles. The attacking Confederates lost 6,134 killed and wounded, while the defending Federals lost 5,031. The next day, June 1, General Smith stepped down for medical reasons, and Gen. Robert E. Lee was appointed commander of the troops in front of Richmond.

The battles of Seven Pines and Fair Oaks failed to dislodge the enemy from Henrico's soil. Each side began to entrench in earnest, and those citizens caught behind the federal lines or in between the opposing forces found it unsafe. Their personal property was subject to confiscation, and their homes and outbuildings were taken over as needed. Many of the slaves in the occupied area were encouraged to leave by the Federal soldiers, and they took the opportunity to go north. Isabella Atkins, a free black, encountered a perplexing situation. When the Federal soldiers first came to her fifty-acre farm near Malvern Hill, they treated Mrs. Atkins and her husband and seven children with kindness. Having received the land from her freeborn father, she did not want to leave. It was not until after the battle that the Federals came and took foodstuffs, fodder, fence rails, wood, and animals. Even the furniture in her house was taken. Some slaveowners removed their slaves to Richmond or sent them to work on farms in the counties west of the city. Francis Adams left his farm at Fair Oaks and moved to Richmond with his twenty slaves when the Union army came. The presence of the armies contributed to a depopulation of Henrico as citizens left to escape the ravages of war. Two of Henrico's justices were caught behind the Federal lines and were required to take the oath of allegiance to the government of the United States. When the area returned to Confederate control, they were charged with disloyalty. The charges were dropped after they renounced the oath to the United States and reaffirmed their allegiance to the Confederate cause. Dr.

E. H. Poindexter did so in open court. Justice George M. Savage reaffirmed his loyalty to the southern cause by taking the oath of allegiance to the Confederate States after presenting a statement to the court:

Richmond, July 4th, 1862. On Friday, the 23rd of May last, two Yankee pickets came to my door and enquired for milk and butter; I told them I had none to spare. They then enquired as to when our pickets left. I replied; I did not know exactly. One was very insolent, remarking that the rebels were cowards and would not stand. I replied that that was a matter on which we could not agree. They very soon left. The next morning they appeared in considerable force, some coming to the house and insulting me and my family. Soon after a skirmish occurred about a mile or little more above me. When they soon appeared with their wounded, and then approaching my dwelling. When I told them that my family were there, and they must not enter my house, but that they could use the barn if they were determined to make a hospital of my premises. The next day (Sunday), the 25th, Gen'l. Keys and staff came up, dismounted, and approached the house. The Gen'l. introduced himself and signified his purpose to make that his headquarters, to which I made no objection. He then introduced the subject of this war. I replied that on this subject I did not care to converse, as I was sure that we would not agree: he however urging an expression of opinion, I gave my views frankly and fearlessly as I have over and over again expressed them among my own people. When I had gotten through, he turned to his staff and said: "this gentleman is an honest and candid man, and I wish you to see that his property is thoroughly protected," and to me that he respected me for my independence. He left on the following Tuesday, and Gen'l. Heinzelman making my house his headquarters the same day. Up to this time my crop and premises were not very much damaged: the officers with some exceptions were tolerably civil, but I could not at any time go fifty yards from my house without being denounced by the men as a "damned rebel and secesh." After the battle of the 31st of May their wounded came pouring in like an avalanche. They took almost entire possession of my dwelling, and when I appealed to the Adj. Gen'l. for protection, he replied to me that "he had no protection to give, nor did I deserve any," "that I was a damned secessionist, and had been instrumental in bringing about this state of things, and my head ought to be cut off, and the sooner I got away, the better." On Monday, the 2d of June, I was obliged to send my three children to a neighbor's, together with a lady living in my family. The next day my wife had to leave, none of whom have yet returned, the place being still used as a hospital. The work of thorough destruction to my property commenced on the night of the 31st of May. They forced nearly every lock on the place and stole very nearly all my stores, together with crockery and innumerable articles of furniture, forced my corncribs and took all the corn, all long forage, ground and cut all my oats and wheat and hay, burned my enclosures of every description, destroyed my fruit trees, took the boards from my buildings for every use they could apply them, broke up and destroyed my farming implements, stole two horses, about 80 hogs, some sheep and cattle, and appeared to try how much they could damage me. In the meantime my wife had been twice confined to a bed of sickness from excitement and anxiety on my account, apprehending that they would do something with me. On the 12th of June I was taken sick, and on the 16th, being better, returned home. On the night of that day I was arrested on the order of Gen'l. McClellan, taken to his headquarters, where I remained until the next day, without being able to learn what charge there was against me. About 10 o'clock on the 17th I was informed that on that afternoon I would be sent to Fortress Monroe; I remarked that my wife was exceedingly delicate, and to take me off without my seeing her I apprehended would result to her very seriously, that she was at my sister's near by and I hoped I would be allowed to have an interview with her, if they chose, in the presence of any of their officers. This was denied. What to do under the circumstances I did not know, Feeling profoundly convinced that to be taken up under these circumstances would kill my wife, I told the officer that, although feeling that my allegiance was due to the Southern Confederacy, that I would take their oath, which I did, however, without kissing the Book. I feel that my conscience justified me under the circumstances; no mercenary consideration could have influenced me, for I was already damaged as far as I well could be without the burning of my buildings. I have not then nor have I since received one cent for anything from them, and I do here declare that I have not at any time up to this hour knowingly done or said anything the least prejudicial to the Southern cause, and that all my sympathies, interest and feelings, are today, as ever, with the South, and I now hold myself ready and willing to do whatever the interests or laws of the Confederacy may require of me, and in conclusion I do hereby declare upon my honor and conscience that at the time of taking the oath I did not regard it, nor do I now regard it, as binding upon me, but laboring under a profound conviction that the life of my wife would be sacrificed, leaving three little children in the power of a merciless enemy, I was tempted in an evil hour to take the hated oath.[6]

Scene near the Trent house, General McClellan's headquarters, June 29, 1862. Franklin's Federal corps is retiring toward the James River. From *Harper's Weekly*, August 16, 1862.

After establishing his headquarters at the Dabbs house on the Nine Mile Road, Lee began the necessary work of strengthening the defenses in front of Richmond and in improving the organization of the army he inherited. The first thing he did was to order his subordinate commanders to have their commands dig in and strengthen the earthworks to stabilize the line; his men soon referred to him as the "King of Spades." On the Federal side of the line, McClellan ordered the balance of Sumner's corps and all of William B. Franklin's VI Corps to cross to the right, or south, bank of the Chickahominy to strengthen and extend the Seven Pines line. This left only Fitz-John Porter's corps on the north bank of the Chickahominy in the Gaine's Mill–Mechanicsville area. Units from Heintzelman's corps advanced up the Williamsburg Road on June 25 and engaged elements of Huger's division in what became known variously as the battle of French's Field, Oak Grove, King's Schoolhouse, or the Orchard. This hotly contested engagement resulted in little change in the lines, but it was the beginning of the Seven Days' Battle before Richmond. Lee had planned to concentrate his army against McClellan's right under Porter at Mechanicsville, and he had moved three divisions into place on the left of the Confederate line. D. H. Hill's division was placed on the Meadow Bridge Road, and Longstreet's and A. P. Hill's divisions were concentrated on the Mechanicsville Turnpike at Chickahominy Bluffs overlooking the town of Mechanicsville. Lee's battle plan called for Stonewall Jackson's troops from the Shenandoah Valley to move down on the right and rear of Porter's position, while D. H. Hill moved his men over Meadow Bridge to drive the Federals from Mechanicsville to open the crossing for Longstreet's and A. P. Hill's troops. The orders called for the movement to commence on the morning of June 26. The divisions under Benjamin Huger and John Magruder were left in the entrenchments in front of Richmond to defend the approaches to the city from the Seven Pines–Fair Oaks area.

The movements of Lee's troops north of the Chickahominy succeeded in driving Porter's corps back after hard fighting at Mechanicsville and Beaver Dam Creek, June 26, and Gaine's Mill, June 27. Following the last battle, Porter's corps retired across the Chickahominy to join the main army.

Porter's determined stand had given McClellan the time he needed to change his base of supply from White House on the Pamunkey River to Harrison's Landing on the James. South of the Chickahominy there had been only minor skirmishing at Fair Oaks during the heavy fighting north of the river. To keep McClellan from launching a counteroffensive against the thin line of defense under Generals Magruder and Huger, a sporadic skirmish fire was maintained. On the twenty-sixth Gen. Robert Toombs's brigade of Georgians moved out to attack the Federal position at Golding's farm. This unauthorized attack met with stiff opposition, and after losing about four hundred men, Toombs withdrew. While the army north of the Chickahominy regrouped on June 28, Toombs, supported by another brigade, led his Georgians against the positions at Golding's farm one more time. Again, the resistance from what he thought was a retreating enemy convinced him that the position was heavily manned, and he was forced to retire after an unsuccessful assault. Toombs had to report the failure of a second unauthorized attack to his already anxious commander, "Prince John" Magruder.

Anticipating McClellan's route of retreat and his change of base, Lee issued orders to his subordinate commanders. While some were to maintain pressure on McClellan's rear guard, the rest were to move to intercept the enemy's main force at Glendale. Longstreet and A. P. Hill were ordered to move across New Bridge, march to the Darbytown Road, proceed down that road to the Long Bridge Road. Huger was directed to move his troops from his lines on the Williamsburg Road to the Charles City Road and down that road to Glendale. Theophilus Homes, with his brigades from the Department of North Carolina, was ordered to cross over from south of the James to move down the New Market Road. While these three columns marched eastward on three separate roads toward McClellan's flank and front, Magruder was to advance down the Williamsburg Road to engage McClellan's rear guard. Lee hoped that Magruder's attack would slow McClellan's march and allow time for the other units to get into position. Jackson, with D. H. Hill's command, was ordered to cross the Chickahominy at Grapevine Bridge and support Magruder's left. Drawing in his troops from either side of the Nine Mile Road, Magruder moved his men down that road early on the morning of June 29 to Fair Oaks Station. Expecting Jackson to come in on his left between the railroad and the river, Magruder moved between the railroad and the Williamsburg Road.

Assuming that Jackson would be on his left and that Huger would be supporting his right, Magruder moved down the railroad. A mile from Fair Oaks Station, he encountered McClellan's rear guard strongly entrenched with artillery support on Allen's farm. Sumner's entire corps occupied the defensive line, with Smith's division of Franklin's corps in close support. To the left and rear of Sumner's position, Heintzelman's corps extended the Federal line to the Williamsburg Road. Outnumbered two to one, but assuming that Jackson and Huger were in position, Magruder began his move. As his artillery wheeled into position, Magruder brought into action the first piece of railroad artillery ever used in warfare. Designed by Lee when he first assumed command of the forces in front of Richmond, the railroad gun consisted of a siege gun mounted on a railroad flatcar behind an angled shield of railroad rails. After it was pushed within range by a locomotive engine, the firepower of the big gun had an immediate effect on the enemy. As the Confederate infantry moved forward, the men of Sumner's corps retired toward Savage's Station.

Meanwhile, at Savage's Station, named for the farm whose cleared fields extended on both sides of the track, the Federals were busy caring for the 2,500 wounded in field hospitals and appropriated buildings and destroying the vast accumulation of supplies to prevent their capture and later use by the Confederates. Magruder continued to advance until he learned that Huger was not on his right. Sending word to Lee of Huger's absence, Magruder requested the support of two brigades from Huger's command. Lee complied and ordered Huger to send two brigades. Moving down the Williamsburg Road, these two brigades took up a position on Magruder's right. Finding that Jackson still needed two hours to reconstruct Grapevine Bridge, Magruder postponed his attack after forming his brigades in line with two in reserve. After two hours passed, Magruder assumed that Jackson had crossed over the river and was on his left. It was at that time that Magruder received word that Huger had withdrawn his two

Battle of Savage's Station, June 29, 1862. Sumner's Federal corps is shown advancing to repel the Confederate attack. From *Harper's Weekly*, July 26, 1862.

brigades because of inaction. Magruder then ordered one of his reserve brigades to his right to cover the Williamsburg Road and to protect the right of Kershaw's brigade of South Carolinians on the right of the railroad. Ironically, General Heintzelman had withdrawn his corps from Sumner's left. When Generals Franklin and Sedgwick rode over to the left of the Federal line, they saw Magruder's right brigade moving into position and quickly ordered up troops from the reserves.

The attack on the Federal position at Savage's Station was not well coordinated. Magruder's line moved forward as independent brigades in line. There was no attempt to coordinate the attack, and when Magruder heard that Jackson was still on the left or north side of the river, he resigned himself to the fact that he would not have support on his left and let his brigades continue the advance. After moving forward about two miles, the Confederates came to the edge of the woods east of Savage's Station. The railroad gun was brought up again and, supported by field artillery units, fired into the Federal positions at Savage's Station. Federal artillery replied. With a shout, Kershaw's South Carolinians moved forward over the open field with Paul Seemes's brigade on their right. The three brigades north of the railroad failed to advance. Kershaw's men succeeded in penetrating the Federal line, but they could not hold the position and were forced to retire back across the field. Darkness was settling in and brought with it a heavy rainstorm. Under the cover of darkness, the Federals retired from Savage's Station, leaving over 2,500 sick and wounded and 500 medical personnel behind. Around 3:30 A.M. Jackson arrived at Magruder's headquarters to tell him that his men would be up by daylight. The battle of Savage's Station was over, and after all the effort, only two brigades and two regiments of a third took part in the attack. They sustained 354 casualties in the futile effort.

The engagement at Savage's Station was minor when compared to the two remaining battles of the Seven Days that took place on Henrico soil. Early on the morning of June 30, Magruder received orders to move his troops to the Darby-town Road. The responsibility for pressuring McCellan's rear guard was to be given to Jackson. Confederate cavalry had been driven back from the crossroads at Glendale on the twenty-ninth. Realizing that Lee had discovered a weak link in his route of retreat, McClellan gave orders to defend the crossroads. Glendale was the place-name given the intersection of the Charles City Road and the Long Bridge Road and the junction with the Willis Church Road from the south. The only sign of settlement was a blacksmith shop which also gave the intersection the name Riddell's Shop. The battle that took place there has been generally referred to as the battle of Glendale, but it has also been called the battle of Frayser's Farm after the farm on the Willis Church Road nearest the intersection and the battle of Nelson's Farm, which was to the west on the Long Bridge Road. Believing that the Long Bridge Road was an extension of the New Market Road, some reports refer to the engagement as the battle of New Market Road. Other names given to the battle are White Oak Swamp, Nelson's Crossroads, Charles City Crossroads, Willis's Church, and Turkey Bridge.

McClellan positioned his troops in an arc extending from south of the intersection and across the Charles City and Long Bridge roads north to the White Oak Swamp Bridge. Behind this line, his wagons were moved over the Willis Church Road to join the balance of his army. In all, five Federal divisions protected the crossroads, and two divisions defended the crossing at White Oak Swamp Bridge. Moving down the Charles City Road, Huger's command bivouacked three miles from the crossroads on the night of June 29-30. Longstreet and A. P. Hill moved down the Darbytown Road to its junction with the Long Bridge Road. From that point they turned to the left and moved toward the crossroads. Jackson's troops followed McClellan's rear guard to the crossing of White Oak Swamp, where he found the bridge destroyed and the high ground on the opposite bank occupied by Federal infantry and artillery.

On the morning of June 30, Huger's command moved down the Charles City Road about a mile and encountered trees felled across the road. Rather than remove the trees, Huger's lead brigadier, Billy Mahone, decided to cut a road through the woods parallel to the road. This decision delayed not only Huger's advance but also the entire attack because the sound of Huger's guns was to be the signal for Longstreet and Hill to advance down the Long Bridge Road

Savage's Station, June 1862. Confederate prisoners are forced to unload supplies for McClellan's army. From Marcus J. Wright et al., *Official and Illustrated War Record* (Washington, D.C., 1899), p. 215.

to Glendale. By two o'clock, Mahone's men cut back to the Charles City Road beyond the felled trees. After deploying Mahone's brigade, a battery of artillery was brought up. The signal gun was fired around 2:30 P.M. The artillery on Longstreet's and Hill's front joined in. Lee expected Huger to advance against the position at Glendale to force the Federals to concentrate against the attacking column. Unknown to Lee, Huger did not issue orders for his infantry to advance. He withdrew his men under cover of the woods and continued the artillery duel. Lee was with Longstreet and Hill. Just before the artillery commenced firing, President Davis came on the field. Lee and Davis retired to a safe distance. It was at this time that Lee was informed about activity on the extreme right. Gen. Theophilus Holmes's command, on the River Road, had witnessed the Federal column retreating across Malvern Hill. Holmes brought his artillery to his front and ordered it to open fire on the Federal column. Almost instantly the Confederates were showered with shells from Malvern Hill and the gunboats in the James. The fire was so intense that Holmes had to withdraw.

The inactivity in Huger's front gave McClellan's army time to retire unmolested to Malvern Hill and beyond to Harrison's Landing. Just before 5 o'clock, Lee gave Longstreet the signal to advance. No word had been received from Huger or Jackson, but Lee assumed they would join in the attack. Longstreet's men plunged into the dark woods. It had been a hot day and the humidity under the trees was oppressive. Longstreet's men overwhelmed elements of McCall's division around the Whitlock house, and the Federal line broke. Here members of the Henrico Guards, Henrico Rifles, and the Henrico Southern Guards engaged the enemy in a fierce bayonet charge as they and other Confederate units sought to wrestle the guns of a Federal artillery battery away from their adversaries. After severe hand-to-hand fighting, the first bayonet charge ended in victory for Lee's men. They seized the artillery pieces and turned them on the retiring Federals. Huger's and Jackson's inactivity allowed the Federals to transfer brigades from other parts of the line to counter the Confederate thrust. As Longstreet's men began to bog down, Lee ordered Longstreet to commit A. P. Hill's division. When the center of the line appeared weak, Longstreet sent his reserve brigade in. Longstreet's and Hill's combined force numbered about 18,000 men. They encountered an enemy force of approximately 40,000 and succeeded in capturing fourteen pieces of artillery, shattering a portion of McCall's division, and capturing Gen. George A. McCall. The price they paid was high. Except for artillery fire on Holmes's, Huger's, and Jackson's fronts and some skirmishing on Huger's and Jackson's part of the line, little support was given by the other 50,000 Confederates to relieve the pressure on Longstreet's front. The battle of Glendale, which had been fought in the darkness of ignorance, ended in the darkness of night. Under the cover of that darkness, McClellan's divisions retired from the field down the Willis Church Road to Malvern Hill. There they filed into defensive lines strongly fortified with field artillery to take advantage of the high terrain. To their backs, the Federal fleet of gunboats lay at anchor in the James ready to provide artillery support when needed.

The Willis Church Road runs in a southwesterly direction. After this road crosses Western Run, a farm road enters it on the right. This farm road connects with the Long Bridge Road. The Willis Church Road turns south just beyond the farm road and begins climbing the steep slope to the crest of Malvern Hill. On the plateau, it crossed between two farms. On the right, the Crew house and its outbuildings perched near the edge of Malvern cliff. Facing west, this feature commanded a wheat field below and the River Road beyond. On the left of the road stood the West house, facing the Crew house. McClellan's front line, facing north, stretched across the plateau for about a half a mile on the flat, cultivated lands of the Crew and West farms. His left, from the Crew house to the Willis Church Road, was held by two divisions of Fitz-John Porter's corps with some sixty pieces of artillery. On the West house side of the road, seven divisions continued McClellan's line in an arc running north to east from the Willis Church Road to Western Run. One mile south of the line on the plateau, the siege guns of the Army of the Potomac were placed in positions around the seventeenth-century brick Malvern house that was serving as a hospital.

Lee's forces around Glendale moved forward cautiously on the morning of July 1. With the exception of a skirmish line

General Lee's railroad battery in action during the Seven Days' Battle. (National Archives and Records Service)

which they captured, they found that the Federals had left only their dead behind. Jackson's men had reconstructed White Oak Swamp Bridge, and he rode forward to confer with Lee. Since his troops were fresh, Lee directed Jackson to take his and D. H. Hill's division down the Willis Church Road toward Malvern Hill. When Hill's division came to the base of the hill, it filed to the left and went into position in front of the Federal line on the West farm. Two brigades from Huger's command were moved into position on the right of the road. To their right, Magruder's troops were eventually brought up to extend the line to the right. These movements placed the Confederates directly in front of the Federal defensive line from the West house to the Crew house. After reconnoitering the line, Lee issued orders for his artillery to move into position on both sides of his line to direct a converging fire on the Union artillery. Gen. Lewis A. Armistead, commanding one of Huger's brigades just to the right of the road, was ordered to advance with a shout if he determined that the artillery fire damaged the Union artillery. The Confederate artillerists failed to bring up sufficient artillery, and when the batteries went into action piecemeal, the Federal gunners concentrated their superior firepower and disabled the Confederate units.

Skirmishing with Berdan's sharpshooters in their front, Armistead's men got carried away and charged up the slope under the arc of the enemy artillery firing from the plateau. This was not intended to be the signal. The general feeling among the Confederate line officers was that the defensive position on Malvern Hill was too strong. They did not believe that an attack would be made against such a formidable position. However, around 5 o'clock, when Magruder moved his brigades in on Huger's right, he saw Armistead's men in the advanced position and assumed the assault had started. He ordered his men forward. Huger's brigades followed on his left, and D. H. Hill's men moved out on the north side of the road. The artillery on the plateau showed no mercy. Those few who survived the charges were met by a sheet of musket fire. Many of the attackers took advantage of any fold in the ground to drop behind or into, from which they continued to fire. The estimated loss was 5,000 Confederates and 3,000 Federals. The firing continued until darkness set in and the flash of the musket or cannon gave way to the lantern lights of the survivors on both sides, as they sought to care for the wounded and looked for friends and relatives.

The battle of Malvern Hill marked the end of the Seven Days' Battle around Richmond. McClellan's army retired to Harrison's Landing, under the protection of his gunboats and after reconnoitering that position, Lee withdrew back to the vicinity of Malvern Hill. Detachments were sent to retrace the routes of the armies to gather all supplies and equipment that had been discarded. Burial details carried out their grim work. Stragglers continued to come in to rejoin their units or to surrender. By mid-July, Lee's army was back in its camps in front of Richmond. In August, McCellan advanced his troops as far as Malvern Hill, but he withdrew when Lee's brigades began to move up to confront him. When McClellan withdrew from Malvern Hill this second time, the Federal army left Henrico soil. A period of about two years would pass before the men in blue returned. When they did, they stayed until victory was won.[7]

The military activity in Henrico in 1862 had halted the functions of government and had disrupted the election process. As a precautionary measure, the governmental records had been removed from the courthouse when the Federal army advanced on Richmond. Even the unused poll books were returned from the voting places to the courthouse for future use. When the court did meet, it had to address a number of administrative problems and to institute measures to care for those citizens of the county who had suffered as a result of the military action. Committees were appointed to examine the populous places around the city to see "whether any nuisances exist affecting the public roads or the public health." The question of who should pay for rebuilding the New Bridge over the Chickahominy River was raised. The court decided that since the Confederate authorities had destroyed the bridge, they should be approached to see if they would rebuild it. Commissioners of roads were ordered to make out new road books numbering each road precinct and assigning hands to work on each road. Where the fortifications cut across the New Market Road, the court directed the surveyor of roads to put up an obstruction and construct a turnout as a public road.[8]

By act of the General Assembly, the justices of the county

courts were authorized to purchase salt and to distribute it to the needy citizens. This necessity of life was in short supply because of the blockade and the demands of the military. In August 1862 the Henrico court appointed Elijah Baker as agent of the court to purchase salt from Preston and King of Saltville. A total purchase of 5,000 sacks at one hundred pounds per sack was authorized. Miles C. Eggleston was appointed by the court to distribute the salt to the people of the county in quantities of twenty pounds per person at cost. Preston and King agreed to deliver the salt in installments over a twelve-month period, but the company did not want cash; payment was made in county bonds that carried interest from the date of purchase payable two years later. When the state government made salt available in December 1862, the county court agreed to sell it to Henricoans at ten cents a pound and to pay the difference to the state. Sheriff George D. Pleasants was directed to transport Henrico's quota to the courthouse and to distribute six pounds to each person.[9]

The year 1863 opened with bitter cold and an epidemic of smallpox. To combat the epidemic, the court established the Sunday School Church near Fairfield Race Track as a smallpox hospital. Dr. Peterfield Trent was appointed physician to the hospital "at the compensation of ninety dollars per month for his services, including medicines, to be paid by the County." Justices John E. Friend and George H. King were appointed a committee to employ Dr. Trent or "some other Physician at a sum not exceeding that price, if they can procure one who is competent; and if not, then they are to employ one at the most reasonable rate for which they can obtain one who is competent." The committee was to impress on the physician employed "that every regard shall be paid to economy in the employment of superintendent, cook, nurses, etc., and in all expenses attending said hospital" and that he could draw on the sheriff for any sums needed to establish and maintain the hospital. Patients were to bear the cost of their transportation to the hospital and the charge of twelve dollars a week "for maintenance, nursing, etc."[10]

About this time a shortage of laborers led the state to begin to draw on the large pool of manpower offered by the slave population. By act of the General Assembly, the governor could requisition slaves to work on fortification, or in govern-

General McClellan's forces crossing the White Oak Swamp on their retreat to the James River. From Marcus J. Wright et al., *Official and Illustrated War Record* (Washington, D.C. 1899), p. 408.

ment departments as needed, but no more than 5 percent of the slave population of an individual county or city could be impressed. The owners received $16 per month for each slave. Any slaves hired by a slaveowner were considered to be still in the possession of their owners; thus, if a slaveowner in Henrico hired slaves from a slaveowner in Hanover, the hired slaves would still be considered part of the Hanover population. They were to be called out only during the non-growing season unless required by an emergency.

The first request submitted to Henrico was in January 1863, and 350 slaves between the ages of eighteen and forty-five were called to work on the fortifications around the city for a period of sixty days. The slave population of Henrico had been 6,557 in 1862, but the court reported that while the Federal army was in the county, "large numbers of slaves escaped or were enticed off" and because of the military activity "large districts" of the county "have been almost depopulated, and large numbers of its citizens have removed from it carrying their slaves with them." The court also noted that "a great many of the slaves now in it are not liable to the operation of the law in the quota to be furnished by this county." Because of these reasons, the court requested and received a reduction of 100 from the quota of 350 requisitioned. Obtaining 250 ablebodied slaves was no easy task. The court had to meet throughout the month of February, as some slaveowners appealed the quota placed on them and others reported the loss, sale, or removal of slaves. Those who were ordered to deliver their slaves had to do so to the sheriff or appear before the court. Failure to comply resulted in the seizure of the slave and an extension of the requisition period from sixty to ninety days. Most slaveholders were required to send one slave. Some had to send two, three, or four, but only large slaveholding farmers, commercial establishments, and those citizens involved with such businesses were required to send more than one. Even the Old Dominion Nail Works and the Virginia Iron Manufacturing Company had to send only five slaves each. Only Dunlop and McCance, millers and commission merchants, had to send ten.[11]

Those blacks in Henrico or Richmond, whether slave or free, found their activities restricted because of the war.

They had to register each year, and some found it necessary to renew their registration. Any free born black had to have a white person appear before the justices to swear that he or she was free born and to give their place of birth. Those who had been freed had to have someone appear for them, also. If they could not prove their free state, they faced the possibility of jail. Any runaway slaves were automatically detained in the county jail. The sheriff advertised the fact in the Richmond newspapers and provided a description so the owner could claim him or her. If an owner failed to come forth, for whatever reason, the prisoner was sold. Those free blacks caught stealing faced similar punishment. When James King, a free black, was found guilty of stealing a cow valued at $400, he was sentenced to be sold into slavery, as was Tom Charles for stealing two sides of beef valued at $350.

The need to care for the poor and the families of soldiers continued to be a problem the court had to face. In March 1863 each of the four magisterial district treasurers received $1,000 from the county treasurer, Thomas T. Duke, by order of the court for use of and relief of families of soldiers. The county levy for 1863 included $6,000 for the poor and $12,000 for the families of soldiers on active duty or who had died in service. The court even reported a $50 gift from Gen. William H. Richardson for the benefit of families of "soldiers of the County as are now in service with the Army (not on home service)." An additional $50,000 in bonds of the county was authorized by the court for the express purpose of relief of the poor in November 1863. The Church and Union Hill Humane Association received $27,500 of the funds raised, and the Sidney Relief Association received the balance of $22,500. The county was divided east and west by a line running up Seventeenth Street to the Mechanicsville Turnpike and out that road to the Chickahominy River. The former association was responsible for the eastern half, and the latter for the western half.[12]

The salt situation became more severe as the county found it difficult to obtain supplies through the channels already set up. Accordingly, the court authorized Elijah Baker, one of the justices and the contracting agent for the county, to hire two slaves or free blacks or to purchase two slaves on behalf of the county and to hire them to John N. Clarkson, superin-

tendent of the Salt Works in Smyth County, at the rate of
$300 per annum through June 8, 1864. The two men were
to supplement the work force at the Salt Works. Although
their labor helped expedite the filling of the county's order,
they did not work to mine salt just for the county. To cover
every contingency, the court stipulated that if he had to hire
slaves, Baker was "authorized to have them valued and to
pledge this County to pay such value to the owners thereof,
in case they escape to, or are otherwise carried off by, the
Public Enemy, while so hired at the Salt Works." The court
further declared that the county was "not to be liable for any
other casualty to said slaves."[13]

In some ways, the war directly affected the administration
of local government. Frequently the court had to petition the
Confederate authorities to exempt sheriff's deputies and
other local officials from conscription so that they could
carry out the functions of government. It was also necessary
to raise salaries and fees to keep up with inflation; the cost of
keeping a prisoner in the county jail rose from $1 a day in
1861 to $2.50 in 1863 and to $4.00 in 1864. As if the problems connected with the war effort were not enough, the
justices were confronted with a renewed old problem in early
February 1864 when a bill was introduced into the Senate by
George W. Randolph of Richmond to extend and define the
southern boundary of the city. At the request of the city
delegation in the House of Delegates, the Henrico delegate,
Joseph J. English, appeared before the court to ascertain its
opinion of the measure. The justices were quick to respond.
They unanimously advised Delegate English to oppose the
measure and agreed to instruct John R. Garnett, the senator
representing Henrico and Hanover, to do so. John G.
Young, the Commonwealth's attorney for Henrico, was instructed by the court to take every action necessary including
appearing before any committee considering the matter.
Young was to act as the counsel for the county in resisting
the proposed extension. The county's efforts were successful
once again, and the resolution was laid on the table.[14]

While the court was occupied with the annexation issue,
another call for slaves to work on the fortifications was received. This time approximately two hundred slaves between
the ages of eighteen and fifty-five were requested, and as

General Robert E. Lee commanded the Army of Northern Virginia. He was particularly active in Henrico during the Seven Days' Battle in 1862 and during the 1864 campaign. (Virginia State Library)

before, the court did not find it easy to fill the quota even with the threat of fines. As it turned out, the activity of the "Public Enemy" would cause more response than the threat of fines. Henricoans had escaped the war for a year and a half, but they were soon to get a taste of what the future held. The news that a Federal cavalry column under Gen. Judson Kilpatrick had slipped around the right flank of Lee's army posted on the Rapidan River and was heading toward Richmond stirred the local defense units into action. The object of Kilpatrick's cavalry raid was to free the Federal prisoners in Richmond and to set fire to the city. While enroute, Kilpatrick detached a force of 500 men under Col. Ulric Dahlgren to move by way of Goochland Courthouse and across the James River to attack the city from the south. Kilpatrick's main force of 3,000 continued toward the Brook Turnpike to attack the city from the north. Each force was to be in striking position by 10:00 A.M. on March 1. On the march, Kilpatrick detailed a force of 450 men to occupy a Confederate detachment at a railroad bridge near Ashland.

General Kilpatrick's column succeeded in getting into position on the Brook Turnpike early on the morning of March 1. As the column advanced across Brook Run, some of the defenders were taken prisoner while their comrades retired to a fortified line. As they advanced, Kilpatrick's men stripped the farms along the road of poultry, mules, horses, and food. Some slaves attached themselves to the column willingly, while others were forced to do so. When his column encountered the defensive works across what is today Chamberlayne Avenue in the vicinity of Union Theological Seminary, Kilpatrick halted. The defenders, supported by artillery, began pouring heavy fire into the Union ranks from behind the earthworks. The ground was soft from rain, and Kilpatrick's men had to dismount and advance on foot. As the dismounted cavalry moved into position, preparations were made for a cavalry charge down the road, but before all dispositions were made, Kilpatrick decided to break off the encounter. The resistance indicated that the element of surprise was lost, and Kilpatrick feared that regular troops were manning the works. Added to this, the lack of any word from or about Dahlgren led Kilpatrick to decide to retire across Meadow Bridge to the vicinity of

Jefferson Davis, president of the Confederate States of America, rode out to confer with General Lee during the action at Frayser's farm, June 30, 1862. (Virginia State Library)

Mechanicsville. While in camp there, Kilpatrick decided to try one more time. Thinking the city's defenders would be concentrated on the Brook Turnpike, he ordered two detachments to prepare to move down the Mechanicsville Turnpike toward the city. Before these detachments could be organized, Wade Hampton's regular cavalry began driving in Kilpatrick's skirmishes from the direction of Hanover Courthouse. Confusion reigned as Kilpatrick gave orders to break camp and retire to Old Church. From there he moved down the peninsula.

Meanwhile, Dahlgren had occupied Goochland Courthouse and had divided his force. He sent a detachment of 100 men down the north bank of the James, under Capt. John F. B. Mitchell, with orders to destroy buildings and homes along the road and locks, boats, and equipment on the canal. Mitchell was to advance as far as Westham Creek and await developments on the south side of the river. Dahlgren planned to cross the James by a ford with the balance of his force and to advance down the south bank and attack the city from the Manchester side.

The same rains that had turned the ground to mud on the Brook Turnpike had caused the river to rise. When his black guide showed him the ford, Dahlgren refused to believe him. He felt the guide, Martin Robinson, had betrayed him, so he ordered him hanged. Dahlgren then led his troopers to Short Pump where he awaited the arrival of Mitchell's detachment. Mitchell passed the swinging corpse as he advanced toward Westham Creek with his men, but it was not until 3:30 P.M. when, to his surprise, he came upon Dahlgren's men at Short Pump that he learned what had happened.

After sending his wagons, ambulances, and prisoners toward Hungary Station in the direction of the firing on the Brook Turnpike, Dahlgren ordered the horses fed some corn confiscated earlier during the march. Around 5 o'clock, Dahlgren's troopers mounted and prepared to advance on Richmond. The weather had been cold and rainy, and as they advanced the soft rain turned into light snow. Moving down the Three Chopt Road toward Westham and the Westham Plank Road (River Road), the column began to encounter sporadic firing from uncoordinated home guard and

General Thomas Jonathan ("Stonewall") Jackson commanded one wing of Lee's army during the Seven Days' Battle. His inability to move his men through White Oak Swamp during the battle of Frayser's Farm has never been adequately explained. (Virginia State Library)

local militia units. The Federal advance continued for about 2½ miles as Dahlgren's men pushed aside, captured, or drove the defenders before them. Several units of the Armory Battalion had been rushed forward to meet the enemy, and they fell back on the rest of the battalion, which was reinforced by the City Battalion, composed of employees from various government departments.

When Dahlgren's men moved against the skirmishers thrown out in front of the position held by the two battalions, the skirmishers fired one round and retired. It was cold and dark as the Federal troopers moved through the mixture of rain, sleet, and snow. The concentrated firepower from out of the darknesss caught them completely by surprise. Dahlgren gave the order to retreat, and during the movement, he and about a hundred of his troopers were separated from the main column. Captain Mitchell assumed command of the main detachment; continuing the retreat, he eventually joined General Kilpatrick's command. Within a few days, Colonel Dahlgren's detachment was overtaken by a force of Confederate regulars and militia in King and Queen County, and he was killed. His body was brought back to Richmond where it was buried secretly below Oakwood Cemetery. It remained there until it was discovered by some agents of Elizabeth Van Lew, the gardener now turned Federal agent who still lived in Richmond on Church Hill. After digging up the body, Miss Van Lew's agents transported it in a cart under some young peach trees to the farm of Robert Orrock near Hungary Station. Dahlgren's body was secretly buried on this Scottish-born Union sympathizer's farm and remained there until after the war; it was then exhumed and transported to Philadelphia for burial in the family plot.

Robert Orrock's involvement in the removal of Dahlgren's body was not the only incident where Henricoans aided the Union cause. By this time, many people had grown tired of the war, and those who had opposed it and who had remained loyal to the Union became more active and vocal. A number of Henricoans assisted Federal prisoners of war on their own or in cooperation with Miss Van Lew's agents. One celebrated case was that of James Duke, a farmer in the eastern part of the county. After losing one son, he smuggled his other sons out of the county and sent them

General George B. McClellan commanded the Army of the Potomac during the Seven Days' Battle. He established his headquarters at Dr. Peterfield Trent's house on Grapevine Road during May and June 1862. From Alexander H. Stephens, *A Comprehensive and Popular History of the United States* (Philadelphia, 1882), p. 618.

north. There they remained until after the war. Duke actively aided escaped Union prisoners of war, and during the 1864 campaign he helped those Union soldiers who had become separated from their units and Confederate deserters by directing them safely through the Confederate pickets to the Federal lines. After the Federal army crossed the James and established a base at City Point, Duke carried information and dispatches about conditions in Richmond, the defenses around the city, and Confederate troop movements to the Union intelligence service at City Point. His activities did not go unnoticed. After being apprehended, he was confined in Castle Thunder prison for several months.

Following the successful repulse of Dahlgren's and Kilpatrick's poorly managed attacks, the citizens of Henrico received a brief respite before the war was brought home to them again. In May 1864 Gen. Phil Sheridan led his Federal cavalry, some 13,000 strong, on a raid on Richmond. The column stretched some thirteen miles in length as it moved south destroying supplies, tearing up railroad tracks, and demolishing bridges. Gen. J. E. B. Stuart moved three Confederate cavalry brigades, numbering around 4,000 effectives, in an effort to get between Sheridan and the capital. The balance of his command remained with the Army of Northern Virginia to observe the enemy's movements and to protect the flanks of Lee's army. With William C. Wickham's and Lunsford L. Lomax's brigades, Stuart marched to cut in front of Sheridan. Gen. James G. Gordon's brigade was given the difficult task of attacking Sheridan's rear guard to slow down the advancing column.

Around 8:00 A.M. on the morning of May 11, 1864, Stuart's weary troopers moved into Henrico County by the Telegraph Road and trotted past Yellow Tavern, just north of the junction with the Brook Turnpike. Just across the turnpike, Sheridan's column was moving down the Mountain Road, which entered the turnpike from the northwest. Stuart found that he had succeeded in getting in front of Sheridan and began moving his men into a line of battle. Placing Wickham's brigade on the right, parallel to the Telegraph Road, and Lomax's brigade on the left, west of the road and almost at a right angle to it, Stuart awaited his adversary. They

Malvern Hill, looking down across the fields over which the Confederates advanced. (Photograph by John S. Salmon)

could hear the firing as Gordon's men harassed the rear guard of Sheridan's column. As the two brigades waited in the vicinity of the tavern that got its name from the yellowish unpainted pine-board siding, they knew they had to fight a delaying action to give the defenders of Richmond time to move reinforcements into the fortifications around the city.

Outnumbered three to one, Stuart's cavalry put up a stubborn fight. As Sheridan's regiments charged the Confederate defensive positions at Yellow Tavern, Stuart rode along the line encourage his troopers to hold. With one regiment in reserve to counterattack, Stuart rode to the left. Sheridan's troopers reeled back, and as they retired, Stuart was mortally wounded. While he was being taken from the field, his horse artillery pieces were overrun, and the cavalry troopers retired to stronger positions east and west of the turnpike. Taking advantage of the gap in the Confederate line, Sheridan's cavalry slipped by and continued the march down the Brook Turnpike toward the city's outer defenses. Stuart's men drew back and regrouped. Among those captured at Yellow Tavern was Capt. George Hopkins of the Henrico Light Dragoons. Blind in his right eye and with the sight of the other much impaired, he had been detailed for light duty in 1863. He returned to active field duty upon receipt of the news of Sheridan's raiding party, but his poor eyesight negated his effectiveness. General Stuart was transported by a circuitous route to Richmond where he died the next day.

Stuart's gallant defensive stand at Yellow Tavern did give Gen. Braxton Bragg time to get the local defense troops into position behind the inner fortification. Three brigades of regular infantry moved up from south of the James to give the defenders numerical superiority and the firepower of veterans. Sheridan crossed Brook Run and pushed the light force of militia skirmishers from the outer defenses. He then moved toward the inner line but decided against a frontal attack. The accuracy of the gunners proved to him that they were well trained. Retiring out of range, Sheridan massed his command on the plateau at Meadow Bridge. On the morning of May 12 he sent one division to rebuild the bridge. After finishing the bridge, the division crossed over and moved in the direction of Gaine's Mill. With the rest of his command, Sheridan began to move down the south bank of

General J. E. B. Stuart commanded the Confederate cavalry at Yellow Tavern where he was mortally wounded, May 11, 1864. (Valentine Museum)

the Chickahominy. On the Mechanicsville Turnpike, where the defensive works extended close to the river, the Federal cavalry encountered two Confederate infantry brigades supported by some cavalry. The units had advanced in front of the defensive line and were supported by the guns in the line. After driving the Confederates back into the defenses, Sheridan's men retired across the Chickahominy. Moving down the north bank of the river, Sheridan recrossed into Henrico at Bottom's Bridge on May 13. On the fourteenth he reached the vicinity of Haxall's Landing where he remained until May 17 when he began the trek back to join the Army of the Potomac by way of the White House on the Pamunkey River.

The cavalry raids in early 1864 brought the war back to Henrico for a brief period of time. However, it was not long before the two opposing armies crossed through the county on the way to Petersburg. Unsuccessful in his efforts to capture Petersburg, Grant laid siege, and defensive lines were built around the city and north to Richmond. Eventually, the defensive lines were extended north to connect with the earthworks already standing in Henrico. The war came back to Henrico and left deep scars in the life of the county. By 1864 its effects were being shown in the county's efforts to assist the poor and distressed. Although the county appropriated $10,000 for the purchase of shoes and socks for soldiers from the county and appointed Col. Sherwin McRae as agent for the county for procuring raw cotton, cotton yarn, cotton cloth, and cotton and woolen cards, there was little to be had. The rate of inflation forced the county to extend the period of payment on county bonds. When an additional $50,000 in bonds was authorized for relief of the poor in April 1864, the bonds were divided into several issues redeemable eleven to fifteen years after date of sale. The interest rate of 6 percent every six months did not attract buyers because the rate of inflation was such that they needed money to meet current expenses. When the court appropriated $40,000 to purchase corn for the poor, the committee was authorized to borrow the money if necessary and to contact the Confederate authorities to try to borrow the corn if they could not buy it on the open market. The county levy for the poor was raised to $10,000 and for relief of families of soldiers in

Battle of the Darbytown Road, October 7, 1864. From *Harper's Weekly*, October 29, 1864

service to $40,000 in 1864. Later, as the winter months set in, the county sought to obtain wood for the indigent families.

Federal infantry returned to Henrico in June 1864, as Gen. G. K. Warren's V Corps crossed the Chickahominy by the Long Bridge after the battle of Cold Harbor. Warren's corps covered Grant's army as it moved to cross the James River. Advancing down the Long Bridge Road with James H. Wilson's cavalry, Warren sent his cavalry forward. At Riddell's Shop on June 13, the cavalry of both armies clashed. Lee had discovered the absence of Grant's army in his front at Cold Harbor and moved the Army of Northern Virginia to the vicinity of Malvern Hill and White Oak Swamp to block the approaches to Richmond. The infantry of the two armies skirmished at White Oak Swamp and on the Charles City and Williamsburg roads before Warren moved his corps across the James to take part in Grant's advance on Petersburg. Lee ordered units from the Army of Northern Virginia to cross the pontoon bridge at Chaffin's Bluff and march to Petersburg. When he was convinced that Grant's whole army was in front of Petersburg, Lee left the north side of the James. The defensive lines in front of Richmond continued to be held by troops in the Department of Richmond and local militia and home guard units. At Petersburg, Grant's attempt to carry the city by assault failed, and the two armies entrenched. The long siege of Petersburg began on June 18.

To add mobility to his operation, Grant used his superior numbers to launch attacks against the left and right of Lee's line. On July 25 Gen. Winfield S. Hancock was ordered to move his corps to the north side of the James to demonstrate against the lines in front of Richmond. The action was designed to force Lee to send reinforcements from the Petersburg line. Supported by two divisions of cavalry, Hancock's infantry crossed the James at Deep Bottom early on the morning of July 27 on pontoon bridges built by units of the X Corps, which also held a bridgehead on the Henrico side. When Hancock's infantry began the advance on Richmond by the New Market Road, they encountered two divisions of infantry transferred from the Petersburg front. Lee had anticipated the move. A third division, with cavalry supports, was on the way and arrived on the twenty-eighth. Heavy fighting

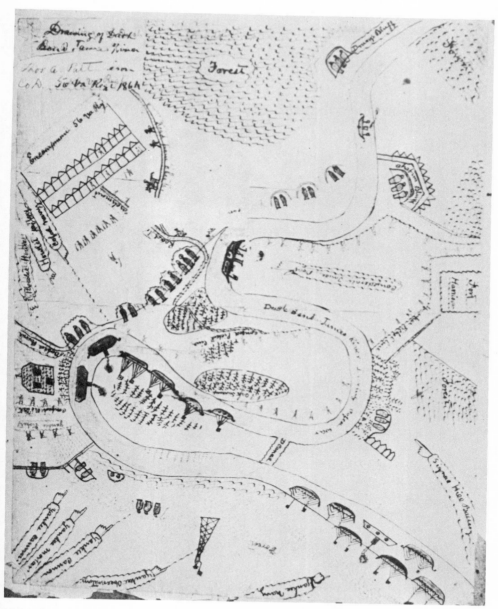

1864 sketch of the defenses along James River drawn by Thomas A. Pattison, Company D, Fifty-sixth Regiment, Virginia Infantry. (Virginia State Library)

occurred on the Darbytown and New Market roads before Hancock withdrew to return to the Petersburg front on July 29.

The month of August opened with a skirmish at Deep Bottom. A second assault on the lines north of the James occurred soon thereafter. Hancock's corps embarked on steamers at City Point late in the evening of August 13. Their destination was the lower pontoon bridge at Deep Bottom. While the infantry moved by steamer, the artillery and cavalry moved by land. After disembarking around nine o'clock, Hancock's men advanced up the New Market and Darbytown roads against the Confederate line at Bailey's Creek and Fussell's Mill. Two Confederate divisions, Charles W. Field's at Bailey's Creek and Cadmus M. Wilcox's at Chaffin's Bluff, held the front. As Hancock's three divisions moved forward, Davis Gregg's division of cavalry moved up on Hancock's right with the intention of dashing into Richmond while the infantry occupied the attention of the defenders. Wilcox's division moved from Chaffin's Bluff to support Field while William Mahone's division of infantry and Wade Hampton's and W. H. F. Lee's divisions of cavalry moved from south of the James to reinforce the defensive line. The disjointed attacks by the Federal infantry on August 16 met with limited success, particularly at Fussell's Mill. There the Confederate line broke, but it was restored before the Federals could exploit the situation. Meanwhile, on the right, at White's Tavern, Gregg's cavalry, flushed with victory after driving a small force in front of them, encountered the Confederate cavalry reinforcements from south of the James. During the engagement, Confederate Gen. John R. Chambliss was killed. Gregg's men and their infantry supports were driven back, and Hancock's right was driven in on his main body of infantry. Even though the attacking units met with limited successes, the campaign failed. Hancock remained north of the James until August 20, when his troops were again withdrawn to the south side of the river.

Except for the bridgehead at Deep Bottom, the Federal forces did not remain in the New Market Heights area. However, those citizens caught in the lines of the opposing armies found that their personal property was subject to the will of the army at hand. The local agencies of government were powerless and unable to help. Gregg's Federal troops

Ditch in front of breastworks near Fort Harrison. (Photograph by John S. Salmon)

stripped William James's fifteen-acre farm in search of food. James, a free black, fled with his family to City Point and returned to his farm after the war. Isaac James, another free black, owned a twenty-acre farm in the same area. When the Federals arrived, they appropriated his house and turned it into a hospital for the wounded. While encamped on his farm, the Federal soldiers consumed his entire ten-acre crop of corn, and when they withdrew back across the James, they took all the furniture from his house. Similar incidents occurred all along the line. After the Federals retired, some of the local citizenry took the opportunity to leave their farms for safer areas behind the lines while others braced themselves for further interruptions.

Grant's third diversionary thrust north of the James resulted in permanent occupation of a portion of the defensive line in front of Richmond. The objective was Chaffin's Bluff, which commanded the river and protected the Confederate pontoon bridge used to cross troops over the river. It was the anchor of the Confederate defensive line north of the James. About a mile and a quarter north of the works at Chaffin's Bluff on the front line of entrenchments was Fort Harrison. While one line of advanced entrenchments ran from Fort Harrison in a northeasterly direction, the main line ran north about three-fourths of a mile to Fort Gilmer. Behind Fort Harrison, the Confederates had constructed two entrenched lines to connect the works on the river at Chaffin's Bluff with those at Fort Gilmer. The main line of Richmond defenses continued north from Fort Gilmer about three-fourths of a mile and then ran northeasterly to the Chickahominy at New Bridge. The occupation of Fort Harrison by a Federal force would not provide them with access to the defenses at Chaffin's Bluff, but the capture of Fort Gilmer would have allowed them to move down the connecting works to the position on Chaffin's Bluff. On the advanced, or Fort Harrison, line, the Confederates had approximately 4,500 men. These troops were supported by some 4,000 locals in the main defensive line of fortifications. Before Grant's third offensive north of the James, only a small bridgehead of 4,300 Federal troops held the area around the bridges at Deep Bottom.

Gen. Benjamin F. Butler, commanding the Army of the

The storming of Fort Harrison. Painting by Sidney King. (National Park Service)

James, which consisted of the troops at the Deep Bottom bridgehead and those on the Bermuda Hundred line south of the river, proposed an assault on the Chaffin Farm position to occupy the bluff and to neutralize the artillery fire directed at the workers constructing the Dutch Gap Canal. This project had also been Butler's idea. To nullify the Confederate batteries that commanded Trent Reach, a wide, shallow part of the James which flowed around Farrar's Island, Butler decided to cut a canal across the narrow neck of land known as Dutch Gap to allow the Federal monitors to move up the river. The narrow neck of land had been fortified by Sir Thomas Dale as part of the defenses for the town of Henrico in 1611. On August 10, 1864, Butler's men started work on the 175-yard-long canal, which required the removal of 67,000 cubic yards of earth. The excavation and later work on the site not only obliterated Dale's moatlike ditch, dubbed Dutch Gap, but probably the site of the town of Henrico also. As Butler's engineers dug and moved the earth off in barges, they were subjected to heavy artillery fire. The dredge and steam pump were bombproofed, but as the work progressed, the Confederates brought up mortars to lob shells into the excavation.

Grant approved Butler's plan to assault the lines on the north side of the river, and ten brigades were put in motion for Deep Bottom. An additional seven brigades were directed to cross the river to Aiken's Landing where a new bridge was to be laid during the night of September 28-29. Aiken's Landing was a principal point of prisoner exchange, as was Cox's Landing nearby. Not far from Aiken's Landing was the site of the town of Varina where the first Henrico County Courthouse stood. Gen. Edward O. C. Ord was ordered to command the 8,000-man force selected to cross the bridge at Aiken's. Downriver at Deep Bottom, so called because of the deep channel, a 16,000-man force under Gen. David B. Birney was assembled to form the right wing of the attack. The initial phase of the attack went off as scheduled. Ord, with the left wing, crossed the bridge at Aiken's Landing and was ready to advance at 4:30 A.M. on the twenty-ninth. The right wing under Birney was in position and ready to move at the same time. The Confederate position on New Market Heights, against which Birney was to concentrate, was under

General U. S. Grant commanded the Federal forces in 1864 and visited Fort Harrison shortly after it was captured. From *One Hundred Americans* (n.p., n.d.,), unpaged.

the command of Gen. John Gregg. Gen. Richard S. Ewell, commanding the Department of Richmond, feared that the enemy would try to capture the right of the line at Chaffin's Bluff, so he concentrated his force there. The center, against which Ord would be moving, was held by detachments at strategic artillery positions. As Ord moved his men out, they took the Varina Road, which led them directly to Battery No. 9, more familiarly known as Fort Harrison. A dry moat at the base of the eighteen-foot walls of this massive earthen fort provided an obstacle to any attacker. The ramparts were un-crenellated, but the steep exterior walls would prove to be a further obstacle to any attackers who made it across the dry moat. Some six or seven pieces of heavy ordnance, in varying conditions of readiness, provided the main defensive power for the position. On either side of the fort were supporting batteries. The entire front line of fortifications did not muster more than 800 defenders on the morning of September 29 as Ord's 8,000-man force advanced.

The mass of bluecoats in Henry Cox's woods on the Varina Road opposite the open field in front of Fort Harrison caused Ewell to realize that the bluffs were not the first objective. He ordered reinforcements, but it was too late. On New Market Heights, John Gregg, although pressured by Birney, saw the threat on his right and began moving men toward Fort Gilmer. As the Federal infantry moved across the open field toward Fort Harrison, the gunners began to find the range. What started out as a walk at trail arms turned into a run. Reaching the dry moat, some of the attackers drove their bayonets into the wall and constructed a ladder up the face of the fort. The disorganized garrison responded to the commands of their unit leaders or took it upon themselves to respond to the emergency. Some broke and ran while others stood to fight. Outnumbered to begin with, the small number that remained found themselves surrounded as they sought to ward off the frontal assault. Some 594 Federal casualties were suffered by the attacking force. One of these was Gen. Hiram Burnham, for whom the fort was renamed after its capture.

With the capture of Fort Harrison, the Federals had broken through the outer defenses, and this breakthrough rendered the New Market Heights line untenable. The cap-

Blowing out the bulkhead of the Dutch Gap Canal, January 1, 1865. From Frank Leslie, *Famous Leaders and Battle Scenes of the Civil War* (New York, 1896), p. 429.

ture of Fort Harrison was considered of such significance that General Grant crossed the James during the morning to inspect the fort. General Ord endeavored to sweep down the captured entrenchments toward the river to capture the Confederate pontoon bridge, but the line was covered by the forces on Chaffin's Bluff and Confederate gunboats in the James. Ord's attempt met with no success, and in the attack he was severely wounded in the leg. Gen. Charles A. Heckman assumed command and moved against Fort Gilmer. This position had been reinforced by three infantry brigades, and Heckman's attack was repulsed with heavy loss. On the right, General Birney's men occupied the outer entrenchments of the New Market Heights line. The attack on Fort Gilmer and the line extending to the New Market Road occurred around 3 o'clock on September 29. Following this repulse, the Federal infantry dug in. On their right, Gen. August V. Kautz's cavalry anchored the right of the Federal assault line on the Darbytown Road. Birney's command was drawn in on the New Market Road, and a line of entrenchments was thrown up extending to Fort Harrison and from that stronghold to the river just above Dutch Gap. Gen. Godfrey Weitzel was placed in command of the XVIII Corps on the north side of the river. The next day, September 30, Lee ordered a counterattack on Fort Harrison. Three unsuccessful assaults were launched against the fort at a terrible loss to Lee's already understrength brigades. Confederate losses on September 30 were estimated at 2,000. The Federal losses for the two days of September 29-30 were reported as 2,272.

Although they failed to carry Fort Gilmer and to break the line that would have enfiladed the Chaffin's Bluff position, the Federals had succeeded in establishing an entrenched line north of the river from which they could protect the Dutch Gap operation and launch any future attacks on Richmond. In an attempt to drive in the Federal right flank, portions of Fields's and Robert F. Hoke's divisions were concentrated on the Darbytown Road on the night of October 6. These infantry troops were supported on their right by Gen. Martin W. Gary's brigade of cavalry. The Henrico Mounted Guard, Companies A and B, served in this brigade. On the morning of October 7, the Confederate infantry advanced and drove General Kautz's cavalry back on the infantry of

Aiken's Landing was one of the main prisoner exchange points late in the war. The sketch depicts the embarkation of exchanged Union prisoners on February 21, 1865. From *Harper's Weekly*, March 18, 1865.

the X Corps on the New Market Road. After an unsuccessful attack on the infantry position, the Confederates retired. During this brief action, Kautz reported 72 killed and wounded and 202 captured. On the Confederate side, Gen. John Gregg, commander of the famous Texas Brigade, was killed while reconnoitering on the Charles City Road. On October 13 Butler sent a reconnaisance in force against the Confederate entrenchments on the Darbytown Road, and it was repulsed.

The last major activity on the north side of the river occured in late October. In conjunction with a move south of Petersburg, General Butler was ordered to carry out a demonstration north of the James. With part of the XVIII Corps, General Weitzel was ordered to cross over to the Williamsburg Road and to make a demonstration north of White Oak Swamp. Gen. Alfred H. Terry, with part of the X Corps, was directed to demonstrate on the Charles City and Darbytown roads. Arriving on the Williamsburg Road near the old Seven Pines battlefield, General Weitzel moved up the Williamsburg Road and sent one brigade over to the York River Railroad to find the left of the Confederate line with orders to turn it.

Perceiving that General Terry's skirmishing on the Charles City and Darbytown roads was too heavy, Gen. James Longstreet, now commanding the Confederate troops at Bermuda Hundred and north of the James, decided that it was a feint and ordered his infantry to move to the left, thus leaving only a heavy skirmish line in front of Terry's men. When Weitzel advanced up the Williamsburg Road, he ran into veteran troops behind the entrenchments. As the men of the XVIII Corps charged over the open ground, they were sent reeling back by a heavy barrage of musketry. The Federal brigade sent north across the York River Railroad met with limited success when they assaulted a defensive salient on the New Bridge Road. After capturing two guns, and as they were driving the defenders out, they were hit hard by a Confederate counterattack. Confederate General Gary arrived with the balance of his brigade and charged along the line of the entrenchments. His men struck the attackers in flank, driving them from the works. Having received orders to retire to the Charles City Road, Weitzel recalled the brigade north of the railroad and moved his command down the Williamsburg Road. While the withdrawal was being conducted, General Terry was ordered to assault the entrenchments in his front, and he did so, only to be repulsed. During this action of October 27, the Federals lost 516 men killed and wounded and 587 missing. About 500 of the missing were accounted for by Capt. J. Banks Lyle of the Fifth South Carolina Infantry, who penetrated the Federal defensive line and moved down the line taking prisoners as he went. Armed with only a shotgun, he managed to subdue his opponents and to convince them to return with him to the Confederate line. The Confederate loss was about 100 men killed and wounded.

Except for some occasional skirmishing, no major encounters occurred north of the James for the balance of 1864. The two armies went into winter quarters soon after the fighting on October 27. Work on the Dutch Gap Canal continued at a slow pace after the capture of Fort Harrison, and it was not completed until December 30, 1864. The large bulkhead at the northwest end, containing nearly 6,000 cubic yards of earth, was all that remained. To remove the bulkhead so the water could flow through the canal, the Federals dug a mine under the bulkhead and inserted 12,000 pounds of powder. After everything was ready, the mine was exploded at 3:50 P.M. on January 1, 1865. When the dust had settled, it became apparent that a great deal of the earth had fallen into the cut, and that it would be necessary to remove all the earth before the canal could be used. As events transpired, the canal was not servicable during the war. However, it was enlarged in the 1880s when it rerouted the James river and became its main channel.

The area of Henrico occupied by and behind the Union entrenchments after October 1864 constituted approximately one-third of the landmass of the county. Add to this the area occupied by the outer defenses of Richmond and the land between the opposing entrenched lines, which was virtually uninhabited after the engagement of 1864, and well over one-third of the farming and slaveholding area of the county was uprooted. Those citizens who remained in the occupied area found that they could not retain possession of their personal property. The Aiken family of Aiken's Landing lost 5,000 cords of wood, 5,000 bushels of wheat, some steam machinery, and farm animals before the war was over. Horace Kent lost all his wood and tobacco, and John S. Atlee lost his medical books and library in addition to his corn, fodder, and animals. Ellen E. Evans lost her horses, mules, corn, and fodder as well as the food and carpets taken from her home. Even James Duke, the Union sympathizer, did not escape the requisitioning agents of Grant's army. Although he had aided the Union cause when the Yankees came in October 1864, they took his fences, hogs, oats, fodder, potatoes, and cut wood. Even some vinegar stored in his barn did not escape their grasp.[15]

The war and all its miseries was experienced by Henricoans on both sides of the lines. Even those who felt relatively comfortable behind the Confederate lines found that war produces more than just battlefield casualties. The suburbs around Richmond expanded into the county as the population and military activities increased during the war. In addition to the training camps, Henricoans saw military and civilian hospitals, convalescent camps, and manufacturing establishments go up outside of the city's limits. The hard times brought on by the war of attrition did not bring the best out in some members of society. The inhabitants of the suburbs found that "persons supposed to be soldiers" were disrupting the general peace, and they complained to the justices, who in turn called on the Confederate authorities to do something about the situation. To control any possible problems with the greatly diminished slave population, the court directed the patrols appointed in November 1864 to visit "negro quarters and other places suspected of having therein unlawful assemblies or such slaves as may stroll from one plantation to another without permission." Any free Negro had to prove that he or she was free; anyone who failed to do so could be sold into slavery. In one case, William Henry, a free Negro, was put in jail as a runaway on May 27, 1864. He remained in jail until August 9 when the gentlemen justices found out that he was indeed a free man. However, before he was released, he was charged $324.50 for his jail fees. When he advised the court that he could not pay the fees, the justices ordered that he be hired out until the fees could be paid. They did give him the option of being hired out to a private individual, a manufacturing concern, or a government or private institution. He chose to go to a private individual, and the sheriff hired him out to John M. Daly for five years. Daly paid all his jail fees, and William Henry agreed to serve through August 9, 1869. Of course, the events of April 1865 terminated the contract.[16]

In January 1865 when the governor requisitioned 130 slaves from the county to labor on the fortifications and public defenses for sixty days, the court petitioned him for relief. Noting the occupation of a large part of the county, the court advised the governor that many slaveholders had lost, removed, sold, or hired out their slaves. Those slaveholders in the western and northern parts of the county had lost their horses and mules to Kilpatrick's and Sheridan's men. They declared that it was necessary for them to retain the slaves they had. A census of ablebodied slaves between the ages of eighteen and fifty-five was ordered by the court. Only 102 slaves were requisitioned, and 36 of them were from the hospitals in and around Richmond while 15 were from the reactivated Westham Iron Works. As the weather began to warm up and winter became spring, additional requisitions came to the court for slaves to work on the fortifications. The court was considering the matter when the end came. After the battle at Five Forks on April 1, 1865, Lee's line south of Petersburg was open to a flanking movement. On April 2 a general assault on the Confederate lines at Petersburg forced the evacuation of the line. When notified of this, Jefferson Davis and the Confederate authorities in Richmond were forced to evacuate the city. During the night of April 2-3, as the last Confederate units left the city over the bridges to Manchester, the cotton and military stores were set on fire. Gen. Godfrey Weitzel, commanding the Union forces north of the James, moved his troops forward up the Osborne Turnpike and encountered the mayor, Joseph Mayo, and a party sent out to surrender the city near Fulton. The city was occupied on April 3, and on that day the clerk of court was busy trying to save the court's records. When he did transcribe the minutes of the April 1 session, the entry was incomplete. It reads: "The Court having again met pursuant to their adjournment, to further consider the . . . ."[17]

Sowing New Seeds

It would take many years for Henrico's economy to recover from the ravages of the war. Recovery would be
delayed by the lack of a strong monetary system, the
struggle for political control, and economic recessions of
national impact. Henrico's economy was based on agriculture, and a ready market a short distance away in the city of
Richmond provided the citizens of the county with the opportunity to sustain themselves and to acquire the necessities of life. Land values dropped, but there was a market
for what was produced.

Some property owners in the county were required to relin-
quish the use of their property by the occupying army. During
the period from April 1865 to 1870, when the troops were
withdrawn, citizens of Henrico and Richmond had to "rent"
their property for campsites, barracks, officers' quarters, depots, wharves, hospitals, repair shops, or general military use
for various periods of time. When Gen. John Schofield assumed command of the military department, he ordered that
all owners be paid for the use of their private property at a
rate set by a board of officers. However, after a portion of the
rents had been paid, Gen. Montgomery C. Meigs, chief quar-
termaster, stopped the payments. Isaac Davenport, Jr., of
Strawberry Hill was one of twenty-six petitioners who asked
Congress to pass a law paying them for the use of their property. A Senate committee was not too sympathetic to their
request and, refusing the prayer of the petitioners, asked to be
discharged from further consideration of the case. Thus,
some property that could have been used to produce revenue
was not available to the property owners.[1]

The presence of other natural resources provided some
diversity in the county's economic base. Until the development of the coalfields in southwestern Virginia, the Richmond Basin continued to provide large quantitites of coal

Dutch Gap Canal as it appeared after the Civil War and before it was made navigable in the 1870s. From Alexander Gardner, *Gardner's Photographic Sketch Book of the War* (Washington, D.C., 1865–66), vol. 2, plate 87.

and coke for domestic and foreign markets. The large clay deposits along the north bank of the James were excavated to supply the brickmaking industry that flourished in Henrico after the war, manufacturing bricks for use in Richmond, Norfolk, and other cities and towns in the Commonwealth. The presence of a large deposit of granite also proved important to the economic life of the county. Large quantities of granite were used in Richmond, and the quarries in Henrico and Chesterfield supplied the granite blocks used in the construction of Army and Navy (old War Department) Building in Washington, D.C.

As before the war, Henrico's economic life continued to be tied to the city of Richmond. The suburbs of the city had continued to extend out into the county, and it was not long before the city renewed its efforts to annex the suburbs to increase its tax receipts. Soon after the Federal troops occupied the city and the Army of Northern Virginia surrendered, the Restored Government under Francis H. Pierpont was recognized by President Andrew Johnson as the legal government of Virginia. Desiring to carry out the mild presidential reconstruction policy and to reconcile Virginia to the North, Pierpont sought to reestablish local government. He appointed commissioners and conductors of county elections, and the justices elected were ordered not to appoint or allow anyone who participated in the former Confederate government to hold office. Elections were held in Henrico in July 1865, and the new county court met on August 7. No change had been made in the procedures to be followed by the court, so the new justices conducted business as had been done before and during the war. Special courts were opened to handle all cases concerning blacks. These courts were under the auspices of the Freedman's Bureau, and black participation on the bench was required by federal law. These courts were limited to imposing a fine of $100 or three months in jail. They did not have a long life, however, and were discontinued in May 1866. The regular county court continued to act on all cases and to conduct the administrative matters of local government. It paid particular attention to the removal of fortifications and obstructions from the roads to make them accessible for commercial travel. Actions taken by the General Assembly of June 1865 increasing the legal rate of interest, the assessment of taxes, and legalizing the marital status of the freed blacks helped economic recovery and improved the status of blacks in the community.

In October 1865 elections were held to fill the congressional seats and to select delegates and senators for the General Assembly that convened on December 4, 1865. During the first session of the new Assembly, the city renewed its efforts to annex a portion of the county. After some political and parliamentary procedural maneuverings, the bill was rejected. Recognizing the need to increase the city's revenues, its officials continued to agitate for annexation. The city officials also believed that the acquisition of land would cause city dwellers to move into the annexed areas, thus reducing the demand for housing in the old city and lowering rents.[2] During the 1866–67 session the issue was renewed. Two days after the December 1866 session started, T. J. Evans, one of the Richmond delegates, introduced a bill to extend the southern boundary of the city. Two similar bills were introduced by N. M. Lee of Richmond in the House of Delegates and one in the Senate by Robert Ould of Richmond before the month was out. Petitions from Henrico citizens opposing the bills were introduced by J. J. White, delegate from Henrico, but on January 12 on a motion of Lee, the House agreed to send all papers relating to the annexation issue to the Senate. There the bill introduced by Ould was reported out of committee on January 25. Clayton G. Coleman, senator from Louisa, Hanover, and Henrico, attempted to amend the bill to allow the voters of Henrico an opportunity to vote for or against annexation. When Coleman lost his bid to have the voters express their desire, Ould attempted to amend the bill by increasing the amount of land to be annexed. Ould's amendment was voted down by the members of the Senate, and his original bill was passed, engrossed, and ordered to be reported to the House. But neither Ould or Coleman was willing to concede, and the action on the floor became hectic.

On motion of Mr. Elisha F. Keen, the vote by which the bill was ordered to be communicated, was reconsidered. And on his further motion, the vote by which the bill was passed, was reconsidered, and on his further motion, the vote by which the bill was ordered to its engrossment and third reading, was reconsidered. Thereupon,

Mr. Keen moved to reconsider the vote by which the amendment proposed by Mr. Ould to the first section of the bill (to extend the boundary further) was rejected—when,

Mrs. Christopher C. McRae made an unsuccessful motion to adjourn.

The question recurring on the said motion to reconsider and being put, was determined in the affirmative—ayes 12; noes 8.

On motion of Mr. George H. Peck, the vote was recorded as follows:

Ayes—Messrs. Nathaniel Alexander, Peter Belew, George W. Bolling, Dale Carter, Charles L. Crockett, Elisha F. Keen, John H. Lee, Francis W. Lemosy, Christopher C. McRae, William Richmond, Philip W. Strother, and Warner T. Taliaferro—12

Noes—Messrs. David S. G. Cabell, Clayton G. Coleman, Joseph W. Davis, Daniel F. Dulany, Robert C. Mitchell, George H. Peck, Nicholas K. Trout and Lawrence Washington—8

Thereupon,

Mr. Coleman moved to lay the bill on the table, and the question being put thereon, was determined in the negative—on division—yes 4; noes 14.

The question recurring on the amendment offered by Mr. Ould to the 1st section of the bill, and being put, was determined in the negative—on division—ayes 8; noes 10.

Thereupon,

Mr. Coleman made an unsuccessful motion to adjourn.

The bill as amended was then ordered to be engrossed and read a third time, and being forthwith engrossed was on motion of Mr. Ould, (two-thirds concurring), read the third time and passed with its title.

On motion of Mr. Ould, it was

Ordered, That he inform the house of delegates thereof and request their concurrence therein.[3]

A fourth annexation bill was introduced in the House by R. B. Davis of Louisa before the Senate bill was reported to the House, but this House bill was referred to committee were it apparently died. When the Senate bill was brought up in the House, J. J. White of Henrico tried to amend it by offering a duplicate of Senator Coleman's amendment to allow the citizens of the county to vote on the issue. White's amendment was rejected, but he did succeed in having some minor amendments made. The bill was sent back to the Senate where an attempt to have it lay on the table was rejected.

Dutch Gap Canal several years after the channel was made navigable. (Virginia State Library)

On February 13, 1867, the Senate agreed to the House amendments. The act was to go into effect July 1, 1867.

Under the provisions of the act, the size of the city was doubled from 2.4 to 4.9 square miles. Of the 2.5 square miles annexed to the city, approximately one-third was the James River and the islands therein. Although there was an increase in the city's population as a result of the addition of the land and the inhabitants thereon, there was no marked loss of voter population in the county or significant gain in the city's as a result of the annexation. Senator Coleman had managed to obtain some concessions for the citizens in the annexed area. They were not liable for city debts contracted before the annexation for five years, and all taxes levied and collected from them were to be applied to the needs of the area for the next three years. The county retained the right to collect all fees due and to levy and collect the taxes for 1867. The city could not levy any taxes in the area for the year 1867, but the citizens in the annexed area were provided representation on the City Council effective July 1, 1867.[4]

The General Assembly of 1866–67 acted on many measures, but it failed to grant the freed blacks all the rights of citizenship. The Assembly decisively rejected the Fourteenth Amendment on January 9, 1867, by a vote of 27 to 0 in the Senate and of 74 to 1 in the House of Delegates. Failure of the southern states to recognize the civil and political equality of the blacks resulted in the passage by Congress of the Reconstruction Act of March 2, 1867, under which the state of Virginia became Military District No. 1. Gen. John M. Schofield, who had been military commander of the state, became military commander of the district and assumed control on March 13, 1867. The Reconstruction Acts of March 2 and 23, 1867, admitted the freed blacks to suffrage, excluded many former Confederates from voting, and required a test-oath of all officeholders. This latter requirement excluded nearly all former Confederates from any public office. General Schofield appointed a board to supervise voter registration and issued an order suspending all elections until it was completed. All vacancies that occurred in the meantime were to be filled by temporary appointments made by General Schofield. Military control and the registration of blacks were

Seal of the Henrico County Court, 1875. (Sketch by Robert Y. Clay)

preliminary to the election of the constitutional convention called to draw up a new constitution for the state.

Under the watchful eye of the military and the Freedmen's Bureau, a total of 1,229 whites and 1,879 blacks registered to vote for the one delegate for Henrico and an additional delegate designated to represent both Henrico and Hanover counties. Since delegates were assigned by voting population, Henrico received one and a half. The campaign pitted the blacks and Republicans in the Radical ranks against the white Whigs and Democrats on the Conservative side. The Freedmen's Bureau and the Union League served to unite the black voters with the white Republicans. The disfranchisement of many whites and the refusal of many registered whites to vote resulted in a constitutional convention that was controlled by the Radical Republicans. Of the 105 members elected, 81 were white and 24 black; 72 were Radicals and 33 were Conservatives. Of the 3,108 registered voters in Henrico, 2,329 cast their votes on the convention issue; 722 whites out of the 1,229 registered and 1,607 blacks out of the 1,879 registered. Of the total votes cast, 53 whites and 1,606 blacks voted for the convention, and 669 whites and 1 black voted against it.

George W. Swan, a native of England, was elected to represent Henrico. Swan (sometimes spelled Swann) was a carpenter by trade and worked as a "mechanic" in Richmond where he was active as a Union Leaguer and popular among the city's blacks. His popularity was enhanced by the allegation that he deserted from the Confederate army. General Schofield labeled him "unprincipled" and "Radical." The floater delegate for Henrico and Hanover was Burwell Toler, a former slave from Hanover County who sometimes served as a minister to black churches. General Schofield noted his occupation as "laborer" and labeled him "illiterate and ignorant" and a "Radical." The constitutional convention met from December 3, 1867, until April 17, 1868, and produced what became known as the Underwood Constitution because Judge John C. Underwood served as chairman of the convention. Although Henrico was affected by the general provisions of the proposed constitution like all other counties and cities, it was directly affected by the apportionment of representatives. The convention's committee on apportionment had originally recommended that Henrico be given two delegates and Richmond six, but the final report called for eight delegates and three senators to represent a district composed of Henrico and Richmond combined. This was the arrangement until 1871 when Henrico received two delegates, but the county and the city continued to share senators until 1904.[5]

During the turbulent Reconstruction period, the Henrico County Court continued to function without any drastic changes. When vacancies occurred on the court from resignation or death, the justices simply recommended a candidate to General Schofield, and he filled the vacancy with the individual recommended by the court. After the passage of the annexation act, General Schofield issued an order continuing the authority of "those officers of the County of Henrico who reside within that portion of the county recently included within the limits of the City of Richmond . . . within those portions of the County or districts for which they were elected and which are not included within the city limits." The gentlemen justices continued to hear felony cases and to carry out the administrative functions of local government such as determining the local tax levy and appointing many of the local officials. Their calendar contained an unusually heavy number of estate settlement and debt default cases, which were a sign of the times. However, the issuance of licenses for stores and ordinaries continued, and the number of naturalization requests rose dramatically. There was a large influx of immigrants from Prussian Hesse-Cassel and Bavaria and other Germanic states and a steady stream of immigrants from Ireland and England. Some of these newcomers to the area settled in the city, but many purchased established farms in Henrico and began cultivating the soil again.[6]

The Underwood Constitution went before the people in a referendum in 1869. The disfranchisement and test-oath clauses of the constitution were defeated, but the rest of the instrument was ratified by an almost unanimous vote. Gilbert C. Walker, a New Yorker and moderate Republican, was elected governor, but the General Assembly chosen in the same election was overwhelmingly Conservative. When the newly elected General Assembly convened in October 1869,

Forest Lodge, Glen Allen. (Virginia State Library)

Forest Lodge, Glen Allen. (Virginia State Library)

it complied with one of the requirements for readmission to the Union by ratifying the Fourteenth and Fifteenth Amendments to the Constitution of the United States. These amendments recognized and protected the voting and citizenship rights of the former slaves. In January 1870 Military District No. 1 ceased to exist, and Governor Walker and the other state officials assumed control of the reins of government.

The new constitution contained some far-reaching changes in Virginia's local government. Notable among these was the establishment in each county of an administrative body, the Board of Supervisors, to take over the administrative functions of local government and thus relieve the court of this burden. Another notable requirement was a statewide system of public schools. There was also a provision for the dividing of counties into townships. Each township in a county was to elect a supervisor along with numerous other local officials, and the supervisors from all the county's townships were to meet as the Board of Supervisors. When the township provision was abolished by constitutional amendment in 1874, the Assembly reestablished the magisterial district. The legal duties of the justices under the old court system were assigned to local township officials known as justices of the peace after the old county court was abolished and a new county court system was established as provided in the constitution. The judge of the new county court was elected by the General Assembly. In addition, each county was placed in a judicial circuit, and a circuit court was established to hear specific cases.[7]

The year 1870 was a new begining for Henrico County and for the Commonwealth. However, the vestiges of the war and Reconstruction remained for many years, and there continued to be a struggle for power and equality among political, social, economic, and racial groups. William Kennedy was one of the first casualties of the new era. Kennedy, a black, had been appointed a justice of the peace by Gen. Edward R. S. Canby, the last military commander, just before the end of military control. When Kennedy served a warrant for the arrest of Luther S. Irvine, a well-known butcher who lived on Brook Turnpike, his authority was challenged because he had taken the oath before a notary public, William

E. Wade, who had been disqualified from administering the oath. Kennedy "deported himself with a considerable show of dignity and authority," but no less a figure than former governor Henry A. Wise argued successfully in Irvine's defense "that Kennedy is not a magistrate, and had no right to issue the warrant for his arrest."[8]

Following the mandates of the constitution and those from federal authorities, the governor appointed commissioners to divide the county into townships and to designate polling places in each township. George D. Pleasants, John A. Hutcheson, James T. Redd, Henry J. Smith, and Joseph Redwood took the oath before Justice of the Peace J. W. Lewellen on April 18, 1870, and reported back to the newly appointed judge of the Henrico County Court, Edmund Christian Minor, on May 2. Judge Minor had seen service in the Third Regiment Virginia Cavalry during the Civil War and had lost an arm in service. After the war, he attended the law school at the University of Virginia where he recevied his law degree in 1868. He was elected judge by the General Assembly in April 1870 at the age of twenty-six.[9]

The commissioners divided the county into four townships: Tuckahoe, Brookland, Fairfield, and Varina. These townships became districts after townships were abolished, and except for the brief life of Lee District in 1891–92, the districts remained the same for the rest of the century. Moran's Store at the forks of River Road and Three Chopt Road and Erin Shades's on Broad Street Road (the old Richmond and Deep Run Turnpike) were designated polling places in Tuckahoe Township. Burns's Store on Brook Turnpike and Hungary Station on the RF&P were designated as such in Brookland Township. In Fairfield Township polling places were set up in the Franklin house near Hardin's Shop on the New Bridge Road and at Chadwick's Store on the Williamsburg Road. Sweeney's on the New Market Road and Carter's Store at the forks of the Williamsburg and Central turnpikes were designated polling places in Varina Township. The commissioners regarded the site of the courthouse as part of Fairfield Township. Acting under their instructions, the commissioners also appointed registrars for each polling place. After their report was received and accepted, the citizens of Henrico began to register for the elections for local officials under the new constitution.[10]

Two parties emerged in Henrico during the summer of 1870, and a number of public hearings and rallies were held by both the Conservative and Republican parties. The court-house was frequently used for such meetings, but barbecues, picnics, and other social events were also visited by those contending for office. All of the candidates for Common-wealth's attorney held forth at Jimmy Throg's on River Road where the citizens of the county "enjoyed the triple luxury of a barbecue, cockfight, and political meeting." The *Daily Dispatch* noted that "one cock was killed, five sheep and several goats devoured, and stirring speeches were made." Doubtless many of the candidates witnessed the prizefight between two employees of the Tredegar Works, William Taylor, a pud-dler, and John Bennett, an iron molder. Taylor won the three-round affair. When the first township elections were held in June 1870, the Conservative party won Tuckahoe, Brookland, and Varina townships. The Republican party succeeded in capturing about half of the offices in Fairfield Township. The members of Henrico's first Board of Super-visors were Dr. Carthon Archer, Varina Township, Dr. A. J. Terrel, Brookland Township, and Jeremiah T. Jones, Tucka-hoe Township, all Conservatives, and Major Samuel Anable, Fairfield Township, a Republican. The board elected Dr. Archer as its chairman. The election of countywide officers was held in November, and the Conservatives gained control of those offices also.[11]

The board met in the courthouse at Twenty-second and Main. Their first official act after electing a chairman was to authorize a seal for the county. During the meeting, they discussed the general economic conditions, and John K. Fus-sell was appointed superintendent of the poor to deal with the deplorable condition of the poor in the county. Notable among this group were the blacks, even though some of them had tried to better their condition by leasing land. Usu-ally they leased the land for two years and agreed to pay the lease price out of the sale of crops raised. Many of the blacks who leased land worked to clear it but failed to plant a crop, and the cleared land reverted to the owner. When the land-owners refused to assist the former lease holders by provid-

Forest Lodge as it appears today. (Virginia State Library)

ing them with food, they had to appeal to the county for help. Arrangements were made by the superintendent of the poor to house some of the more destitute citizens in the city's Alms House, but the county had to devise a program to help those in greater need. To fund a local program, the overseers of the poor decided not to subsidize the farmers who were taking advantage of those citizens who were "easily imposed upon." When the county levy was determined in November 1870, $13,000 was set aside for the poor. By comparison, the levy for administering the rest of county government for the same period of one year was $10,523.93. Each township overseer of the poor was given funds from the general levy and given responsibility for helping the poor in his district while the county superintendent of the poor sought to place destitute cases with citizens who were willing to provide assistance. Township overseers placed some cases with citzens in the district and reimbursed them for their expenses. When smallpox broke out in January 1873, the county turned to the city for use of the city's hospital for treatment of patients, but when no agreement could be reached, the county board authorized a levy of $1,000 for a hospital for treating patients and vaccinating those unable to pay. After the townships were abolished in 1875, the board assumed responsibility for levying for the poor. A system was established whereby those in need appeared before the board to apply for aid. Tickets for supplies were issued, and the county purchased quantities of supplies or arranged for dealers to redeem the tickets. This system worked so well that by the end of the decade the county took steps to sell the old poorhouse property and to purchase a farm site on Nine Mile Road to cultivate and grow crops for distribution to the poor.

One problem that confronted the board was the suit brought by Stuart, Buchanan and Company for salt provided during the war. The company had won a judgment against the county in the amount of $5,941.99. Believing that the city should pay a portion of the judgment because of the annexation, the board employed E. C. Minor to bring suit against the city. The board's efforts apparently were not successful, because on June 12, 1875, it authorized the payment of $2,500 to Stuart, Buchanan and Company as the first installment of the amount due. In 1880 the General Assembly provided relief on the salt payment debt by passing legislation granting the county "a right to contribution against the city of Richmond in proportion to the amount of taxable property of the said county taken within the limits of the said city . . . For all debts contracted . . . before the passage of said [annexation] act."[12]

Before they were abolished, the townships had responsibility for the secondary roads, but the major thoroughfares and bridges came under the jurisdiction of the Board of Supervisors. The concept of township and later district road authorities survived into the twentieth century, but the responsibility for all the public roads was transferred to the board when the townships were abolished in 1875. To provide a labor force to maintain the roads, a chain gang of jail inmates was made available in 1876. Major construction work was contracted out, and in 1877 the General Assembly authorized the governor to hire out convicts to the county for work on public roads.

A special levy of 15¢ on each $100 taxable value was passed by the board to raise $3,000 for expenses involved in transporting, guarding, and providing medical needs of convicts hired. The final arrangements called for the county to hire twenty convicts at a range of 35¢ to 40¢ a day each. The convicts were picked up at the penitentiary in Richmond in the morning and returned to it at night. They were fed at the penitentiary in the morning and evening. Their noon meal was supplied by the state, but the county had to provide the pail for each man to carry it in. All guards hired by the county had to provide their own guns and ammunition, and they received $1.25 a day in wages. The county purchased a plow, two scoops, eight picks, twenty shovels, two axes, and two grubbing hoes and contracted for the use of several wagons. Gustavus G. Carter was elected by the board to superintend the work that began on September 17, 1877, on the old Westham Plank Road. On October 6 the board agreed to hire ten additional convicts and to house them in the county jail after the sheriff notified the board that it would cost 20¢ a day to do so. On that day, the board authorized the use of convict labor on Creighton Road. In December an annual contract was entered into with the state for

twenty convicts. Even with the convict labor, the board continued to use the county chain gang of all jailed males over
sixteen for work on roads and public property. The first
"road machine" purchased by the county in 1880 was manufactured by S. Pemock and Sons. The availability of state
funds under the special road law passed that year allowed
the county to make the purchase. The machine proved to be
satisfactory, so the Board authorized the purchase of two
more "road machines" in July 1880.

In 1870 Henrico had a population of 15,741 and during
the next ten years experienced only a modest increase to
18,905. One reason for the slow rate of growth was the general economic condition of the country, but also influential
was the close proximity of a large city which attracted country folk like a magnet. A large part of the county's population was school-age children, and the new public school system established by the Underwood Constitution found a
rather lukewarm reception among some of the county's adult
citizens, who felt it was unnecessary and a waste of money.
Each township was responsible for contributing to the financial needs of the system in the township, and the county had
a general levy for schools to supplement the township levies.
The initial levy of 5¢ per $100 of property value for the
township and later district levies was increased to 7½¢ and to
10¢ by the end of the decade. By that time, additional funds
were being received from a tax the county was allowed to
assess on the property of railroads. Part of the tax collected
from railroads went into the county's coffers, and about one
third of it went to the schools. J. N. Powell was Henrico's first
superintendent of schools under the new public school system. From the beginning, each township had a dual system
of school—one for whites and one for blacks. Each township
was responsible for construction and maintenance of its
schools and for hiring the necessary teachers. Frequently,
they competed against each other for the services of a particular teacher. Powell recognized that although only eighteen votes were cast against the school tax levy, establishing a
sound education system was going to be a slow process. One-
third of the population of the county and city could not read
and write.[13]

The number of schools varied from year to year, but as the

Lakeside Park, one of the many amusement parks in the county that served citizens of Richmond and Henrico. From *Richmond, Virginia—Yesterday and Today, 1911* (Richmond, 1911), p. 35.

townships began to build schools, the system took hold. There were twenty-three white and ten black schools operating in the county in 1871 with 821 whites and 467 blacks enrolled. The average salary for teachers was $28.66, and the average tuition per month per pupil was 81¢. Powell noted that sentiment was in favor of the public free schools, "but the people are much disposed to grumble, because the schools are sometimes discontinued before the close of the session for the want of funds, and also because every man cannot have a school at his own door." Most of the schools were primary schools, usually consisting of no more than six elementary grades taught by one teacher. There was also one graded school at Harvie, a school in which there was a prescribed course of study divided into definite periods and progressive steps, which had to be taken in regular order. By 1873, his last year as superintendent, Powell reported that the "schools are looked upon now as a success, and great desire is shown on the part of the people to render them as efficient as practicable." He did note that there were still a few who "murmur and complain," but he felt that they were either "too ignorant to appreciate the advantages of education" or did not "take the trouble to read and comprehend the law." Only 30 percent of the school-age population (861 whites and 385 blacks) was enrolled in the twenty-four white and nine black school in 1873.[14]

When he assumed his duties in 1874, the new superintendent, Daniel E. Gardner, "found great dissatisfaction among all classes." No schools had been opened in Varina, and the other three townships were "languishing, chiefly from a want of ready means to pay teachers and to supply the necessary paraphernalia for school houses." He lamented the presence of "a deep-seated prejudice with some against the system" and the fact that "this can never be removed while the abominable 'civil rights' agitation is an open question." Nevertheless, he reported a "gradual and steady increase of better feeling among the intelligent and thinking people" and "confidently expect[ed] more substantial results for the ensuing year."[15]

In 1878 he reported: "The old Bourbons, few in number and weakening in influence, are still growling away in opposition to almost everything in general, and the free school system especially. There is also a class of persons who neither oppose nor favor the system, except as it may happen to affect them personally. If in any way they can derive incidental benefit from it, they are loud in its praises; but if somebody else's cousin is appointed teacher, they are ready to cry out humbug, no account, break 'em up, &c., &c." But he felt assured that a great majority of the people, "especially the females (who of course have great influence) regard the schools with the highest degree of favor, and are determined to sustain them to the utmost of their power." The demand for schools continued to grow, and the citizens responded by voting the school levy tax for the districts and the county. Funds received from the state supplemented those raised locally. Gardner concluded that "after five years of severe struggle against circumstances, we have come out with flying banner and a resolute purpose," but "oh, for a little more means." By 1880 there were 1,250 whites and 851 blacks being taught in thirty-one white and sixteen black schools at a cost per pupil of 85¢ per month. The system had made great strides. Four grade schools, three white and one black, had been established. The former were at Sidney, Brook Turnpike, and Union Mill, and the latter was at Woodville. A collegiate department had been authorized for the graded school on Brook Turnpike, and it was referred to as a "high school."[16]

The public schools throughout the Commonwealth eventually received additional support from the state through increased appropriations to the Literary Fund, part of the legislation adopted by a new political party known as the Readjusters. Virginia politics in the 1870s centered on the issues of funding the state's prewar debt in full or readjusting it. Supported by those who wished to return the state back to the prewar party leadership, old-line Virginia Democrats, having formed the Conservative, or Democratic Conservative, party, led the fight for full payment of the state's prewar debts. By 1870 the state's prewar debt had risen to $45 millon, and in that year Governor Gilbert C. Walker succeeded in obtaining the passage of the Funding Act, which required the state to pay two-thirds of the debt while West Virginia was to assume payment of the other third. The act provided for the issuance of bonds bearing 6 percent interest to help pay the debt. The sums required for payment of the debt severely crippled the Commonwealth's ability to maintain other mandated governmental programs. This problem was compounded as the country slipped into an economic depression during the mid-1870s. Not only were there insufficient funds to meet the needs of government, but the public school system was left with inadequate financial support from the state.

Virginia's ultraconservatives, or "Bourbons," supported full payment of the debt, as did the whites in the black belt, large landowners, members of the old Virginia families and the well-to-do citizens in the cities. Opposing the idea of full funding were a large number of Virginians from the rural areas of the state. Most of them felt that the debt should be adjusted down to a more reasonable figure by taking into consideration the devastation that occurred during the war. This group found support from those blacks who felt they had no part in creating the debt and who did not see why they should have to pay for it. The different philosophies over payment of the prewar debt became an issue in the 1877 gubernatorial campaign. William Mahone, an opponent of full funding, became a candidate for the nomination, and he assumed the lead in urging readjustment of the state debt.

Failing in his effort to become governor, Mahone began organizing those opposed to full funding. The idea of voluntary readjustment had been tried and had failed. In February 1879 at a Readjuster Convention in Richmond, the movement was formally launched, and the elections in the latter part of the year were targeted for a push to elect Readjuster candidates. Henricoans gathered at the courthouse in early September 1879 to hear candidates who were seeking their parties' nominations for the Assembly. During the meeting "a lively spat occurred" between William Taylor, an incumbent Independent, and John N. Hopkins, a Conservative, over the funding question. Taylor supported an act passed during the preceding session of the legislature reducing the interest on the debt, for he felt it was the best compromise that could have been secured between the funders and the Readjusters. Hopkins charged Taylor with being a Radical. Henry A. Atkinson, Jr., the incumbent state senator, campaigned on the Conservative platform and vowed that the state senate would not send Mahone to the United States

Residence of Joseph M. Fourqurean. From William B. Burford, *Richmond, Virginia, Illustrated* (Indianapolis, 1891), opp. p. 12.

Senate. At that time, the state legislature elected the state's senators to sit in the United States Senate. The term of Robert E. Withers, a full funder, was expiring, and the politicians knew that the next legislature would have to decide either to return him or to send someone else. The Conservative party campaigned to stop Mahone's bid for the office. When the Conservative party primary was held in Henrico on September 13, both Atkinson and Hopkins won their nominations for the state Senate and the House of Delegates respectively.[17]

The Republican party in each of the county's districts appointed five delegates to meet at the courthouse to nominate a Republican candidate for the House of Delegates. At their first meeting, only the delegates from Fairfield, Tuckahoe, and Brookland were present; the delegates from Varina had not been appointed because of some "hocus pocus." Ten days later all twenty delegates, eighteen blacks and two whites, met to pick a candidate, but they could not agree. Feeling that the rest of the delegates would not support their choice, William Taylor, the five Brookland delegates withdrew from the meeting. The remaining fifteen delegates unanimously elected J. Wilbor Southward of Varina as the Republican candidate. Both Taylor and Southward had served in previous legislative sessions as delegates from Henrico.[18]

In the city of Richmond, the Conservative party was so strong that the Republicans did not put up any candidates. Henrico and Richmond shared two senators, so when the elections were held on November 4, two Conservatives, Henry A. Atkinson, Jr., and William Wirt Henry, won. The race for the one Henrico delegate seat better reflects the attitudes of Henricoans. They went to the polls with the admonition to "let measures not men, principles not candidates, be their motto." When the ballots were counted, Hopkins, the Conservative, was elected (633) votes over Taylor, the Independent (344 votes), and Southward, the Republican (272 votes). However, Henrico's Conservative representatives found themselves in the minority when the General Assembly convened in December. The Readjusters held 56 of the 100 seats in the House of Delegates and 24 of the 40 seats in the Senate. As Senator Atkinson was soon to find out, there was no way he or any Conservative in the legislature could prevent the election of Mahone as United States senator.[19]

Even though Mahone had built a strong party organization, he found his plans to readjust the debt through legislation thwarted by the incumbent governor, F. W. M. Holliday, who vetoed the legislation. Because of this action, Mahone realized that the Readjusters had to gain control of the Governor's Mansion at the next election in 1881. For this campaign the Conservative Democrats nominated John W. Daniel of Lynchburg, and Mahone and the Republican Readjusters nominated William E. Cameron of Petersburg.

The Conservative Democrats in Henrico held their primary early in September 1881 and concurred with the Richmond party by nominating Henry A. Atkinson, Jr., and William Lovenstein for the two Senate seats from the Richmond-Henrico district. J. E. Broaddus was nominated for the House of Delegates. The Conservative Democrats represented the established families, business and industry, and all others who supported full funding. The Republicans in Henrico drew their strength from the black community, some of the laboring whites, and northern whites who had settled in the county after the war. When they held their convention, the *Daily Dispatch* of September 15 termed it "a field-day for the colored orators of Henrico." Thirty-two of the thirty-five delegates elected at the district level were blacks.

During their nominating convention, Henrico Republicans debated whether to remain Republican or to turn Readjuster. A committee of conference, appointed by the chairman, failed to resolve the issue, but the Readjuster members of the committee agreed to support the nominee of the convention. After much debate and political rhetoric, Martin W. Hazlewood, "a well-known Republican with Readjuster proclivities" was nominated to run for the House of Delegate's seat. The convention adjourned without making any nominations for the two Senate seats. Later, William Taylor was nominated to run for the Senate by a meeting of Richmond and Henrico Republicans.[20]

The real test of local sentiment was displayed in the gubernatorial and House of Delegates races in Henrico. In the city the Conservative Democracts were still in control, and the Republican Readjusters did not put up a strong slate. In the county the Conservative Democrats brought in state political leaders to drum up support for their candidates. At Womelsdorf Grove near the Deep Run pits, a mass meeting and barbecue was held on October 12. Notices in the *Daily Dispatch* of October 5 mentioned that refreshments would be prepared for at least six hundred. John Gode of Bedford, a former Confederate officer and member of Congress, and Charles T. O'Ferrall, a vigorous young Democratic orator, were billed as speakers along with the party's candidates.[21]

Henricoans were not swayed by the Conservative Democratic argument for full funding. Like many in the Commonwealth, they had reversed their earlier stand and felt the need to readjust the debt down to allow for more money to finance essential governmental services. Unlike their neighbors in the city, Henricoans gave a majority of their votes (1,538 to 1,249) to Cameron and a majority of 226 to Hazlewood, both Republican Readjusters. With strong support from city voters, Conservative Democrats Atkinson and Lovenstein easily won the two Senate seats. Running well across the state, Readjusters won majorities in both legislative branches.[22]

The Readjusters succeeded in reducing the debt down to $21 million, and eventually West Virginia assumed responsibility for the remaining one-third. The Readjuster General Assembly also passed significant legislation in the areas of public education, tax relief on real estate, and tax increases on corporations and struck down some antiblack laws. However, at the same time, Mahone and his political cronies abused their power and ruthlessly removed Conservatives from office and replaced them with Readjusters. These activities mobilized the Conservatives in a statewide effort to remove Mahone, and the first step was taken in 1883 when they succeeded in winning control of both houses of the legislature. For all practical purposes the debt question had been settled, but Henricoans continued to return Hazlewood to the House of Delegates even after the Readjuster hold on state government had been broken.[23]

Throughout the first decade after Reconstruction, Henricoans found it necessary to reestabish the economic base of their way of life. The monetary support for the new school system and the expanded services of county government had to come from the citizens. They could control the sums raised by public levy through their votes, but many citizens

Deep Run Hunt Club in front of Rosedale Lodge, its clubhouse from 1896 to 1910. From *Harper's Weekly*, December 21, 1901.

found that they could not survive during the economic hard times of the 1870s. Those who could not had to file for bankruptcy. During the month of March 1870 forty-eight citizens did so, and the court records contain numerous lists of bankruptcies throughout the period. Land was sold at auction, or facilities were rented out in hopes of being able to hold on to them. The sale of land brought hard money and new citizens into the county. "Gentlemen from northern states, attracted by our fine climate and the promising future of Virginia," purchased many parcels that had been placed on the auction block. The *Daily Dispatch* of January 10, 1870, reported the sale of 1,238 acres on the James River for $40,000, 150 acres for $7,500, and a "county-seat" for $6,000. That same month, 25 acres in the upper part of the county sold for $5 an acre, and 177 acres eight miles below the city sold for $4 an acre. When the owner of Aiken's Landing, Albert M. Aiken, died, his 1,219-acre estate in Varina was sold for $42,681.90, or $35 per acre, to R. B. Chaffin of Amelia County. At the same auction, Locust Hill, some 337¼ acres, was purchased by Rush Burgess of Richmond for $6.50 an acre. In May 1872 David Tennant of Petersburg acquired Strawberry Plains, consisting of some 1,033 acres on Curles Neck, for $30,000. William Allen tried to rent his warehouse, store, and wharf in January 1870 and considered renting his steam corn mill and blacksmith and wheelwright shops with full sets of tools "if sufficient inducements are offered."[24]

One sign of the depressed times was the increase in crime in the county. In April 1870 it was noted that "not a night passes without the farm of someone below the city being invaded and everything edible or otherwise which can be carried off taken." A gang of thieves active in the county took hogs, poultry, harnesses, plows, and just about anything else they could carry away. By digging under the fence around the enclosure, they were even able to enter and steal a dozen of Senator Normand Smith's chickens. Frank Hall, caught for stealing oats, was sent to jail for ninety days. Andrew J. Byrnes was caught using grain for another purpose; he was confined for violating the revenue laws and for failing to pay the license taxes on his distillery. Even Emmanuel Episcopal Church was "invaded by burglars . . . and robbed."

Housebreaking, garrotings, malicious acts of destruction, and several acts of knifing and snipping were reported. Several crimes attracted the attention of the public and the press. In a dispute over the rent on some land, Milton Ladd stabbed Isaac P. Mayo, and the family connections made for a rather sensational trial. County Court Clerk William J. Annable was sentenced to three years in the penitentiary for "fraudulently erasing, altering, secreting and destroying a certain record then in his keeping . . . a list of names of the grand jurors selected according to law" and for embezzling $1,300. These crimes did not directly affect the general populace, but the "depredations committed by a large number of roving thieves" were dealt with by an organized effort. To meet the threat to public safety, Judge Minor appointed seventeen citizens as policemen to assist in enforcing the laws of the Commonwealth. These policemen were appointed for one-year terms and were subject to reappointment.[25]

Even in hard times, Henricoans found time for entertainment. The church was still the center of community activity, and it was there that citizens gathered for regular worship, revivals, picnics, barbeques, and festivals. At Ridge Church, where one of the early schools had been established, local political leaders held forth at barbeques. A festival at New Bridge Baptist Church included the auction of several plows donated by Watt and Knoght, C. T. Palmer, and P. H. Starke, with the proceeds going to the church. Several recreational parks under private management were in operation, and a new park, called Riverside Park, was opened in June 1872. The pleasure boat *Dolly Varden* was available for trips up the canal to the three-mile locks, where passengers could disembark and stroll over the new park. Special constables were appointed by the court at the request of the owners to insure that order was preserved in the park. In Glen Allen, Capt. John Cussons, who had married Susan Sheppard Allen, the widow of the man for whom the area was named, began plans for a resort hotel and park, to be financed with money he made from his successful printing business.

Cussons's dream was to develop a resort that would attract visitors from all along the East Coast, so he converted a one-thousand-acre tract of land into a hunting preserve with lakes, driveways, boat houses, and gardens. The centerpiece of his resort was the 135-room Forest Lodge. Many of the rooms were decorated in the Victorian style, and some had large murals of outdoor scenes. Amateur theatricals were held in the lodge's auditorium. Guests could relax on one of the three-story porches and watch the peacocks, deer, turkeys, squirrels, and other animals that populated the grounds, or they could row boats on the artificial lakes, which were stocked with fish. When the resort opened in the early 1880s, guests arrived from Richmond, but to Cussons's disappointment, it did not attract visitors from out of state. Unable to solicit sufficient patronage to make the venture profitable, Cussons closed its doors after two or three years.[26]

Henricoans had always been active in horse racing and a related sport, the fox hunt. Usually some friends would get together and organize a hunt, and sometimes they put a notice in the Richmond newspapers and invited anyone who wished to participate. Participants and spectators would gather to take part in the festivities. Everyone but the fox had a good time, and even the fox did when he managed to elude the hounds. Some of the prominent business and political leaders of Richmond enjoyed the hunt and the social atmosphere surrounding it. In 1887 a group formed the Deep Run Hunt Club. An Irishman by the name of Blacker, two former British army officers, Maj. S. H. Handcock and Capt. S. S. Handcock, and the British vice-consul in Richmond, P. A. S. Brine, were instrumental in the formation of the club. At first they kept the hounds at Blacker's home, Chantilly, about three miles from Richmond on the Deep Run Turnpike, now Broad Street. The name of the club was taken from Deep Run, the stream in the western part of the county that empties into Tuckahoe Creek. The membership grew to about sixty, and the hunts were usually held in the western part of the county. In 1894 the club moved to Major Handcock's home on Staples Mill Road near the millpond, and during the first year there the membership increased to one hundred. Two years later, the membership accepted the offer of Maj. Lewis Ginter and moved to Ginter Park. There they occupied a 127-acre site across from the A. P. Hill monument. In addition to Rosedale Lodge, the facilities included a stable for forty horses, a racetrack, a nine-hole golf

Laburnum, on Hermitage Road, was the suburban home of Joseph Bryan.
From Andrew Morrison, ed., *The City on the James* (Richmond, 1893), p. 72.

course, a speedway and steeplechase course, and pens for the hounds. The club remained in Ginter Park until 1910 when it joined with the Country Club of Virginia. Although the two clubs separated five years later because of growing differences between the fox hunters and the general membership, they remain a part of the Henrico scene today.[27]

The fairgrounds on Broad Street Road continued to be a gathering place for people from all over the state during the annual agricultural fair. A Farmers' Club was organized in the county in June 1871, and in January 1872 the agriculturalists of Fairfield Township organized a township club with neighborhood auxiliaries. These clubs were evidently short-lived, as interest waned depending on the season of the year and the active participation of members of the farming community. A similar group, Henrico Farmers Club, was organized in August 1884 for the purpose of holding "regular meetings for discussion and friendly interchange of opinions . . . as often as the Club may desire and direct." This group believed "husbandry to be the nobelest and most important of all human pursuits" and that "increased and more accurate knowledge of husbandry in all its branches" was "attainable through associated efforts." Corn, wheat, oats, and tobacco remained the principal crops.[28]

There were also several large nurseries and many orchards and vineyards in the county. Large orchards of fruit trees were set out after the war, and the *Daily Dispatch* reported in July 1871 that farmers were "getting in returns for their labor." J. B. Cooley had planted a peach orchard and found a ready market in the city for his fruit. However, the newspaper reported that "the finest specimens of early peaches we have seen this season were from Mr. Beattie, Grove Road." On Mechanicsville Turnpike, John Werth cultivated grapes on his farm know as Glenwerth. His vineyard produced a wine "which is not unlike Rhine wine." Those who wished to purchase some of his wine could have it delivered at $1 a gallon, with 10 percent off for orders of ten gallons. Within fifteen years, the Virginia Department of Agriculture would boast that "the 'Norton' the best of American wine grapes . . . originated just outside of Richmond." Almost all the native grapes did well in Henrico's soil, and some promoters felt that Richmond would probably become the center of a great wine-making district. Large quantities of table grapes from vineyards in the county were sold in Richmond.[29]

Dairy farming was another new agricultural venture in the postwar period. By 1880 there were 2,181 milk cows in the county, and 180,491 gallons of milk were sold. During the same year, 96,561 pounds of butter and 1,400 pounds of cheese were produced. There were 1,130 farms in the county in 1880, and they were valued at $3,788,796. One statistic that reflected the growing population was the cost of fences for 1879—$10,642. The value of farming implements in 1880 was put at $86,627, and the value of livestock at $216, 478. The total value of production was reported at $467,943.[30]

An 1888 publication designed to sell the county to prospective land speculators and farmers described Henrico's climate as "all that can be desired" and noted that "two and three crops can be grown annually on the same land and no soil in the world will respond to generous treatment more quickly than ours." Adding that the general farmer continued to raise stock and crops, the pamphlet remarked that "a large portion of the county is devoted to vegetables and fruit" and "the German gardeners are as a class making money rapidly." Market-gardening and trucking increased in the 1880s and 1890s, as did poultry and dairy farming. Nurseries also abounded in the county. J. D. Mosby's seventy-five-acre nursery employed 25 men and provided fruit trees and ornamental shrubbery. The nursery of Hodd and Winn, located on Brook Turnpike, covered seventy-five acres and employed 30 men and 125 agents. These nurserymen raised large quantities of fruit trees and vegetables for the local and out-of-state markets. Franklin Davis and Company, of Richmond, had a general nursery in the county and one at Baltimore, Maryland. With over two hundred agents, the company distributed nursery products from coast to coast and in Canada.[31]

In addition to private and independent farm clubs, Henrico farmers took an active interest in the national movement known as the Grange, or Patrons of Husbandry. This organization was started in 1867, by some federal postal and agricultural clerks in the Northwest and spread to the West and East Coasts. It was a secret order of farmers, modeled on the

Masonic order, with prescribed rituals, degrees, signs, and passwords. The principal objective of the movement was to unite the farmers and to advance the knowledge of agriculture. Women were admitted, but they had a separate order of degrees. The nominal dues of as low as a dollar per degree did not place a financial burden on the membership. The organization sought to address many of the problems faced by the farmers by encouraging them to cooperate in mutually beneficial ventures. Once united, the farmers could and did take stands on regulating railroads and big corporations. Although the founders agreed that it was not to take part in political issues, the Grange drifted into them and became very active in later years. It also encouraged the establishment of local cooperatives both for the purchase of necessities and the sale of farm products. These cooperatives flourished for a while, but hard times put an end to many such ventures. In addition, the Grange entered into the areas of insurance, manufacturing and testing of farm equipment, and agricultural education.[32]

The local Grange units were known as Subordinate Granges and in Virginia the first such unit was organized at Petersburg in February 1872. By December 29–31, 1873, the movement was sufficiently organized to hold a state meeting in Richmond to establish the State Grange of Virginia. Representing Subordinate Grange No. 16 from the Fairfield District were Martin W. Hazlewood and James W. Lewellen. The Fairfield Grange had been organized on December 16, 1873, with eighteen charter members. Both Hazlewood and Lewellen became very involved in the Grange movement. Hazlewood was elected secretary of the State Grange at its first meeting and served in that post through 1876. Both men served as editor of the *Virginia Patron,* a Grange newspaper published in Richmond in 1875-76.[33]

When the State Grange held its second annual meeting in Richmond in 1875, a total of Six Subordinate Granges were reported in Henrico. On March 30, 1874, No. 127 at Marshall had been chartered with fourteen members; all fourteen were reported as "withdrawn" a year later. Subordinate Grange No. 186 was organized on May 7, 1874, in Brookland District with twenty-three charter members; this lodge grew to thirty-six members in 1875 and to forty-four in 1876. Five days after the Brookland Subordinate Grange was organized, Subordinate Grange No. 202 was chartered at Curles Neck with seventeen members. The Chickahominy Subordinate Grange (No. 247) was chartered on June 4, 1874, with seventeen members, but a year later all seventeen were reported as "withdrawn." The fifth Subordinate Grange organized in Henrico in 1874 was at Glendale, where twenty-two charter members gathered to open the lodge; their numbers grew to sixty in 1875 but dropped back to twenty-four in 1876. When the State Grange met in that year, the secretary reported that a seventh Subordinate Grange (No 484) had been organized at Laurel, but he failed to give the date of organization or the number of charter members.[34]

Little is known about the activities of the Subordinate Granges in Henrico. Each lodge conducted its meetings in secret in accordance with the ritual and ceremonies prescribed by the National Grange. As in other states, blacks were not admitted into the ranks of the Patrons of Husbandry. However, women were actively involved in the Henrico lodges, and Mrs. Hazlewood held the state office of Pomona (Hope). Mrs. Lewellen attained the degree of Flora (Charity) and held that position on the state level. The year 1876 was the high point of the Grange movement in Virginia. The seven Subordinate Granges in Henrico had grown from a total of 135 charter members to 179 members during the three-year period 1873–76. Unlike those in some areas of the country, the local lodges in Henrico did not try to establish or support an independent political party.

As the Grange movement declined, only a semblance of organization was preserved in about fifteen Virginia counties. The need for new programs was met by the Farmers' Assembly, which organized in Richmond in 1885. In 1889 the Farmers' Assembly gave way to the National Farmers' Alliance and Industrial Union. Like the Grange, this organization brought the farmers together to address economic problems, to establish cooperatives, to conduct secret meetings and to take part in social activities. Once established, the movement grew to about forty thousand members statewide. Col. Normand Smith represented the Henrico Alliance at the 1890 annual meeting at Lynchburg, and Lewis Guy was a delegate from the county at the 1891 meeting in Richmond.

During the spring and summer of 1892, the Farmers' Alliance became the Populist party in Virginia. As under the Alliance, the seventeen counties south of the James from the fall line to the mountains known as the Southside were the center of the Populist movement in Virginia. The pressure of hard times made the farmers in areas that depended on a single crop waver in their support of the Democratic party. But Henricoans remained faithful to the Democratic party, even though they had supported the Readjusters earlier. In the 1889 gubernatorial race between Philip W. McKinney, the Democrat, and William Mahone, the Republican Readjuster, Henrico's voters went for McKinney by a majority of 221. In the presidential election of 1892, they went heavily for the Democratic ticket. The Populist presidential ticket received only 113 votes in Henrico. When the Populist party put up E. R. Cocke as a candidate for governor in 1893, Henricoans cast their votes for the Democrat, Charles T. O'Ferrall, 2,183 to 1,211.[35]

The county also witnessed growth and change in industry during the last three decades of the nineteenth century. Early in the 1870s, the Dutch Gap Canal was opened to larger shipping. This channel cut seven miles off the old river route and allowed the movement of larger shipments in and out of the port of Richmond. A commission set up to compensate Henry Cox, the owner of the Dutch Gap property, did not attempt to fix the commercial value of the land but did assess the value of the land destroyed or used in the construction of Butler's canal at $100 per acre and estimated that Cox sustained $7,500 in damages because of the severance of Farrar's Island, about eight hundred acres, from the rest of his farm. Under contract with the federal government, F. B. Colton of the American Dredging Company of Philadelphia began the dredging work in March 1871. With two dredging machines, an eighteen-foot channel was excavated and cleaned out. The steamer *Norfolk* passed through the canal in July 1871, but the canal was not completed and officially accepted until January 1, 1872. The next day, the 260-foot steamer *Wyanoke* of the Old Dominion Line passed through "unembarrised."[36]

Above Richmond, the operators of the James River and Kanawha Canal were encountering difficulties. Although the canal had been restored and opened to Clifton Forge, damage from floods and competititon from railroads cut into the operations on the waterway. A group of citizens had gathered in Richmond in February 1870 to inaugurate a movement for a new railroad from Clifton Forge through Richmond to Newport News, but the railroad did not become a reality until 1880 when the canal was sold to the organizers of the Richmond and Alleghany Railroad Company. The work of constructing the railroad along the towpath of the canal started almost immediately, and on September 21, 1880, the first train took several celebrities to Maiden's Adventure, Goochland County. The railroad was opened to Clifton Forge on October 15, 1881. The company went into receivership in 1882, and the Chesapeake and Ohio Railway Company, reorganized from the Virginia Central Railroad in 1867, leased the line and later purchased it outright. Richmond was the eastern terminus of this road until the line was extended from Rocketts through Henrico County to Newport News in 1881. The Richmond and Alleghany line provided a means of transporting the coal from western Henrico at Lorraine Station past Westham to Richmond. Later, the Belt Line would be built from the RF&P, crossing the James River and connecting with the Richmond and Petersburg Railroad.

The railroads and steamships transported agricultural produce, coal, granite, and bricks manufactured in the county and a variety of manufactured items produced in the city and its suburbs. The Carbon Hill Coal Company, which had been organized in 1866 by several of the mineowners in western Henrico, continued to mine coal until the James River Coal Company, founded in 1874, began operations in 1875. All coal and coke was transported to the canal on a tramway. After the construction of the Richmond and Alleghany Railroad, the Lorraine Station served the area, and all coal and coke transported on the tramway was transferred there to coal cars for transport to Richmond. Ownership of the mines was transferred to the Richmond Coal Mining Manufacturing Company, Ware B. Gay president, shortly after that company organized in 1882. Under Gay the mine slopes were improved, and new machinery was purchased to improve ventilation and excavation conditions. Four seams of coal and coke were worked, and the small village that grew up around the mines became known as Gayton. The mines continued in operation until 1912. The old Deep Run pits were operated intermittently, also. One sign of urban growth in what was still a very rural county in 1889 was an act of the General Assembly that prohibited the sinking, digging, excavating, or working of any mine or shaft on coal lands within forty feet of an adjacent parcel without consent in writing of every person having interest in the adjacent land.[37]

Along the north bank of the James above the city, granite quarries were opened to extract granite blocks for use in rebuilding the city of Richmond and for the construction of government buildings in Washington. Below the city, a number of brickyards were established. Several brickyards were owned and operated by contractors, and many of the bricks produced were used by them in construction projects. On the Osborne Turnpike there were several brickyards just below the city limits. Powers and Crumps Brickyard, under the management of John Gibson, employed twenty hands and produced about 12,000 bricks a day during the busy season from April to November. Powers and Crump used most of their bricks in their construction business, but they also sold some to other builders. R. Maynard and Brother employed thirty hands and produced about 20,000 bricks a day. Hudgins and Neal worked twenty employees and turned out about 15,000 bricks on an average day. In the same vicinity, West and Lacy, managed by John Gibson, Jr., produced 10,000 bricks. These yards and the yards of Davis and Son and Gideon Ragland on the city's western edge manufactured bricks on tables, using molds. The production of these two city yards was about 21,000 bricks a day. Since both yards were operated by builders, the total production went into the erection of houses and commercial buildings.

Farther down the Osborne Turnpike, at Powhatan, the old Mayo family seat, George S. Price, an enterprising Northerner who had purchased the house and grounds, established a brickyard about two hundred yards from the front door of the mansion house, which he used as a summer home. Price did not use the table method. Using two large brickmaking machines, he could produce 30 bricks a minute on each. Thirty hands were kept busy supplying the machines with clay, and the daily production ran about 26,000 bricks. Price's bricks were shipped to Norfolk and to northern cities. Near Price's was located the Nonpareil Fire Brick Company with a 20,000-brick-capacity kiln. The clay used in the production of firebrick was brought in from New Jersey and mixed with flint from Virginia. These bricks sold for $50 a thousand. Figuring the total production for all the brick-yards as 104,000 a day, and deducting one day a week as lost because of inclement weather, one reporter concluded that 13,520,000 bricks were produced during the normal seven months' season. He concluded that 11,520,000 would be used in the local market to construct 154 houses of average size, or if laid in a pavement four feet wide, they would make nearly 136 miles of sidewalk. Even Brannan and Hagerty, the contractors for the Church Hill tunnel, used locally made bricks for arching the tunnel. The brickyards changed hands and some discontinued operations, but brickmaking continued to be a part of Henrico's economic life into the twentieth century.[38]

A number of manufacturing, canning, woodworking, fertilizer, meat-packing, and similar industries began to appear in Henrico around the city of Richmond. The Richmond Locomotive Works manufactured locomotives, engines, boilers, and heavy machinery. The Richmond Cedar Works produced tubs, buckets, churns, and other wooden items. The Virginia and North Carolina Wheel Company manufactured wheels, hubs, and wagon woodwork. The Richmond Basket Works made various kinds of baskets for domestic use and crates and baskets for fruits and vegetables. The Atlantic and Virginia Fertilizing Company and James G. Tinsley and Company manufactured fertilizers of all kinds. V. Hechler, Jr., and Company operated a pork-packing plant, while J. P. Badenoch and James G. Tinsley managed canning establishments. A number of tobacco factories and general manufacturing businesses were in operation also.

The growth in industry in and around the city naturally led to a greater concentration of people, and this led to the development of new subdivisions whose citizens organized to express the needs of each community. The suburb of Harvie, west of the city, between present-day Hollywood Cemetery and Byrd Park, began seeking help from the county to improve the streets in the neighborhood and the extension of the city rail line to the area in 1872. This area had been the site of two Confederate hospitals during the war, Camps Winder and Jackson. Just west of and adjoining Harvie, the new "town" of Hopedale was "tastefully laid off" in April 1872. To commemorate the good deeds and administration of Governor Gilbert Walker, the citizens named the two principal streets Gilbert and Walker. The lots in Hopedale were 30 by 150 feet and sold from $4.75 to $7.37½ per front foot.[39]

In the rural areas of the county, the freed blacks either formed communities in the general areas where they had labored or moved to the suburbs or city. Blacks employed at the Deep Run Coal Pits and in the coal region along Tuckahoe creek tended to live in their own community. Another group remained in the Mountain Road area. Some 52 blacks purchased 102 acres in White Oak Swamp in January 1872 and employed a surveyor to subdivide it.

Henrico citizens witnessed the purchase and use of county land for a variety of uses other than farming, residential, or commercial developments. The effects of the "late war" could not only be seen in many of the old defensive works that dotted the county but also in the four national cemeteries that were established in Henrico. One, on the Williamsburg Road just east of the city, was opened just after the war. In 1887 Congress appropriated funds to purchase and surface the road leading to it, which became known as Government Road. The other three cemeteries were established at Fort Harrison, Glendale and Seven Pines. Federal money was used to improve the road to Fort Harrison, and the Seven Pines cemetery became important to the development of a rail line to that area. The land was also put to other uses. Not far from Fair Oaks Station, 48 acres were donated for the Virginia Inebriates' Home. In the western end of the county the city of Richmond purchased some 60 acres and built the New Reservoir, completed in 1875. In 1888, 300 acres were added to the tract, and Reservoir Park soon became a favorite recreation resort for Henricoans and Richmonders. Not far from this reservoir on Grove and the Boulevard, 36 acres of land were acquired by Lee Camp, No. 1, Confederate Veterans for the purpose of constructing the Confederate

rook Hill. Although the present structure dates from the late 1860s, an ear-
er dwelling is thought to be incorporated within its walls. This house, located
n U.S. Route 1 near Brook Run, has remained in the same family (William-
ons, Stewarts, Bryans) since the early eighteenth century. (Virginia State
ibrary)

Soldiers' Home. The main building, completed in 1885, served to house the old veterans. A number of cottages and a chapel were built around the main building. Today, the chapel still stands behind the Virginia Museum of Fine Arts.

The growth in population and the development of subdivisions, parks, special-purpose buildings, and points of interest necessitated the improvement of roads and created a demand for public transportation. To meet the needs in one area, the Richmond and Henrico Railway Company was authorized to construct a line out Brook Turnpike in 1870. The company was authorized to use any gauge and to use horses, steam power, or "road engine to draw their cars over the turnpike." This line was also referred to as the Richmond and Henrico Railroad, Turnpike, and Graded Road Company. Citizens of the county protested the charging of tolls until the road was in proper condition in 1872, and the fact that it failed to survive indicates that the venture was unprofitable. In 1882 the Henrico Railroad Company was chartered, with authority to construct a line from the RF&P line at Hungary Station throught the counties of Henrico and Goochland to any point at or near the James River and from Hungary Station through the counties of Henrico and Hanover to any point on the C&O. Failure to attract sufficient capital, between one hundred thousand and one million dollars, made this another paper dream. The Richmond Union Passenger Railway Company, organized in 1887, was the first electric line. It ran from Church Hill through the city to Reservoir Park in the county. The next year, 1888, the Richmond City and Seven Pines Railway Company was chartered.[40]

Except for the Richmond terminal on the northeast corner of twenty-sixth and O streets, virtually the entire line of what became the Seven Pines Railway Company was located in the county. The single-track line ran north on Twenty-sixth Street for about three blocks and then along the south side of Nine Mile Road; it crossed Stony Creek on a wooden trestle and continued east to Fair Oaks and Seven Pines where it crossed the Williamsburg Road and made a loop on the south side of the road. The company purchased a small steam engine and two open coaches. Later, a small flatcar with a roof and side rails was purchased and added to the train. The first run over the tracks of the Seven Pines Railway was in April 1889. Passing sidings were located at several places along the line to allow two-way traffic on the one-track line. One of the sidings was at the forty-acre site of the Masonic Home, a mansion and surrounding grounds donated by A. G. Babcock to serve as a home for distressed Masons and their wives, widows, and orphans. Farther east, another stop was on Oak Avenue in Highland Springs. Founded in 1890 by Edmund S. Read and his sons, Highland Springs, which received its name from the high elevation and number of springs in the area, was a planned community. The streets were laid out on a grid pattern and named alphabetically for different trees and shrubs. Fifty-foot lots sold for $50 to $500 and could be purchased with a down payment of $10 to $20 with the balance due in monthly payments. To entice people to purchase lots, the developers offered them a free railroad pass good for one year.

The Seven Pines line provided access to the city for citizens from the county, and it also provided excursion trains for special trips for city dwellers. Picnic trains ran to New Bridge Baptist Church, Fair Oaks, and Seven Pines. At Fair Oaks a new recreation park became a popular meeting place. At Seven Pines, the national cemetery attracted visitors reliving the days of the war. The company received a charter for a branch line to Cold Harbor in 1890, but construction of this line was never undertaken. The Seven Pines line was electrified in 1892 so that the company could run streetcars instead of trains. In 1894 the company reorganized as the Seven Pines Railway Company, and in 1900 it was purchased by the Virginia Passenger and Power Company. As the suburbs expanded, the Board of Supervisors received requests for charters to construct lines into the country from some of the railway companies operating in the city. The Richmond and Manchester Railway Company and the Manchester Railway and Improvement Company petitioned the board. The latter company received a charter and extended a line to the fairgrounds on Broad Street.[41]

A long procession of military organizations, bands, and many dignitaries marched from downtown Richmond on May 29, 1890, to the Allen property just south of the fairgrounds on Broad Street Road. The occasion was the unveil-

ing of the equestrian statue of Gen. Robert E. Lee at what is
now the intersection of Monument and Allen. The corner-
stone had been laid on October 27, 1887, and the statue by
Jean Antoine Mercie, the French sculptor, had arrived on
May 4, 1890. The area at that time was just an open field in
Tuckahoe District. Some thirty Confederate generals took
part in the parade and ceremony, and Gen. Joseph E. Johnston pulled the rope to unveil the statue before a hundred
thousand witnesses. The statue and the land around it was
not to remain a part of the county for very long. Early that
same year, in January 1890, the General Assembly had established Lee District within Tuckahoe District, and the statue
and the surrounding area were made part of the new district.
Lee District was bounded on the east by the western corporate line of the city, on the north by Broad Street Road, on
the west by the Boulevard and Reservoir Park, and on the
south by Ashland Street. The district was incorporated to
enable the property owners to raise funds by special taxes to
improve streets, drainage, and other local projects. However,
it remained a part of the Tuckahoe District and subject in all
respects to the county government. The act of incorporation
authorized commissioners of roads for Lee District, but no
other local district officers.[42]

The original Lee District had a short life as part of Henrico, because on February 19, 1892, the General Assembly
passed an act annexing that part of the district bounded by
the western boundary of the city, Broad Street Road, Boulevard, and Grove. Upon receipt of word that the city intended
to annex the area, the Board of Supervisors proposed to
submit a protest to the General Assembly because it would
necessitate an increase in taxes on county residents. Copies of
the protest were sent to all senators, but to no avail. The bill
passed with little trouble. Since the act was in force as soon as
it passed both houses of the General Assembly, most of Lee
District became a part of Clay Ward of the city on February
19, 1892. That part of the original Lee District south of
Grove Avenue was reincorporated as Lee District by act of
the General Assembly ten days later, February 29, 1892, and
the act incorporating the original Lee District was repealed
on March 3, 1892. The new Lee District also was incorporated with commissioners of roads.[43]

There was a great deal of activity in the county before the economic downturn of 1893. The Brookland Railway and Improvement Company was chartered on March 4, 1890, to build and operate a railway line in Brookland District. After constructing the Barton Heights and Lakeside lines, the company leased them to the Richmond Railway and Electric Company. On this line, Richmonders could take excursion rides to Lakeside Park north of the city. Here Maj. Lewis Ginter, whose country estate of Westover was nearby, had established a zoological park and the first golf course in the Richmond area. The large lake gave Lakeside Park its name. Major Ginter, a native New Yorker, had served in the Confederate army. After the war, he worked in a New York bank until 1873 when he returned to Richmond and entered the tobacco business with John F. Allen. The firm of Allen and Ginter prospered after the introduction of prepackaged cigarettes. Before his death in 1897, Ginter was involved in many enterprises, including the street railway and the development of what was to become Ginter Park. He chose the site for his county estate, Westover, so that he would not have to ride to and from work facing the sun. Through Ginter's efforts, the body of Gen. A. P. Hill was moved and interred under his statue at the intersection of Laburnum and Hermitage in 1892. Ginter's estate became Westbrook Sanatorium in 1911, the first private hospital in Virginia devoted to the care and treatment of emotional problems. The name was later changed to Westbrook Psychiatric Hospital, and in 1975 Ginter's Queen Anne–style mansion was torn down.[44]

Another popular recreation site of Richmonders and citizens of the county in the 1890s was the eight-acre Westhampton Lake. There people could enjoy boating on the lake or relax under the shade of the stately trees. A large pavilion overlooked the lake. In 1911 the University of Richmond moved to this area, and the lake served to separate the two units of the university, Richmond and Westhampton colleges.

The prominent county citizens who incorporated the Brookland Railway and Improvement Company were also involved with the Northside Development Company, which began the development of Barton Heights, named after James H. Barton, one of the prime movers in the developing the area. In 1891 a viaduct was built over the ravine that

divided the development from the city. Connecting with First
Street, the viaduct gave the residents of Barton Heights direct access to the city. Barton District was created in Brookland District by act of the General Assembly on February 12,
1894.[45] There were a number of subdivisions within Barton
District. In addition to Barton Heights, Barton and T. A.
Lamb were involved in Brookland Park and its surroundings,
and Joseph M. Fourqurean developed the North Street subdivision. Under the act creating Barton District, the county
Board of Supervisors could appoint "improvement commissioners" and could subdivide the district into subdistricts and
appoint improvement commissioners for one or all subdivisions as well as improvement commissioners for the district.
All taxes raised from personal and real property in the district were to be held separate by the county treasurer and
applied to the cost of improvements in the district after the
project received approval of the Board of Supervisors. The
board could appoint other district officials if it deemed them
necessary, and it had complete authority to remove any or all
appointees. As with the commissioners of roads in the Lee
District, the improvement commissioners in Barton District,
after meeting and electing a chairman and secretary to keep
a record of proceedings, were "to fix plans and specifications
for the proper and economical execution of all improvements ordered by the board of supervisors."[46]

In February 1898 Northside District was established in
Brookland District "to provide for lighting and sewage . . .
and for making and maintaining other improvments of a
public nature therein." The General Assembly appointed five
citizens or landowners in the district to a Board of Improvement Commissioners for a period of five years. After that
term, the citizens in the district were to elect the members.
Again, taxes raised from personal and real property in the
district were to be used in the district. The members of the
first Board of Improvement Commissioners were Joseph M.
Fourqurean, A. F. Mosby, W. H. Dunn, C. W. Wingfield, and
C. W. Vaughan. Greater local autonomy was given to this
body than to any previous district board. On January 15,
1900, the Fairmount District in Fairfield District was established with a Board of Improvement Commissioners empowered to make special levies and to use them and road taxes

for "lights, sewerage, and other improvements of a public nature." The General Assembly appointed Johnson F. Newberry. T. J. Teagle, S. A. Allen, J. L. Mitchell, and T. H. Morris to the board. When their term expired after one year, the voters in the district were to elect the members of the board. The term was extended to two years by act of the General Assembly one month later. The board in Fairmount District functioned in the same manner as the board in Northside District.[47]

Two fires in the county courthouse during the month of November 1894 led the Board of Supervisors to consider whether to remodel the old courthouse or to build a new one. The old courthouse had been built in 1825 in the middle of Twenty-second Street just south of Main Street. It was moved to the western side of the street in the 1840s so the street could be opened to traffic. During the evacuation fire of April 1865 the building was badly damaged, and extensive repairs were completed in 1867. After adopting a resolution that the courthouse was inadequate to meet the county's needs, the Board of Supervisors decided that a new courthouse could be constructed for not more than $40,000. It was agreed that the county would issue bonds to pay for the building. Citizen opposition to the cost of a new building led the Board to trim the figure to $25,000. During a debate over whether to build a new one for $25,000 or improve the existing building for $7,000, the board decided to call in engineers to examine the walls to see if they could take additional stress. The report came back that the old building could be reinforced at great expense, but that its appearance would not be changed. The experts recommended that the building be torn down. Again the citizens protested, but the board recognized the need for a new structure and trimmed the amount limit to $20,000. This was in December 1895, one year after the initial proposal.

Carl Ruehrmund was asked to prepare building plans for a new courthouse, and on March 24, 1896, his plan was adopted. When the plans were advertised, it was specifically noted that the cost was not to exceed $20,000. A committee was appointed to sell all material from the old courthouse that could not be used in the new building, and the funds were used to defray some of the costs. The bid of William

Henrico County Courthouse. This red-brick Romanesque structure, located on Twenty-second Street in Richmond, was built in 1896 and served the county until the new courthouse was completed on Parham Road in 1974. (Virginia State Library)

Trexler and Richard E. Elmore for $14,990 was accepted, but changes and additions totaling $3,742.80 and other expenses ran the total cost up to the $20,000 figure. The new courthouse is a neo-Gothic structure of red brick, and it is still standing at Twenty-second and Main in Richmond. After inspecting the building, the board received it from the contractors on November 9, 1896.[48]

Although it was acknowledged that the county owned the land in the middle of Richmond on which the courthouse was erected, the question of whether the county court had the legal right to hold sessions and transact business there was raised. Also, the right of the court to try anyone for crimes committed in the courthouse or the land around it belonging to the county was questioned, as was the right of county officers to assert control over the property. To put these issues to rest, the General Assembly passed an act stating that the "lot of land, known as the Henrico county courthouse property, on the southwest corner of Twenty-second and Main streets, and belonging to said county, shall be, and the same is, declared to be a part of Henrico county, forming a part of Fairfield magisterial district with all the rights, privileges and immunities thereto belonging." Full power was given to the courts to hold their sessions, to transact all business, and to exercise power, control and jurisdiction over the property. County officers were given the same control and authority on the property as they had in the county, but city police had concurrent jurisdiction in special cases. To clarify the issue, the Assembly declared "that so much of the acts extending the corporation limits of the city of Richmond over the property . . . as conflicts with the purpose of this act, be, and the same is hereby, repealed."[49]

The new courthouse was designed to provide space for all county offices. With the growth of the county, an increase in administrative services followed. Roads that had been considered "almost impassable by reason of the depth to which horses and wheels sink into the mud" were now under a general road law with responsibilities for maintenance spelled out. Again, as with the schools, the basic unit was the district. A District Road Board consisting of the district supervisor and a commissioner of roads appointed by the judge had "exclusive control of the roads, bridges, and ferries" within the district's limits. All taxes levied for roads and the building and repairing of bridges was to be expended in the district in which the taxes were levied. A resident of each district was appointed overseer of roads in his district for a one-year term and was responsible for "the less frequented roads" there. The commissioner of roads directed the activities of the district overseers. The principal highways leading out of the city were under the jurisdiction of the District Road Board. Using the low-bid process, each District Road Board approved contracts for the maintenance of the principal and main public roads for a three-year term but restricted the work to three-mile segments at a time. When the private turnpike companies abandoned their roads, the supervisors took the necessary action to give the county control of the roads. When the volume of traffic on the roads, railroads, and street railways reached a point where it became hazardous, the supervisors ruled that guards and crossing gates were required at crossings and petitioned the General Assembly for a law so stating. The board established regulation for specific crossings, at some points requiring the street railway conductors to stop their cars and walk out ahead to insure that the crossings were clear. Gravel was the primary road cover, and stockpiles were maintained for inclement weather.[50]

The county schools remained under the individual districts, and the quality varied according to the amount of money each district levied for its system and the commitment of the district trustees. Daniel E. Gardner was replaced as superintendent on July 1, 1876, by John K. Fussell, who served in that position into the twentieth century. The last two decades of the nineteenth century witnessed an increased commitment to schools in the county and the development of an administrative system to direct the system's growth. The number of schools grew from thirty-one white and nineteen black in 1881 to seventy-four white and thirty-six black in 1900; the number of pupils enrolled rose from 1,172 whites and 987 blacks to 2,812 whites and 1,965 blacks. Even with the increase, the figures represent only about half of the school-age population.

The average cost per pupil per month for all the districts in 1881 was 86¢. The school levies could and did differ from district to district from year to year. The allotment for white and black schools also differed. In 1883 the Varina District started the year with twelve schools for 611 white students and six schools for 432 blacks and spent $1.10 per month for each white student and 60¢ for each black. Fairfield District trustees began with eleven schools for 879 whites and seven schools for 1,175 blacks and spent 80¢ each month per white student and 50¢ per black. In Tuckahoe the trustees had eight schools for 683 whites and six schools for 670 blacks and spend 82¢ per white and 60¢ per black student each month. The greatest difference was in the Brookland District where 686 white students attended nine schools and 755 blacks went to five schools; the cost per white student was $1.31 each month while only 60¢ was spent on each black pupil per month. The total number of school-age blacks in Henrico for 1883 was 3,032, and 1,700 of them were not enrolled. A little over one-half of the total number of whites were not enrolled; of the 2,859 white children of school age, 1,457 did not attend school.[51]

These figures are representative of the number of school-age children during the two decades, and even though Superintendent Gardner concluded that "the universal demand for school privileges assures us of the success and acceptability of our work," there were still many to be reached. However, there never was enough money to build the schools that were needed for those who wished to attend. The schoolhouses were generally wood-frame structures containing one or two rooms. A few brick buildings were constructed, while some were built of logs. Fussell surveyed the situation in 1889 and concluded that "additional funds for the erection of better schoolhouses and improvement of school furniture and apparatus" were needed. He also felt that "school officials should receive increased pay to enable them to devote more time to their duties." Most of the schools were not graded, but occasionally a two- or three-grade school was opened. In 1889 the graded school at Brookland had six grades for the 46 pupils enrolled. In 1895 a graded school with four grades, four teachers, and 172 pupils opened in Barton Heights. The total cost for schools in the county in 1889 was $24,232.14, about twice what it was in 1881. By 1895 it had risen to $34,821.19, and in 1900 it was $41,630.19. The increased expenditures for schools does not necessarily reflect the growth of the system, but the fact that more of the schools were built and owned by the districts indicated greater commitment by the districts to the school system. In 1883 only thirty-three of the sixty-four schools were owned by the district trustees; by 1900 all seventy-five school buildings were the property of the districts.[52]

The subjects taught in Henrico's schools were arithmetic, geography, grammar, history, eclectic, reading, and spelling. Annual teachers' meetings, called summer normals, were held for black and white teachers separately to familiarize them with changes in regulations and to provide them with an opportunity to learn about new textbooks and discuss mutual interests. Occasionally, an annual conference was held for both black and white teachers. Most of the teachers had little education beyond high school. Some had received certificates from normal schools, but many of them were the product of the city's schools. Superintendent Fussell "insist[ed] that teachers shall read good educational literature and attend summer normals." He visited the schools and "made short talks on the importance of moral as well as intellectual culture." After a number of such visits, he observed that "the discipline is of higher order than formerly, and that our teachers are doing better work, both morally and intellectually." Although it only remained in existence for one year, the first school library was reported in 1899.[53]

One statistic reflects a demand on the county's government that was brought about by population density. Of the sixty-four schools in 1883, only the twenty-three owned by the districts had outhouses. In 1900 all seventy-five schools were equipped with such facilities. Public health problems were only addressed when a crisis occurred. As in the past, when a smallpox epidemic broke out in 1881–82 steps were taken to hire a doctor to vaccinate the poor. A hospital was established for the crisis, and those who could pay did so while the poor received free care. When the city tried to purchase land in the county on which to build a small pox hospital in 1881, 1883, 1886, and 1887, the Board of Supervisors refused to give the city authority to establish a hospital. In 1899 the supervisors agreed to accept the city's smallpox hospital as the county's and appointed W. T. Oppenheimer as health officer of the county. As early as 1893, the supervisors ac-knowledged that public health needs required the appoint-ment of someone to look after sanitary conditions in the county. W. T. Hockerworth was appointed to make inspec-tions, to report any dangerous conditions, and to superin-tend the removal of any dangerous matter. The next year, John Wooldridge was engaged to remove "night soil" from the suburbs for 70¢ per closet when packed in boxes and $1.00 when in loose condition. About the same time, R. C. Mosby, a constable in Brookland District, was directed to look after sanitary conditions and to order the removal of all night soil and other matter likely to create a nuisance. Sepa-rate contracts were negotiated to remove night soil until the General Assembly authorized the Board of Supervisors to adopt sanitary rules and regulations for that portion of the county lying within three-fourths of a mile of the corporate limits of the city. Using the C&O Railway tracks as the divid-ing line, the supervisors divided the county into two sanitary districts, and contracts were awarded in both the upper and lower districts, and special police were authorized to ascer-tain the sanitary conditions of all premises. Written notices of any violations were given to the occupants and the sanitary contractors. On July 6, 1900, the board passed a resolution requiring all persons within three-fourths of a mile of the city to have their water closets connected to boxes.[54]

The effects of urbanization were realized in other aspects of administration and county life. Special police had to be assigned to night duty in Barton Heights. Fire was always a hazard to life and property, and many buildings were lost because of the lack of fire-fighting equipment. By 1895 ar-rangements were made with the city to have the Richmond Fire Department respond to fires in the suburbs. The county reimbursed the city whenever the city firemen fought fires in the county. In the more rural areas of the county, fires had to be fought by volunteer bucket brigades. Their efforts usu-ally led to preventing the spread of fires, not saving a burn-ing building; usually the discovery of fire meant the total loss of the building. The city police also were available to assist in the preservation of order when they were "in attendance at a race-course, fair-grounds, base-ball or foot-ball park, and other places where athletic sports are held, situated within the county of Henrico." Restrictions were placed on keeping hogs in certain areas of the county near the corporate limits. The extension of existing cemeteries and the establishment of new ones were strictly regulated in 1900 because of suburban growth.[55]

Henrico was ending the century in a state of transition. There were many areas of the county that were rural, and they would not become urban communities until after World War II; but the demands of urbanization around the city and the introduction of the new technologies were forcing the county administration to cope with the changes that were occurring. One of the last actions of the board in 1900 was to approve the requests of the Richmond Telephone Company and the Newport News and Richmond Telephone and Telegraph Company to erect telephone poles and lines along the public roads of the county. Other changes were to come.

CHAPTER IX

Beginning the Fourth Century

Henrico County entered the twentieth century as a predominantly rural county with farming, coal mining, and industry as the foundation of its economy. The county government was in a state of transition as the people sought more services and the government attempted to finds ways administratively and financially not only to meet the needs expressed by citizens but also to plan for future expectations. The people of the county would see great changes in the political, economic, governmental, educational, and social life in Henrico.

The first decade of the century witnessed a revitalization of the coal industry in the western part of the county. The quality of soft coal and coke seams was found to be satisfactory, and the owners of the mines thought that the market for heating fuel warranted the investment of additional capital. Steps were taken to improve conditions in the mines and to provide more modern facilities aboveground. A branch rail line was built from the Chesapeake and Ohio Railway from Gayton Junction to the village of Gayton, and extensive preparations were made to mine coal. In addition to a new mine ventilation system, three 120 and two 200 horsepower boilers, a three-story breaker building used to break up the chunks of coal, boiler and engine buildings, machine shops, and storage bins were built to process and store the coal removed from the mines. Numerous houses were built for the workmen at a cost of $20,000. Commissary buildings, more commonly known as company stores, and stables were also built. As in the past, when mining was actively pursued in the area, the mining village became a self-contained community.[1]

A sad but historic event in the history of the county occurred on July 16, 1912, when William Donnelly, the shot-firer, lit his pipe and went to the face of No. 2 slope of the

Carbon Hill Mine (formerly Gayton Mine) owned by the Old Dominion Development Company, where he had discovered a gas pocket. Although he had been instructed to use a battery and connecting wires to fire a charge of dynamite to dislodge the coal, he decide to use a fuse. Remarking that "he had a hard shot to fire but was going to take a chance," he went to the face, charged the hole, and then ignited the first fuse with his pipe. Failing to light the second fuse from the first one, he struck a match. Both charges exploded, and so did the pocket of gas. Some ninety men were working in the mine at the time of the explosion, and all but ten were evacuated as word of the explosion spread. Superintendent A. G. McGowan rushed down the slope with a rescue party. When they reached the men, they forced some whiskey into each of their mouths and started to carry them out, but McGowan and some members of the rescue party were forced to give up the effort when they were overcome by the afterdamp. As word of the disaster spread, a large crowd of families and friends gathered at the mouth of the shaft. Delay in recovery of the injured led the crowd to pressure for answers, and the mine officials had to resort to force to keep the crowd from entering the shaft. Some of the badly burned miners, including a fifteen-year-old boy, managed to struggle to safety only to die later from their burns. William Donnelly and seven other miners lost their lives as a result of his careless act.

The presence of gas had always been a problem with the mines in the area, but it became increasingly difficult to prevent as the slopes were extended deeper. The shaft of No. 2 slope extended about 2,400 feet down on about a 35° incline. On the 1,350-foot level, a tunnel 900 feet long extended in an eastward direction. A ventilation fan nine feet in diameter had been set on a substantial concrete base and was well cased in concrete and metal with connecting ducts to remove the gases and stale air.[2] Numerous problems were encountered as the main shaft was extended and the danger of disaster increased. Before William Donnelly fired the fatal shot on July 16, 1912, a number of accidents and explosions had been reported. In January 1909 six men were killed in a careless accident. Seven men were killed from a gas and dust explosion on the main gangway on January 21, 1911, when

FORT HARRISON

LAUREL HILL

VARINA HIGH SCHOOL

TOWN HALL

OSBORNE

As Henrico's school population increased, the one-room schools were consolidated into centrally located multiroom structures. (Henrico County)

the men walked into a gas pocket with an open light. In January 1912 some men were putting in the first round of shots for the No. 3 tunnel and charged six holes with eight sticks of dynamite each. They left the box of dynamite 160 feet behind them in the tunnel. They returned to the box to set the charges off, and when they did so, the flame flashed back to the box and ignited the dynamite in it. Four men were killed outright and one died later. On June 19, 1912, four weeks before the fatal accident, a miner walked into a pocket of gas with an open light. The resulting explosion killed two men.[3]

Ironically, the General Assembly had provided for a mine inspector, but funds were not appropriated to fill the position. The only inspections that were made, and they were reported as being made on a daily basis, were conducted by the employees of the mine. Because of the dangerous conditions in the mine and the cost of upgrading the mining equipment and life-support system, the Carbon Hill mine was closed in 1912. A. G. Lucas, who worked in the mine and later served as a mine inspector, summed up the conditions when he wrote: "Apparently from the beginning there has been entire absence of knowledge on the part of successive owners of this property, in dealing with dangerous conditions, such as they have in this mine." He concluded that the stockholders and directors "should be informed of the dangerous conditions that prevail and the horrible conditions that have existed in the past. In fact, it seems incredible that such mining conditions should have been permitted in any state."[4]

Except for small pits mined for local consumption, deep-slope mining ceased in western Henrico except for one brief period. In 1920 a mine was opened, and as much as 50,000 tons of coal were mined the twelve months before it was closed in 1923. The availability of harder coal from southwestern Virginia and the abundance of coal from that region in the coalyards in the city made the possibility of reopening the Henrico mines remote. Some interest in the coalfield was expressed in the late 1920s, when representatives of the Du Pont Company were reported to be interested in the coal in connection with their Rayon Silk Department, and the Sement Solvay Company and engineers of Koppers Company

First Highland Springs School. (Henrico County)

of Pittsburg inspected the area in 1928. However, available information indicated that it was not practical to start coal-mining operations in the Richmond Basin. The crash of 1929 brought an end to any speculation that investment money would be available for beginning any new mining operations. In 1935 Frank R. Wadleigh, a mining engineer, completed an extensive study of the Gayton, Carbon Hill, and Cole-brook mines and concluded that although there no doubt was a large body of mineable coal of fair to good quality, the failure to mine it successfully was due to lack of knowledge and mining experience, ignorance and misunderstanding of underground conditions, insufficient financial resources, and misdirected use of the funds available. In later years the vacant buildings fell into decay. During World War II coal samples were taken from the area for experiments that only proved what had been discovered many years earlier—that the coal could not generate enough heat to be efficiently used in heating boilers. Interest in reopening the mines disappeared. The mines faded from memory and remained relatively unknown until a developer began constructing a housing subdivision in the area in the 1970s. Now the area that once was the scene of a vast mining camp has been suburbanized.[5]

In addition to the coal industry, farming was still the primary economic activity in the county at the turn of the century. It continued to be the backbone of the county's economy for the first half of the century. Farm products were varied and extensive. Corn, oats, wheat, and tobacco were the main crops, while barley and rye were also raised to some extent. Clover and timothy grasses and hay were also grown in quantity. Nurseries, orchards, and vineyards continued to occupy a part of the agricultural scene. Although market-gardening and trucking were carried on extensively, dairy and poultry farms increased and eventually captured 56 percent of the county's agricultural sales. Dairy farming became so extensive that Henrico became known as the "Dairy County of Virginia." A large number of the dairy cows were Holsteins, but Jerseys were also popular. The Curles Neck Farm was one of the largest dairy farms in the county, but there were many smaller farms. The agriculturalists in the county could boast in 1919: "Sanitary and up-to-date barns

Second Highland Springs School, erected in 1906. (Henrico County)

are found on every farm. A large number of herds of dairy cattle is registered, while nearly everyone has some registered dairy cattle. Many of the herds are tuberculin tested and are on the accredited list. Alfalfa fields may be found on nearly all dairy farms and ensilage plays an important part in the dairy ration." The same group noted that "the scarity of farm labor under present abnormal conditions has been obviated by the introduction of many tractors and other labor-saving machinery."[6]

There were 1,508 farms in the county in 1910, and the number increased to 1,841 in 1925. The depression period saw a drop to 1,032 in 1930 and then an increase to 1,318 in 1935. The figure fluctuated, but 1,311 farms were reported in 1945. The number dropped in 1950 to 1,049, to 715 in 1955, and to 518 in 1960. The number of cattle increased during 1910–60 from around 7,000 to 10,000, while the number of milk cows dropped from around 5,000 to 3,000. The number of hogs and pigs dropped from 5,800 to 3,600, and sheep and lambs dropped from 590 to 250. The year 1929 was the high point for milk production. On the other hand, the volume of chickens rose from 27,519 in 1919 to 124,181 in 1929 to 2,189,086 in 1959. As early as 1919, "poultry plants" were reported in the county. From 1944 to 1954 turkey farming was very active, but from a high of 7,657 in 1954, the volume dropped to 221 in 1959.[7]

The county farm demonstrator was very active in the county during the 1920s, and Henrico farmers took an active interest in a number of farming organizations on the county and state level. Many of the farmers were members of the Producers' Cooperative Exchange in addition to being involved in such organizations as the Henrico County Fair Association, County Council of Cooperation and Conference, Henrico Farmers' Union, Henrico Holstein Club, Farmers' Milk Producers' Association, and the Henrico County Health Unit. Farming clubs were also organized in the schools for the children, and the 4-H Club was very popular.

Education had a great deal to do with the increased production of Henrico's farms and with the ability of its citizens to compete in a diversified labor market. Henrico began the century with seventy-four white and thirty-six black schools. John K. Fussell was still superintendent, but his salary had

Chickahominy School, also known as Union Chapel, was located on the Oak Hall property. The school was closed in 1906. (Henrico County)

increased from $400 to $700 a year. He continued to serve until July 1, 1905, when Jackson Davis succeeded him. By 1904 there were only sixty-four schools in the county, but among these were three high schools—Fairfield High School, Barton Heights High School, Sidney High School—and four graded schools teaching some high school branches—Highland Park Graded School, Dumbarton Graded School, Glen Allen Graded School, and Yellow Tavern Graded School. The school population for that year was 5,908 whites and 4,524 blacks; however, the thirty-eight white schools had a seating capacity of 3,900 while the twenty-six black schools would only seat 1,850. The cost per pupil per month was estimated at $1.03. The amount per pupil for each district system was not reported; but in 1907 the cost each month per white pupil was $1.58, while per black pupil it was 76¢.

The one-room schoolhouse was still predominant throughout the county. Teachers like Jenny Culton would meet their students as they walked to school. She would begin her instruction even before they reached the schoolhouse and the bell was rung to call all the students to begin classes. In the one-room schoolhouse, the teacher was responsible for the instructional program for all the classes and for the general administration and maintenance of the building. With all the students in the one room, the teacher worked with one class while the others were studying. Mary Thompson Parks recalled that "when Miss Jenny was busy with another class, we would get out our geography book (because that was the biggest) and prop it up and eat those delightful, delectable, delicious sour pickles." The children were also responsibile for certain chores like bringing in the wood and coal and fetching the drinking water. A tin dipper was generally used for drinking water from the water bucket, but in some schools each student had his or her own tin cup. The entire student body took part in such activities as spelling bees and parent-night programs. The latter included special exhibits of student work, plays, recitations, singing, and speeches.[8]

When the schools were established, the prevailing philosophy had been to provide schoolhouses for basic educational needs where the students could easily attend. The need to expand the educational program and to provide additional opportunities for higher education necessitated facing the

Glen Allen School on Mountain Road. The left wing was built in 1899, and the right wing was added in 1901. (Henrico County)

problems of transportation and consolidation. The one-room schoolhouse could not provide the graded structure needed, and the population density in the county was not sufficient to support a number of larger schoolhouses. To provide the greatest opportunity for the largest number of students, the school trustees had to face the question of consolidation of small one-room schoolhouses into a centrally located multi-room school. Once the decision was made to consolidate, the trustees had to provide transportation for those students who lived too far away from the school to walk to it. In some areas of the county, consolidation was not the answer because of the distance between communities and schools and because of the local opposition to transporting children great distances. At the time, the idea of consolidation was an emotional issue, for some parents did not like the idea of closing their neighborhood school and transporting their children to a larger school in another neighborhood. Wagons were not used for transporting pupils until the school year of 1906–7. Three wagons were used in 1906. In 1907 fourteen wagons were employed regularly during the year, and an additional one was employed in bad weather. Streetcars and trains were also used to transport the children. The result of consolidation was the abandonment of some of the old one-room schoolhouses and the concentration of resources into the construction of better buildings. E. H. Russell, the state examiner on transportation and consolidation, reported during the first year of the effort that "whatever may have been the sentiment at the start, there is now practically no complaint on account of transportation or consolidation where it has been tried." Consolidation efforts resulted in larger enrollments, more regular attendance, and an increased interest on the part of parents and children. By 1910 the sum of $2,265.95 was expended for transportation.[9]

The individual school districts still were responsible for raising the funds to construct the buildings, and it was not unusual for them to ask the Board of Supervisors to place a bond referendum before the voters in their district to raise funds for the construction of new schools. The Fairfield school board constructed Highland Springs and Glen Lea schools in 1908 for $16,000 and $14,000 respectively. Two years earlier the school board had decided to close the old

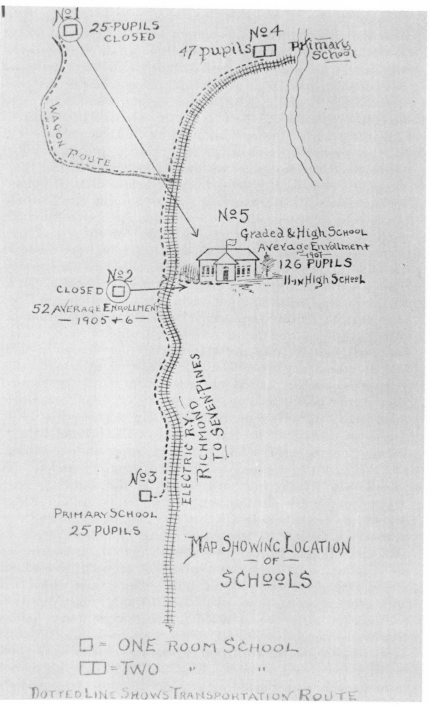

Map showing the consolidation of four one-room and two-room schools into one larger graded and high school. From *Annual Reports of the Superintendent of Public Instruction, 1905–1907* (Richmond, 1907), p. 42.

one-room Highland Springs School and the Union Chapel at Oak Hill and to transport the pupils to a newly constructed building at Highland Springs. Although this new building was "deemed too large at the time of its erection," it was overcrowded by the end of the first session when enrollment increased from 88 to 175. This led the district school trustees to plan for and construct the building which was opened in 1908 to "draw within its doors the grammar and high school pupils from the limits of Richmond to Seven Pines." This school, known as Highland Springs School and Highland Springs High School, was free to any pupil in the Fairfield District. In addition, a normal training class, established by the State Board of Education, was offered at the school, free to any pupil in the county. Several additions were made to the building in later years, and today it serves as the county's School Administration Building.[10] Glen Lea School began in 1876 in a little brick building on an acre of land bought from John Wright. Located between Harvie Road and Mechanicsville Turnpike, the school served the Creighton Road, Cool Lane, Highland Park, and Hanover County line area. The new building constructed in 1908 was on Mechanicsville Turnpike just beyond Montezuma Farms and was named after the farm the land was once a part of, Glen Lea. Here, the Glen Lea Improvement League was organized in 1908. These leagues were the forerunners of the present Parent-Teachers Associations. The Glen Lea Improvement League was the first to be organized in Henrico and was later referred to as "The Mother of Leagues" in the county.[11]

The year 1908 also witnessed the renovation of Ridge School in Tuckahoe District at the cost of $4,000. Ridge School was originally started in Ridge Baptist Church in 1867, and it continued under the system established under the Underwood Constitution of 1870. In 1882 the school moved out of the church and into a schoolhouse which had been erected on property purchased from Mr. and Mrs. Willis J. Carter. After a fire in 1903, classes were held in James Urban's general store at Three Chopt and Ridge Roads. After renovation, the two-room school was expanded in 1908 to offer two years of high school. In 1913 the high school students were transported by wagon to Barton Heights High School.[12]

Highland Park, an incorporated subdivision with its own school trustees, built the Highland Park School in 1909 for $35,000. That same year, in February, Varina School was dedicated with an address by Governor William H. Mann. The school was built as a result of the consolidation effort. Four one-room schools, Osborne, Fort Harrison, Laurel Hill, and Town Hall, were closed, and the pupils were sent to the new two-story school, which served both the elementary and high school for eleven years. In 1916 Varina School was accredited as a four-year high school. In 1920 a separate stucco building was built next to the two-story building with funds provided under the Smith-Hughes Act to foster the study of vocational agriculture. Varina School now had its own high school building and was known as the Varina Agricultural High School. Its first class had twenty students of whom seventeen were boys majoring in agriculture. The principal, George Baker, served as the first agricultural teacher, and the course was offered until 1941 when it was discontinued, the year after Baker retired.

The history of Varina School mirrors the growth of the public school system in the county. In 1928 its primary, or auditorium, building was completed, housing six classrooms and an auditorium with a seating capacity of six hundred. At that time, the stage in the auditorium usually served a dual function as stage and gymnasium. A separate shop building was constructed for industrial arts classes in 1934. Later, the old stucco high school building was condemned, and a new high school building and home economics cottage were completed in 1939. A small cannery building built near the athletic field in 1945 was converted into two classrooms in 1951. Two years later a new wing was added to the high school which included a cafeteria, seven classrooms, and administrative offices. The new Varina High School was built in 1962, and the old one became Varina Elementary School.[13]

The year 1907 witnessed several changes and innovations in Henrico's school system. Six consolidations were accomplished during the year, and even though the annexation of the previous year had reduced the tax base by about one-third and had removed several schools and a large number of children living in the annexed area, the county school authorities continued to improve the program. Two fairly

Ridge School. This building was replaced in 1907 by a two-story frame structure. (Henrico County)

Ridge School, erected in 1907. (Henrico County)

well equipped kindergartens, maintained by private funds, were opened. Manual training, industrial work, and a new method of instruction in drawing were introduced. That year the schools of the county received a bronze medal for an exhibit of "Buildings and Pupils' Work" at the Jamestown Exposition. The exhibit include a number of pictures of county schools, interior views showing the kindergarten at Barton Heights, maps, a copy of *The Dumbarton Bulletin*, studies of the butterfly, specimens of the cocoon and moth, dolls representing different nations dressed by the pupils, a dollhouse with furniture made by paper cutting and folding, and many other items from the county schools.[14]

After 1910 there was a marked increase in the number of schoolrooms with libraries and in the number of volumes in each room. Provisions were made for libraries in the newer school buildings, but the purchase and student use of the books was still considered a responsibility assumed by or delegated to the individual teacher. It would be several years before separate rooms were set aside for libraries and the library program was administered on a systemwide basis with professional librarians. Two new schools were built in 1912, Glen Allen and Short Pump, and in 1913 Barton Heights, White Oak, and Westwood were built. Glen Echo, High Park, Yellow Tavern, and Laurel were built in 1914. Glen Allen High School, Virginia Randolph, Coal Pits, Highland Springs, and Glendale were added to the system in 1915. The next year, Henrico adopted a compulsory attendance rule, and in Fairfield District an addition was made to Montrose and Woodville School was constructed. The costs per pupil enrolled in 1917–18 was $17.54 for white students and $8.54 for blacks. In 1919–20 it cost $247,370.09 to support the 81 white and 30 black schoolrooms in the county. In 1929–30 the cost was $600,690.52 to support 135 white and 46 black schoolrooms. During that year, the new Westhampton High School was built. The five accredited four-year high schools in 1930 were Glen Allen, Highland Springs, Varina Agricultural, Virginia Randolph Training and Westhampton. The one accredited junior high school was Dumbarton. Under the county School Board, the system continued to develop throughout the 1930s. By 1940 there were thirty public schools with a total enrollment of 7,817. The school libraries contained 35,887

Short Pump School around 1930. (Henrico County)

books. The total value of the white school plants was $1,220,000 as compared to $163,000 for the black schools. The 1940 per capita costs for students in elementary and high schools combined was $84.17 for whites and $54.42 for blacks.

Another significant innovation in the educational program occurred in 1908, and it provided the added dimension of teaching the students useful skills. At Mountain Road School that year Virginia Estelle Randolph gathered her pupils to plant twelve sycamore trees on the school grounds. The planting of the trees, named after the twelve disciples, was the start of a long tradition, Arbor Day. (Ten of the trees are still standing and have been named the first National Historic Trees in Virginia.) Miss Randolph, a native Richmonder born of ex-slave parents in 1874, had been educated in Richmond at Baker School and the Richmond Colored Normal School. She started teaching at the age of sixteen in Goochland County, and in 1892 she opened a one-room school for black children on Mountain Road which became know as the Old Mountain Road School. As a child, she had learned to cook and sew from her mother. She combined teaching of regular subjects with instruction in such practical skills as cooking, sewing, washing, gardening, and woodworking. She often said: "I believe in educating the hands, the eyes, the feet and the soul." In advocating the teaching of practical skills, she remarked "that a child must learn to use his hands. There is no need for a mind if you can't use your hands."[15]

Although she never admitted to having a philosophy of education, Miss Randolph considered that teaching a work skill was just as important as basic instruction in reading, writing, and arithmetic. In teaching work skills, she used what was at hand. She taught the girls how to make dresses and bed sheets using feed sacks after she showed the pupils how to wash them to make them soft. When she decided to teach the children how to cook, she borrowed a neighbor's cooking stove. Honeysuckle vines rather than expensive reeds were used for basket weaving. Sometimes she would use what the student made for instructional purposes: napkins were made from feed sacks, and then she used the napkins to teach them how to set a table and how to utilize them. She often spent her own money to provide needed supplies, and on one occasion she purchased gravel for the school-

Virginia Estelle Randolph (1874–1958). As a teacher and a social worker, she emphasized the importance of vocational education for youth. (Virginia State Library)

yard. At her home in Richmond, she opened a small store and sold some of the baked goods and handicrafts made by the children. The proceeds from the sales were used in her school.[16] An added dimension of Miss Randolph's teaching was her personal concern for the welfare of the children. She rode the railway to the Glen Allen station and walked to the school. As she walked, the children would join her. For those who were in need, she would open her house. Sometimes she had as many as twelve "guests" living in her home, and one time she had seventeen of her students staying with her. When asked about this, she recollected that over the years she gave a home to as many as fifty-nine children.

Superintendent Davis visited the Mountain Road School, and after seeing Miss Randolph at work, he was convinced that her ideas should be transmitted to other teachers. County funds were not available, so he applied for a grant from the Jeanes Fund, set up by Anna T. Jeanes, a Philadelphia Quaker, for the "one purpose of assisting in the Southern United States community, county or rural schools, for that great class of Negroes, to whom the smaller rural or community schools are alone available." Davis's application was approved, and the county received a grant for a salary of $40 a month for nine months. On October 26, 1908, Superintendent Davis wrote: "I have secured Miss Virginia E. Randolph (colored) as the industrial teacher for the Negro school in the county, and her work in this field began today. I think we are fortunate in securing her. . . . She possesses common sense and tact in an unusual degree and has the confidence of all who know her."[17]

The position entitled Jeanes Supervising Industrial Teacher thus became a reality. Davis believed that with Miss Randolph's experience and ability, she could organize a School Improvement League at each school and could encourage the black citizens to provide the industrial equipment. He was convinced that she would direct the work in a way that would build on the principle of self-help and that in doing so she would make use of whatever material she might have at hand. She was assigned to the staff of the county superintendent of schools to work with all the teachers of the Negro schools to help them improve their schools and communities and to develop the industrial arts. This rather revolutionary

Highland Springs. Visible in the picture are the electric railway station, post office, and stores. Note the price of lots on the billboard. From Andrew Morrison, ed., *The City on the James* (Richmond, 1893), p. 306.

idea became known as the "Henrico Plan." The state superintendent of public instruction reported in 1917 that "Henrico is known as the home of the industrial work, having had it on an organized plan longer than any of the other counties. . . . Virginia Randolph has served as industrial supervisor since 1908." In 1918 there were eighteen "Industrial Colored Schools" in the county, staffed by thirty teachers under Miss Randolph's supervision. During that year, there were 514 girls enrolled in the schools, and they preserved 8,258 quarts of fruits and vegetables produced from forty-nine gardens. Adult classes were also offered, and 75 women were enrolled; they preserved 5,147 quarts estimated in value at $2,681. The pupils were encouraged to join canning, poultry, and farming clubs. To defray the expenses of the clubs and the supplies for the different "industrial" courses, Miss Randolph established the Industrial Exchange on Broad Street in Richmond to sell the products of the canning and poultry clubs.[18]

In honor of her efforts, a school was named after her in 1915. To provide a residence for some of the pupils, the Anna T. Jeanes Memorial Dormitory was added in 1923. The two-room school building was destroyed by fire in 1929, but it was replaced the same year with a nine-classroom brick building with a seating capacity of 160. The building cost $33,000 and also had an auditorium that would seat 360 and boasted a central heating plant. The Caldwell-Creighton Home Economics Cottage was added in 1939. Virginia Randolph School became the only black high school in the county, and its pupils were required to travel long distances from all areas in the county. After the closing of all black schools, Virginia Randolph was reopened as the Virginia Randolph Education Centers. The Home Economics Cottage was set aside to house a museum in Miss Randolph's memory in 1970 and six years later was dedicated as a National Historic Landmark.

Miss Randolph continued working with Henrico students until she retired in 1949 after fifty-seven years of service. She died on March 16, 1958, and is buried on the grounds of the museum. She had received a number of awards during her life, including the Harmon Awared for meritorious achievement in education from the Southern Education

Foundation and the Certificate of Meritorious Service from Virginia State College. In 1960 the Virginia E. Randolph Elementary School was built. But, as D. Tennant Bryan said at her funeral: "No one person in our generation has done more to bring about goodwill and sympathetic understanding between the races in Virginia than has the late Miss Randolph. . . . Virginia Randolph's greatness is not to be measured in the honors that came to her during her life, but rather it is to be found in the boys and girls, men and women who, thanks to her interest and leadership, have attained the better life she, almost alone in her time, foresaw for them."[19]

In addition to the public schools, there were three private schools reported in the county by the superintendent of schools in 1911. The Methodist Orphanage under the Reverend A. B. Sharpe had three teachers and enrolled seventy pupils. The Masonic Home under E. W. Skinner enrolled sixty students and had two teachers. The third private school was Emanuel Parish School under Annie Kuyk with one teacher and forty students. Even with the expansion of the public school system, these private schools continued to increase their enrollment.

Jenny Culton's one-room public school was located at the forks formed by the junction of Cary Street Road, River Road, and Three Chopt Road. John Lennox's drugstore, housing the Rio Vista Post Office, was also situated at the forks, along with the Robert Browning's grocery and variety store and Lazarus Lee's blacksmith shop. Rio Vista was a little village in the area generally referred to as Westhampton. This quiet country community was accessible by trolley and was also the site of Westhampton Park, which soon became the home of the University of Richmond.[20]

Early in 1910 the Board of Trustees of the Richmond College appointed a committee on location to examine possible sites for the institution. M. M. Blacker's farm on Broad Street was under consideration by the board when the committee on location asked it to view some land in Westhampton. Although several members of the board were not overly impressed by the run-down condition of the old park, there was general agreement that the property could accommodate the new college for women, which became Westhampton Col-

Brickworks established by E. T. Mankin on Oakleys Lane. All the bricks were made by hand. The domed, hivelike brick kilns have been demolished. (Dementi Studios)

The Mankin mansion, built in 1921 with bricks manufactured on the site, still stands. (Dementi Studios)

lege, and Richmond College. It was also felt by some that the lake would serve as a natural barrier between the two institutions. Two hundred acres of land were given to the college by the Landstreet and Gunn syndicates with the condition that the college begin construction of buildings within eighteen months. Accepting this offer, the trustees purchased an additional parcel of ninety-three acres for $18,000.

On Christmas night, 1910, fire swept through the north wing, Ryland Hall, of the Main Building at the old site of Richmond College on Lombardy and Grace streets. Although the fire did not destroy the building, it did precipitate construction activity at the new campus. The plans called for a women's college building, an academic building, two dormitories for men, a refectory, science hall, president's house, assembly hall, stadium, powerhouse, water and sewer lines, landscaping and grading, and a spur line for the railroad. It took a couple of years to raise the money and to construct buildings, but by the fall of 1914 the move was made. When students and faculty viewed the new campus, they saw a single building, Westhampton College, on the south side of the lake. Among the pines on the north side of the lake, there was an administration building, two dormitories, a stadium, a refectory, a chapel, a science building, and several student recreational buildings. The two colleges continued to grow and to expand, and in 1920 the old Richmond College charter was amended and the name was changed to the University of Richmond. The land to which the university moved in 1914 remained a part of Henrico County until 1942 when the area was included in the city annexation of that year.[21]

The same year the college moved to Westhampton, 1914, the Chamberlayne School for Boys moved to Westhampton to an area called The Pines. This school had been opened in Richmond in September 1911 by Churchill Gibson Chamberlayne in his home at 3311 (now 3211) Grove Avenue with an enrollment of sixteen boys. The school was divided into an upper school of eight classes and a lower school, also called the Primary Department, of four classes. In addition, there was a "primer" class for boys six to seven years old. The two schools provided "continuous and systematic courses of instruction for boys from the time they are seven years old

Greenhouses and residence of W. A. Hammond, Brook Road. These were advertised as the largest greenhouses in the South. Approximately 95,000 square feet of land were under glass. From *Richmond, Virginia: Her Advantages and Attractions* (Richmond, 1895), p. 94.

until they are ready for college." The Chamberlayne School for Boys began to develop and grow at Westhampton. In addition to the buildings for the upper and lower schools, a gymnasium was constructed and houses were built for the headmaster and the staff. Academic studies were given priority, but the school also emphasized sports and compiled an enviable record in athletics. In 1920 the Chamberlayne School was acquired by the Episcopal church and incorporated into its system of church schools as St. Christopher's School.[22]

A second private school moved into the area in 1917. The Virginia Randolph Ellett School for girls had been founded by Miss Ellett in Richmond in 1890. As the enrollment increased, the school outgrew three successive buildings, so Miss Ellett moved the school to Westhampton in 1917. It was at that time that the school was incorporated as a Country Day School. At Westhampton, the lower school was originally housed in three cottages, and the upper school was housed in a private home. The purpose of the school was two-fold: "First, to develop the 'Country Day' and 'Open Air' plan at its best; and second, to offer a well-organized course of study from the beginning of a child's school life to the end of the high school years." The advantages offered by the school's new location were voiced in the school catalogue for the 1917–18 academic year: "The children spend the whole day in the country, breathing in the pure air and doing their academic work the better for it, spending their recreation in wholesome activities under expert guidance, instead of on the city streets and at the motion picture theatres, and learning how to study under careful supervision. They come home late in the afternoon with plenty of red blood in their veins, their work accomplished except in the case of the older girls, and eager to bring to the less fortunate members of their families the joys of their day in the country." In 1920 the school was acquired by the Episcopal church and became St. Catherine's. In 1923 it became a boarding school. Miss Ellett continued her association with the school until her death in 1939.[23]

In 1921 the Virginia Industrial School at School, present-day Laurel, moved to Beaumont, Goochland County. This school and the community in which it stood are an interesting part of Henrico's history. Originally, the area was known as Hungary Station; later it was called Jenningsville after a man named Jennings who laid off some lots at the cross-roads, and still later it was known as School because of the presence of the Industrial School. In 1933 the name was changed to Laurel because of the number of flowering trees in the area. The Virginia Industrial School was established by the state around 1899 as a boy's reformatory. Ranging in age from seven to eighteen, about 300 boys lived at the school in dormitories. They received three hours of instruction in the classroom and worked in the school garden, dairy barn, tailor shop, or blacksmith shop. The school was largely self-supporting. After the school was moved, some of the buildings were converted to other uses. Some of them are still standing, and plans for their future use are being developed. A public golf course was opened on the grounds in later years, and the old tailor shop served as the Laurel Gold Clubhouse until the golf course was closed in 1979.[24]

The offer made to Richmond College by Landstreet and Gunn syndicates was typical of actions taken by land developers. They hoped to sell surrounding land to the college staff and to city dwellers who wished to move to the country. Another attraction promoted by land speculators was the rail and trolley lines. Frequently, landowners and developers contributed financially to the construction of such lines both for the expected return on their investment from the profits earned in the operation of the line and to make their land more attractive to potential buyers. Those early carriers helped open the country land and made the city more accessible for those who worked in and around the city and for those who had business in the city. The early rail and trolley lines were the first step in urban mass transportation.

The street railways continued to extend out into the county as promoters and developers sought to lure home buyers. In 1905 the Richmond and Chesapeake Bay Railway was chartered to build an interurban electric railroad from Richmond to Washington and points north. The line was the first high-voltage, high-speed electric line in the state and was built from Richmond to Ashland with terminals at Laurel and Broad streets in Richmond and Maple and England streets in Ashland. A powerhouse containing the generators was located at Twelfth Street. In addition to running the trains, the company sold its surplus electricity to the town of Ashland. The line was never extended beyond Ashland, and the company terminated service on December 21, 1917. The shorter independently owned lines ran from the city to a specific suburban development, and as the system of lines developed, mergers occurred. Eventually, the independent lines were either disbanded or became part of a trolley network controlled by one company. The Westhampton Park Railway, chartered in 1900, constructed a line out Grove Avenue. In 1902 it merged with the Virginia Passenger and Power Company, which had acquired some of the independent lines in Henrico that same year. In 1904 the Virginia Passenger and Power Company merged with the Richmond Traction Company. After being placed into the hands of receivers, these two companies emerged as part of the Virginia Railway and Power Company. The Brookland Railway and Improvement Company continued to operate the lines to Barton Heights and Lakeside until it leased them to the Richmond Railway and Electric Company in 1927. The Northside Viaduct Company built the Fifth Street Viaduct over which the Highland Park Line ran until the line was leased to the Richmond and Manchester Railway Company, and eventually it became part of the Virginia Electric and Power Company. East of the city, the Richmond and Henrico Railway Company built a toll viaduct on Marshall Street and a viaduct at Spring Street and ran a line along Marshall Street to Fulton. This company was chartered in 1906 and continued to operate until it became a part of the Virginia Railway and Power Company in 1916. This later corporation had been organized by Frank Jay Gould and Associates after the consolidation of several independent companies in 1909. In 1925 the Virginia Electric and Power Company acquired the Virginia Railway and Power Company operation and added several other streetcar lines and the Richmond Rapid Transit Company, which had started bus service in 1922. The introduction of buses eventually led to the abandonment of some of the rail lines. For many citizens of the county it was a sad day when the lakeside trolley line was abandoned in 1929 and buses replaced the old trolley cars. This was just the beginning. Buses provided a cheaper and more flexible

Charles F. Senff mansion, Curles Neck Farm. (Virginia State Library)

means of transportation. It was not long after the Virginia Transit Company took over the operations of the Virginia Electric and Power Company in 1944 that the streetcar lines were abandoned; the last of the cars were burned in 1949. The Westhampton line was abandoned in 1947, and the Ginter Park and Highland Park runs terminated in 1949. The fixed-track streetcar with its high maintenance and up-keep gave way to the more mobile and more efficient bus. Today citizens of the county can park their cars in fringe parking areas at no cost and ride the buses of the Greater Richmond Transit Company.[25]

Several rail projects were undertaken in the county during the early part of the century with various degrees of success. In 1911 the Henrico and Chesterfield Railway Company was chartered to connect Ridge Church in western Henrico with the village of Bon Air in Chesterfield County. Tracks were laid on the South Hampton Bridge (also known as the West-ham Bridge) across the James, but the line, which was under-taken to promote the sale of country lots, was never com-pleted. The old Seven Pines Railway, which had been acquired by the Virginia Railway and Power Company and by its succes-sor, Virginia Passenger and Power Company, was offered for sale to the Richmond Urbanna and Peninsular Railway Com-pany in 1911. This sale was never concluded, and in 1912 the line was sold to the Richmond and Rappahannock River Rail-way Company. The idea of a deepwater terminal at Urbanna connected by rail with Richmond had been a topic of specula-tion for a number of years, but it was not until Joseph E. Willard provided the financial backing that work was started on such a project. The first section of the line was built from Richmond through the battlefields of Gaine's Mill and Cold Harbor to Rock Castle on the Pamunkey River. This part of the line was completed in July 1914. A connector line with the C&O Railway was constructed in Henrico for the transfer of freight cars from one line to the other. This steam railroad was never completed beyond Pamunkey Station, and the vol-ume of freight business never reached the expectations of the promoters. On December 17, 1917, the line was sold at auc-tion. Willard, who had backed the line financially and who had served as its president, was the high bidder. He had chartered a new company, Richmond and Seven Pines Rail-

Mowing hay, Curles Neck Farm. (Virginia State Library)

way, and wanted the abandoned and dismantled Seven Pines line owned by the Rappahannock line. Willard's Richmond and Seven Pines Railway was purchased by the United States Housing Corporation in September 1918 to provide rail service to a housing community under construction for the workers at the new federal powder-bagging plant. In 1920 Oliver J. Sands organized the Richmond and Fairfield Railway Company and purchased the old Seven Pines streetcar line from the government. The Sandston Railway Company assumed control of the line in 1926, and in July 1933 the streetcar line was replaced by a busline, and service on the old Seven Pines line was terminated.[26]

The rail lines helped develop the county, brought in new people, and made the citizens more mobile. The growth in population created some problems and placed greater demands for services on the Board of Supervisors. Early in this century, the board resolved some of the sanitary conditions by requiring the removal of hogs within a three-quarter-mile area around the city. At the request of the city or private citizens in the county, water and sewer lines were extended into certain areas of the county. The welfare of citizens and prisoners also were addressed. Each overseer of the poor was allowed $5 a month for poor families, and provision was made to house some cases at the Richmond Alms House and on the county poor farm. An operating room was authorized at the Alms House "not to exceed the sum of $75." At the county jail provision was made for padding a cell for confinement of lunatics. A sanitary force was established, and $2,000 was appropriated for cleaning the areas of the county adjacent to the city. In 1902, by act of the General Assembly, all dogs had to be licensed. The collections of the 5¢-license fee produced an administrative nightmare in Henrico. Finally, Charles W. Childrey and L. H. Kemp were paid $185 for listing 3,700 dogs in the county.[27]

In January 1902 William J. Vaughan introduced a new way of handling his rural mail route. As rural carrier no. 2, Vaughan carried the mail on Route No. 2 in Tuckahoe District. He traveled out Cary Street Road to Ridge Church, then to Lawrence's Store, and back to the post office in Richmond. The route covered 26½ miles. During the cold and wet weather, he was exposed to the elements in his open buggy, so he had

Barns and dairy herd, Curles Neck Farm. (Virginia State Library)

Thomas Duke build a wagon with closed sides and sliding glass doors to separate the driver's seat from the interior mail-sorting area. A small heater kept him warm as he handled the reins through holes in the front panel. Post office officials liked Vaughan's wagon and ordered several for other routes.[28]

The road situation continued to occupy the attention of the supervisors. In support of the Good Roads Association, the board authorized $250 for the associational meeting in Richmond. Requests for new roads and repairs to old roads were handled through the district road commissioners, but to insure accountability, the board resolved that no expenditure was to be incurred for construction of roads without its approval. Next, it required that any petitioner for a new public road submit a report to the board with an analysis of all factors involved. Soon after this ruling, the board directed that a deposit of $30 be filed with any road petition. If the road was established, the petitioner would be reimbursed; if the petition was rejected, the petitioner forfeited the deposit. Even with this provision, roads, bridges, and culverts continued to occupy the board's attention.[29]

Although the county granted the city permission to run gas, water, and sewer lines along the public roads at no expense to the county, it fought tenaciously when the city attempted to annex land from it. When the city expressed a desire to do so in 1902, the board resolved itself into a committee to work with a committee of citizens from the county to resist extension of the city's corporate limits. The city notified the board officially of its intentions in 1905, and the supervisors appointed an engineer to collect data to make a proper defense on the part of the county. Under the new state constitution of 1902, the city could bring suit in court, and when it did, the county employed an attorney. By decree of the Henrico County Circuit Court, entered February 17, 1906, 4.45 square miles of the county on both the eastern and western ends of the city were awarded to the city. Under the decree, the city had to compensate the county.

A problem that would later recur confronted the board in 1906. Sanitary conditions at the county jail necessitated enlargement of the facility. Accordingly, an architect was employed to draw plans for remodeling the jail at a cost not to exceed $10,000. It was decided that the jail should include

Haystacks, Curles Neck Farm. (Virginia State Library)

cells with a capacity for about 116 prisoners, two burglar-proof cells, two insane cells, a hospital, a women's department, witness cells, and a place for juveniles. Generally, the building was to have sanitary and safe conditions, proper ventilation, and a heating system independent of the court-house. But Judge Carter Scott refused to accept any plans for remodeling and directed that a new jail be constructed. Accepting the plan of Stewart Jail Works for a new jail at $48,000, the board received approval from the court to issue the necessary bonds. Temporary quarters had to be found for the prisoners; they were housed at the Richmond jail for three cents per day while the new building was under construction, and two iron cells from the old jail were placed in the basement of the courthouse as holding cells for prisoners during court sessions. Upon notification from the architect, the board refused to accept the concrete work and ordered that the walls be torn down. An inspector was hired to insure that the concrete used in the new walls was mixed to specifications. When Stewart Jail Works submitted a statement amounting to $1,380.40 for extra work, the board allowed $160.77 and rejected the balance.

Exactly when the first automobile traveled over the county's roads is not known. However, by July 3, 1906, traffic conditions became so dangerous that the Board of Supervisors adopted the provisions of an act of the General Assembly of March 17, 1906, requiring the registration of and regulating the running of automobiles, locomobiles, and other vehicles powered by other than animals. The addition of the automobile to the wagons and other horse-drawn vehicles on the county roads eventually created problems. The crisscrossing of roads, railroads, and streetcar tracks added to the complexity of the situation. When the fairgrounds moved from Broad Street to Boulveard early in the century, there were no real traffic problems until the pedestrians, streetcars, trains, wagons, and automobiles converged during the fair. Special police had to be sent; wooden bridges and sidings had to be constructed. Each problem tended to be settled separately. Finally, the board appointed a general superintendent of roads to coordinate operations and road maintenance. Surfacing materials did not provide a cover hard enough to resist narrow-width wheels and tires, so restrictions were set on the width of the size of wagon

'LIBERTY DAY'

Opening
U. S. Gov't
Bag Loading Plant

SEVEN PINES
October 12, 1918
1:30-5 P. M.

ADMISSION BY PASS ONLY

Airship Flights—Military Band
Interesting Speakers

Hon. Josephus Daniels, Secretary of the Navy
WILL BE PRESENT

Watch Newspapers for
Announcement of
Special Trains

Frederic H. Tippet

WOMEN'S MUNITION RESERVE

Billboard poster announcing the opening of the bag loading plant at Seven
Pines. (Virginia State Library)

wheels and tires. State funds made available by the General Assembly were accepted and used to improve the surface of the county's roads. A more mobile society required a more mobile police force. Special police were mounted on horses to assist in patrolling the roads, and telephones were placed in the homes of some of the officers. A pair of bloodhounds was requested from the state for detection of criminals, and the sheriff was authorized to employ as many men as necessary at $2.50 a day to assist the police in arresting persons violating the speed limits for automobiles. When the board established road use regulations, it specified that it was unlawful to leave glass, metal, nails, etc., on roads. The speed limit was set at twenty miles per hour except on curves, down sharp inclines, or at intersections, where it was ten miles per hour. Brakes and a horn were required, along with one white light on the front that would throw a beam one hundred feet and one red light in the rear to illuminate the tag. Both lights had to be on from one hour after sunset until one hour before sunrise. Fines for speeding violations were set at not less than $2.50 and not more than $50.

The increased traffic on the unsurfaced roads necessitated action by the board. Funds for road projects had to be raised by levies. However, additional funds were received from the city when the old problem of annexation was brought up again. In 1914 the city of Richmond more than doubled in size when it annexed 12.21 square miles from Henrico and Chesterfield. The district of Ginter Park, incorporated in 1912 with John Garland Pollard as its mayor, was included in this annexation, along with Barton Heights, Laburnum, Highland Park, and part of Bellevue on the north side. On the west end, the city line was extended to, and in some sections beyond, the beltline railroad. Along a narrow corridor northeast and east of the city, just beyond Fairmount and Fulton Hill, which had been annexed in 1906, the city acquired the Oakwood and Evergreen cemeteries and a part of Woodville. The Board of Supervisors withdrew its appeal of the annexation decree when the city agreed to compensate the county by appropriating $100,000 for permanent improvement of highways leading to and from the city. In addition, the city agreed to pay for the school property taken and to assume all school indebtedness for the schools in the annexed area. The board divided the $100,000 by designating

Some Henricoans who served in World War I saw action on the Western front and, after the Armistice, traveled throughout Europe. Pfc. Clarence R. Lechler poses in front of some barges on the Rhine. (Virginia State Library)

specific sums to be used on fifteen different roads from River Road on the west to Osborne Turnpike on the east. To supervise the work, the board contracted with the state highway commissioner for the services of an engineer at $75 per month. Rather than hire a second engineer, the board authorized the purchase of a Ford automobile at $515 to enable the engineer to travel and supervise all of the projects. The car was to be sold after the work was completed.

The county was receiving some state aid for road construction and maintenance as well as money from local levies and fees from automobile tags, but the roads were not surfaced. Mud and ruts were common sights. It became necessary to declare unlawful the use of the public roads when they were soft or spongy unless the size of the load was not in excess of the amount specified for the size of wheels on the vehicle. Any vehicle with wheels less than three inches wide could not carry more than 2,000 pounds. A three-inch-wheeled vehicle could carry up to 4,000 pounds, and a four-inch-wheeled vehicle could carry up to 5,000. A 6,000-pound load was the maximum allowed, and the tires had to be twelve inches wide. On November 12, 1918, the state highway commissioner advised the board on the condition of the roads in the county and specified certain highways that would be taken into the state highway system to be maintained by the state. He also advised that the state would take over maintenance of other roads if the county provided the necessary supplies for the maintenance work. The county roads were still under the district road commissioners, but the Board of Supervisors administered the road program through its authority to approve funding. The increased activity of the state in developing the state road system and in establishing regulations on the users removed some of the authority and responsibility from the local jurisdictions. As the state began assuming this responsibility and others that transcended county and city boundaries, the local units of government could concentrate on internal matters.

The entry of the United States into World War I affected Henrico, as it did the rest of the Commonwealth. The Board of Supervisors appropriated $100 for an armory for Company H, Fourth Regiment at Highland Springs. Red Cross auxiliaries were organized at Ridge Church, Fort Harrison,

Monument marking the area where Gen. J. E. B. Stuart was mortally wounded during the battle of Yellow Tavern, May 11, 1864. (Virginia State Library)

Glen Allen, New Bridge Church, and by many other church and local civic groups. The children took part in patriotic programs, cultivated gardens, raised money for relief work, and collected old clothes and books. Many of the women organized knitting circles and made caps, leggings, and sweaters for the soldiers. Conservation of food and fuel was practiced by many. A war savings stamp campaign was launched to raise $350,000 from citizens in the county in conjunction with the national war bonds campaign. By August 10, 1918, $82,000 had been raised, and a second campaign was underway to raise the balance.[30]

Through the efforts of K. T. Crawley, president of the Chesapeake and Ohio Railroad, negotiations were entered into between the Du Pont Engineering Company and the federal government for the construction of a powder-packing plant in the Seven Pines area. Between the railroad, where the army had established Fort Lee, and Seven Pines, the federal government purchased a twelve-square-mile area. On August 17, 1918, the government announced that it intended to purchase an additional four hundred acres adjoining the powder-packing plant for the construction of approximately two thousand homes for housing the workers to be employed in the plant. The Richmond Real Estate Exchange was directed to appoint a committee to appraise the property at its prewar value to discourage speculators from trying to move in and profit from the purchase.[31]

When the plant was proposed, it was estimated that it would take fifteen months to complete the work. Within three months, the tangle of woods and vines had been cleared by an army of some six thousand workers. As one reporter noted: "Industry has come. The sleepy days are over for the old battle site." Row after row of warehouses were built, and miles of railroad track were laid "to create the mightiest munition-packing plant in all the world." The construction work proceeded on schedule with a few minor interruptions. One such interruption occurred on August 15 when Sheriff W. Webb Sydnor, accompanied by his deputies and several officers from the U.S. Army, arrested 163 men on the charge of evading the draft law. The men were turned over to the military authorities at Camp Lee, near Petersburg, where they were held until friends or relatives

Architect's drawing of the bungalows for the Montessori and lower schools for the Virginia Randolph Ellett School. The buildings were started early in 1917 and were ready for occupancy by the beginning of the 1917–18 school year. From *The Virginia Randolph Ellett School Catalogue, 1917–1918* (Richmond, 1917), p. 2.

arrived with their registration cards or other evidence that they were not in violation of the law. When the influenza epidemic hit the county in September and October, all churches and schools were closed, and members of the families in which there was one or more flu cases were asked to remain at home. A number of the workers at the plant contracted the disease, and for several weeks large numbers of them were unable to report for work.

In September, the federal government decided to exercise its option to buy and operate the Richmond–Seven Pines electric rail line as an auxiliary to the powder-packing plant. The traffic on the line had increased greatly. City residents traveled it daily to and from work at the plant. Plans were proposed to build a giant rail terminal in the city which would include a new passenger depot. Additional acreage was secured by the federal government near the terminus of the electric line for the construction of houses for the workers. At this six-hundred-acre site, the United States Housing Corporation began constructing the town of Fairfield. The plans called for 230 six-room (with bath) bungalows, several community buildings, and utilities. Only about half of the houses were completed before the armistice was signed.

Even before work was completed on the entire plant complex, women in the county and city were encouraged to enlist in the Women's Munition Reserve. By doing so, they had "the right to don a uniform and to demonstrate their loyalty to the nation by working with their own hands at the United States bag-loading plant, No. 3, at Seven Pines." Mrs. Westmoreland Davis, wife of the governor of the Commonwealth, accepted the presidency of the reserve, and on August 22 twenty-five of the women were called into active service to begin their training course at Plant No. 3. A Munition Workers' Special was placed in operation on the C&O to carry the workers to and from the plant. By August 29 some two thousand women had volunteered to serve, and on that day Mrs. Davis dressed in the work uniform and, carrying her lunch, journeyed to Plant No. 3 to enter the training school to become a full-fledged munitions worker.[33]

Elaborate plans were made for the formal opening of the plant on October 12, but they had to be abandoned because

Unable to obtain sufficient money for the proposed large central buildings, the trustees of the Virginia Randolph Ellett School secured a house very near the school grounds to accommodate the upper school. From *The Virginia Randolph Ellett School Catalogue, 1917–1918* (Richmond, 1917), p. 17.

of the prevalence of influenza. Josephus Daniels, secretary of the navy, was the principal speaker at the ceremony, which was under the auspices of the Women's Munition Reserve. The day was designated "Liberty Day," and the workers were given a half-day off. After the flag-raising ceremony and the patriotic speeches, members of the reserve conducted tours through the plants.

Activity at the plant continued for a short time after the armistice was signed, but many workers began leaving before official word was received that the plant would be closed. On November 26, the Du Pont Engineering Company announced that it had been advised to cut production by 50 percent, and the process of laying off employees began in earnest. Those who were salaried employees received a cash bonus, while all others were given money for their transportation home. When word was received that the plant would be converted into an ordnance depot, arrangements were made to recall the employees. These plans never materialized to the degree that was hoped for, and the plans for revitalizing the plant site, which by now included about fifty miles of track and many miles of improved roads, were eventually abandoned.

The men of the county had responded willingly to their county's call. On July 23, 1917, the *Times-Dispatch* announced that Henrico's quota for the first national draft was 138 men. Many of the men from the county were sent to Camp Lee, below Petersburg, where they received their basic training. The men from Henrico saw their military service as a duty to their country. Joseph Ewell Perross of School remarked: "I was never in favor of military or naval discipline, although at the beginning of the [war, when the] U.S. declared war, I was perfectly satisfied with my lot." William James Gentry of Glen Allen felt that "it was every man's duty and I only did my duty." Pleasant Edmund Gentry of Glen Allen "thought it my duty I owed to America." Military training and camp life were new experiences for most of the men from the county, and French Graham, who was a rural letter carrier before the war, considered his camp experiences "mentally demoralizing" and "physically beneficial," while Pleasant Edmund Gentry felt that camp life "taught me how to live under any condition and complain about nothing." From the training

Main School Building · Old Athletic Building · Main Dormitory · New Gymnasium

The Chamberlayne School Cadet Company, 1917–18. The school curriculum included a course on military training during the two sessions of 1917–18 and 1918–19. A school company was formed and drilled by the school commandant, Capt. C. G. Puller, Jr. From *The Chamberlayne School Catalogue, 1919–1920* (Richmond, 1919), frontispiece.

camps, those who were assigned to units were sent to France where many of them saw action in the Muese-Argonne offensive in September 1918. Cpl. Martin Luther Harris of Highland Springs and Pfc. Clarence R. Lechler of Dumbarton and others were wounded during that offensive. Pfc. Lechler remained with the army of occupation. His experiences under fire taught him "that we are all dependent in so much as we need the support and protection of our fellow man. In unity there is strength." Pfc. Perross was wounded at Belicourt, France, September 30, 1918. When asked about his impressions under fire, he replied: "No impressions to any extent, for a little while under shell fire harden a fellow to the extent of being a Savage Indian." In all, the Henrico County Draft Board inducted 518 men and sent them to camp. Of this total, 34 were rejected and discharged.[34]

When the men from Henrico returned after the war, they generally resumed working where they had been employed before they left. There was no great impact on the county except in the Seven Pines area where the powder-bag plant was constructed. The American Locomotive Company works just outside the city limits were converted for the production of munitions, as were other plants in and around Richmond, but these companies reconverted to peacetime production.

The town of Fairfield, built by the United States Housing Corporation for the workers and military personnel at the powder plant, was only partially finished when the war ended. Oliver J. Sands, heading a group of investors, purchased the property and buildings for resale. The presence of the streetcar line made it an inviting opportunity for families of moderate means, and before long the town began to develop. The old hospital building was converted and served as a school and community center until 1939 when the first section of the present Sandston Elementary School was opened. North of the highway, opposite the bungalows built by the Housing Corporation, the houses were larger and a little more expensive. Locally this area is referred to as Strainersville, and it is said that the name was given to the area because the purchasers had to strain a little to pay for their homes. As the town began to develop, the citzens voted to change the name from Fairfield to Sandston in honor of Oliver J. Sands.[35]

Byrd Airport shortly after Pitcairn Aviation of Virginia, Inc., began operations. (Virginia State Library)

The first flight of a heavier-than-air craft witnessed by Henricoans and Richmonders was made at the fairgrounds in 1909. Foster Willard flew his Curtiss Golden Flyer around the grounds after his first attempt failed. For several years, such flights were regular occurrences at the annual fair. Before a publicly owned airfield was established, local aviation enthusiasts used a landing strip at the end of Chamberlayne Avenue known as Charles Field. This open-pasture landing field gave way to residential development. In later years, a small private airfield known as North Field served local pilots. This too had to give way to housing, and today the North Field community of Chamberlayne Farms occupies the site. In 1927 the Richmond City Council purchased 100 acres and leased an additional 300 acres east of the city for a municipal airfield. This was to become Byrd Field. The city built two runways and a frame administration building. The airport was officially opened on October 15, 1927, when Colonel Charles A. Lindbergh circled and landed in the *Spirit of St. Louis*. Thousands of citizens came to watch, and as air traffic increased, airplane-watching became a favorite Sunday pastime. The city leased the field to Pitcairn Aviation, and it became a stop on a mail route flown by Pitcairn. The company became Eastern Air Transport, and later Eastern Air Lines. The airport was turned over to the army during World War II and was used as a fighter-training center. During the war, the army added improvements and 1,568 acres to the airport, which had grown to 1,274 acres. When the army returned the field to the city, the county claimed rights to the land, but it lost the fight when the War Assets Administration awarded the property to the city.

The year 1927 was also a significant year in the evolution of county government, as the Board of Supervisors sought administratively to meet the needs of the citizens. The western and northern areas of the county had traditionally been the growth areas. In the West End, a number of smaller communities had contracted to construct their own water and sewer systems. Some members of the communities wanted to take the next step and incorporate, while others in the area opposed the idea. When some citizens of Westhampton Village petitioned the board to be incorporated as the town of Westhampton, the board refused the request be-

A promotional photograph depicting the three methods of transportation available in the county in 1929. (Virginia State Library)

cause a majority of the citizens within and adjacent to the community opposed any steps to incorporate. By act of the legislature, the board was given authority to establish Sanitary District No. 1 on April 11, 1927. On April 20, the board resolved to issue bonds for $300,000 to construct and operate a water supply, sewerage, light, and gas system within the district. After entering into an agreement with an engineer to build the system, the board purchased the Hampton Gardens and Gordon Wallace sewer systems and acquired the necessary land. A contract was negotiated with the city for water for the district, and $5,500 was approved for fire apparatus for use in the district. In July 1930 a contract for the construction of a firehouse at Westhampton was approved, and on September 2, 1930, a resolution calling for the creation of a fire department for Tuckahoe District was approved. The resolution called for employing a regularly paid fireman and created a volunteer force as a separate organization. The process of developing and implementing the plans for Sanitary District No. 1 were followed by ordinances providing for building permits in subdivided areas and the establishment of zoning districts and a Zoning Commission for the county. Additional sanitary districts were established in later years, and they were later reduced in size as the population density increased.

As the county administration attempted to cope with the growing demands for services, it was apparent that the Board of Supervisors could not keep pace. The funds of the county were controlled by the commissioner of revenue and the treasurer, both of whom were elected. The Board of Supervisors served part-time and could not keep abreast of all the programs. In response to citizen demands, a special grand jury was impaneled to investigate the complaints. The grand jury in January 1932 declared the county financially sound and found the county offices to be efficiently operated.

The report of the auditor of public accounts for 1931–32 disagreed sharply with the grand jury's findings. The auditor found a number of careless accounting practices, some of which were the product of inefficient administrative management and some of which were the result of questionable ethical practices. One of the four district road superintendents had a working fund which he mingled with his per-

BIRDSEYE VIEW DRAWING OF "DUMBARTON PLAZA"

AIRPLANE VIEW OF CABELL RESIDENCE AND LAWN

NOTE — DIAGRAM OF SUBDIVISION IS NOT MEANT TO BE ACCURATE BUT MERELY TO GIVE GENERAL IDEA OF STREET AND LOT LINES.

Dumbarton Plaza was a "scientifically subdivided" community proposed on land at the corner of Dumbarton and Staples Mill roads. The property, including the James Branch Cabell residence, was offered at auction on January 10, 1928. (Virginia Commonwealth University)

sonal funds. No sinking fund had been set up to retire the bond issue for Sanitary District No. 1. Apparently some of the supervisors felt that the district would eventually be annexed by Richmond and the debt would be Richmond's problem. Several other debt funds did not have enough to pay off the indebtedness. In addition to a $4,000 shortage, it was reported that the treasurer was employing some unusual accounting practices. Members of the Board of Supervisors did not escape the auditor's eye; it was discovered that they were selling county supplies and deducting the money received from their paychecks. The auditor concluded: "it is apparent to us that the volume and variety of the county's activities are such that the affairs of the county are not, and probably cannot be, properly administered under the form of government that has been followed. The county is practically an urban one. . . . And there is every indication that day to day administrative control, which is not had under present form of government, is necessary for the accomplishment of efficient administration of the county's affairs." He considered Henrico as a prime example of "the indefiniteness of responsibility that is inherent in the Board of Supervisors form of government."[36]

The General Assembly of 1932 passed legislation authorizing counties to adopt the county manager form of government. The Board of Supervisors would retain responsibility for determining the policies of the county, enacting local legislation, levying taxes, making appropriations, and directing and controlling in a general way the activities of county agencies; however, it would place the county's day-to-day business operation entirely in the hands of a county manager whom it selected. The county manager was to be a full-time officer, serving at the pleasure of the board, who would carry out the policies determined by the board and coordinate the business affairs of the county by proper administrative procedures. The new form of government could be adopted only if approved by the voters. Forming the Henrico Citizens League, a group of citizens organized to support a referendum on the issue. In September 1933 the voters of the county let it be known that they wanted a change by a vote of 1,683 to 1,321.

Under the county manager form of government as it was

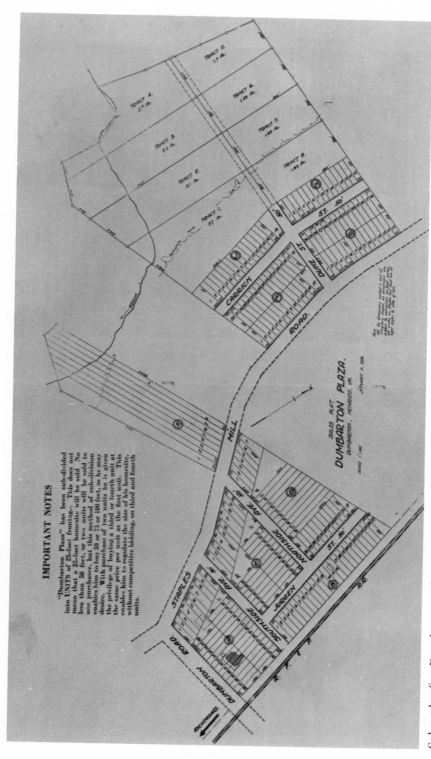

Sales plat for Dumbarton Plaza, 1928. (Virginia Commonwealth University)

originally outlined in the legislative act, each district was to be represented by a supervisor who was to be elected at large. The Henrico Citizens League next mounted a campaign to elect candidates who were sympathetic to the new form of government. The league was successful in its campaign and elected all four of its candidates in November 1933. The former incumbents, believing that they were entitled to serve the complete four years for which they had been elected in 1931, filed suit. Judge Julien Gunn agreed and ruled in their favor, but the Virginia Supreme Court of Appeals reversed his ruling, and the new board was allowed to sit. Thus Henrico had the distinction of being the first Virginia county to adopt the county manager system.

The new form of government went into effect on March 25, 1934. Willard F. Day, former city manager of Staunton, was Henrico's first county manager. When the new form of government was adopted, the elected positions of commissioner of revenue and treasurer were abolished, and the two positions were consolidated into a director of finance, filled by appointment of the county manager. Before Day's appointment, the county had decided to maintain its own roads under the newly established Department of Public Works; consequently, the county roads did not come under the State Department of Highways. The Department of Public Works was assigned many unrelated functions as the new government began to cope with the county's needs. It was administered for many years by County Engineer Tazewell Ellett. The department was responsible for maintaining the water and sewerage systems, building inspection, fire protection, and assisting the zoning and planning boards. Separate departments were established after World War II to administer these operations, and Public Works assumed its original function of maintaining the roads. The four district road forces were abolished and a countywide system was adopted. This was not done with ease, however, and Day found that some of the old ways died hard.

The county manager initiated a program to centralize the purchasing of supplies used by all departments, and many other steps were taken to centralize the county administration during particularly hard economic times. Day instituted the practice of monthly and annual reports, and many of the changes and growth problems are reported therein. The Depression affected the entire economy of the county, and frequent requests were made for emergency relief funds. Civil works service projects were instituted to provide citizens with jobs; painting and plastering jobs at the courthouse, jail, and schools were available as well as road and septic tank work. Many county citizens found work under the WPA roadbuilding program. Although many were severely hit by the economic depression, the agricultural base of the county's economy served to reduce the impact. In the middle of the 1930s, the city of Richmond paid the final payments on the 1906 and 1914 annexations, totaling $30,530.01. Despite hard times, citizens of the county were not immune to popular crazes that provided opportunities to win cash prizes. However, the board found it necessary to prohibit marathons, walking contests, and other physical endurance contests between midnight and 8:00 A.M.

Opponents of the manager form of government continued to speak out against it and organized their own citizens' organization, the Henrico County Good Government Association. This group spoke out against the economics of the manager form, and opposed the method of electing the supervisors at large. They pointed out that in the 1935 election the pro–county manager candidates won in Fairfield and Brookland districts without receiving a majority of votes in those districts. Battle lines were drawn between the Good Government forces and the Citizens League, and in 1937 a referendum was held on the question of abolishing the county manager form of government. The Citizens League won a second victory on the issue, but in both Brookland and Fairfield, a majority of the voters were in favor of returning to the old system of government. Although the Good Government Association failed to change the form of government, they did win a victory when the General Assembly passed legislation to amend the county manager act by providing that supervisors were to be elected by district rather than at large. Once this issue was settled, a period of calm and stability settled over the county. This was to be shattered when the country was compelled to enter World War II.

CHAPTER X

Vibrant Urban County

Late on a peaceful Sunday morning while Henricoans were busily preparing for the day's activities, the word quickly spread that the American fleet at Pearl Harbor had been attacked. Like so many Americans, citizens of the county turned on their radios to hear the latest reports. They knew it meant war, and doubtless many of them knew that their lives would never be the same. Although the scenes of battle were played out on other soil, the county and its citizens would feel the impact of the war. Before it was over, men from the county would serve on foreign fields in all branches of the armed services.

At the time, Henrico officials were awaiting the implementation of court rulings after a long and bitter annexation fight with the City Council over the annexation of more land on the western and northern boundaries of the city. This annexation dispute had started as early as September 27, 1927, when the City Council considered the establishment of a committee to study the advisability of enlarging the city. Even though the council considered the establishment of such a committee every two years after that date, it was not until February 18, 1938, that an ordinance was approved directing city officials to institute annexation suits for about seven square miles of land in Henrico and about five square miles in Chesterfield. The area sought in Henrico extended westward to the University of Richmond and included Paxton-Hill Crest, Sanitary District No. 1, West Broad Street and Monument Avenue, Grove Avenue Crest, Windsor Farms, Belt Line Angle, Roghesay, Hermitage Road, Rosedale, Laburnum Avenue, Joseph Bryan Park–Flying Field, Bellevue, part of North Ginter Park, Hood's Nursey, Highland Park Addition, part of Mechanicsville Turnpike, and Woodville.

The ordinance stipulated that the city agreed to assume and to pay a just proportion of any existing debts and to reimburse the county for any permanent public improvements made in the annexed area in accordance with the value at the time of annexation. The city ordinance also carried the provision that all revenues derived from taxes paid by residences of the area would be used for street, sewer, light, water, and other public improvements in the area for five years. In addition, 12 percent of the assessed value of the territory at the time of annexation was to be set aside from the proceeds of the sale of the city's next bond issue for use in the annexed area. Once this sum was expended, the city tax rate was to be applied to the property in the area. As soon as practicable after annexation, the city promised to provide garbage disposal, police and fire protection, and school facilities to the citizens in the area.

The suit was filed in the Henrico circuit court on February 7, 1939, and three judges were assigned to hear the case. Judge Julien Gunn of Henrico was joined by Judge Frederick W. Coleman of the Fifteenth Circuit, which covered the Fredericksburg area, and Judge A. D. Barksdale of the Sixth Circuit, the Lynchburg area. Trial of the case began October 24, 1939. Thomas B. Gay was selected as the chief counsel for the county. His counterpart for the city was Horace H. Edwards.

The political status of about fifteen thousand people and property with an assessed value of $18 million was involved, and the trial continued with a few short adjournments for fifteen weeks until February 1, 1940. Over five thousand pages of testimony were taken, and more than three hundred maps and charts were presented in evidence. Gay and Commonwealth's Attorney Harold M. Ratcliffe were aided by Allen J. Saville, former director of public works of Richmond; Ernest P. Goodrich of New York, a city planning engineer; and Walter J. Millard, field secretary of the National Municipal League.

Arguing that Henrico was able to perform every public service function and could do so more economically than the city, Henrico's counsel attacked the city's government and demanded that Richmond put its own municipal house in order before trying to take more land from the county. Because he felt the city had failed to make its government adequate and efficient, Goodrich charged that it had failed to live up to the old equity axiom that required it to come into court with clean hands. Millard charged that the city had a "fossilized" government. Goodrich agreed and suggested that the city should reform its government before trying to annex more land. He saw no reason for Richmond to seek to preserve its economic stability at the expense of the county. Believing that annexation was not the best solution for either the county or the city, Goodrich testified that he thought the most practical and feasible arrangement for the city and the suburbs would be a contractual relationship under which the suburbs could pay the city for public services.

The city experts testified that Henrico could not operate a government for a half-rural, half-urban county. These two elements were irreconcilable, declared Thomas H. Reed of New York, an authority on municipal government. City planner Harland Bartholomew of St. Louis argued that annexation was necessary because the amount of land within the city available for residential development had been exhausted in 1930. He testified that in his opinion satellite communities around a city were harmful.

Goodrich countered this argument by stating that cities could get too large for their own good. He charged that Richmond had no real city plan for the future and pointed out several steps that the city government should take to be more responsive to the needs of its citizens. The experts on both sides rebutted each other, and in his cross-examination of Saville, Edwards was particularly critical of his testimony and pointed out how it conflicted with previous statements he had made. Testimony, supporting documents, and exhibits were presented for fifteen weeks to prove the city's need and the county's ability to govern the area adequately. The topics ranged from administration of government to welfare, schools, police, fire protection, health, slums, congestion, and the effects of annexation on the loss or gain of revenue.

On January 22, 1940, the court announced its two-to-one decision giving the city a little more than it had petitioned for. Judge Gunn of Henrico filed his forty-page dissenting opinion a week later. Calling Richmond the "Queen of the South," he charged that the city was run by an "outmoded and fossilized government." Concluding that the city had failed to prove its case, Judge Gunn noted that "no one has testified that persons desiring to live in Richmond have been unable to find suitable places to live or build. . . . The fact that the annexation lines encompass the most highly developed part of the county lends strong support to the view that the real and only purpose of this annexation proceeding is to obtain additional revenue for the City of Richmond."[1]

Neither party was satisfied with the court's rulings on specific areas of contention. The county vigorously denied that the city had shown the necessity of annexation and filed a list of exceptions which included challenges to several technical points of law ruled on by the court during the case and disagreements as to the amount of money the city should pay for improvements made by the county. The city challenged the price tag, about $2.3 million, that the court ordered it to pay for the annexed area. Included in this figure was $93,000 of a $207,000 county school bond issue. In addition, the city was ordered to pay $220,000 of Sanitary District No. 1 sewer bonds issued to finance a recently constructed sewer disposal system. Arguing that the sewer bond issue money actually was spent to defeat annexation, the city objected to having to pay the money. In all, the court ruled that the city was to assume more than $500,000 of the county's bonded debt. Also, the city was ordered to pay $235,000 for schools in the areas annexed and $17,976 for the Westhampton fire station and fire-fighting equipment. The county claimed that the roads in the annexed areas cost $556,091, but the court ruled that the city would only have to assume $62,144 of the bonds issued for the construction of Grove Avenue. In addition to the money to be paid directly to the county and the bonded debts assumed, the city was directed to negotiage for the purchase of privately owned utilities in the area annexed. This figure was estimated at the time as between $400,000 and $500,000.

Even though the city authorities felt they could show a profit on the new areas after five years, they objected to the court's failure to give them all of Sanitary District No. 1. The order did not include the Country Club of Virginia and the University of Richmond or the development lying between them. In all, the court awarded the city 92.7 percent of Sanitary District No. 1 and ordered the city to provide sewer and water services to the unannexed portion of the district. Judge

Barksdale agreed with the city's argument that it was necessary to annex all of the district to have a compact body of
land as set down by the governing statutes. However, Judges
Gunn and Coleman opposed the inclusion of the remaining
7.3 percent of the district. Later, after the decision had been
announced, representatives from the University of Richmond asked that the college be included in the annexed area,
because they believed that the county was not in a position to
provide an adequate sewage system, lights, and fire and police protection.

The court also ruled that all children who lived outside of
the annexed area but had been attending schools within it
could continue to attend those schools through the 1942–43
school session. The city authorities objected to having to educate county children as well as to having to reimburse the
county for the school furniture in the several school buildings in the annexed area.

The final court decree also provided that the county had to
maintain public properties in the area until the effective date
of annexation and that the county and district taxes in the
awarded area were to be paid to the county for the fiscal year
ending June 30, 1941. Annexation was to take effect on mid-
night, December 31, 1940. Because of the disagreement over
various parts of the decree by both parties, appeal of the
court's ruling to the state Supreme Court was inevitable.
Judge Barksdale's term of office was due to terminate on
February 9 because of his appointment to the federal bench,
so the city began proceedings. At the same time it submitted
legislation to the General Assembly authorizing the appointment of a substitute judge to annexation courts when one of
the original judges had to withdraw. These maneuvers were
calculated to prevent the county from seeking a mistrial on
grounds that it did not have the right to appeal. Pending the
outcome of the appeal process, the date of annexation was
stayed.

The Supreme Court of Virginia heard oral arguments on
April 23, 1941, limiting each side to three hours. After reviewing seven volumes of around five thousand printed pages and
more than three hundred maps and charts, the high court
issued its opinion in a fifty-five-page report on June 9, 1941.
Affirming most of the annexation court's findings and rul-

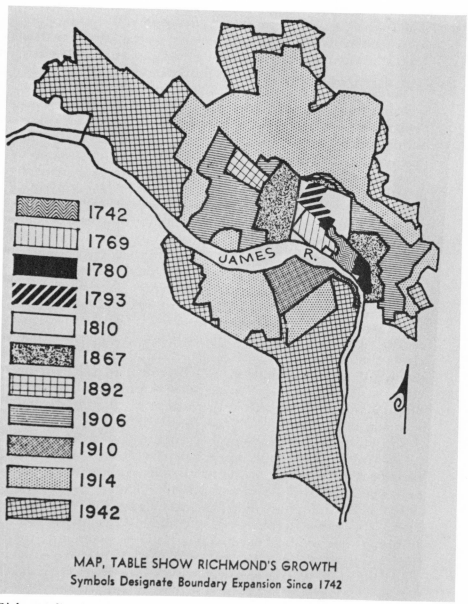

MAP, TABLE SHOW RICHMOND'S GROWTH
Symbols Designate Boundary Expansion Since 1742

Richmond's growth since 1742. (The Metropolitan Richmond Chamber of Commerce)

ings, the Supreme Court added all of Sanitary District No. 1 to
the city, including the area left out by the lower court. Richmond won 8.29 square miles from the county. By order of the
court, annexation was to take effect December 31, 1941.
Thus, the city was to receive the land on January 1, 1942, the
year of the city's two-hundredth birthday.

On the plus side, the annexation brought about an approximately 66 percent reduction of the county's bonded indebtedness, the receipt of $251,000, and savings on other
budget items. On the minus side, the county lost 8.29 square
miles and approximately 47 percent of the county's assessed
valuation, 32 percent of its school population. and 30 percent
of its total population. County Manager S. J. Mahaffey was
optimistic that "with wise planning, however, with our encouraging new developments and building construction, and
by designing plans whereby land may be properly utilized,
the loss through annexation can be overcome." His optimism
was based in part on the increase in building permits for
single-family dwellings. From 1938, when 562 permits were
issued, there was a steady increase to 762 in 1939, 901 in
1940, and 1,091 in 1941. Even with the annexation loss, assessed valuation increased approximately $2,605,000. The
chairman of the Board of Supervisors, B. H. Martin, lamented the loss of so much land to the city and called on the
citizens of the county to "make what is left of old Henrico
Shire that which she was destined to be by the efforts and
sacrifices of her founders."[2]

Recognizing that they must accept the loss of land and
people to the city, county leaders made plans to continue to
provide for the needs of the county's citizens. Planning for
new sanitary districts and further development of existing
ones by providing fire departments, sewer and water services, and other improvements continued. A permanent
planning and zoning board with a full-time planning engineer was busy making a survey and map of the whole county.
The county's resources and opportunities for farming, trucking, dairying, cattle and poultry raising, manufacturing, and
other businesses were studied. Careful and long-range planning also was under way to select the most advantageous
locations for community centers, parks, churches, and
homes. The county's Planning Commission began considera-

tion of studies that vitally concerned the future development of the entire county. Some of the property owners located in areas adjacent to the new city boundaries began to subdivide their land. To meet the potential growth, particular attention was given to improvement of the methods used in subdividing land into building sites, the sanitation and public utility needs, and traffic access. Zoning ordinance revision was also given consideration, along with a master plan for parks.

Henrico had no incorporated towns within its borders. The sanitary districts, of which there were five in 1942, functioned as semi-independent communities. Theoretically, all the services provided in a city were available in the districts, and the people in the district paid for the services they received. Construction of major sewer and water projects were paid by special taxes after the voters in a district approved the project. The county manager's office provided general services in the administration of the government. Thus, the manager found himself dealing with problems varying from those of a strictly rural nature to those of communities of an urban character which existed as distinct entities.

The wartime shortage of building materials and the strict regulation of existing supplies led to a decline of building permits after 1941. The war had a marked effect on many county activities, particularly in the construction of roads, water and sewer lines, and buildings. Some remodeling was done to the Dabbs house, the county Alms House converted for county government use, but little else in the way of public building construction took place during the war. County Manager Mahaffey reported that "this curtailment has been due to a desire to do only the necessary things, to aid the war effort in every way possible, and to the lack of personnel and materials."[3] Nothing was done to extend fire protection during the war. After the loss of the fire station in Sanitary District No. 1 by annexation, there were only two fire departments in the county, one in the Lakeside Sanitary District and the other in the Highland Springs–Sandston Sanitary District. Each department had one pumper, and each station was manned by a paid chief and assistant chief and unpaid volunteers from the community. Because each department was paid for out of sanitary district funds, it only responded to emergency calls within its district. The county did own a third pumper, paid for out of county general funds, and this pumper, which was stationed at Lakeside, could be used anywhere in the county.

The only area to experience rapid growth during the war was around Byrd Airport. The City Council voted to lease the facility, an area of 1,274 acres, to the U.S. Army for twenty years for $1 a year on January 19, 1942. The federal government lost no time in transforming Byrd Airport into the Richmond Army Air Base. In February 1942 the Unites States District Court awarded the army 1,518 acres adjacent to the airport, giving the installation a total of 2,800 acres. The county received $32,000 for portions of roads taken into the expanded base. The development of the air base resulted in the erection of residential structures that had been granted a priority by the government on the basis of military need. On May 10 Eastern Air Lines temporarily suspended service, and an air of secrecy surrounded the airport. Armed guards were stationed on all roads soon after the army took over, and several citizens who ventured too close learned that the army meant business. Approximately $10,115,000 was spent to build and equip the new air base. The facility was primarily used for training pilots, and the citizens who lived near the airport could see the men put to practice in the air what they learned on the ground. On a number of occasions, citizens also witnessed crashes. Richmond Army Air Base remained a training facility until November 1944 when it underwent a drastic change in status, becoming a redistribution center where officers and men with combat service were sent for reassignment. On January 4, 1945, Richmond Army Air Base was declared surplus, and the barracks were converted to apartments to meet housing needs.[4]

The people in the neighborhood around the air base, especially in Sandston, opened their community centers and homes to the young men stationed there. However, the existence of a large military installation presented problems for the local officials. Police Chief W. J. Hedrick complained that the presence of the air base increased police work appreciably. At the time, the force consisted of eight officers, three dispatchers, and four special officers. They were equipped with eight radio cars and one motor cycle. In addition to the military facility at the airport, there were several military

Dabbs House. The date the original part of the house was constructed is not known. Before the Civil War it was known as High Meadow when Josiah Dabbs acquired the house. In 1862 the house served as General Lee's headquarters, and in 1883 it was acquired by the county for use as the county Alms House. Over the years, a number of additions were made, and today the Division of Police occupies the house. (Photograph by John S. Salmon)

installations in the city of Richmond. To make space available in Washington, D.C., the Patent Department was moved to Richmond during the war.

Shortly after war was declared in December 1941, directives were sent out from Washington to organize the civilian population for defensive measures. Under the Civil Defense Program in Henrico, the county manager was designated director, and all the divisions of the Civil Defense Organization were commanded by employees of the county. Tazewell Ellett, engineer of public works, was coordinator, and Police Chief Hedrick was head of the police, fire, and air raid wardens. To mobilize farm production, the Henrico County Board of Agriculture was established in 1942 to carry the agricultural programs to the people. The county was divided into six white communities with a chairman and vice-chairman in each. These communities were divided into 196 neighborhoods with leaders. The black communities were organized separately under the Negro agricultural agent and the vocational agricultural teacher at Virginia Randolph School. There were eighteen black communities with 45 neighborhoods. The victory home food supply campaign was the first program started. Nonfarmers were urged to plant Victory Gardens while the farmers were encouraged to increase production. The Henrico County Agricultural War Board, through the efforts of the United States Department of Agriculture, was organized to include professional agricultural workers. This board reviewed all applications from farmers for materials on the government's restricted list, assisted farmers in arranging credit, assisted them in locating labor, and reviewed applications for farm machinery and tractor fuel.

The Agricultural War Board had another rather special function, to pass on the draft status of farm workers before the two Selective Service Boards in the county could take action. These citizen boards were charged with reviewing the applications for draft deferral filed by county residents. To insure that they were free from political pressure, the boards were not required to report to the Board of Supervisors. Appointed by the county manager, three citizens served on the War Price and Rationing Board, assisting county residents in obtaining their ration coupons and in filing applications for ration books. Citizen volunteers took nursing courses, rolled bandages, conducted scrap metal and paper drives, and entertained military personnel. Clinics on food conservation and sewing were conducted by the county's Department of Agriculture and Home Economics. In 1944 the women of Henrico gave 18,810 hours of their time to Red Cross work; this included the sewing of 3,405 articles of clothing for distribution and use by the Red Cross. In addition, 30,695 volunteer hours were devoted to the Office of Price Administration, Office of Civil Defense, Rationing Board, and USO.

The war effort had a marked effect on county government. To save money and increase efficiency, the Public Works Department and the Police Department reorganized, and the Probation and Parole Department was consolidated with the Department of Public Welfare. All maintenance and construction of buildings, including school buildings, was consolidated in the Department of Building and Grounds, and school bus maintenance was transferred to the Engineering Department. The total number of county employees dropped from 607 in 1941 to 431 in 1945. Keeping qualified personnel was a problem, and the county manager reported that he had to raise salaries to keep experienced and capable employees in key positions. White schoolteachers' salaries were raised 20 percent, and male and female black teachers' salaries were made equal. Although the number of students dropped about one-third after annexation, the school population increased during the war. The demands of supporting a dual system of white and black schools and the lack of construction material created a problem for school administrators. Sites were acquired for new elementary schools in Tuckahoe, Brookland, and Fairfield, but construction was delayed until after the war.

While men from Henrico saw service in all branches of the armed forces on both the European and Pacific fronts, the county was also represented by the *USS Henrico*. This attack transport was constructed by the Ingalls Shipbuilding Company, Pascagoula, Mississippi, and was launced on March 31, 1943, as the *Sea Darter*. It was acquired June 23, 1943, by the U.S. Navy and the next day was commissioned the *USS Henrico*. At the Bethlehem Steel Company, Hoboken, New Jersey, the ship was converted into an attack transport. On November 23, 1943, under the command of Comdr. J. H. Willis, the *Henrico* was recommissioned and assigned to Norfolk where it took part in training exercises for army combat teams. On February 2, 1944, the *Henrico* departed for New York where it embarked troops and sailed for Scotland on February 11. There the ship's crew began strenuous amphibious training in preparation for the invasion of Normandy.

On June 6, 1944, the *Henrico* landed her troops in the first assault wave on Omaha Beach in the face of heavy seas and strong enemy fire. As the beachhead was secured, the ship stood by to receive casualties from shore. It remained on shuttle duty until the advance inland began. In August the *Henrico* took part in the invasion of the southern coast of France and then remained in the Mediterranean trans- porting troops and cargo to the beachhead. In October the *Henrico* returned to the United States and departed from Norfolk with troops and replacement boats for the Pacific theater. There the ship took part in the invasion of Oki- nawa on March 26, 1945. During this action, the *Henrico* was attacked by a suicide bomber. Efforts to shoot down the enemy plane before its pilot accomplished his mission failed. The plane crashed into the starboard side of the bridge, her bombs exploding as she hit. Forty-nine officers and men were killed, including the *Henrico*'s captain. After regaining power, the ship sailed for San Francisco for repairs. Return- ing to the western Pacific, the *Henrico* took part in the op- eration to return American soldiers after the war ended. The *Henrico* earned three battle stars for her World War II service.

After the war, the *Henrico* took part in the atomic tests at Bikini in 1946 and remained in the Pacific, stationed at San Francisco. During the Korean conflict, the *Henrico* trans- ported troops and participated in the Inchon landing on September 15, 1950. In December the *Henrico* and other ships evacuated thousands of troops from the Wonsan- Hungnam area after they were cut off by a massive Chinese attack. For outstanding performance during three tours of duty in Korean water, the *Henrico* received nine battle stars and a Navy Unit Commendation. Following the Korean con- flict, the *Henrico* continued as a training vessel and partici-

U.S.S. *Henrico*, after her service in the Korean War. (Department of the Navy, Office of Information)

pated in amphibious war training exercises. In 1962 she transported a contingent of marines to the Caribbean Sea and served with the force organized to quarantine Cuba after the deployment of Russian missiles there. Returning to the West Coast, the *Henrico* joined the Seventh Fleet in southeast Asia. There she transported troops from Okinawa to Da Nang and Chu Lai, South Vietnam. After transporting additional troops from San Diego, Okinawa, and the Phillippines, the *Henrico* ranged the coastal waters of Vietnam until March 1967 when she returned to San Diego. She was laid up at Olympia, Washington, on July 3, 1968, and transferred to the Maritime Administration on December 3. In 1972 the ship was moved to Fuisum Bay where she was laid up as part of the National Defense Reserve Fleet. After being struck from the Naval Vessel Register in June 1973, the *Henrico* was sold for scrap.[5]

Changing from a wartime to a peacetime economy did not come easy after the end of World War II. There was a surplus of manpower as the armed services began reducing their ranks. Men and women returned home, but there were not enough jobs to absorb all of them into the labor market. The new county manager, Carlton C. Massey, who had assumed the top administrative position in 1944, found himself confronted with a multiplicity of problems. The end of the war brought a residential building boom, but the scarcity of building materials and labor delayed housing starts and completions. Many dwellings started during the war remained unfinished. Materials that had been rationed during the war were hard to obtain, and as industry converted to peacetime needs, it could not supply enough to meet the needs of consumers across the nation. County officials found it difficult to extend water mains because of the lack of materials. At the same time, the shortage of supplies and skilled labor retarded the county's road program, particularly new construction. Only 279 building permits were issued during the fiscal year prior to the end of the war, 127 of them for single-family dwellings. The total value of buildings constructed during that period was $60,828.

The year July 1945 through June 1946 witnessed an explosion in new construction. It was only the beginning. During that year, the county acquired approximately five thousand new residents. By comparison with the previous year, there were 1,252 building permits issued for the period July 1945 through June 1946; of these, 1,012 were for single-family dwellings. The total value of building construction was $269,735. To insure that the dramatic increase in construction did not get out of hand, the Board of Supervisors adopted zoning and building code ordinances. The zoning ordinance was designed to insure an orderly growth in accordance with the county's approved land use plan. The building code ordinance required that the quality of construction meet specific standards. A third ordinance, relating to water works, sought to insure that adequate measures were taken to protect the health and welfare of the residents receiving water. The enforcement of the ordinances rested with the Department of Public Works. This department was concerned with the physical development of the county and the maintenance of existing facilities. Its responsibilities included construction and maintenance of county roads and bridges and water and sewer systems, maintenance of all county equipment, machinery, and public buildings, administration of building and zoning ordinances, and operation of the school transportation system and the various fire departments.

Between 1945 and 1950 the county's population almost doubled from approximately 30,000 to 57,165. The increase in population adversely affected the farming economy in the county because the demand for land resulted in the sale of farmland for subdivision development. It also brought increased demands on county services ranging from schools, to health and life-support services, to the administration of county government. The total number of new dwellings for the period July 1945 through June 1950 was 7,052. The total number of permits issued during the same period was 9,904. The total assessed value of new construction was $50,845,859. Subdivisions like Glenbrooke Hills, Highland Gardens, Monument Avenue Crest, Westview Manor, Norcliffe, and Chatham Place, to name a few, began to dot the landscape. Again, to insure controlled development, the Board of Supervisors passed a subdivision ordinance. In 1949 the board created a permanent Board of Assessors to review all assessments. New sanitary districts were created, and new water and sewer lines were installed.

An interesting phenomenon in the late forties was the appearance of apartment developments. Only five permits were issued for apartment units in 1946–47, but the number issued jumped to 49 in 1947–48, 156 in 1948–49, 102 in 1949–50, and 185 in 1950–51. After that year there was a brief halt to apartment construction. During this period the increased construction created a demand for new road construction and resurfacing of existing roads, all of which was paid for out of the gasoline tax returned to the county from the state. Until 1949–50 the county road crews concentrated on resurfacing and constructing new roads to facilitate access to and through new subdivisions. In 1949–50 an extensive program of rebuilding and improving major county roads was started. Darbytown Road, Osborne Turnpike, Francis Road, Meadow Bridge Road, and Military Road were just a few of the road-resurfacing projects started that year.

During these same years the number of county employees increased from 431 to 693. Of this figure, the largest area of increase was in education. In 1944–45, 301 of the 431 were school employees, and in 1949–50, 454 of the 693 were employed in the schools. As a result of the population increase, there was a corresponding increase in the number of students.

	1944–45	1949–50
White high schools	1,361	1,948
Black high school	240	303
White elementary schools	3,334	5,360
Black elementary schools	969	936

The per capita costs for the same period were:

	1944–45	1949–50
White high schools	84.86	$121.14
Black high school	54.39	75.96
White elementary schools	100.98	136.74
Black elementary schools	54.38	76.77[6]

To meet the cost of construction of new schools, the voters approved bond issues in 1947 and 1949. New elementary schools were started in Tuckahoe and Brookland districts in 1946 and 1947, and plans were made for a new elementary school in Fairfield. In addition, the School Board prepared long-range plans for new high schools. Tuckahoe Elementary opened in September 1947; a year later, Lakeside Elementary opened, and a year later, in September 1949, Glen Lea Elementary opened. An addition to Ridge Elementary was completed in April 1948.

Along with the increased residential construction, the county experienced a growth in new construction for small businesses like garages, gas stations, and grocery and general merchandise stores. These businesses provided employment for some Henricoans, but the major part of the working population found employment in the city of Richmond. Farming was still a major factor in the county's economy. Dairy products were the largest single source of income for Henrico farmers; the county ranked twenty-first in the state in dairy production. Poultry was the second largest source of income for Henrico farmers; the county ranked sixth in production of chickens and twenty-eighth in production of eggs. The poultry industry in Henrico included not only broilers and eggs but breeding stock and baby chicks. The production of beef cattle and swine, while not as extensive as the dairy and poultry industry, did contribute to the county's agricultural industry. Henrico farmers also produced quantities of hybrid corn, barley, and small grains, as well as hay for livestock consumption.

Farmers in the county received advice and assistance from the county's Department of Agriculture and Home Economics. Here as in the schools, there was a biracial system. All of the employees of the department were members of the Agricultural Extension Service of Virginia Polytechnic Institute, and they were joint employees of the state, the United States Department of Agriculture, and Henrico County. Along with the county agent and the home demonstration agent for white residents, there was an "agent for colored farmers" and a "colored home demonstration agent." While the agents worked directly with the farmers and their families, the home demonstration agents worked with both farm and non-farm families, conducting workshops in canning, food preparation, sewing, furniture reupholstering, and repairs of household equipment and appliances and clinics on refurbishing old clothing. The assistant to the county agent worked with the boys' 4-H Clubs. These clubs, numbering as many as thirteen, were very active, preparing exhibits for the State Fair, attending the Jamestown 4-H Club Camp, and cultivating their own crops. The assistant home demonstration agent worked with the girls' 4-H Clubs, which numbered up to twenty-five clubs. Project work with the girls included housekeeping, food preparation, canning, gardening, clothing, and laundry. They conducted exhibits at a Harvest Show, camped, and participated in gardening and canning contests. Most of the teaching phase of these clubs was conducted at the schools as part of the educational curriculum.

The period from 1945 to 1950 was just the beginning of the county's tremendous growth. From 1950 to 1955 the county's population grew from 57,165 to 86,750. In the words of County Manager E. A. Beck, who assumed the duties after Massey resigned to become county manager in Fairfax County in 1952, the county was undergoing a transformation from rural to urban which sometimes was referred to as "rurban." Henrico had become a "rurban society with all the problems of a city and the limitations of a county." He remarked that "the tremendous growth in population is explained by the national trend toward so-called 'casual suburban living.' "[7]

It was an extremely difficult period of growth for the county administration, the School Board, and the people. Skillful administrators and planners within the county government utilized the available financial resources from local, state, and federal sources to provide the citizens with the services they needed and desired. It was not always done to everyone's satisfaction; sometimes conditions had to dictate priority needs, particularly in the area of school construction. Everyone had to be convinced about the size of bond issues; but through it all, a stronger, more responsive government evolved.

The school population rose from 8,547 in 1950 to 14,613 in 1955, and the average cost per student during the same period rose from $23.30 to $58.09. To meet the expanding enrollment, the School Board had to plan additions to existing school buildings and the construction of new ones. The overall plans had to anticipate geographic areas of need for elementary or secondary schools. Additions were completed

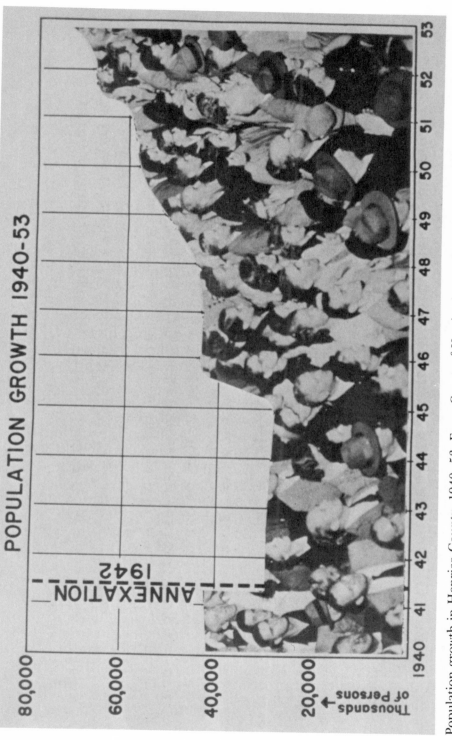

Population growth in Henrico County, 1940–53. From *County of Henrico Annual Report, 1952–1953* (Henrico, 1953), p. 9.

to Tuckahoe Elementary in 1950 and to Short Pump Elementary in 1952, but the critical need was for high schools. Hermitage High School (now Moody Middle School) was completed in 1951, and Highland Springs High School was finished in 1952. By the end of the 1952–53 fiscal year, additions to Varina Elementary and Lakeside Elementary were completed, and a new high school, Douglas Southall Freeman, was under contract. This school was completed during the 1954–55 fiscal year, and by that time five new elementary schools were in various stages of construction— Crestview, Harold Macon Ratcliffe, Henrico Central, Laburnum, and William Leroy Vandervall. Additions to five others were also reported—Dumbarton, Glen Lea, Montrose, Sandston, and Short Pump. The construction of buildings was only part of the problem facing school administrators. New teachers had to be hired, the curriculum had to be developed, new programs had to be organized, and support services to teachers and students had to be expanded to meet the needs. The availability of state and federal funds helped, but school administrators and county officials found it necessary to call on the people to vote for school construction bond issues.

This period witnessed growth not only in the county schools but also in county government. This growth was tempered with administrative reorganization to make the government more efficient. Construction in the county continued. From July 1950 through June 1955, a total of 11,440 building permits were issued, 8,670 of these for single-family dwellings at an appraised value of $93,080,969. Between 1942 and 1953, more than 640 new subdivisions were developed in the county, and indications at the time were that many more would be built. Four new sanitary districts were created and three were merged into one in 1952–53. Near the corner of Lakeside Avenue and Hilliard Road, the Lakeside Water tank and Pumping Station was completed. Bids had been received for this 750,000-gallon storage tank in March 1952. It was necessitated by the lack of storage space in the lines caused by poor pressures and the lack of water during periods of peak demand. Water emergencies had been declared during the summers of 1947 and 1949–52 because of the lack of pressure to supply the needs.[8]

By June 30, 1955, there were ten sanitary districts with 172 miles of water mains, 116.97 miles of sewer mains, 13 sewage treatment plants, and 60 deepwater wells. In addition, the county operated two landfills and one open dump. Trash pickup service was provided to approximately 8,000 county residents. Road construction continued, and some 520 miles of roads were maintained by the county. The newest additon to the county's road system was the two-lane divided extension of Monument Avenue to Glenside Avenue. It was along this road that the county's first traffic light was installed at the intersection of Monument and Libbie avenues in 1955. The three rooms added to the courthouse for the county's Finance Department in 1951 proved to be only a temporary measure. A complete reorganization of the Finance Department occurred in 1952–53. By 1955 the county had a new County Office Building at twenty-first and Main streets near the courthouse. These facilities were needed to house the growth of county government, which was a direct result of the population growth in the county.

The county's health and welfare departments experienced corresponding growth. Additional firehouses were built, and on July 1, 1952, the county's five fire stations were placed directly under the newly created administrative office of fire chief. Before that time, there had been an acting chief who also did regular tours of duty in a fire station. In Varina, the Varina Fire Protection Association was formed, and the members provided their own firehouse. The fire stations were manned by a few paid fire fighters supported by volunteers. The Police Department activated its new 250-watt radio transmitter in 1955, and for the first time Henrico's police and fire departments had complete coverage of the entire county for reporting fire and police emergencies. The police force had increased to twenty-five officers and five dispatchers by 1955. This increase corresponded to an increase in complaints and investigations and an increase in traffic accidents.

The office of fire chief was not the only central administrative office created at this time. It was apparent to the Board of Supervisors and the county administrator that the urbanization of Henrico necessitated some streamlining in county government. The Planning Commission was reorganized and reactivated October 14, 1953, and the office of planning administrator was created in the county manager's office. The office of purchasing agent was also established as a separate office, and the office of general registrar was established and filled in March 1953. The purchasing for county agencies was centralized to obtain the most suitable services and commodities at the lowest prices and to provide a channel through which to exercise better control of expenditures. The general registrar, authorized by an act of the General Assembly, was to maintain a central office for the registration of voters and the records of persons registered.

The second half of the 1950s witnessed a further increase in population. Starting with 57,165 residents in 1950, the county grew to 86,750 citizens in 1955 and to 117,339 in 1960. The major portion of new construction was still single-family dwellings, but there was a marked increase in office buildings, stores, and shopping centers. Between 1950 and 1956 an average of forty-six subdivisions were built per year. There was a general economic downturn after 1956, but in 1959 there were forty-two subdivision plats (1,083 lots) and thirty-two (693 lots) in 1960. By 1960 an addition was built to Willow Lawn Shopping Center, and during that year the River Road Shopping Center, Willow Lawn Apartments, Three Chopt Apartments, Miracle Mart Shopping Center, Azalea Shopping Center, several large motels, two bowling alleys and the Dominion Chevrolet and Richmond Motor Company buildings were built. The growth that the county experienced after World War II had an adverse effect on both the city and the county. The growth in Henrico placed a strain on county government to provide adequate service to the new residents. Those who moved into the county from the city left behind a city that was experiencing a growing problem of providing services to a large economically poor population with diminished revenues.

Proceeding on the assumption that "the future of Henrico is bright if we continue to plan and prepare for it," County Manager Beck and the Board of Supervisors took steps to insure some order and control over the county's growth. A land use and zoning study was undertaken to lay the groundwork for a plan of development to meet the growing needs of the county for the next twenty-five years. Efforts were made to require that the development of land be consistent with an orderly plan of growth for the county. The land use plan was approved by the Zoning Board on February 13, 1958. Such planning was undertaken to insure some order to growth and to save time and money for roads and streets, water and sanitary facilities, schools and school services, police and fire protection, drainage, and other public and semi-public services.[9]

School enrollment increased over a thousand pupils a year during the last half of the 1950s. Planning allowed school administrators to keep pace. Education was the county's biggest job and one of the most important. No sooner was construction completed on five new elementary schools and additions to four others in 1955–56 than construction was started on three new elementary schools and additions to two high schools and three elementary schools in 1956–57. During that same fiscal year, sites were purchased for five elementary and three junior high schools for grades seven, eight and nine. Between 1947 and 1957 the citizens had approved three bond issues for school construction, and twenty-two new schools and twenty-four additions to existing schools were built. Even with all this new construction, school administrators were still having a difficult time keeping pace with the school-age population increase. Even the completion of Bethlehem and Maybeury elementary schools and Brookland, Fairfield, and Tuckahoe junior high schools and the start of Seven Pines Elementary in 1958–59 did not provide enough classrooms; the county was still 136 rooms short. To meet this need, the citizens of Henrico approved another school bond issue for $9.5 million on June 3, 1960.

By 1960 there were 23,588 pupils in the Henrico school system, which had thirty-four schools with 858 classrooms. The average cost per pupil had risen to $283.72; however, this figure did not reflect the difference in the expenditures by race. The average spent for each white student in an elementary school was about $90 more than for a black pupil. On the high school level, the difference was about $55 more per white student. A dramatic change in the type of construction was witnessed during this period. Instead of the conventional design, where all facilities were under one roof, the campus-style school was introduced. These schools consist of a series of separate buildings connected by covered walkways. The construction followed the contour of the ground, thus reducing the grading costs. The buildings were one-story high, and a roof overhang provided protection for students and eliminated glare on the windows. In the junior high schools the school-within-a-school feature was adopted, and separate buildings were arranged in clusters by grades, with separate dining areas for each grade. Food was transported from a central kitchen by hot-food carts, and the dining areas were converted to multipurpose use for the rest of the day.

The campus-style school provided a better learning environment and a feeling of individuality, and at the same time it gave the students a sense of community. They were also less expensive to construct; by incorporating the latest construction methods, including prestressed concrete, three-inch Insulrock roof decks, and terrazzo floors, the average cost per elementary classroom was reduced from $25,000 to $20,965. The construction economies enabled school administrators to build 185 classroom from the $8.5 million bond issue approved in 1957, 60 more classrooms than originally planned when the bond issue was proposed. In addition, there was enough money left to build two cafeterias and a sewer line. One of the additions was a fourteen-room elementary school addition at Virginia Randolph combined school. The construction of this addition allowed the removal of all elementary students from the overcrowded high school, the only black high school in the county.

An improved program of library services was instituted for elementary schools during the 1956–57 school year, when three librarians were employed to serve nine schools. All the high schools had libraries with a professional librarian in charge, and there was one librarian for every two elementary schools by the end of 1958. To insure that the teachers could keep abreast of current technology and curriculum philosophy, the school administration began providing increased teacher in-service education. Both teachers and principals were given an opportunity to attend local, state, and federal workshops on general curriculum, science, math, history, government, language, guidance, and civil defense. In addition, some teachers were able to take regular college and extension courses.

The Varina Fire Station was erected on Gregg Road one block north of Route 5 on property owned by E. G. Gaulding of the Varina Electric Company by the Varina Fire Protective Association and other volunteers in the community. From *Annual Report, 1952–1953* (Henrico, 1953), p. 28.

The growth of the school system and the county government in general necessitated an increase in the number of county employees—1,436 by June 1956 (1,002 of these were in the school system). Although the major increase was in the area of education, each of the other county departments experienced limited growth. Recognizing the need to insure uniform hiring practices and the administration of personnel policies, a personnel officer for county personnel was appointed January 1, 1956.

In another effort to control and coordinate related aspects of county government, the police, fire, and building inspection departments were combined into the Department of Public Safety, and on December 19, 1956, the Board of Supervisors passed a resolution establishing a Department of Public Utilities to replace the Department of Sanitary Districts. The new department was made responsible for the administration of the water and sewer systems operated by the county and the affairs of the various sanitary districts including water, sewer, and sewage disposal systems and refuse collection. All fire protection functions, formerly a responsibility of the sanitary district, were assigned to the Fire Division, Department of Public Safety. By 1959 four of the sanitary districts were combined to form a new Sanitary District Brookland B. Later, two sanitary districts were combined into Sanitary District C in 1959–60. Negotiations were opened with the city for disposal of sewage from Sanitary District Brookland B. Other evidence of the administrative development of county government was the creation of the Animal Protection Section, July 1, 1958, the Research and Public Information Office, March 16, 1959, the real property agent, January 1, 1960, and the codification of all Board of Supervisor ordinances into *The Code of the County of Henrico, Virginia,* June 22, 1960.

The Research and Information Office was charged with the responsibility of public enlightenment about Henrico's governmental functions. A *Guide to Henrico* was published for all new citizens to inform them of available county services. The real property agent was responsible for the appraisal, negotiation, and acquisition of all real estate required by county agencies, such as school sites, rights of way for widening and improving roads, drainage easements, and utility

easements for water and sewer, and the appraisal and disposition of surplus county property. These new offices and the
increase in schools contributed to a work force of 2,011 in
June 1960. A total of 1,508 of these were in the educational
system.

In addition to the commercial recreational facilities in
the county and in the city of Richmond, Henricoans took
advantage of the recreational programs offered by the
county's Recreation Department. This department had
been established in 1934 when there were only three playgrounds in operation. After World War II, as the county's
population increased, the department found its services in
demand. Utilizing the playgrounds at the schools, school
buildings, and separate athletic fields, it developed a
variety of programs for Henricoans. Included in the day
programs were arts and crafts, sports, games, storytelling,
dancing, skating, ceramics, band instruction, and music.
Night programs featured organized softball and baseball
leagues, horseshoe tournaments, games, dancing and band
instruction. By 1959 the department operated thirty-five
playgrounds, eleven softball fields, eight baseball fields,
nine softball and baseball combination fields, three tennis
courts, two shelter houses, and twenty-one hard-top areas
for multiple use. In addition to activities conducted under
the supervision of department personnel, the fields were
made available to such community groups as church
leagues, the Babe Ruth League, and the Little League. In
1955, 135,629 people took advantage of the county's recreational facilities. This figure grew to about 250,000 by the
end of the decade.

The growth of the suburbs around the city created population density, some at the city's expense, and a duplication in
services among the local governments. To bring about more
coordinated planning for Richmond, Henrico, and Chesterfield, leaders in the three political jurisdictions agreed to create a Richmond Regional Planning and Economic Development Commission. This group hired Public Administration
Service of Chicago, a consulting firm, to conduct a study.
Their report, presented January 26, 1959, proposed consolidation of Richmond and Henrico County, because of the
similarity in population density. Chesterfield County was not

included in the recommended merger because of its basically rural nature.

R. C. Logan, chairman of the Henrico Board of Supervisors, accepted the report philosophically with the comment: "The two communities are essentially one and might as well combine their resources." City Councilman J. Edward Lawler championed the merger suggestion, believing that it would be the way to recapture the "young and progressive leadership of the area that is growing up in the county instead of the central city." Thomas R. Jacobi, field representative for the consulting firm, recognized that there would be "hundreds of details that would have to be ironed out when and if the consolidation idea is accepted." He pointed out that taxes could be equalized between rural and urban areas by charging for various services such as water, garbage collection, and sewers; and he suggested that the governing body of the enlarged city should initially consist of all the members of the City Council and the Board of Supervisors. How they were to be elected and how the various units of government were to be combined were just part of the problem. Some saw the merger as a solution to Richmond's racial problem, but J. Malcolm Bridges, executive manager of the Richmond Chamber of Commerce, concluded that merger "might be realized in the future so far off none of us can foresee it."[10]

The members of the Regional Planning Commission took the consultant's report under advisement and began exploring the various aspects of merging the city and Henrico. As members of the commission, Chesterfield's representatives took part in the investigation. Various departments from Henrico and Richmond were asked to examine the pros and cons of merger and to report to the commission. When they compared the personnel situation, they found that Henrico's pay scale was approximately 10 percent lower than Richmond's; Henrico had no retirement system; and Richmond's workmen's compensation was more liberal than Henrico's. It was estimated that it would cost approximately $191,200 more a year to bring Henrico's salaries up to the city's and $143,000 more a year to put Henrico's employees under the city's retirement system.

The safety director from Richmond and the police chief from the county believed that combining their police depart-

The Lakeside Fire Company, 6911 Lakeside Avenue, had three pumpers in addition to this 1,000-gallon water-tank truck. From *Annual Report, 1953–1954* (Henrico, 1954), p. 30.

ments would offer some advantages and some disadvantages. Although the police training programs, shooting ranges, radio systems, and other facilities could be combined to their mutual advantage, it was reported that merger would result in the loss of assistance in the county from the state police, who accounted for about 10 percent of all of the county's accident investigations and arrests. A similar viewpoint was taken in the report on merger of the fire departments of the two jurisdictions. It was concluded that the combining of the fire departments "would provide strength in depth which would mean more flexibility and reserve power," but such a move would result in the loss of help from state forest wardens in the county. The transit committee reported that the Virginia Transit Company's exclusive right to operate in Richmond would automatically force the urban bus companies out of business without any provision for protecting their investments. The committee concluded that the existing city ordinance giving the Virginia Transit Company exclusive rights would have to be amended.[11]

The report of the committee that studied the effects of possible merger on the welfare systems of the two jurisdictions acknowledged that there "was vivid evidence of the great social and economic differences between the city and the county." Again, the representatives from both the city and the county recognized that no real advantages or disadvantages could be foreseen regarding consolidation of the two departments. Because the committee decided to accept the city's level of service and cost figures as the basic level of services and costs to be provided by the new city after merger, the county residents would have to pay six times what they were paying. To add insult to injury, county residents would experience a reduction in the level of some county welfare services. At the time, Henrico was spending 71¢ per capita in local funds for welfare services, and the city was spending $5.61. The per capita cost for the merged city was estimated to be $4.18, an increase of $3.47 for Henrico and a decrease of $1.43 for the city. Even though the county was providing 100 percent of the needs in all recipient categories, the committee concluded that the level of service would have to be reduced to the city's level wherever the city's service was below 100 percent. Because the city only provided 80 percent of the need of persons in the aid-to-dependent children category and 70 percent of the need of general welfare recipients, the report called for Henrico to reduce its efforts to the same level as the city's. Julian P. Garber, member of the Board of Supervisors and chairman of the Welfare Board, testified to the commission that the projected welfare burden on county residents was "too much of a sacrifice for Henrico to make." Edwin P. Conquest, chairman of the Regional Planning Commission, remarked that Richmond must "look like big rock candy mountain" to persons seeking welfare assistance. The welfare directors from the two jurisdictions agreed that the differences in costs were due to socioeconomic and personnel factors.[12]

The commission discovered that deciding on a method of taxation to differentiate between the urban and rural areas was particularly difficult. The question of whether a charter and a constitutional amendment were necessary to allow the new super city to have separate taxes for urban and rural areas created concern. Any amendments would have to be approved by the General Assembly, which was controlled by county delegates. Tensions ran high as charges and counter-charges were made. Race was voiced as a reason for merger because some city leaders felt that without expansion of the city blacks would soon be able to exert powerful influence on its government. City dwellers felt that county residents should be called on to contribute more directly to the support of the city because they derived benefits from it. Opponents of merger replied that county residents contributed financially to the city's progress when they traded with business establishments in the city. County residents also felt that the city had failed to provide adequate services to the areas annexed in 1942. Garber believed that county residents "contribute more to the city than they receive." Richmond appeared convinced that it had to expand, whereas Henrico felt it had a choice between negotiated merger and an all-out annexation fight. As one observer notes: "There seems to be no other issue." One reporter concluded that "relations between Richmond and Henrico county appear ready to burst into open war. . . . if war comes it is almost certain to last until the city, hungry for new land and new citizens, has absorbed a part or all of Henrico."[13]

The Regional Planning Commission met to review the pros and cons of merger after hearing testimony from representatives and citizens from both jurisdictions. After three hours of debate, the commission approved a resolution declaring that a merger would not be agreeable to those concerned. The resolution which passed by a five-to-four vote, was approved by one representative from the city and two from each of the counties. Three members of the opposition (two from the city and one from Henrico) felt that the concept of the merger should be approved with a recommendation that the city and the county work out a merger plan to be submitted to the voters. J. J. Jewett of Chesterfield, the fourth member opposing the resolution, felt that a factual report should be submitted to the governing bodies with a recommendation that they appoint citizens' committees to study the plan. The commission concluded that the city and county were one community and that they should continue to cooperate.[14]

Citizen groups began to study the merger issue. In the city, the Richmond First Club, the Richmond Chamber of Commerce, and the Junior Chamber of Commerce appointed committees and study groups to examine the commission's report. They generally concluded that some form of expansion was necessary. A committee representing black businessmen was also appointed. In the western end of the county, a joint council representing some twenty-five civic organizations appointed study groups to work on merger problems. Across the county, in the eastern end, the Sandston Rotary Club and the Varina Ruritan Club organized study committees to gather information. Their primary concern was to insure that citizens received information so that they could make an intelligent decision.[15]

As tempers continued to flare, the idea of directing the city manager to prepare a plan for annexation was discussed, and members of the City Council considered introducing a resolution calling for annexation. Thought was given also to raising the charges for water, sewer, and gas services to county citizens. Approximately 33,000 Henricoans were connected to the city's sewer system, while 51,516 were receiving their water from the city. The outgoing chairman of the Board of Supervisors, R. C. Logan, spoke out for annexation of the urban areas of the county. When the General Assembly considered the questions of merger and annexation, A. Tredway Lane, president of the Henrico Citizens Committee, testified: "The Henrico Citizens group favors legislation which allows merger of any part of the city with the county, provided legislation can also be introduced to prevent annexation."[16]

Groups in the city were frustrated by the complex problems that needed to be worked out before merger could become a reality, so they proposed that Richmond file an annexation suit by December 1 if the merger plan had not moved forward by then. On July 28, 1960, the Henrico Board of Supervisors took the first step in the next phase of merger proceedings. The consolidation laws passed by the General Assembly provided for the appointment of negotiators, and on that day the board appointed Garland M. Harwood, a lawyer, Aubrey L. Lawrence, a businessman, and W. N. Stoneman, a farmer, as an advisory committee to assist with the formulation of a consolidation plan. The three-man committee was charged with the responsibility of negotiating for and under the direction of the board. Under state law, any agreement between the negotiators had to be submitted to the two governing bodies and then to the people for a vote. The board expressed a willingness to negotiate with the city "for the purpose of determining whether a mutually agreeable and satisfactory plan of consolidation can be developed for the consolidation of the county of Henrico and the city of Richmond into a city of the first class under terms and conditions which are in the best interests of the people of each." However, some citizens groups in the county were opposed to "a railroaded merger" and called mass meetings to voice their displeasure.[17]

The action taken by the Henrico supervisors caused a great deal of speculation, but city officials had already decided that the city would have to expand either by merger or annexation. They referred to Henrico's decision as "a concession to reality." Pointing out that the courts rarely failed to permit a city to annex, a reporter voiced what many county residents considered a reality: "The political views of county citizens are never sought, and their opposition is no defense to annexation. . . . the citizens of the annexed areas would have nothing to say about such vital issues as taxation and representation." Consolidation was a bargaining procedure, and both sides believed that if it failed, annexation was the only recourse. The City Council responded to the Henrico offer by appointing a three-man advisory committee to represent the council in consolidation talks. The three city negotiators were Walter W. Craigie, an investment banker, John S. Davenport III, an attorney, and David J. Mays, a constitutional lawyer. Later, in August, one of the county negotiators, Aubrey L. Lawrence, had to resign on the advice of his physician, and W. C. Schermerhorn, Jr., a former supervisor and electrical contractor, was appointed by the board.[18]

As the negotiators began to meet, it was generally speculated that if the county and city merged, Richmond would be the fifth largest city in area in the nation and the thirty-sixth largest in population. If the merger became a reality, Richmond would stretch 27.1 miles from Goochland County to Charles City County. However, 85 percent of the land in the county was undeveloped and open land. Just 28 square miles of the county's 245 square miles were urbanized. In the county at the time, building construction was down, but the total value was up because of the increased number of new office buildings and combination office and warehouse buildings, some twenty-four in all. Construction also started on needed schools after the passage of a $9.5 million school bond issue on June 7, 1960. Planning already had been completed, so construction started in the summer and fall on Pinchbeck, Central Gardens, and Chamberlayne elementary schools. Ground was also broken for the new Varina Junior-Senior High School, and plans were started for two new 1,600-student junior-senior high schools, one on Parham Road and the other on Azalea Avenue, to be constructed during the 1961–62 school year. At the same time, planning started on a thirty-room elementary school to be located on Nesslewood Drive, near Parham Road. In addition to the new construction started in the second half of 1960, additions were made to Freeman High School, Ridge and Skipwith elementary schools, and Virginia Randolph High School. The latter received a new administration building and science, homemaking, music, choral, language lab, shop, and library facilities.[19]

As the negotiators deliberated, citizens in the city and

To meet the increase in school population, new schools were constructed throughout the county. Highland Springs High School was completed during the 1952–53 fiscal year. From *Annual Report, 1952–1953* (Henrico, 1953), p. 77.

county began to take sides on the issue. The Greater Metropolitan Committee, organized by a group of Richmond-area business and professional leaders, promised nonpartisan efforts to stimulate public interest and discussion on the merits of the merger plan. Twenty-five civic groups in Henrico banded together to form the Henrico Citizens Committee and charged that the city was acting in "bad faith" when city officials reported that "a merger or annexation is 'inevitable.'" Edwin H. Ragsdale, chairman of the committee, which represented groups in the Fairfield and Varina districts, addressed the groups' complaints to the Board of Supervisors and asked for clarification on specific issues. "We would request," he stated, "that the city be advised that formal opposition has been voiced by representatives of the public in Henrico to the extent that the representatives ask that the city desist from any further acts or statements which would be interpreted as a failure to act in good faith."[20]

City officials became apprehensive as the negotiators continued to consider all aspects of merger. The City Council instructed the city manager to gather information should Richmond seek to acquire land from Chesterfield either by annexation or by merger. Chesterfield County officials countered by hiring the law firm that had defended Roanoke County in an annexation suit brought by the city of Roanoke. Willing to explore the merger proposal, Chesterfield County decided to fight any attempt to annex some of its territory. Some city officials were anxious to resolve the mergers before the start of the 1962 session of the General Assembly in January. If the localities agreed to a merger, the legislature would have to authorize a new consolidated city. If annexation suits were instituted because the merger talks failed, then the General Assembly might enact legislation to make annexation more difficult. However, before the legislature could act on any merger, the negotiators, the two governing bodies, the voters would have to approve it.

After more than one hundred meetings, the six-member negotiating committee completed its work and presented a plan for the consolidation of Richmond and Henrico at a joint meeting of the board and council on July 30, 1961, one year and two days after the Henrico Board of Supervisors had appointed its negotiators. W. C. Schermerhorn, Jr., presented the report on behalf of the negotiators. The merger plan called for the consolidation to take effect on January 1, 1963. The new city, to be known as Richmond, was to consist of four boroughs, which were created by extending the existing county magisterial district lines of Tuckahoe, Brookland, Fairfield, and Varina into the old city. The governing body was to consist of nine members, all of them elected at large. The one candidate in each borough who received the highest number of votes was automatically elected, and the five remaining councilmen were to be determined by the number of votes they received, regardless of the borough in which they lived. On the tax question, the negotiators recommended that county taxes be elevated to the city level over a fourteen-year period. They recommended also that lower tax rates on rural property be adopted if a plan could be devised. A special department of rural affairs was suggested to handle the problems of the rural areas of Henrico. The Richmond circuit court was to remain, but the Henrico circuit court and the city's hustings court were to be combined into a new hustings court. The committee also urged that city and county employees be retained, that their salaries not be reduced, and that city services be extended to urban areas of the county as promptly as possible.[21]

The borough plan drew some criticism, because it was possible that all the councilmen could be residents of the original city. It was felt that Henrico should be guaranteed representation on council. The merger negotiators met again and proposed a new borough plan which called for the city to be divided into two boroughs—Lee and Madison—and the consolidation of Varina and Fairfield into one borough and Tuckahoe and Brookland into another one. The City Council and the Board of Supervisors met to discuss the new plan on October 4. They reached a "precarious agreement" which provided for a transitional period of five and a half years. During that time, the new city was to be governed by an eleven-man council. County and city voters were to elect four members each, and three councilmen were to be elected at large. At the end of the transition period, the council was to be reduced to nine, and they were to be elected at large, but each borough was to have at least one representative on council. Later, this was changed, and the county's four magisterial districts were designated as separate boroughs with each to have one councilman. The city was designated as one borough, and four councilmen were to be elected from it. Three additional councilmen were to be elected at large.[22]

Additional minor changes were made, particularly in the tax differential between the county rate and the city rate, but the fourteen-year period for adjusting the rates remained. At the request of the county board, the City Council agreed not to institute an annexation suit until after the voter referendum. On October 10 the two governing bodies met separately and voted to submit the plan to the citizens for a vote. Board Chairman S. A. Burnette of Fairfield and Supervisor B. Earl Dunn of Brookland voted to submit the agreement but announced that they would oppose adoption. Supervisors Tollie H. Quinn of Varina and L. McCarthy Downs, Jr., of Tuckahoe favored the agreement. On October 18 Mayor Claude W. Woodward and Chairman S. A. Burnette signed eight copies of the merger document.

Calling the merger "the most important issue to confront area residents in generations," the Richmond newspapers ran numerous articles in an effort to inform citizens of both jurisdictions of the pros and cons of the merger. The city was referred to as the "center of urban galaxy," and citizens were advised that annexation was the "only alternative to consolidation." The referendum was set for December 12, and although some city and county residents were supporting the idea of merger, there was strong opposition from members of the Board of Supervisors and citizen groups in the county. The Merger Opposition Group, with T. Dix Sutton as temporary chairman was organized the day before the agreement was signed. Sutton promised "a vigorous campaign against the proposed merger plan" and expressed the feeling that the "citizens of Henrico county will reject the proposal." The group's principal objection to the merger plan was that the county would be paying more and more taxes with no assurances of corresponding benefits. Sutton argued: "The last time Richmond annexed county territory was in 1942, when it took over 10 square miles. They still haven't brought them up to city standards. If the same ratio is followed for the 235 square miles they now want to merge, it would take 1,500 years to extend city services into the county." Merger oppo-

Located on Three Chopt Road in the county's West End, Douglas Southall Freeman High School was completed in 1954 and is the home of the Rebels. From *Annual Report, 1953–1954* (Henrico, 1954), p. 77.

nents also expressed fears that county interests would be jeop-
ardized by a city-dominated council. The group elected chairmen for each magisterial district and agreed to coordinate the
various committees and community groups who opposed the
merger and to utilize the advertising media to inform the
people of Henrico. The leadership of the group determined
to counter the promerger campaign launched by the Richmond-Henrico group—the Greater Metropolitan Committee.
In the county, a Citizens for Merger group was formed. As the
consolidation campaign progressed, both proponents and opponents launched intensive educational campaigns and often
presented conflicting "facts."[23]

On the Board of Supervisors, B. Earl Dunn of Brookland,
Tollie Quinn of Varina, and S. A. Burnette of Fairfield reserved the right to oppose the merger proposal. L. McCarthy
Downs, Jr., of Tuckahoe was the only board member who
publicly favored the merger proposal. Burnette came out
against the plan because he objected to the taxation, representation, and services portions of the plan. He felt the negotiators had come to a "crash closing" and cautioned against
the possibility of a constitutional amendment to provide a tax
differential between urban and rural areas. Quinn concluded
that the plan was "as good an agreement as we could expect
to get within the framework of the present laws governing
consolidation" and became a proponent of the plan. Dunn
became an outspoken critic of the plan and urged citizens
not to be "lulled by sweet opium." Thus, the Board of Supervisors was evenly divided over the merger issue.[24]

Public meetings held to discuss the issues became debates
and in some instances degenerated into sarcastic innuendos,
vague charges, and unnecessary personal references. The
voters went to the polls on December 12 amid threats of an
annexation suit if the merger was not approved, appeals for
a new consolidation plan, and demands that an annexation
court be allowed to hear a suit. In the city, where the proponents of the measure were confident of approval, voter
apathy kept the turnout low, but the merger plan was approved 15,051 to 6,700. Fearing that the addition of the
county's white voters would dilute their rising political
strength, black voters in the city opposed the merger. Approval by both electorates was necessary to make the plan a

reality, however, and in Henrico only the voters of Tuckahoe District endorsed the plan. The votes received in Tuckahoe were not enough to offset the opposition votes in the other three districts, and the plan was defeated 13,647 to 8,862. Some 5,146 of the 8,862 votes for the plan came from Tuckahoe. Only one other precinct, Byran Park in Brookland District, voted for the merger. In all, only nine of the county's thirty-four precincts voted for merger.

As predicted, rejection of the merger plan plunged Richmond and Henrico into an annexation fight. On December 18, 1961, the Richmond City Council received separate ordinances calling for the annexation of 142 square miles of Henrico and 51 square miles of Chesterfield. While discussing the possibility of adopting a resolution expressing a willingness to meet with Henrico's supervisors to renew merger discussions, the City Council approved by a vote of seven to two the annexation ordinance concerning Henrico; and on December 27, 1961, the city attorney filed suit in Henrico circuit court. Judge Edmund W. Hening, Jr., entered an order requesting the Virginia Supreme Court to appoint a three-judge annexation court. By order of the court, the annexation ordinance was published once a week for four successive weeks. Basically, the annexation suit called for the extension of city government over 142 of Henrico's 245 square miles where 115,000 of the county's 123,372 citizens resided. The suit called for no change in the composition of the City Council, the assessment of county property at the same rate as city property, no guarantee to county employees that they would be retained, and the placement of all schools under the city's School Board. The proposed annexation would have left Henrico divided with a small area (17.8 square miles) in the western part of the county next to Goochland and Hanover counties and a larger area (72.5 square miles) in eastern Henrico, east of Seven Pines and bordering on Charles City and New Kent counties. The city acknowledged that its annexation of 142 square miles of the county might leave the remainder of Henrico with insufficient area, population, or sources of revenues to justify a separate government. The city's petition, therefore, requested that the city be allowed to annex the whole county if the remainder of the county could not sustain itself.[25]

Although the Board of Supervisors met the same day the suit was filed, it did not discuss it; but when Chairman Burnette was advised that the suit had been filed, he reportedly told the clerk to "put it in file 13." When the board finally addressed the issue, it decided to retain counsel to defend and advance the county's interests vigorously in the proceedings. County Manager Beck concluded that "the expressed objective of the city, if successful, would demolish Henrico as an outstanding and nationally recognized county unit of government." The proceedings proved to be long; and in fighting the annexation suit, it was necessary to review existing county services to present a picture of the county's operations to the court. Instead of just waiting, county officials continued to provide the basic services and increased efforts and capital outlay to extend services where necessary.[26]

The special annexation court did not announce its decision until April 1964. During the three years that had passed, there was a slight decline in the number of new single-family dwellings constructed but an increase in the number of apartments. The county's population increased by approximately 9,000, and there was a marked increase in the number of business establishments, executive offices, and light manufacturing and industrial plants. Varina, Henrico, and Tucker high schools and Jackson-Davis Elementary School were started during the 1961–62 school year. A new capital improvement program to provide major circumferential roads, libraries, parks, and additional fire stations and fire equipment was approved by the voters on July 9, 1963. Plans were developed to make Parham Road, Glenside Avenue, and Laburnum Avenue circumferential routes around the city. However, initial efforts were directed toward extending Laburnum Avenue eastward from the city line on the north side and Parham Road eastward from the western part of the county.

Even though residential construction continued to decline during the three-year annexation court hearing, from 1,187 in 1961–62 to 948 1963–64, the number of students in the schools increased approximately 3,000. During 1961–62, the School Board and the school administration moved to Hechler Village. School administrators and teachers continued the annual training conferences started in 1959, the year

Henrico County builds and maintains all county roads within its boundaries. This is the Gayton Road improvement project undertaken in the early 1950s. From *Annual Report, 1953–1954* (Henrico, 1954), p. 47.

the Long-Range Comprehensive School Improvement Program for Better Curriculum and Teaching started. Principals, supervisors, teachers, and members of the central office staff took part in the summer conferences, and in-service training programs were conducted for administrators, supervisors, and guidance workers. Internal studies on curriculum were undertaken. The music program was expanded to provide every elementary school child with some exposure to music under trained music instructors. High school students were given the opportunity to continue with music in band, chorus, and a cappella choir. Summer programs in instrumental music were also offered.

Library services in the schools were increased, and in December 1963 a central book-processing service was started, providing more uniform procedures in ordering and cataloging books and releasing the school librarians from clerical duties so they could work more closely with the instructional program. By the end of the 1963–64 school year, there were forty-five librarians in the school system and 209,164 books. The ratio of books per student was 7.5 During the same year 19,000 of the 29,000 students were transported to school, When the school bus fleet was first publicly owned and operated by the School Board in 1933–34 school year, there were 26 buses transporting 2,283 students daily. The number of buses increased to 118 during the 1959–60 school year, when a policy of staggering the opening and closing hours of elementary and secondary schools was established. In the 1963–64 school year, 158 buses were in daily operation. Through sound management, the transportation cost per pupil per day had only doubled, from five to ten cents, during the thirty-year period. Under the direction of the superintendent of schools, George H. Moody, greater emphasis was placed on the purpose of education, the scope of current and future curriculum, new and improved techniques of teaching, and the development of new and better equipment and facilities for learning. The publication of the school report *And Take One More Step* defining the Henrico school program was enthusiastically received by educators throughout the state and country.

The county continued to maintain health, welfare, sanitation, and safety programs and increased efforts wherever the need existed. Agriculture continued to be a major factor in the county's economic picture. Of the four million dollars earned annually, about one-third was received by those farmers who were in the poultry business. The rest of the annual income was from beef, dairy, grain, and vegetables. With the increase in homeowners, a program to help them with lawn development, insect control, disease control, and use of plant materials was developed through clinics offered by the Farm and Home Demonstration Unit. A central communications system for the Division of Fire was put into operation on July 1, 1962, when the county operated seven fire companies. Three new fire stations were under construction a year later. The Division of Police was increased to fifty-nine officers in 1962, and in that year plans were laid for construction of the Civil Defense Emergency Operating Center at Dabbs House on Nine Mile Road. A full-time civil defense coordinator, P. L. Burnett, Sr., was appointed November 1, 1962, with the responsibility of establishing radiological monitoring stations, first-aid stations, and fallout shelters and preparing a mobilization plan and communications network in the event of an atomic or conventional weapons attack. He also had the important duty of informing the public about the civil defense program. The Emergency Operating Center, built with 50 percent federal funds, was constructed underground with a protection factor of 5,000 from radioactive fallout and was later used by the Division of Fire, the Division of Police, and the civil defense coordinator. When the building was completed in 1965, it was dedicated by Governor Albertis S. Harrison, Jr.[27]

While the Emergency Operating Center was still under construction, the three-judge annexation court handed down its decision on April 27, 1964. Composed of Judges Edmund W. Hening, Jr., of Henrico, Gus E. Mitchell, Jr., of Halifax, and Joseph N. Crindlin of Lee, the court awarded the city only 17 square miles with 45,000 residents, and not the 142 square miles with 115,000 inhabitants as requested. Noting that the city's suit complied with the state constitution and the annexation statutes, the court ruled that Richmond had proved a need for additional territory; that it had shown a community of interest between the city and the area to be annexed; that it had demonstrated a need for governmental services in the area; and that it had proved its financial ability to annex. City officials were disappointed that the court did not award Richmond more undeveloped land for commercial and industrial growth, and county officials were distressed over the loss of valuable tax sources. Recognizing that there were a number of points to be settled, the court set the week of November 2, 1964, during which it would hear arguments. Before any of the disputed points could be settled, a survey had to be made. Both the city and the county prepared briefs on the location and estimated value of public improvements in the area, the amount of county debt to be assumed by the city, and the amount of assessable real and personal property. While the county officials had to make a decision about retaining the schools, the city officials had to prepare a plan for extending services to the area awarded by the court.[28]

Within the boundaries of the area awarded were several major shopping centers, including Willow Lawn and Azalea Mall, the Robertshaw Controls Company, the Reynolds Metals Company headquarters building, four discount stores and two major automobile agencies. Also included in the area were the residences of a number of county officials, including Supervisor L. Ray Shadwell, Jr., Judge E. Ballard Baker, County Manager A. E. Beck, School Superintendent George H. Moody, and State Senator William F. Parkerson, Jr. Under state law elected officials living in an annexed area could serve out their terms but would have to move to the county before running for reelection.

After reviewing all the reports and hearing additional arguments from both sides, the court awarded Richmond the 17-square-mile area on January 20, 1965. The court also decreed that the city should assume a portion of the county's debt and make other payments amounting to about $55 million to the county. The city had the options of paying the amount decreed by the court, appealing the decision to the state Supreme Court, or dropping its bid to annex and paying the county's defense costs. Under the ruling, if the city decided to annex, it would have to pay about $15 million in cash on the day that annexation was to take effect, January 1, 1966. In addition, the city would have to undertake a five-year public improvement program in the area and pay the county an installment of about $3 million for each of the five years to compensate it for its net loss of tax revenue. The balance of the $55 million would have to be paid for public improvements.

County officials were not pleased because the court decree did not include an additional $20 million. City officials greeted the decision with mixed emotions. Some felt that the amount of money was excessive but that the city should pay it. Others felt the figure was too high and that the city could not afford it because there was no vacant land included for industrial development. After reviewing the expected revenue and anticipated costs, the city estimated the operating loss to provide government services to the area would be $1.3 million annually. Reluctantly the City Council dropped its bid to annex Henrico and turned to press its annexation suit for Chesterfield land. On March 8, 1965, the council decided to decline the annexation award under the conditions laid down by the court on the grounds that it was too costly in view of the area awarded. The annexation court entered an order dismissing the city's motion for the annexation of a portion of Henrico on May 19, 1965. As stipulated by the court, the city reimbursed the county for the slightly more than $404,000 paid by the county for its defense during the annexation suit.

Convinced of the need to acquire additional land, city officials continued to keep alive the possibility of acquiring a part of Henrico, even as they persisted in their annexation suit for Chesterfield land. The base of political power was beginning to shift to the black voters, and annexation was looked on by some as a means to gain additional revenue-producing land and additional white voters. The fear that the government of the capital would become black was voiced by both sides during the Richmond-Henrico merger-annexation fights. The black voters in the city opposed the merger because they saw it as a means of diluting their voting strength. Eventually, a new element, the federal government, would intervene to protect their rights.

In April 1966 the county negotiated a new contract for utilities from the city, and plans for a county sewage disposal system were drawn up. In January 1967, while the county was exploring the possibilities of a joint water authority with

Hanover County, another overture from the city to consider working on a new plan for merger was rejected by the board as not being "in the best interest of the citizens of Henrico at this time." The supervisors stated that they were ready to cooperate with the city on matters of mutual interest that did not jeopardize the best interests of the citizens of Henrico. They also affirmed that they would oppose any effort to change the laws controlling merger or consolidation allowing a majority vote of the entire area to control the outcome of the question.[29]

In 1968 a bill was introduced in the Senate calling for the merger of Henrico and Richmond. Calling the bill "a coercive measure," the Board of Supervisors opposed it. Amid fears that the measure was an attempt to "head off an impending political dominance in Richmond by the rapidly increasing Negro voting bloc," the City Council barely endorsed the bill by a five-to-four vote. After the bill died in committee, the General Assembly adopted a resolution establishing the Richmond Boundary Expansion Study Commission. Under the chairmanship of state Senator George S. Aldhizer II, the commission listened to testimony from officials from all three jurisdictions. Following extensive hearings, the commission concluded that Henrico, Richmond, and Chesterfield should undertake voluntary actions to expand Richmond's boundaries and that the General Assembly should have the authority to designate and determine the boundaries of the capital. The commission recommended that such authority should be given in the new state constitution currently before the General Assembly. The commission also reported that it had a consolidation bill prepared by one of its members which would include all three jurisdictions, and it listed the bill as a possible recommendation for the next session of the General Assembly.[30]

The proposed constitutional amendment to allow the General Assembly to expand Richmond's boundaries every ten years as necessary after July 1, 1971, was approved by both the houses of the legislature during the constitutional revision session of 1969. The amendment became Article XIII of the proposed constitution, and it was left up to the 1970 session of the General Assembly to determine how the amendment was to be presented to the voters. As events transpired, the Rich-

With urbanization comes the need to provide trash disposal. This is the county's first landfill, located on Dabbs House Road behind the county equipment depot. From *Annual Report, 1953–1954* (Henrico, 1954), p. 73.

mond boundary measure was introduced in the 1970 session as a separate resolution, and it died in committee. The entire annexation issue was becoming a political and administrative nightmare. Under state law only cities could annex counties. To avoid annexation, some counties became cities by legislative action. During the 1971 session of the General Assembly, both Henrico and Chesterfield officials had bills introduced in the General Assembly calling for charter changes and referendums to make them cities. Instead, the legislative committee considering the bills proposed that a study commission be established to study annexation techniques and statutes. This proposal was adopted, and Henrico's bid to become a city died in committee. In the meantime, Richmond, having waited the necessary five years after its last efforts to annex Henrico, reinstituted a suit to annex the county. However, under the federal Voting Rights Act of 1965, any annexation award adding white voters would have to be approved by federal authorities. The General Assembly placed a moratorium on annexation suits pending the study, but it did allow the Richmond-Chesterfield suit to continue, and Richmond did receive a portion of Chesterfield land.

The annexation issue dominated the county scene like a dark cloud over the administration of government. Henrico officials realized, however, that they could not wait for the issue to be resolved. By July 1971 the population of Henrico had increased to 154,364. The enrollment in the schools had increased to 35,654. After an $11 million bond issue was approved by the voters in December 1965, two new elementary schools were constructed. The special education and summer school programs were expanded. A new Resource Material Center was established with such teaching aids as films, tapes, records, and later video players for use throughout the school system. Two new schools, Hermitage High and H. F. Byrd Middle Schools were scheduled for construction during the 1968–69 school year after the voters approved a $15 million bond issue; they were to be completed by 1971 when the middle schools for grades six, seven, and eight started. Over 32,000 new books were added to school libraries, bringing the total to 355,777 in 1970. The cost of education increased to $712 per pupil during the 1970–71 school year.

The dual system of schools was maintained until the 1969–70 school year. During that year all of the black schools were closed, and the black students were assigned to white schools in the district in which they lived. From the United States Supreme Court ruling in 1954 until 1969–70, black and white students had been allowed "freedom of choice." This practice of allowing black students to attend white schools if they desired did not result in an integrated system. The continued existence of separate districts for white students and a countywide "district" for black students resulted in pressure from federal authorities to abolish the freedom-of-choice approach by abolishing the countywide "district" for black students and integrating the white districts system. After the 1969–70 school year, some of the former black schools were reopened as integrated schools. Many of the older black schools were closed permanently, and some of the names of those that reopened were changed. Virginia Randolph, the only black high school, became the Virginia Randolph Education Centers. Vandervall Elementary was used temporarily as a branch library and later became Pemberton Elementary.

An attempt to consolidate the county schools with those of the city and to introduce forced busing was successfully defeated by the county. In August 1973 a countywide kindergarten program was started based on three-hour shifts with team teaching in order to fit the attention span of young children, to make efficient use of teacher competencies, and to conserve classroom space. By 1975 there were forty-two schools in the system with 34,540 students enrolled. The cost per pupil had increased to a little over one thousand dollars, and the total expense for education, including debt retirement, was 72 percent of the county's budget. By 1977 education was 80 percent of the county's budget.

In addition to the school bond issue in 1965, the voters approved a $5 million road bond for circumferential highways. Construction of the initial leg of the Laburnum Avenue extension, from Route 360 to Route 60, was started; and during the 1970s Laburnum was extended to Route 5. Work on Parham Road from River Road to Interstate 95 was also completed during this time. These two roads, plus Interstates 95 and 64, opened new vistas for growth in the county. In addition to new commercial and industrial development, the county witnessed the construction of its first modern hospital when St. Mary's Hospital was opened in 1965. Later, Henrico Doctors' Hospital and St. Luke's Hospital would be constructed and opened in the 1970s.

All this increase in population and economic growth necessitated a reevaluation of the existing representative system. On November 8, 1966, the voters approved an additional supervisor to be elected at large, thus increasing the number of supervisors to five. All were elected for a four-year term. In 1969 a fifth district, The Three Chopt District, was created with its own supervisor, and for a time there were six supervisors. However, when the term of the at-large supervisor expired, the position was abolished, and the number of supervisors was reduced to five, each elected from one district.

In March 1968 the county entered into a long-term contract with the city of Richmond for the purchase of water and the disposal of sewage. The contract enabled the county to expand and improve utility service. The services started on July 1, 1968, and in October the county entered into a contract with the thirteen sanitary districts to operate the water, sewer, and sewage systems as a unified system. Under this agreement, the county's Department of Utilities began operating all of the districts as a total system. Approximately 90 percent of the water consumed by county residents came from the city at 15.5¢ per 100 cubic feet. The remaining 10 percent came from wells. The county installed and maintained all storage facilities, pumping stations, and distribution lines from the wells and from the city line. Approximately 90 percent of the county's sewage was transmitted to the city's treatment facilities. The remaining 10 percent was treated at six treatment plants located generally in the eastern section of the county. This contract with the city was one example of the attempt to handle regional problems through cooperation. However, any move toward annexation threatened to destroy such cooperative ventures.

The Henrico County Free Library System was established by the Board of Supervisors on August 24, 1966, and a five-member Board of Trustees was created to manage and control the system. On October 4, 1967, the trustees accepted the deed to the Sandston Public Library, which had been

Federal cemetery near Fort Harrison. The building is now used by the Henrico County Bicentennial Committee. (Photograph by John S. Salmon)

operated by the Sandston Woman's Club since 1923. Temporary branch library quarters were found in all but the Varina District during the first year, and a site was purchased in Varina District for a branch there. A building to house administrative offices, centralized book processing, and a temporary branch was leased at the corner of Nine Mile Road and Laburnum Avenue. The Fairfield Branch opened there on June 29, 1968, with over fifteen thousand volumes. The Lakeside and Tuckahoe branches were opened a year later. Contracts for branch buildings in the Varina and Tuckahoe districts were awarded during the 1969–70 fiscal year. With the infusion of state, federal, and local funds, the system continued to expand, and during the 1970s branch libraries were constructed in all the districts, and additional programs were introduced to serve the citizens of the county.

The need to plan for future as well as present needs became a critical factor in countywide administrative efforts. The county's old courthouse could no longer serve the needs, and agencies were scattered throughout the county in some sixteen locations. The need to centralize county government and to provide adequate jail facilities led the governing authorities to initiate steps to move the courthouse from the old location at Main and Twenty-second streets. By referendum on February 23, 1971, the voters approved the removal of the courthouse to Parham and Hungary Spring roads. Construction started in 1973, and the building was dedicated December 2, 1974. Construction of the juvenile court center and probation office building and the county administration building followed. Farther north on Parham Road, construction of a new community college, to be called J. Sargeant Reynolds, was started in 1973. This institution is part of the state community college system, and eventually it received authorization to build a satellite campus in the city of Richmond. The institution serves citizens of Henrico and Richmond as well as residents of surrounding counties.

During the last half of the 1960s and on into the 1970s, new industry moved into the county, including the Union Camp plant, A. H. Robins Corporate Distribution Center, and the Nabisco and Western Electric plants. To facilitate planning, an updated industrial site survey was completed by the county with the cooperation of the Virginia Electric and

The present Henrico County Courthouse. (Virginia State Library)

Power Company. The growth in industrial and commercial sites and in population and residential areas caused a decline in the number of acres devoted to farming and a change in the economic base. The value of farmland more than doubled from 1930 to 1960, from $142.42 an acre to $316.96 an acre. During that same period, the number of citizens engaged in farming dropped from 6,834, or 22.5 percent of the 20,310 total population in 1930, to 1,506, or 1.3 percent of the 117,339 total population in 1960. In addition to the numerical decline, there was a significant change in the farming population during that period. Approximately 60 percent of the farms in 1959 were classed as part-time or part-retirement farms. Two-thirds of the farm families had other income exceeding the value of farm products sold. The number of farms dropped to 224 in 1969 when the total acreage in farms was 40,192, or 21.8 percent of the county's land mass. By 1974 the number of farms had dropped to 187 and the acreage to 37,885, or 20.5 percent of the land in the county. Cattle, dairy products, hogs, and poultry, along with grain and vegetable production, were still the major farming activities. Even though the quantity of production had dropped, the annual value of farm products sold remained around $4 million. Although some of the production of Henrico farms made its way to the markets in Richmond, Henrico had become a consumer rather than a producer/seller of agricultural products. What had been the foundation of the county's economic base and a way of life for Henricoans from its beginning in 1611 gave way to a mosaic of industrial, professional, construction, and service-oriented businesses. The movement of people into the county created a demand for housing with the resulting growth of suburban communities, increased land values and a reduction of the acreage in farming activities. The county changed from a rural to an urban to a metropolitan community.[31]

The population of Henrico grew steadily from the turn of the century. The annexations of 1906 and 1914 had reduced the county's population rather drastically, but it continued to grow. In 1900 the population was 30,062. It dropped to 23,437 in 1910 and to 18,972 in 1920. By 1930 it was back up to 30,310, and in 1940 there were 41,960 residents. Even with the annexation of 1942, the county population continued to

In the midst of superhighways and subdivision development, this stretch of Wilmer Avenue between U.S. 1 and U.S. 301 captures the essence of the old country lanes that used to abound in the county. (Photograph by John S. Salmon)

show an increase, and by 1950 it was 57,340. There was a dramatic jump during the decade of the 1950s to 117,339 in 1960. In the 1960s the increase continued, and there were 154,463 residents by the end of that decade. By 1980 the population had increased to 180,315.

The population increase necessitated modernization, re-structuring, and development of additional governmental programs. Data processing was instituted under the county manager in 1969–70 to maintain information on financial matters and to insure more efficient management of the billing process for taxes and services. Automatic voting machines were purchased and used for the first time in the November 1971 elections. On May 27, 1972, the Board of Supervisors voted to affiliate with the Virginia Department of Health, and on July 1 the joint operation of the county's welfare program was inaugurated. Although the county had started a recreational program in the 1930s, the first county recreational area was dedicated at Glen Lea during the 1975–76 fiscal year. The previous year the county had accepted Mrs. Elizabeth Adam Crump's generous gift of Meadow Farm. A portion of this 165-acre historic farm was developed into a recreational park and designated the General Sheppard Crump Memorial Park. The house became the Meadow Farm Museum, exhibiting memorabilia from the Crump family and artifacts relating to the history of the area and to agriculture in general. A portion of the original farm was set aside for a county-owned nursing home, and Crump Manor was constructed and opened to receive elderly citizens of the county. In 1977 county voters approved a $7.5 million bond referendum for recreation and parks. Under the Division of Recreation and Parks a number of community, neighborhood, playground, and pocket parks had been developed, and a master plan was prepared. The money from the bond issue was designated for county parks for citizens from throughout the county. The first such park established was Belmont Park, the old Hermitage Country Club, which was purchased by the county in 1978. Additional county parks include Dorey Park in Varina and Deep Run Park in Tuckahoe. Acquisition of land for Four Mile Creek Park to preserve the watershed is currently underway. Land was acquired for Vawter Street Park, but it has not yet been developed. In addition to the county park system, citizens enjoy the National Battlefield Parks in the eastern end of the county.

During the period of growth and development in Henrico, County Manager E. A. Beck, who served from 1952 to 1976, fathered the changes in administrative growth necessary to respond to and plan for the needs of Henrico and its citizens. During that time, also, a spirit of cooperation evolved between the county and the city even after some bitter disagreements over annexation and merger. Population increase, economic development, and growth of government played an important part in the county's long duel with the city. Only after the General Assembly passed legislation on the annexation issue and the county's population reached a certain density could the county be declared immune from annexation. In fact, the density of 740 people per square mile in 1980 was 600 more than the minimum established by the General Assembly in a 1980 law dealing with immunity from annexation. Responding to a petition filed by the Board of Supervisors, Judge E. Ballard Baker signed an order declaring the county immune from annexation on March 21, 1981. As he noted at the time, it was indeed "an historic moment for this county."[32]

Freed from the cloud of annexation, planning continues as the Board of Supervisors, the county manager, county employees, and the citizens of Henrico seek to meet the challenges of present and projected future needs. In the words of former county manager Frank A. Faison, Henrico has become a "vibrant urban county." As citizens of the county have done ever since Sir Thomas Dale first established the town of Henrico, Henricoans of today are striving to insure that the county remains, in Dale's words, "a Convenient, Strong, Healthie and Sweete Seate."

Appendix

Adams, Colonel Richard
Adams, Richard, Jr.
Adams, Thomas Bowler
Adkins, David
Akin, John
Allen, David
Allen, Isham
Allen, James
Allen, John
Allen, Thomas
Alley, David
Alley, Samuel
Alvis, Zack
Ambler, Jacquelin
Anderson, William
Archer, Thomas
Armistead, Isaac
Armistead, William
Atkins, David
Atkinson, John
Austin, John
Austin, Thomas

Bacon, Izard
Bacon, William
Bailey, Joseph
Bailey, Moses
Bailey, Noah
Bailey, Peter
Bailey, Pierce

Baker, Henry
Ball, William
Ballentine, John
Banks, John
Barker, William
Barksdale, Daniel
Barret, John
Battrell, William
Beckley, John
Bennet, James
Bennett, William
Beville, Robert
Bilboe, Peter
Binford, James
Binford, John
Binford, William
Blair, Archibald
Blair, Reverend John F.
Blakey, Morris
Blakey, Smith
Booth, Captain Thomas
Boulware, Obediah
Bowles, David
Bowles, Elijah
Bowles, Richard
Bowles, Thomas
Bowman, James
Boyd, Robert
Bracket, John
Bradley, William

Brannon, Daniel
Braxton, James
Bridgewater, Daniel
Bridgewater, Jonathan
Bridgewater, Levi
Bridgewater, Sanl
Bridgewater, William
Brittain, James
Brittain, Ludwell
Brooke, Christo
Brooke, George
Brooke, John
Brown, John
Brown, Joseph
Brown, Doctor Robert
Brownley, John
Buchannon, Alexander
Buchannon, Reverend John
Buchannon, James
Buckins, Richard
Bullington, William
Burton, John
Burton, Martin
Burton, William

Camp, William
Campin, William
Carden, Robert
Cardwell, George
Carrington, Colonel
   Edmond
Carrington, Mayo
Carter, Charles
Carter, Jacob
Carter, John
Carter, Robert
Carter, Sherwood
Carter, William
Cary, Nathaniel
Charles, Thomas
Childers, Alex

Childers, Meredith
Clark, Frederick
Clarke, John
Clarke, Obediah
Clarke, Peter
Clarkson, John
Clopton, Thomas
Cocke, Boler
Cocke, James Powell
Cocke, William
Coleman, Lieutenant Sam
Conner, John
Connor, Timothy
Consolver, John
Conway, John
Cook, William
Cooper, John
Corbet, John Cornet
Cornet, Francis
Cornet, William
Cottrell, Charles
Cottrell, Richard
Coutts, Reuben
Coutts, William
Cox, Mrs. Mary
Craig, Adam
Craig, David
Craighton, Elizabeth
Crew, Andrew
Crew, Elizabeth
Crew, John, Sr.
Crew, Samuel
Crittenden, Jared
Crouch, Richard
Crow, Abernathy
Crow, Natlaniel S.
Crump, Abner
Crutchfield, Douglas
Crutchfield, Robert
Culbertson, Dev
Culbertson, James

Culbertson, Joseph
Cullen, Daniel
Cunningham, Sam Baron
Currie, Dr. John

Dalton, Mary
Dandridge, William, Jr.
Daugherty, Lieutenant
  James
Davenport, Ambrose
Davis, Augustine
Denholm, Archibold
Dennis, Nathaniel
Denoon, James S.
Depriest, William
Dixon, John, Sr.
Dorton, John
Dougherty, James
Drewin, Samuel
Dunlop, John
Dunn, Jamie
Dunscomb, Andrew
Durham, John
DuVal, Joseph
DuVal, Samuel
DuVal, William

Ege, Dorothy
Ege, Jacob
Ege, Samuel
Ege, Mrs. Samuel
Eggleston, John
Ellis, David
Ellis, John
Ellis, Joseph
Ellis, Thomas
Ellis, William
Ellyson, Gerrard
Ellyson, Gideon
Ellyson, John
Ellyson, Thomas

Ellyson, William
Emmonds, John
Eskridge, Malicai
Eubank, James
Eubank, Thomas
Evans, John
Evans, William

Faris, John
Faris, William, Jr.
Faris, William, Sr.
Fitzgerald, George
Fleming, Tarleton
Folks, Thomas
Ford, David
Ford, Samuel
Fordell, Charles
Foushee, Dr. William
Franklin, Elijah
Franklin, James
Franklin, Francis
Franklin, Thomas
Franklin, Zebilin
Frayser, William
Frazier, Jackson
Freeman, Isam
Froggett, William
Fry, Nathan
Fuzzell, John

Gait, George
Gait, Robert
Gamble, Robert
Gammon, John
Gathright, Anselm
Gathright, Ephraim
Gathright, Benjamin
Gathright, John
Gathright, Samuel
Gathright, William
Geehagan, Anthony

Gibbons, Captain James
Gibson, Major James
Giles, Arthur
Giles, Nicholas
Giles, William
Gilliam, Hugh
Glover, Richard
Golson, W.
Goode, Benjamin
Goode, Joseph
Goode, Samuel
Goodman, Thomas
Gordon, John
Graves, Ralph
Green, William
Gregory, Charles
Gregory, John
Gregory, William
Griffin, Pierce
Grinstead, Jesse
Grinstead, John
Grymes, Benjamin
Gunn, John

Hales, John
Harold, Houson
Harris, Thomas
Harrison, Benjamin, Jr.
Hartwell, John
Harvey, Reverend John
Harwood, James
Harwood, Samuel
Harwood, Thomas
Hatcher, John
Hay, John
Hay, William
Hayes, Charles
Hayes, James
Hendrick, Zack
Hening, William
Henley, Ezekial

Henley, Leonard
Henley, William
Herbert, William
Heth, Captain John
Heth, Colonel William
Hicks, Daniel
Hicks, William
Hill, Amos
Hilton, Dan Lawrence
Hilton, Daniel
Hobson, Matt
Hobson, William
Hogg, Richard
Holbert, Robert
Holliman, Nathaniel
Holloway, James
Holt, Robert
Holt, William
Hooper, James
Hooper, Richard
Hooper, Richard B.
Hopkins, Fras
Hopkins, John
Hudson, John
Hughes, Robert
Hunter, James
Hyde, Robert
Hyland, Mrs. Frances
Hylton, Dan L.

Irvin, Charles

Jackson, Reuben
Jamison, John
Jefferson, Thomas
Jennett, Thomas
Johnson, Benjamin
Johnson, John
Johnson, Nathan
Johnson, Robert
Johnson, Thomas

Johnson, Winifred
Jolly, Joseph
Jones, Elizabeth
Jones, Joseph
Jones, Sam
Jones, William
Jordan, Nobel
Jordan, William
Joy, Dan
Joyce, Richard
Jude, George
Jude, John

Kauman, Captain C. C.
Kearns, John
Kelly, William
Kemp, William
Kendall, John
Kendrick, Robert
Kilby, William
King, John
King, Phillip
King, William

Lacy, John
Ladd, John
Ladd, William
Lambert, David
Lancaster, John
Lancaster, Joseph
Lane, Anna Marie
Lane, John
Lawrence, Absolom
Leonard, Mary
Lewis, Ben
Lewis, Charles
Lewis, Joseph
Lewis, Thomas
Liggon, John
Liggon, Samuel
Lightfoot, H. B.

Lindsay, James
Lindsay, John
Littleberry, Stovall
Logan, Charles
Loving, Richard
Lucas, William
Lyle, James

McCargo, H.
McCarty, Timothy
McCaul, Alexander
McCauslans, Andrew
McClure, Robert
McCoy, William
McCraw, Samuel
McDonald, Terrence
McKeand, John
McNickel, Dr. John
Maddox, William
Madison, Roland
Mahoney, Florence
Marchanes, Tarpley
Marshall, John
Mason, Thomas
Massie, Thomas
Mathews, Ann
Mathews, Hutchens
Mathews, Thomas
Mathews, William
Mauzy, Peter
Mayo, John
Menton, Mary
Mercer, James
Meriweather, Lieutenant
  David
Miller, Dabney
Miller, Henry
Miller, James
Miller, John
Miller, William
Mills, John

Minton, John
Mitchell, Robert
Mitchell, Samuel
Moore, Captain Peter
Moore, Lieutenant William
Morgan, John
Morgan, William
Morris, John
Morris, Joshua
Morris, Nathaniel
Morton, David
Mosby, John
Mosby, Josiah
Mosby, Major William
Mosley, Joseph
Mosley, Robert
Mosley, William
Munday, Thomas

Nance, Massie
Nelson, Robert
Nestill, Mrs. Mary
New, William
Newman, Edmund
Nicholas, Colonel Robert
Nicholson, George
Norvell, Lipscomb

O'Brian, Lieutenant Rush
Otey, John
Overtonlt, Thomas
Owen, Hobson
Owen, John
Owen, Colonel Richardson
Owen, Thomas
Owen, William

Parsons, Samuel
Parsons, Mrs. Susanna
Patman, William
Paut, Thomas

Payne, Samuel
Peake, Isaac
Pearce, Francis
Pearce, William
Pearman, James
Pearson, Charles
Pendleton, John, Jr.
Perry, Hilderburt
Perryman, Daniel
Phillips, Mourning
Picket, George
Pleasants, John
Pleasants, Joseph
Pleasants, Mary
Pleasants, Robert
Pleasants, Robert, Jr.
Pleasants, Thomas
Plowman, Robert
Poe, Thomas
Pollard, Captain Robert
Pollock, Oliver
Povall, Robin
Povall, Robert
Powell, Dr. John
Price, Barret
Price, Charles
Price, James
Price, Jesse
Price, John
Price, Joseph
Price, Robert
Price, Samuel
Price, Lieutenant William
Pride, Berry
Pride, Burton
Pritchett, Thomas
Prosser, Captain Thomas
Pruett, Ambrose
Pryor, John
Puckett, George
Pulliam, Mosby

Puryear, Susanna
Putnam, William

Randolph, Lucy
Randolph, Mary Grimes
Randolph, Peyton
Randolph, Robert
Randolph, Ryland
Rawlings, Robert
Reddie, Isham
Redford, John
Redford, Milner
Redford, William
Revelly, John
Reynolds, John
Rice, Bennett
Rice, Richard
Richardson, George
Robertson, John
Robertson, Cherito
Robertson, George
Rogers, Bolling
Rogers, Sarah
Rogers, Shadrack
Rogers, Sol
Rogers, Thomas
Ronald, Andrew
Roper, Jesse
Roper, John
Rose, James
Roundtree, John
Roundtree, William
Rowland, Zack
Royal, Joseph
Royall, James
Royster, Corporal John
Ruffin, Captain Thomas

Sadler, Henry
Sanders, John
Saunders, Robert H.

Scherer, Samuel
Scott, James
Scott, John
Scott, Littleberry
Scott, Samuel
Scott, Thomas
Seabrook, Nicholas Brown
Seaton, Augustine
Seldon, Joseph
Seldon, Captain Miles (Rev.)
Seldon, Lieutenant Sam
Sharpe, John
Sharpe, Richard
Sharpin, James
Shelton, Captain Eliphaz
Shepherd, Benjamin
Shepherd, John
Shepherd, John Mosby
Shepherd, William
Shermer, Robert
Short, Samuel
Slate, James
Slate, Thomas
Sledd, John
Smith, Elizabeth
Smith, Francis
Smith, Isabella
Smith, Jacob
Smith, Lieutenant James
Smith, Jesse
Smith, Obediah
Smith, Susanna
Smith, William Sterling
Snead, Charles
Snead, John
Snead, Robert
Soleleather, Phillip
Southall, Thomas
Southall, William
Spears, Daniel
Spears, John

Spears, Robert
Stagg, John
Stodner, John
Stone, Lucy
Stone, Prudence
Storrs, Susanna
Street, William
Striker, William
Sullivan, Mary
Swinton, James

Tait, Zenus
Tally, Billy
Tandy, Smith
Tankard, Stephen
Tatum, Lieutenant Henry
Taylor, James
Taylor, Miles
Tench, William
Thomas, Frederick
Thomas, James
Thomas, John
Thomason, Samuel
Throckmorton, Richard
Thurman, John
Tinsley, James
Tinsley, John
Tomlin, William
Tomlinson, Benjamin
Tompkins, Anne
Totty, Daniel, Jr.
Tredway, Moses
Trent, Peterfield
Truman, John
Truman, Richard
Turner, John
Turpin, Alexander
Turpin, John
Turpin, Lusby
Turpin, Dr. Thomas
Tyler, Benjamin

Valentine, Jacob
Valentine, James
Vanderwall, Anne
Vanderwall, David
Vanderwall, Lieutenant
  Mark
Varner, William
Vaughan, James
Vaughan, Lieutenant John

Wade, Richard
Wade, William
Walker, Francis
Wallace, Adam
Walton, John
Warriner, John
Warrington, John
Warrington, Rachel
Watkins, Joseph
Watkins, Mary
Watkins, Thomas
Watson, Rebecca
Webb, Foster
Webb, George
Webb, John
Wescott, Wright
West, Drury
West, Francis
West, John
Whaler, John
Wheeler, Thomas
Whitaker, Lieutenant
  William
White, Catherine
White, Elisha
White, Henry
White, John
White, Mary
White, William
Whitlock, Anna
Whitlock, John

Whitlock, Reuben
Wiley, Alexander
Wilkinson, Colonel
  Nathaniel
Wilkinson, Thomas
Williams, Andrew
Williams, Benjamin
Williams, Durrell
Williams, Elisha
Williams, Robin
Williams, William
Williamson, Allen
Williamson, John
Williamson, Samuel
Williamson, Susanna
Williamson, Thomas
Winston, Peter
Winston, William

Wood, Drury
Wood, Governor James
Wood, John
Wood, Thomas
Wood, William
Woodfin, John James
Woodson, Charles
Woodson, Frederick
Woodson, John
Woodson, Tarleton
Wright, Henry
Wylie, Alexander

Yancy, Jeremiah
Young, Alexander
Young, Henry
Younghusband, Isaac

This list was compiled by the late Ann Waller Reddy of Richmond, Virginia, a noted genealogist and local historian of the area. A typed copy of the list appears in Pauline Warner's manuscript history of Henrico on file in the county manager's records stored in the Henrico County Records Center.

Notes

Chapter I

[1]David I. Bushnell, *Virginia before Jamestown* (Washington, D.C., 1940), pp. 125–26.

[2]Ben C. McCary, *Indians in Seventeenth-Century Virginia* (Richmond, 1957), p. 10. Samuel Rivers Hendren, *Government and Religion of the Virginia Indians* (Baltimore, 1895), should be consulted for general responsibilities of the various leaders.

[3]Bushnell, *Virginia before Jamestown*, p. 130. There were at least five Indian villages within the present confines of the county of Henrico. On the south side of the Chickahominy River running east to west were Pas-Pa-Hegh, Rich-Ka-Hauk, and Ne-Chan-I-Cok. Along the north bank of the James River running east to west were Ar-Ro-Ha-Teck and Pow-Ha-Tan. Conway Whittle Sams, *The Conquest of Virginia the Forest Primeval* (New York, 1916); McCary, *Indians in Seventeenth-Century Virginia*.

[4]David Freeman Hawke, ed., *Captain John Smith's History of Virginia* (New York, 1970), p. 25.

[5]The name of this group was also spelled Arrohateck. Although they did not live on land that became a part of Henrico County, the Chickahominy Indians played a significant part in the settlement of the colony and gave their name to the river that forms part of the boundary line of the county. The name Chickahominy means "coarse-pounded corn people," or "hominy people."

[6]The present-day Three Chopt Road follows part of this trail. Margaret Ethel Kelley Kern, *The Trail of the Three Notched Road* (Richmond, 1928).

[7]Edward E. Hale, ed., *Original Documents from the State Papers Office, London, and the British Museum; Illustrating the History of Sir Walter Raleigh's First American Colony, and the Colony at Jamestown, with an Appendix, Containing a Memoir of Sir Ralph Lane, the Governor of the Colony of Roanoke*, Transactions and Collections of the American Antiquarian Society (Boston, 1860), 4:63.

[8]Powhatan related that his father had unfriendly encounters with the Spanish, but no evidence has been found that the Spanish explored in the area that became Henrico County.

[9]Captain Newport listed the men in the party he commanded in his account: "Gentlemen: George Percye, Esq., Capt. Gabriell Archer, Capt. Jhon Smyth, Mr. Jhon Brooks, Mr. Tho. Wotten; Mariners: Francys Nellson, John Collson, Robert Tyndall, Mathew Fytch; Sailors: Jonas Poole,

John Crookdeck, Benjamyn White, Tho. Turnbrydg, Robert Jackson, Stephen, Jeremy Deale, Robert Markham, Olyver Browne, Rych Genoway, Tho. Godword, Charles Clarke, Thomas Skynner, Danyell." Hale, *Original Documents*, pp. 40–41.

[10]Ibid. These day dates are those of the old calendar. The year dates used in this study are those of the new calendar, which went into effect in the colonies in 1752.

[11]Ibid., p. 43.

[12]Ibid., pp. 44–45.

[13]Ibid.

[14]John Smith, *True Relations, 1608*, ed. Albert Bushnell Hart and Edward Channing (New York, 1896), p. 3.

[15]Hale, *Original Documents*, p. 45; Alexander Brown, *The Genesis of the United States*, 2 vols. (New York, 1890), 1:164.

[16]Brown, *Genesis*, 1:164; Hale, *Original Documents*, p. 49.

[17]Hawke, *John Smith's History*, pp. 69–70, 100.

[18]Ibid., p. 109.

[19]William Strachey, *The Historie of Travell into Virginia Britania (1612)*, ed. Louis B. Wright and Virginia Freund (London, 1953), p. 56; Hawke, *John Smith's History*, pp. 109, 111; Brown, *Genesis*, 1:484. Henry Spelman reported that "Capt Smith at that time repliede litell but afterward conspired with Powhatan to kill Capt. Weste."

[20]Brown, Genesis, 1:481; Hawke, *John Smith's History*, p. 122.

[21]William Strachey, comp., *Lawes Divine, Morall and Martiall, etc.*, ed. David H. Flaherty (Charlottesville, Va., 1969); Brown, *Genesis*, 1:492, 503–4.

[22]Robert Beverley, *The History and Present State of Virginia*, ed. Louis B. Wright (Chapel Hill, N.C., 1947), p. 37; Brown, *Genesis*, 1:498.

[23]Ralph Hamor, *A True Discourse of the Present State of Virginia* (1615; rept. Richmond, 1957), pp. 27–30; Brown, *Genesis*, 1:504, Beverley *History*, p. 37; Hawke, *John Smith's History*, pp. 123, 125. The area was called Henrico and Henricus throughout the colonial period. The term *Henricopolis* first appeared in nineteenth-century writings; there is no historical evidence that it was ever used during the colonial period. George Carrington Mason, "The Case against Henricopolis," *Virginia Magazine of History and Biography* 56(1948): 350–53.

[24]*A Briefe Declaration of the Plantation of Virginia duringe the First Twelve Yeares, When Sir Thomas Smith Was Governor of the Companie, & Downe to This Present Tyme. By the Ancient Planters Nowe Remaining Alive in Virginia*, in *Colonial Records of Virginia, Senate Document (Extra)* (Richmond, 1874), p. 74.

[25]Hamor, *A True Discourse*, pp. 29–30; Robert Johnson, *The New Life of Virginia*, in Peter Force, *Tracts and Other Papers Relating Principally to the Origin, Settlement, and Progress of the Colonies in North America, from the Discovery of the Country to the Year 1776*, 4 vols. (Washington, D.C., 1836–46), 1:14.

[26]Johnson, *New Life*, 1:14; Hamor, *A True Discourse*, p. 30; Robert Hunt Land, "Henrico and Its College," *William and Mary Quarterly*, 2d ser., 18(1938): 467–68; William Stith, *The History of the First Discovery and Settlement of Virginia*, 3 vols. (1747; rept. Spartanburg, S.C., 1965), 3:124.

[27]Hamor, *A True Discourse*, p.31; Johnson, *New Life*, 1:14.

[28]Alden Vaughan, *American Genesis: Captain John Smith and the Founding of Virginia* (Boston, 1975), p. 99.

[29]Little is known of the married life of John Rolfe and Pocahontas. They did have a son, Thomas, while living in the colony. Tradition has it that they lived in Henrico below the town of Henrico in an area that was given to them by Powhatan which they called Varina after a tobacco region in Spain, but available records do not show that they ever owned land in the Varina area. After the death of his wife in England in 1617, Rolfe returned to the colony, remarried about 1619, and resided in James City where he died before the massacre of 1622. In his will, dated March 10, 1622, he left land south of the James to his son, Thomas, who had been left in England under the care of his uncle, Henry Rolfe. Thomas came to the colony around 1635, and by March 1640 he was in possession of the land south of the James. He married Jane Poythress, and they had two daughters, Anne and Jane. Jane married Robert Bolling of Charles City, and their son, John, lived in Henrico before settling on the Appomattox River below Petersburg. A daughter, Jane, married Colonel Richard Randolph of Curles in Henrico, and they had six children. Frances Mossiker, *Pocahontas: The Life and the Legend* (New York, 1976), p. 169; Grace Steele Woodward, *Pocahontas* (Norman, Okla., 1969), p. 165; Marguerite Stuart Quarles, *Pocahontas (Bright Stream between Two Hills)* (Richmond, 1939), p. 25; John Rolfe, *A True Relation of the State of Virginia Left by Sir Thomas Dale, Knight, in May Last 1616* ed. John Melville Jennings (Charlottesville, Va., 1951), p. xxiii; John Rolfe File, First Families of Virginia Papers, Archives and Records Division, Virginia State Library (hereafter cited VSL), Richmond.

[30]*A Briefe Declaration*, p. 75; John Rolfe, *A True Relation of the State of Virginia Left by Sir Thomas Dale* (New Haven, 1951), p. 9. In his account, Rolfe reported a total of 351 settlers (including 65 women and children) in six settlements: "Henrico and the lymittes, Bermuda Nether Hundred, West and Sherley Hundred, James Towne, Kequoughtan, and Dales Fifte."

[31]Brown, *Genesis*, 2:1050; Philip L. Barbour, *Pocahontas and Her World* (Boston, 1970), pp. 117–18; Land, "Henrico and Its College," p. 473.

[32]Susan Myra Kingsbury, *The Records of the Virginia Company of London*, 4 vols. (Washington, D.C., 1906–35), 3:1–2.

[33]Ibid., 3:100, 276; *A Briefe Declaration*, p. 80.

[34]Alexander Brown, *The First Republic in America* (Boston, 1898), p. 260; Land, "Henrico and Its College," p. 475.

[35]The General Assembly consisted of the Council chosen by the Virginia Company and the House of Burgesses chosen by the freemen of the colony. The Assembly could make laws, give advice, and serve as a court of justice. The governor had veto power, and all laws had to be ratified by the Virginia Company court. Kingsbury, *Records*, 3:482–84; Henry R. McIlwaine and John Pendleton Kennedy, eds., *Journals of the House of Burgesses of Virginia, 1619–1658/59*, 13 vols. (Richmond, 1905–15), pp. 31, 43.

[36]Kingsbury, *Records*, 1:517, 603, 3:123–25, 226–27, 245, 246, 305, 452–53; Clifford Dowdey, *The Great Plantation* (New York, 1957), p. 40.

[37]Land, "Henrico and Its College," p. 487; J. Frederick Fausz, "George Thorpe, Nema Ttanew, and the Powhatan Uprising of 1622," *Virginia Cavalcade* 28(1979): 115.

[38]Francis Earle Lutz, *Chesterfield—An Old Virginia County* (Richmond, 1954).

[39]Kingsbury, *Records,* 3:264, 546, 4:13; Richard L. Morton, *Colonial Virginia,* 2 vols. (Chapel Hill, N.C., 1960), 1:64.

[40]Kingsbury, *Records,* 3:553, 365–71.

[41]Ibid., 3:611.

[42]Ibid., 3:670–71, 4:16.

[43]Ibid., 4:259–60.

[44]*Journals of House of Burgesses, 1619–1658/59,* pp. 26–27; Kingsbury, *Records,* 4:493; see also Morton's *Colonial Virginia,* 1:chap. 7.

[45]Brown, *First Republic,* pp. 617–18; Kingsbury, *Records,* 4:551–52. Beginning from the falls on the south side of the river, land had been patented to John Petterson (100 acres), Anthony Edwards (100 acres), Nathaniell Norton (100 acres), John Proctor (200 acres), Thomas Tracy (100 acres), John Hilliard (100 acres), Francis Weston (300 acres), Phettiplate Close (100 acres), John Price (150 acres), Peter Neinmart (150 acres), William Perry (100 acres), John Blower (100 acres), Edward Hudson (100 acres), Thomas Morgan (150 acres), Thomas Sheffield (150 acres), Lieutenant Edward Barkley (12 acres), Richard Boulton (100 acres), Robert Aukland (200 acres), John Griffin (50 acres), Thomas Tindall (100 acres), Thomas Read (100 acres), and John Layden (200 acres).

Petterson and Sheffield had been killed by the Indians; Edwards, Norton, Tracy, Neinmart, Morgan, Aukland, Griffin, Read, and Tindall were probably dead. Still living were Proctor Perry (then in England) and Close, "over the river from Jamestown"; Hilliard, Boulton, and Layden, in "Elizabeth City": Price, in "the Neck of Land Charles City"; Lieutenant Barkley, on "Hog Island"; and Blower, who had surrendered his patent on "Falling Creek" to the use of the ironworks on "the Eastern Shore."

Chapter II

[1]Henry R. McIlwaine, ed., *Minutes of the Council and General Court of Colonial Virginia, 1622–1632, 1670–1676* (Richmond, 1924), p. 106; William Waller Hening, comp., *The Statutes at Large; Being a Collection of All the Laws of Virginia from the First Session of the Legislature in the Year 1619,* 13 vols. (Richmond, etc., 1809–23), 1:169; Philip Alexander Bruce, *Institutional History of Virginia,* 2 vols. (New York, 1910), 1:541.

[2]The shire of Warwick River became Warwick County, incorporated as the city of Warwick in 1952 and then incorporated into the city of Newport News in 1958. Warosquoyacke became Isle of Wight in 1627. The shire of Charles River became York County in 1643. Elizabeth City County was incorporated into the city of Hampton in 1952. Charles City County and Henrico County still exist, though reduced in size. *Minutes of Council and General Court,* p. 481; Hening, *Statutes,* 1:224; see also Albert Ogden

Porter, *County Government of Virginia: A Legislative History, 1607–1904* (New York, 1947).

[3]Charles Francis Cocke, *Parish Lines, Diocese of Virginia* (Richmond, 1967), pp. 10–11.

[4]Patent Book I, p. 330, Virginia Land Office Records, Archives and Records Division, VSL.

[5]*Journals of the House of Burgesses, 1659/60–1693,* pp. 135, 137; Hening, *Statutes,* 2:471–78.

[6]Patent Book I, pp. 304, 436, 512, 836, 707.

[7]The glebe land was referred to in Elizabeth Parker's patent of Feb. 12, 1635, and William Farrar's patent of June 11, 1637. The patent on the glebe lands of April 16, 1666, for 198 acres was recorded on Oct. 7, 1672. Patent Book I, pp. 330, 436; Patent Book IV, p. 427. In an article entitled "Varina" in the *Virginia Historical Register and Literary Advertiser* 1(1848): 161–62, Richard Randolph reported that the original courthouse was built in 1636. No primary evidence was found to substantiate the date. The courthouse is referred to in the April 16, 1666, patent on the glebe lands.

[8]Henrico County Order Book, 1678–93, p. 22, Archives and Records Division, VSL; Randolph, "Varina," p. 162.

[9]*Minutes of Council and General Court,* p. 476.

[10]Hening, *Statutes,* 1:273, 303.

[11]The parish court was a court of record. The court was discontinued before the end of the century, and its records passed into the custody of the clerk of the Henrico County court. Bruce, *Institutional History,* 1:482–83; Hening, *Statutes,* 1:251, 376; Cocke, *Parish Lines,* p. 54; *Journals of House of Burgesses, 1619–1658/59,* p. 85.

[12]Hening, *Statutes,* 1:237; Beverley, *History,* pp. 60–61.

[13]Hening, *Statutes,* 1:315, 317–19; "Acts, Orders and Resolutions of the General Assembly of Virginia at Sessions of March 1643–1646," *Virginia Magazine of History and Biography* 23(1915): 231.

[14]Hening, *Statutes,* 1:323–27.

[15]Ibid., 1:326–27; Edwin Randolph Turner III, "An Ethnohistorical Study of the Powhatan of Tidewater, Virginia" (M.A. thesis, Pennsylvania State University, 1972).

[16]*Journals of House of Burgesses, 1619–1658/59,* p. 101; John P. Little, *History of Richmond* (Richmond, 1933), p. 24; Charles Campbell, *History of the Colony and Ancient Dominion of Virginia* (Philadelphia, 1860), pp. 233–34; Matthew Page Andrews, *Virginia, the Old Dominion* (Richmond, 1949), pp. 148–50.

[17]Hening, *Statutes,* 2:237, 274–76, 289; Richard Randolph, "Henrico," *Southern Literary Messenger* 25(1857): 66.

[18]Charles McLean Andrews, *Narratives of the Insurrections, 1675–1690* (New York, 1952), pp. 19–20; Mrs. Bacon's letter to her sister, June 29, 1676, in "Bacon's Rebellion," *William and Mary Quarterly,* 1st. ser., 9(1900): 4.

[19]Andrews, *Narratives,* p. 110; Thomas Jefferson Wertenbaker, *Torchbearer of the Revolution: The Story of Bacon's Rebellion and Its Leader* (Princeton, N.J., 1940), pp. 52–53, 215; Philip Alexander Bruce, *Social Life of*

Virginia in the Seventeenth Century (Lynchburg, Va., 1927), p. 138. For more detailed genealogies of these and other early Henrico County families, see William Clayton Torrence, "Henrico County, Virginia: Beginnings of Its Families," *William and Mary Quarterly*, 1st ser., 24(1915–16): 116–42, 202–19, 262–83, 25(1916): 52–58.

[20]Wilcomb E. Washburn, *The Governor and the Rebel: A History of Bacon's Rebellion in Virginia* (Chapel Hill, N.C., 1957), p. 18.

[21]Mrs. Byrd fled to Bacon's house at Curles after the attack. Later, Byrd sent her to England to stay with relatives. "Bacon's Rebellion," *William and Mary Quarterly*, 1st ser., 9(1900): 10.

[22]Andrews, *Narratives*, p. 20.

[23]Beverley, *History*, p. 78.

[24]Andrews, *Narratives*, p. 108.

[25]Ibid., p. 111.

[26]"Bacon's Rebellion," *William and Mary Quarterly*, 1st ser., 9(1900): 5.

[27]Andrews, *Narratives*, pp.118, 123.

[28]William Hatcher had represented the county in the House of Burgesses during the sessions of 1644, 1645, 1646, 1649, 1652, and 1659. John Pleasants was a Quaker and suffered persecution because of his religious beliefs.

[29]The list of grievances is published in Pauline Pearce Warner, *The County of Henrico, Virginia* (Richmond, 1959), pp. 42–43, and John Davenport Neville, *Bacon's Rebellion: Abstracts of Materials in the Colonial Records Project* (Richmond, 1976), pp. 359–60. A transcript of the original manuscript is in the Winder Manuscripts, Archives and Records Division, VSL. All quotes are taken from this transcript, which is accessioned as Winder Transcripts, From the Public Record Office, London, vol. II, Bacon's Rebellion.

[30]Bruce, *Social Life*, p. 138.

[31]Winder Transcripts, 2:103.

[32]Hening, *Statutes*, 2:326–36, 336–37.

[33]Ibid., 2:343, 347.

[34]Andrews, *Narratives*, p. 134.

[35]*Minutes of Council and General Court*, pp. 416, 520; Henry R. McIlwaine, ed., *Executive Journals of the Council of Colonial Virginia*, 6 vols. (Richmond, 1925–66), 2:33. In 1687 Colonel Byrd was granted a patent for 956 acres beginning on the east side of Shockoe Creek at its mouth and extending up the creek and down the river. On a part of this grant, the town of Richmond was started. Later, Byrd acquired two patents for land escheated from Nathaniel Bacon, Jr., "by his attainer for high treason." Patent Book VI, p. 604; Patent Book IX, pp. 270, 318.

[36]Letters and Papers concerning American Plantations, Feb. 5, 1678/79–Dec. 19, 1679, C.O. 1/43, f. 29, and Entry Book of Letters, Commissions, Instructions, Charters, Warrants, Patents, and Grants concerning Virginia, and Especially the Rebellion of Nathaniel Bacon There and the Governorship of Berkeley and Culpeper and Lieutenant Governor Jeffreys, 1675–82, C.O. 5/1355, pp. 264, 265, Public Record Office, London (hereafter cited as PRO).

[37]The storehouse was to be sixty feet long and twenty-two feet wide, and the small house was to be the same width by ten feet long. All of the troops raised in Henrico were to be sent to the fort on the James. They were to be reinforced by the troops raised in that part of Charles City County on the north side of the river and those raised in Warwick, Elizabeth City, and James City counties. In addition, Lower Norfolk, Nansemond, and Isle of Wight counties were to send four men each. Surry County was directed to send three men, and the area of Charles City County on the south side of the river was to send two men. Hening, *Statutes*, 2:433–40; Torrence, "Henrico County, Virginia: Beginnings of Its Families," pp. 131–33.

[38]Letters and Papers concerning American Plantations, Jan. 12, 1679/80–May 2, 1680, C.O. 1/44, PRO; Hening, *Statutes*, 2:469–71; *Executive Journals of Council*, 1:7.

[39]Hening, *Statutes*, 2:47–52, 498–501; William P. Palmer, ed., *Calendar of Virginia State Papers and Other Manuscripts, 1652–1781, Preserved in the Capitol at Richmond*, 11 vols. (Richmond, 1875), 1:14; *Executive Journals of Council*, 1:57; Henry R. McIlwaine, ed., *Legislative Journals of the Council of Colonial Virginia*, 3 vols. (Richmond, 1918–19), 1:111–12.

[40]Pierre Marambaud, *William Byrd of Westover, 1674–1744*, (Charlottesville, Va., 1971), p. 16; Randolph, "Henrico," p. 66; Philip Alexander Bruce, *Economic History of Virginia in the Seventeenth Century*, 2 vols. (1895; rept. New York, 1935), 2:556.

[41]Randolph, "Henrico," p. 66; Bruce, *Economic History*, 2:556.

[42]Randolph, "Henrico," pp. 66–67; Henrico County Records, Deeds and Wills, 1688–97, p. 429, Archives and Records Division, VSL.

[43]Hening, *Statutes*, 1:269, 348, 411; Henrico County Records, Deeds and Wills, 1688–97, pp. 151, 257.

[44]Kern, *Trail of the Three Notched Road*, p. 7; Hening, *Statutes*, 1:436, 2:103, 163; Edward Graham Roberts, "The Roads of Virginia, 1607–1840" (Ph.D. diss., University of Virginia, 1950). "A table of fines was set under which all parties, from the justices of the county court to the individual labourers on the road, might be penalized for neglect of duty" (ibid., p. 19).

[45]Henrico County Records, 1677–92, p. 330, Archives and Records Division, VSL; "Letters of William Byrd, First," *Virginia Magazine of History and Biography* 26(1918): 254.

[46]W. G. Stanard, "Racing in Colonial Virginia," *Virginia Magazine of History and Biography* 2(1895): 294.

[47]Henrico County Records, 1677–92, p. 65, 254; Henrico County Order Book, 1678–93, p. 65.

[48]Henrico County Order Book, 1678–93, p. 313; Henrico County Records, 1677–92, p. 466; Henrico County Records, Deeds and Wills, 1688–97, p. 147.

[49]Henrico County Records, Deeds and Wills, 1688–97, pp. 74–75.

[50]Henrico County Records, 1677–92, p. 181; Henrico County Order Book, 1678–93, p. 340.

[51]Henrico County Order Book, 1678–93, p. 235.

[52]Ibid., p. 351.

[53]Henrico County Records, 1677–92, p. 431.

[54]Cocke, *Parish Lines*, pp. 9–10; Bruce, *Institutional History*, 1:49.

[55]Cocke, *Parish Lines*, p.55; *Colonial Records of Virginia Senate Document* (Extra) (Richmond, 1874), p. 103; Henrico County Records, 1677–92, p. 294; Parke Rouse, Jr., *James Blair of Virginia* (Chapel Hill, N.C., 1971), p. 21.

[56]*Calendar of Virginia State Papers*, 1:49–50; William Stevens Perry, ed., *Historical Collections Relating to the American Colonial Church*, 3 vols. (Hartford, 1870), 1:35.

[57]*Minutes of Council and General Court*, p. 506; Hening, *Statutes*, 1:532–33, 2:48.

[58]Torrence, "Henrico County, Virginia: Beginnings of Its Families," p. 53; Henrico County Records, 1677–92, p. 194; Henrico County Order Book, 1678–93, p. 191.

[59]Henrico County Order Book, 1678–93, pp. 67, 359; Henrico County Records, Deeds and Wills, 1688–97, p. 154.

[60]*Journals of House of Burgesses, 1659/60–1693*, pp. 413, 433; Henrico County Order Book, 1678–93, p. 377; *Journals of the House of Burgesses, 1695–1702*, pp. 78–79.

[61]Henrico County Records, Deeds and Wills, 1688–97, p. 353; Torrence, "Henrico County, Virginia: Beginnings of Its Families," p. 54; Bruce, *Institutional History*, 1:250.

[62]William Gordon McCabe, *Virginia Schools before and after the Revolution* (Charlottesville, Va., 1890), p. 12; Hugh Jones, *Present State of Virginia* (London, 1724), p. 70.

[63]Henrico County Order Book, 1678–93, pp. 213, 223.

[64]Bruce, *Institutional History*, 1:418–20.

[65]Henrico County Records, Deeds and Wills, 1688–97, pp. 284, 606, 706.

[66]Ibid., pp. 85, 88.

[67]Bruce, *Economic History*, 2:152.

[68]Ibid., 2:251–53. Bruce notes: "The personalty owned by Frances Eppes, who combined the trade of a local merchant with the business of planting, was problably as large in volume as that of any citizen in this county; independently of the value of the contents of his store, which at the least added as much again, it amounted to £302. The personalty of Thomas Osborne was inventoried at £208; of William Glover at 23,500 pounds of tobacco; and of John Davis, at 32,435 pounds of tobacco."

[69]*Journals of House of Burgesses, 1695–1702*, pp. 150, 156.

[70]Ibid., p. 139; *Executive Journals of Council*, 1:443, 2:33. The office of coroner was filled by appointment by the governor from nominations made by the county court, which usually would recommend one of its members. John Farrar, Richard Cocke, William Randolph, William Byrd, Abell Gower, and Thomas Battle served in the office before 1700.

Chapter III

[1]*Journals of the House of Burgesses, 1727–40*, p. 14.

[2]Hening, *Statutes*, 3:82–85.

[3]Robert Alonzo Brock, ed., "Communication from Governor Francis Nicholson of Virginia, August 12, 1700," *Collections of the Virginia Historical Society,* n.s., 6(1887): 64.

[4]Beverley, *History,* p.283.

[5]Robert Alonzo Brock, ed., "Documents, Chiefly Unpublished, Relating to the Huguenot Emigration to Virginia and to the Settlement at Manakin-Town, with an Appendix of Genealogies. Presenting Data of the Fontaine, Maury, Dupuy, Trabue, Marye, Chastain, Cocke, and Other Families," *Collections of the Virginia Historical Society,* n.s., 5(1886): ix; Andrews, *Old Dominion,* p. 175.

[6]Brock, "Huguenot Emigration," p. 43.

[7]Beverley, *History,* p. 282; Brock, "Huguenot Emigration," p. ix; Hening, *Statutes,* 3:201, 478.

[8]Morton, *Colonial History,* 1:367; R. H. Fife, ed., "The Vestry Book of King William Parish, Virginia, 1707–1750," *Virginia Magazine of History and Biography* 11(1904): 298, 300, 303, 12(1904–5): 17–32, 243–44; Beverley, *History,* p. 283. Beverley also reported: "The Assembly was very bountiful to those who remain'd at this Town, bestowing on them large Donations, Money, and Provisions for their Support; they likewise freed them from every Publick Tax, for several years to come, and addrest the Governor to grant them a Brief, to entitle them to the Charity, of all well-dispos'd Persons throughout the Country, which together with the Kings Benevolence, supported them very comfortably, till they could sufficiently supply themselves with Necessaries" (p. 282).

[9]*Executive Journals of Council,* 2:209, 360, 3:60; Brock, "Communication from Governor Nicholson," p. 64. See also Charles Washington Baird, *History of the Huguenot Emigration to America,* 2 vols. (Baltimore, 1966); Brock, "Huguenot Emigration"; Fife, "Vestry Book King William Parish."

[10]William Byrd, "The State of the French Refugees," *Collections of the Virginia Historical Society,* n.s., 5(1886): 43–44; Howard N. Eavenson, *The First Century and a Quarter of American Coal Industry* (Pittsburgh, 1942), p. 29. Historians frequently have confused this site with the Dover site near Manakin on the north side of the river.

[11]A. S. Wooldridge, "Geological and Statistical Notice of the Coal Mines in the Vicinity of Richmond, Virginia," *American Journal of Science* 43(1842): 12; *Executive Journal of Council,* 2:244; Eavenson, *Coal Industry,* p. 29; Patent Book IX, pp. 612, 613, 688.

[12]Louis B. Wright and Marion Tinling, eds., *The Secret Diary of William Byrd of Westover, 1709–1712* (Richmond, 1941), p. 351.

[13]Benjamin Henry Latrobe, "An Essay on Landscape," Archives and Records Division, VSL. The Richmond Coal Basin lies in five counties: Henrico, Chesterfield, Powhatan, Goochland, and Amelia.

[14]Joseph K. Roberts, *The Geology of the Virginia Triassic* (Richmond, 1928), p. 115.

[15]Eavenson, *Coal Industry,* pp.31, 441; Beverley, *History,* pp. 125, 294. In the will of John Brumall dated 1746, he left half of the tract of land in the Midlothian area of Chesterfield County, called the "Cole pit," to his wife.

[16]*Journals of House of Burgesses, 1695–1702,* p. 266.

[17]Ibid., pp. 226, 266–67; *Calendar of Virginia State Papers,* 1:145; *Legislative Journals of Council,* 3:1555; *Journals of the House of Burgesses, 1712–26,* pp. 86, 154.

[18]Hening, *Statutes,* 3:218–22; *Journals of House of Burgesses, 1695–1702,* p. 224.

[19]Hening, *Statutes,* 3:392–95.

[20]Beverley, *History,* p. 25; *Executive Journals of Council,* 3:57, 158–59; Wright and Tinling, *Byrd's Diary,* p. 234.

[21]Wright and Tinling, *Byrd's Diary,* pp. 390, 400.

[22]Ibid., p. 415. Colonel Byrd's position was not unpopular with the general government. When several Quakers from Henrico, Charles City, and Nansemond counties petitioned for relief of the militia fines, the Council ruled "that the said fines being imposed on them for their refusing obedience to the law, they ought therefore not to be relieved." *Executive Journals of Council,* 4:150.

[23]Wright and Tinling, *Byrd's Diary,* p. 513; *Executive Journals of Council,* 3:332, 350–51.

[24]*Legislative Journals of Council,* 2:627; *Journals of House of Burgesses, 1712–26,* p. 224; *Executive Journals of Council,* 3:507.

[25]Philip Alexander Bruce, "Public Officers in Virginia, 1702, 1714," *Virginia Magazine of History and Biography* 1(1894): 374. A total of 709 tithables were reported in Varina (Henrico) Parish and 518 in Bristol Parish. There was no report on the number of French refugees.

[26]See J. Staunton Moore, *Annals and History of Henrico Parish, Diocese of Virginia* (Richmond, 1904), p. 10, for a history of the church records. *Journals of House of Burgesses, 1712–26,* p. 155; Waverly K. Winfree, *The Laws of Virginia; Being a Supplement to Hening's Statutes at Large, 1700–1750* (Richmond, 1971), pp. 145–46.

[27]Winfree, *Supplement to Hening,* pp. 196–97; Morgan P. Robinson, "Henrico Parish in the Diocese of Virginia and the Parishes Descended Therefrom," *Virginia Magazine of History and Biography* 43(1935): 17–27, 33–34. See also Cocke, *Parish Lines.* In 1721 New Kent County was divided, and Hanover County was established north of Chickahominy River on Henrico's northern boundary.

[28]There is some question as to when Finnie was assigned to Henrico Parish, but he stated in 1724 that it was about his fourteenth year, and although the signature was cut off of the original report, he was reported as minister in 1714. Philip Alexander Bruce, "Public Officers in Virginia, 1702–1714," *Virginia Magazine of History and Biography* 2(1894): 5; George Maclaren Brydon, *Virginia's Mother Church and the Political Conditions under Which It Grew,* 2 vols. (Richmond, 1947), p. 394.

[29]Perry, *Colonial Church,* 1:304.

[30]Moore, *Annals of Henrico Parish,* p. 12; *Journals of House of Burgesses, 1712–26,* p.155. See also Stith, *History of Virginia:* George Carrington Mason, "The Colonial Churches of Henrico and Chesterfield Counties, Virginia," *Virginia Magazine of History and Biography* 55(1947): 45–60.

[31]Perry, *Colonial Church,* pp. 304–5. Brydon noted that "there were possibly more Quakers in Henrico County than in any other county, and

doubtless it was the strong Quaker influence" that led to this ill attention to "devout postures." *Virginia's Mother Church*, 1:394.

[32]Perry, *Colonial Church*, p. 305.

[33]*Journals of House of Burgesses, 1727–40*, p. 66; Hening, *Statutes*, 4:443–45. The parish was coterminous with the county of Chesterfield, which was not formed from Henrico until 1749.

[34]Hening, *Statutes*, 4:525–26.

[35]Robert Alonzo Brock, "The Vestry Book of Henrico Parish, Virginia, 1730–1773, from the Original Manuscript, with Notes and Appendix," in Moore, *Annals of Henrico Parish*, p. 17; Gavin became rector of St. James's Parish, Goochland County, in 1738 and served that parish until his death in 1749.

[36]Brock, "Vestry Book of Henrico Parish," p. 43.

[37]Ibid., pp. 51, 61.

[38]Ibid., pp. 64–65, 73, 90.

[39]Bishop William Meade, *Old Churches, Ministers, and Families of Virginia*, 2 vols. (Philadelphia, 1857), 1:137; Brock, "Vestry Book of Henrico Parish," pp. 19, 69, 84.

[40]Brock, "Vestry Book of Henrico Parish," p. 83.

[41]Henrico County Deeds, Wills, etc., 1750–67, p. 758, Archives and Records Division, VSL; William Clayton Torrence, ed., *The Edward Pleasants Valentine Papers*, 4 vols. (Richmond, 1927), 2:898–99, 1184–85, 1189.

[42]Perry, *Colonial Church*, 1:381–82.

[43]*Calendar of Virginia State Papers*, 1:145; Perry, *Colonial Church*, 1:26, 305.

[44]Lyon G. Tyler, "Education in Colonial Virginia," *William and Mary Quarterly*, 1st ser., 5(1898): 219–23, 6(1897–98): 1–6, 71–85, 171–87.

[45]Hening, *Statutes*, 4:266.

[46]Louis B. Wright, ed., *The Prose Works of William Byrd of Westover* (Cambridge, Mass., 1966), pp. 342, 388.

[47]Ibid., p. 388; Virginius Dabney, *Richmond: The Story of a City* (New York, 1976), pp. 12–13; *Journals of House of Burgesses, 1727–40*, pp. 200, 202.

[48]*Virginia Gazette*, April 1737, reprinted in Alexander Wilbourne Weddell, *Richmond in Old Prints, 1737–1887* (Richmond, 1932), p. 3.

[49]*Virginia Gazette*, June 9, 1737; Henrico County Order Book, 1737–46, p. 180, Archives and Records Division, VSL; Hening, *Statutes*, 5:191–93; *Journals of the House of Burgesses, 1742–49*, pp. 47, 58, 65–67, 70.

[50]Hening, *Statutes*, 5:191–92. The act stipulated that all fairs "shall continue and be in force four years, from the passing thereof and from thence to the end of the next session of assembly; and no longer."

[51]Ibid., 5:274, 8:657. See John W. Reps, *Tidewater Towns: City Planning in Colonial Virginia and Maryland* (Williamsburg, Va., 1972), for an evaluation of new town acts in colonial Virginia.

[52]*Journals of House of Burgesses, 1742–49*, pp. 263, 269, 299.

[53]Morgan P. Robinson, *Virginia Counties: Those Resulting from Virginia Legislation* (Richmond, 1916), p. 208; *Journals of House of Burgesses, 1742–49*, pp. 377–80, 384, 405; *Legislative Journals of Council*, 2:1043, 1045.

[54]William H. Gaines, Jr., "Courthouse of Henrico and Chesterfield," *Virginia Cavalcade*, 17(1968): 32; *Executive Journals of Council*, 5:311.

[55]Hening, *Statutes*, 6:281.

[56]See Marianne Patricia Baroff Sheldon, "Richmond, Virginia: The Town and Henrico County to 1820" (Ph.D. diss., University of Michigan, 1975), pp. 17–20.

[57]Hening, *Statutes*, 6:273–74; *Journals of the House of Burgesses, 1752–58*, pp. 25, 42, 64, 97–98; *Legislative Journals of Council, 3:1069*.

[58]Philip Alexander Bruce, "Public Officers in Virginia, 1702, 1714," *Virginia Magazine of History and Biography* 1(1894): 366, 2(1894): 5; Beverley, *History*, p. 253; Brydon, *Virginia's Mother Church*, 2:363–64; William Maxwell, ed., "Number of Tithables in Virginia," *Virginia Historical Register* 4(1851): 19, 67, 74; Brock, "Vestry Book of Henrico Parish," pp. 4, 40, 90.

[59]*Journals of House of Burgesses, 1752–58*, p. 512; Jeff Marshall O'Dell, *Inventory of Early Architecture and Historic and Archeological Sites, County of Henrico, Virginia* (Richmond, 1976), pp. 44, 64.

Chapter IV

[1]Robert Alonzo Brock, ed., *The Official Records of Robert Dinwiddie, Lieutenant-Governor of the Colony of Virginia, 1751–1758*, 2 vols. (Richmond, 1883), 1:154.

[2]*Journals of House of Burgesses, 1752–58*, pp. 121, 155.

[3]Ibid., p. 357.

[4]*Virginia Gazette* (Purdie and Dixon), Aug. 20, 1767; Hening, *Statutes*, 8:421–22.

[5]*Virginia Gazette*, (Purdie and Dixon), Aug. 20, 1767.

[6]All records relating to William Byrd III, his trustees, and the lottery were filed with the General Court, whose records were destroyed in the evacuation fire in Richmond in April 1865. The seven trustees of Byrd's estate were John Robinson, Peter Randolph, Peyton Randolph, Presley Thornton, John Page, Charles Carter, and Charles Turnbull.

[7]Hening, *Statutes*, 4:421–22.

[8]Ibid., 8:655–57.

[9]Ibid., 6:223; *Journals of House of Burgesses, 1752–58*, p. 148; ibid., 1758–61, pp. 208, 211.

[10]*Journals of House of Burgesses, 1752–58*, p. 254.

[11]Frank R. Wadleigh, "The Story of the Richmond, Virginia, Coal Field and Its Development, 1700–1934," in Ira Festus Davis and L. S. Evans, comps., *Richmond Coal Basin*, 3 pts. (Richmond, 1934), pt. 2, pp. 8–9.

[12]*Virginia Gazette* (Purdie and Dixon), June 3, 1766.

[13]Westham Foundry Records, Archives and Records Division, VSL; William Hand Browne, et., *Archives of Maryland*, 72 vols. (Baltimore, 1883–1972), 12:353; *Virginia Gazette* (Dixon and Nicholson), Sept. 20, 1780. The Deep Run pits were later operated by David Ross and James Currie (1788), Francis Hyland (1789), and the business partnership of Henry Heth and Andrew Nicholson (1804). William Barton Rogers, *A Reprint of Annual*

Reports and Other Papers, on the Geology of the Virginias (New York, 1884), pp. 483–84; Wadleigh, *Richmond Coal Field*, p. 27.

[14]Fairfax Harrison, "The Equine F.F.Vs.," *Virginia Magazine of History and Biography* 35(1927): 368; William G. Stanard, "Racing in Colonial Virginia," ibid., 2(1895): 302.

[15]*Journals of the House of Burgesses, 1770–72*, pp. 175, 195.

[16] Ibid., p. 127–29; Legislative Petitions, Henrico County, May 13, 1783, General Assembly Records, Archives and Records Division, VSL.

[17]Hening, *Statutes*, 8:493–503.

[18]*Virginia Gazette* (Purdie and Dixon), June 6, 1771. The monument still stands, and tradition says it marks the highest point reached by the flood-waters in that vicinity, some forty-five feet above normal high tide. See O'Dell, *Inventory*.

[19]*Journals of the House of Burgesses, 1766–69*, p. 145.

[20]*Virginia Gazette* (Purdie and Dixon), July 28, 1774, Supplement.

[21]Ibid. (Dixon and Hunter), Feb. 11, 1775; Worthington Chauncey Ford, ed., *Journals of the Continental Congress, 1774–1789*, 34 vols. (Washington, D.C., 1904–37), 1:79.

[22]*Virginia Gazette* (Dixon and Hunter), Feb. 11, 1775; Edmund and Dorothy S. Berkeley, *John Beckley, Zealous Partisan in a Nation Divided* (Philadelphia, 1973).

[23]*Virginia Gazette* (Dixon and Hunter), Feb. 11, 1775.

[24]The newspaper accounts of these sales and the actions taken by the Henrico committee are published in William J. Van Schreeven, Robert L. Scribner, and Brent Tarter, eds., *Revolutionary Virginia: The Road to Independence*, 7 vols. (Charlottesville, Va., 1973–83), 2:213, 220, 237–38, 244, 258, 263–64; see also ibid., 2:265–66, n.2.

[25]*Virginia Gazette* (Purdie), April 28, 1775; *Journals of the House of Burgesses, 1773–76*, pp. 235–36.

[26]Hening, *Statutes*, 9:16.

[27]*Virginia Gazette* (Purdie), Nov. 24, 1775.

[28]Committee of Safety Account Book, General Assembly Records, Archives and Records Division, VSL.

[29]See minutes of the Virginia Committee of Safety published in *Calendar of Virginia State Papers*, vol. 8, for references to Captain DuVal's and Captain Pleasant's companies.

[30]E. M. Sanchez-Saavedra, *A Guide to Virginia Military Organizations in the American Revolution, 1774–1787* (Richmond, 1978), p. 45.

[31]William G. Stanard, ed., "Virginia Legislative Papers," *Virginia Magazine of History and Biography* 18(1910): 35. Three years earlier, in 1773, 2,329 tithables were reported. William G. Stanard, ed., "List of Tithables in Virginia Taken 1773," ibid., 28(1920): 81. See also Appendix.

[32]Van Schreeven et al., *Revolutionary Virginia*, 5:271; *Virginia Gazette* (Pinckney), Dec. 6, 1775; *The Proceedings of the Convention of Delegates, Held at the Capitol, in the City of Williamsburg, in the Colony of Virginia, on Monday the 6th of May, 1776* (Williamsburg, Va., 1776), p. 27. See also Larry D. Bowman, "The Scarcity of Salt in Virginia during the American Revolution," *Virginia Magazine of History and Biography* 77(1969): 464–72.

[33]*Proceedings of Convention Held May 6, 1776*, pp. 26–27.

[34]*Virginia Gazette* (Dixon and Hunter), Aug. 10, 1776.

[35]Legislative Petitions, Henrico County, Oct. 14, 1778; *Journals of House of Burgesses, 1770–72*, p. 192.

[36]Legislative Petitions, Henrico County, Oct. 14, 1778.

[37]Westham Foundry Records. For a detailed description of the construction and operation of the foundry, see Kathleen Bruce, *Virginia Iron Manufacture in the Slave Era* (New York, 1931), and Kathleen Bruce, "The Manufacture of Ordnance in Virginia during the American Revolution," *Army Ordnance* 7(1926–27): 41.

[38]Legislative Petitions, Henrico County, Nov. 27, 1781, Dec. 14, 1780, Nov. 22, 1787.

[39]Hening, *Statutes*, 10:8, 86, 89. The directors, appointed on June 24, 1779, were Turner Southall and James Buchanan of Henrico, Archibald Cary and Robert Goode of Chesterfield County, and Robert Carter Nicholas of Hanover County.

[40]*Virginia Gazette*, (Dixon and Nicholson), March 25, 1780; letter of Eliza J. Ambler to Mrs. Dudley in *Virginia Magazine of History and Biography* 38(1930): 167–69. See also Harry M. Ward and Harold E. Greer, *Richmond during the Revolution, 1775–1783* (Charlottesville, Va., 1977), chap. 3.

[41]Hening, *Statutes*, 9:179–84, 339–49, 445–49, 10:221–26, 326–37, 338–44.

[42]Ibid., 10:573.

[43]Joseph P. Tustin, ed., *Johann Ewald, Diary of the American War: A Hessian Journal* (New Haven, 1979), p. 267.

[44]Ibid., p. 268; Hening, *Statutes*, 10:572–75. See also Bruce, "The Manufacture of Ordnance."

[45]*Calendar of Virginia State Papers*, 1:507–8.

[46]Ibid., 2:102.

[47]Ibid., 2:466.

[48]Tustin, *Ewald's Diary*, p. 268; Robinson, *Virginia Counties*, p. 80; Henrico County Order Book 1, 1781–84, p. 3, Archives and Records Division, VSL; Hening, *Statutes*, 10:452–53; Henrico County, Proceedings of Commissioners respecting the Records of Henrico Court Destroyed by the British, Archives and Records Division, VSL.

[49]Turner Southall to Gov. Thomas Nelson, July 24, 1781, Col. William Davies to Gov. Nelson, Sept. 15, 21, 1781, Letters Received, Gov. Nelson to Col. Davies, Sept. 19, 1781, Letters Sent, Executive Department Records, Archives and Records Division, VSL; Arthur J. Alexander, "A Footnote on Deserters from the Virginia Forces during the American Revolution," *Virginia Magazine of History and Biography* 55(1947): 144.

[50]Col. Davies to Gov. Nelson, Sept. 21, 1781, Letters Received, Executive Department Records. The record is silent as to Humphries's given name.

[51]*The Proceedings of the Convention of Delegates, Held at the Town of Richmond, in the Colony of Virginia, on Friday the 1st of December, 1775, and Afterwards, by Adjournment, in the City of Williamsburg* (Williamsburg, Va., 1776), p. 17. In 1846 Boar Swamp Baptist Church became Antioch Baptist Church.

Chapter V

[1]Ward and Greer, *Richmond during the Revolution,* pp. 126–42.

[2]Porter, *County Government,* p. 152.

[3]Legislative Petitions, City of Richmond, May 28, 1782; Hening, *Statutes,* 11:45–51. The act dealt primarily with the establishment of the city of Richmond. However, the "other purposes" mentioned in the title of the act concerned the enlargement of the territorial limits of the town of Fredericksburg and the court of hustings in Fredericksburg and Alexandria.

[4]Hening, *Statutes,* 12:642–43.

[5]Henrico County Order Book 19, 1815–16, p. 238; Henrico County Order Book 2, 1784–87, pp. 573, 582; Henrico County Order Book 3, 1787–89, p. 51; Henrico County Order Book 4, 1789–91, p. 120; *Calendar of Virginia State Papers,* 5:58.

[6]Henrico County Order Book 1, 1781–84, p. 469; Henrico County Order Book 2, 1784–87, pp. 3, 215, 295, 357, 397, 571; Henrico County Order Book 3, 1787–89, p. 432; Henrico County Order Book 4, 1789–91, p. 21; Legislative Petitions, Henrico County, Oct. 3, 1792.

[7]Henrico County Order Book 2, 1784–87, p. 398; Henrico County Order Book 3, 1787–89, p. 58; Henrico County Order Book 1, 1781–84, pp. 39, 302.

[8]*Legislative Journals of Council,* 3:1573–75.

[9]Henrico County Order Book 2, 1784–87, p. 335; Legislative Petitions, Henrico County, Nov. 10, 12, 1785, Nov. 10, 1786. Another petition filed Oct. 29, 1787, requested that the Assembly not act because of the expense and because it would "serve views of a few interested persons."

[10]Hening, *Statutes,* 12:620–21; Henrico County Order Book 3, 1787–89, pp. 232–78; Legislative Petitions, Henrico County, Dec. 18, 1800.

[11]Legislative Petitions, Henrico County, Nov. 10, 1786, Dec. 28, 1818; *A Collection of All Laws and Resolutions of the General Assembly, Relating to the Board of Public Works; The Report of the Commissioners Appointed to View Certain Rivers within the Commonwealth in 1812; The Reports of 1814–15, from the Committee of Roads and Internal Navigation, to the Legislature; and the Several Annual Reports of the Board of Public Works to the General Assembly, up to 1819* (Richmond, 1819), p. 76.

[12]Hening, *Statutes,* 12:722–23.

[13]Ibid., 13:200; Legislative Petitions, Henrico County, Dec. 11, 1822, Dec. 13, 1827.

[14]Hening, *Statutes,* 13:200–201; *Calendar of Virginia State Papers,* 4:402; Henrico County Order Book 3, 1787–89, p. 133; *Journal of the House of Delegates of Virginai, 1828–1829* (Richmond, 1829). The report of the Adjutant General, on page 28 of the Governor's Message (ibid.) gives the figures for 1820 and 1828. In 1828 the Henrico regiment numbered 20 officers and 459 noncommissioned officers, musicians, and privates.

[15]Hening, *Statutes,* 11:210, 13:479; Henrico County Order Book 2, 1784–87, pp. 4, 386; Henrico County Order Book 4, 1789–91, pp. 20–21, 78; Henrico County Order Book 1, 1781–84, pp. 568, 587.

[16]Hening, *Statutes*, 12:582; Henrico County Order Book 3, 1787–89, p. 434.

[17]François Alexandre Frédéric, duc de La Rochefoucauld-Liancourt, *Travels through the United States of North America, the Country of the Iroquois, and Upper Canada, in the years 1795, 1796, 1797*, 4 vols. (London, 1800), 3:58–59, 125; Henrico County Personal Property Tax Book, 1783, Second Auditor's Records, Archives and Records Division, VSL.

[18]*Journal of the House of Delegates, 1831–32*, Document No. 21, Report of the Auditor of Public Accounts, County and City Census, 1790–1830; Samuel Shepherd, *The Statutes at Large of Virginia from October Session 1792, to December Session 1806, Inclusive*, 3 vols. (Richmond, 1835–56), 1:272–73, 3:189; James K. Sanford, *Richmond: Her Triumphs, Tragedies, and Growth* (Richmond, 1975), p. 171.

[19]Legislative Petitions, Henrico County, June 8, 1782, Nov. 16, 1784; Henrico County Order Book 1, 1781–84, p. 39; Henrico County Order Book 3, 1787–89, pp. 74, 587; *Calendar of Virginia State Papers*, 6:179–80.

[20]William Joel Ernst, "Gabriel's Revolt: Black Freedom, White Fear" (M.A. thesis, University of Virginia, 1968), p. 13.

[21]*Calendar of Virginia State Papers*, 9:78, 82, 84.

[22]James Thomson Callendar to Thomas Jefferson, Sept. 13, 1800, Thomas Jefferson Papers, University of Virginia Library, Charlottesville.

[23]*Richmond Examiner*, Oct. 10, 1800; *Calendar of Virginia State Papers*, 9:138.

[24]Virginius Dabney, *Richmond: The Story of a City* (New York, 1976), p. 54.

[25]*Calendar of Virginia State Papers*, 9:169; Ernst, "Gabriel's Revolt," p. 22.

[26]*Calendar of Virginia State Papers*, 9:155–56, 166–68, 171.

[27]Legislative Petitions, Henrico County, Dec. 20, 1810.

[28]Ibid., Dec. 14, 1816, Dec. 17, 1818, Dec. 11, 1820, Jan. 15, 1828.

[29]Henrico County Order Book 3, 1787–89, p. 168.

[30]Samuel Mordecai, *Virginia, Especially Richmond, in By-Gone Days* (Richmond, 1946), p. 302; Legislative Petitions, Henrico County, Nov. 14, 1789.

[31]Legislative Petitions, Henrico County, Dec. 6, 1798.

[32]Hening, *Statutes*, 11:467–69; Henrico County Order Book 2, 1784–87, p. 24; La Rochefoucauld-Liancourt, *Travels*, p. 59.

[33]Henrico County Order Book 2, 1784–87, pp. 25, 56, 571; Henrico County Order Book 1, 1781–84, pp. 257, 297.

[34]Hening, *Statutes*, 12:174–79, 374–76.

[35]*Calendar of Virginia State Papers*, 4:588.

[36]Henrico County Order Book 1, 1781–84, p. 24: Henrico County Order Book 4, 1789–91, p. 164; Hening, *Statutes*, 12:27–30.

[37]Legislative Petitions, Henrico County, Oct. 31, 1785, Nov. 28, 1785.

[38]Hening, *Statutes*, 12:361. The 1780 law limited the number of ministers to four from each denomination and required that they be recommended by the elders of the sect. By an act of 1784 any minister could be licensed after providing proof of ordination. Henrico County Order Book 1, 1781–84, p. 36; Meade, *Old Churches*, 1:142; Moore, *Annals*, p. 27.

³⁹Henrico Parish Records, p. 33, Archives and Records Division, VSL; Moore, *Annals*, pp. 27–28.

⁴⁰Henrico Parish Records, p. 46.

⁴¹Henrico County Order Book 1, 1781–84, p. 472; Henrico County Order Book 3, 1787–89, pp. 59, 231; Hening, *Statutes*, 12:27–30; Shepherd, *Statutes*, 2:93; *Acts of the General Assembly of Virginia, 1816–1817* (Richmond, 1817), pp. 22–23.

⁴²Henrico County Order Book 2, 1784–87, p. 581.

⁴³Legislative Petitions, Henrico County, Dec. 17, 1817.

⁴⁴A copy of the vestry minutes is on file with the petition of the overseers of the poor cited in the preceding note.

⁴⁵Moore, *Annals*, pp. 35–36; Meade, *Old Churches*, 1:143–44; *Journal of the House of Delegates, 1830–31*, Document No. 9, A Report Containing Abstracts of Overseer of the Poor Reports to the Auditor. John G. Williams, agent for the overseers of Henrico, reported: "The report commences in 1822, no records prior to that time being in the Agent's possession. The annual average expense stated is the net amount levied, after deducting Collector's commissions and insolvencies; but the amount actually expended did not average annually more than about $1,813, or about $30 to each pauper, supposing the average number 60. It appears, however, that nearly one half the paupers were generally either dismissed or bound out, or that they died or eloped in the course of the year, so that the average number maintained would fall below 60, and the cost of maintenance be proportionately increased."

⁴⁶Hening, *Statutes*, 11:140–45; Henrico County Order Book 1, 1781–84, pp. 201, 675; Henrico County Order Book 2, 1784–87, p. 222; Legislative Petitions, Henrico County, June 12, 1784, Nov. 25, 1794; *Calendar of Virginia State Papers*, 4:82, 87, 111, 119, 154, 168.

⁴⁷Eavenson, *Coal Industry*, p. 117; John Bladen, "Report on Coal Lands in Tuckahoe Valley," in Davis and Evans, *Richmond Coal Basin*, pt. 1, p. 1.

⁴⁸*Virginia Gazette*, Jan. 22, 1789; Joseph Scott, "Henrico," *The United States Gazetteer* (Philadelphia, 1795); James Mease, *Geological Account of the United States* (Philadelphia, 1807), pp. 410, 413.

⁴⁹*Muster Rolls of the Virginia Militia in the War of 1812* (Richmond, 1852), p. 651; *Pay Rolls of Militia Entitled to Land Bounty under the Act of Congress of September 28, 1850* (Richmond, 1851), p. 45; *Calendar of Virginia State Papers*, 10:132; Legislative Petitions, Henrico County, Dec. 12, 1813, Oct. 21, 1814. The individual muster rolls of the eleven companies are printed in the *Muster Rolls:* the company of Capt. William Allen, p. 90; Capt. Samuel Brown, p. 177; Capt. William Childrey, p. 215; Capt. Abraham Cowley, p. 250; Capt. Thomas Friend, p. 341; Capt. William Henley, p. 421; Capt. Isaiah Johnson, p. 487; Capt. Morris L. Miller, p. 593; Capt. Martin Smith, p. 729; Capt. Francis Wicker, p. 829; Capt. Dabney Williamson, p. 836.

⁵⁰Legislative Petitions, Henrico County, Dec. 6, 10, 1803.

⁵¹*Acts of the General Assembly, 1803–4*, pp. 79–81; ibid., *1815–16*, pp. 135–41.

⁵²*Richmond Enquirer*, Dec. 5, 1815, Feb. 13, 1810; James Pierce, "Practical

Remarks on the Shell Marl Region of the Eastern Parts of Virginia and Maryland, and upon the Bituminous Coal Formation in Virginia and the Contiguous Region," *American Journal of Science* 11(1826): 58; Eavenson, *Coal Industry,* p. 443.

[53]*Acts of the General Assembly, 1812–13,* pp. 60–64; ibid., *1818–19,* pp. 127–28.

[54]Ibid., *1814–15,* pp. 91–96; Legislative Petitions, Henrico County, Dec. 18, 1815; *Acts of the General Assembly, 1817–18,* pp. 142–43, 143–44, ibid., *1815–16,* pp. 129–34; ibid., *1816–17,* pp. 138–39; *Calendar of Virginia State Papers,* 10:488. Wood's map is on file in the Map Collection, archives and Records Division, VSL.

[55]*Acts of the General Assembly, 1826–27,* pp. 56–58; ibid., *1827–28,* pp. 75–76.

Chapter VI

[1]*Journal of the House of Delegates, 1830–31,* Document No. 1, Governor's Message, p. 7, Voting Returns. In addition to the figures given for 1840, found in Document 48, ibid., *1840–41,* there were six pensioners for military service residing in Henrico. Document 48 also records the breakdown by ages for males and females in each of the three categories: whites, slaves, and free blacks.

[2]G. MacLaren Brydon, *The Story of Emmanuel Church at Brook Hill in the Diocese of Virginia, 1860–1960* (Richmond, 1960), pp. 17–21: H. Douglas Pitts, "Brook Hill Lives," *Henrico County Historical Society Magazine* 2(1978): 5–6.

[3]William Arthur Maddox, *The Free School Idea in Virginia before the Civil War* (New York, 1918), pp. 189–90.

[4]Ibid., p. 41; John H. Rice, ed., *Virginia Evangelical and Literary Magazine* 2(1819): 382–84.

[5]*Virginia Evangelical and Literary Magazine* 6(1823): 285–86.

[6]D. E. Gardner, "History of Public Education in Henrico County," *Annual Report of the Superintendent of Public Instruction* (Richmond, 1885), pp. 198–99. A partial list of teachers for 1820–61 appears in the report.

[7]*Journal of the House of Delegates, 1829,* Document No. 4, Report on the Literary Fund, p. 25; ibid., *1841–42,* Document No. 4, Report on the Literary Fund, p. 29.

[8]Ibid., *1850,* Document No. 40, Report on the Literary Fund, pp. 50–51; ibid., *1855–56,* Document No. 4, Report on the Literary Fund; ibid., *1844–45,* Document No. 4, Report on the Literary Fund, p. 32; ibid., *1839,* Document No. 1, Governor's Message, pp. 1–42; ibid., *1840–41,* Document No. 48, Report on 1840 Census.

[9]Ibid., *1840–41,* pp. 62, 119; Charles W. Turner, "Virginia Agricultural Reform, 1815–1860," *Agricultural History* 26(1952): 82; *Richmond Enquirer,* Sept. 18, 1845, Nov. 7, 1847; *Southern Planter* 5(1845): 278–79.

[10]*Proceedings of the Henrico Agricultural and Horticultural Society* (Richmond, 1844), pp. 12, 23–24.

[11]Ibid., p. 19.

[12]Ibid., p. 42. The types and numbers of livestock reported were: horse, 1,245; asses and mules, 820; milk cows, 1,832; working oxen, 314; other cattle, 1,461; sheep, 1,778; and swine, 7,735. *Journal of the House of Delegates, 1852*, Document No. 76, Agricultural Tables.

[13]J. S. Skinner, ed., "The Tree Hill Course," *American Turf Register and Sporting Magazine* 1(1929): 151, 466.

[14]This course appears on Smith's 1853 map of the county. Mordecai, *Richmond in By-Gone Days*, pp. 254–55.

[15]*Acts of the General Assembly, 1834–35*, pp. 46–59; ibid., *1835–36*, pp. 209–10; ibid., *1849–50*, p. 79; *Journal of the House of Delegates, 1855–56*, pp. 50, 100, 194, 303, 344, 408, 416; ibid., *1852*, p. 47; ibid., *1853–54*, pp. 66, 232–33, 237, 285.

[16]*Twentieth Annual Report of the Board of Public Works* (Richmond, 1836), pp. 126, 129.

[17]John B. Mordecai, *A Brief History of the Richmond, Fredericksburg and Potomac Railroad* (Richmond, 1940), pp. 9, 23; *Twentieth Annual Report of the Board of Public Works*, p. 448; *Twenty-third Annual Report of the Board of Public Works* (Richmond, 1839), p. 117.

[18]*Twenty-third Annual Report of the Board of Public Works*, pp. 121–22, 131–32; Mordecai, *RF&P*, p. 13; *Twenty-fourth and Twenty-fifth Annual Reports of the Board of Public Works* (Richmond, 1841), pp. 129–30, 392. On Oct. 1, 1839, DuVal, Burton and Company had a balance of $2,766 and John Barr had a balance of $5.48 left on their credit.

[19]Eavenson, *Coal Industry*, pp. 443–44.

[20]*Seventeenth, Eighteenth, and Nineteenth Annual Reports of the Board of Public Works*, (Richmond, 1835), pp. 414–31, 590; *Twentieth Annual report of the Board of Public Works*, pp. 434–37. The engineer was very graphic in his description of the topography of Henrico in these reports.

[21]Tuckahoe Canal Company Correspondence, Reports, etc., 1830–35, Board of Public Works Records, Archives and Records Division, VSL.

[22]Legislative Petitions, Henrico County, Dec. 18, 1835; *Acts of the General Assembly, 1836–37*, pp. 124–25; ibid., *1838*, pp. 148–49; Eavenson, *Coal Industry*, p. 97. Four of the petitioners owned 32 shares of capital stock in the canal company.

[23]Tuckahoe and James River Railroad Correspondence, Report, 1842, Board of Public Works Records, Archives and Records Division, VSL; I. P. Kimball, "Report on Richmond Coal Basin and Mines, 1866," in Davis and Evans, *Richmond Coal Basin*, pt. 1, pp. 83–99.

[24]*Acts of the General Assembly, 1836–37*, pp. 208–10.

[25]Eavenson, *Coal Industry*, p. 99; Wooldridge, "Coal Mines in the Vicinity of Richmond, Virginia," pp. 12–13. Chesterfield mines produced 983,781 bushels, or 39,351 net tons, and employed 194 men. The figures for the Goochland mines were 433,000 bushels, or 17,320 net tons, and 114 hands; while the mines in Powhatan produced 120,000 bushels, or 4,800 net tons, and employed 59 men.

[26]Wooldridge, "Coal Mines in the Vicinity of Richmond," p. 13; William Barton Rogers, "Observations on the Natural Coke of the Oolite Coal

Region in the Vicinity of Richmond," *Boston Society of Natural History Proceedings* 5(1854–56): 677–78.

[27]*Richmond Times and Compiler*, Nov. 21, 1844.

[28]*Richmond Whig and Public Advertiser*, July 15, 1846; Charles B. Dew, *Ironmaker to the Confederacy* (New Haven, 1966), pp. 99, 150, 239, 258.

Chapter VII

[1]*Calendar of Virginia State Papers*, 11:62–63.

[2]For more detailed histories of the units from Henrico County and the companies from the city of Richmond in which some Henricoans served, see Louis H. Manarin and Lee A. Wallace, Jr., *Richmond Volunteers, 1861–1865* (Richmond, 1969).

[3]Henrico County Minute Book, 1860–61, pp. 381, 446, Archives and Records Division, VSL.

[4]Ibid., p. 457; *Journal of the House of Delegates, Extra Session, 1861*, pp. 6, 34, 50, 57, 69, 75, 91–113; *Journal of the Senate, Extra Session, 1861* (Richmond, 1861), p. 66; Henrico County Minute Book, 1861–63, pp. 6–8.

[5]Henrico County Minute Book, 1861–63, pp. 99–100.

[6]Ibid., p. 109; John H. Moore, "Richmond Area Residents and Southern Claims Commission," *Magazine of History and Biography* 91(1983): 287–88, 292; original records filed in cases nos. 17877 and 2903, Southern Claims Commission, Record Group 217, National Archives and Records Service, Washington, D.C. (hereafter NA).

[7]Greater detail on the Seven Days' battles around Richmond can be found in vol. 2 of Douglas S. Freeman, *R. E. Lee*, 4 vols. (New York, 1934); vol. 1 of Douglas S. Freeman, *Lee's Lieutenants*, 3 vols. (New York, 1951); and Clifford Dowdey, *The Seven Days: The Emergence of Lee* (Boston, 1964).

[8]Henrico County Minute Book, 1861–63, pp. 113–14.

[9]Ibid., pp. 113–14, 196.

[10]Ibid., p. 215.

[11]Ibid., p. 240.

[12]Ibid., p. 329.

[13]Ibid., pp. 421–22.

[14]*Journal of the Senate, 1863–65*, pp. 137, 173, 177.

[15]Southern Claims Commission, Record Group 217, NA.

[16]Henrico County Minute Book, 1864–67, pp. 216, 163.

[17]Ibid., p. 293.

Chapter VIII

[1]Petition of Isaac Davenport, Jr., Henrico County Records, Virginia Historical Society, Richmond; *Senate Report No. 20*, 44th Cong., 1st sess., ser. 1, vol. 1, Jan. 20, 1876.

[2]*Journal of the House of Delegates, 1865–66*, pp. 307, 312, 404, 418, 437;

Michael B. Chesson, *Richmond after the War, 1865–1890* (Richmond, 1981), p. 217.

[3]*Journal of the Senate, 1866–67*, pp. 202–3.

[4]The number of males over 21 in Henrico in 1866 was 2,657 whites and 1,278 blacks in 1867, 2,573 whites and 1,288 blacks; the number of males over 21 in the city was 4,316 whites and 1,292 blacks in 1866 and 4,078 whites and 2,075 blacks in 1867. *Constitutional Convention, 1867–68* (Richmond, 1868), Document 16.

[5]Richard G. Lowe, "Virginia's Reconstruction Convention: General Schofield Rates the Delegates," *Virginia Magazine of History and Biography* 80(1972): 352, 360.

[6]Henrico County Order Book, 1867–68, p. 32.

[7]For the many changes in local government during this period, see Porter, *County Government*, pp. 243–303; *Acts of the General Assembly, 1869–70*, pp. 34–35, 269–87.

[8]*Richmond Daily Dispatch*, Jan. 28, 1870, Feb. 8, 17, 1870.

[9]Ibid., April 23, 1870.

[10]Report filed in Original Deeds, 1870, Henrico County Court Records, Archives and Records Division, VSL.

[11]*Richmond Daily Dispatch*, Sept. 2, Nov. 11, 1870.

[12]*Acts of the General Assembly, 1879–80*, pp. 96–97.

[13]*Virginia School Reports, 1870–1871* (Richmond, 1871), p. 201.

[14]Ibid., *1871–72*, p. 27; ibid., *1872–73*, pp. 27, 94, 105. The 1872–73 report noted that ten additional schools were needed. Of the thirty-two schoolhouses in use, six were log, twenty-five frame, and one was brick. Twenty-three had outhouses.

[15]Ibid., *1873–74, p. 46.*

[16]*Acts of the General Assembly, 1875–76*, p. 187; *Virginia School Reports, 1877–78*, p.71; ibid., *1878–79*, p. vii. On pages 74–75 of the 1878–79 report, Gardner gave a summary of the first ten years: "The effect of popular education upon our population during the past ten years has been very decided, and has become a subject of comment and some curious speculation. Especially have the colored people advanced in civilization. The slovenly, ragged, unwashed personal appearance has given place to tidy, nicely-patched clothes. The general order in their houses and cabins betoken a self-reliance and respect for the proprieties of life, which but few ever accorded to the race. They are beginning to be more reasonable than they used to be. Some of them exhibit tact and skill in the intercourse with the world. That a large majority of them become valuable and useful citizens, under our benign system of education, is not longer a problem to be solved, but a fact to be sneered at only by prejudiced map-caps."

[17]*Richmond Daily Dispatch*, Sept. 9, 12, 14, 1879.

[18]Ibid., Sept. 19, 29, 1879.

[19]Ibid., Nov. 5, 1879.

[20]Ibid., Sept. 15, 1881.

[21]Ibid., Oct. 12, 1881.

[22]Ibid., Nov. 10, 1881.

[23]See Charles Chilton Pearson, *The Readjuster Movement in Virginia* (New

Haven, 1917); Dabney, *Richmond;* Andrews, *Virginia;* Allen W. Moger, *Virginia: Bourbonism to Byrd, 1870–1925* (Charlottesville, Va., 1968).

[24]*Richmond Daily Dispatch,* Jan. 10, 31, 1870.

[25]Ibid., Feb. 8, April 12, 1870.

[26]"The Strange Lodge of Wau-zee-hos-ka: A Tale of Honor Upheld and a Dream That Died," *Virginia Cavalcade* 5(1955): 30–33; *Glen Alan, My Community* (n.p., n.d.); O'Dell, *Inventory,* pp. 88–89; *Richmond Times-Dispatch,* March 13, 1977. A portion of the old lodge still stands. The towers have been removed, and the rooms have been converted into apartments. All that remains of the original building is an L-shaped three-story and four-story wooden building with multitiered verandas. The parkland was reclaimed by the forest. Cusson was bitter over the failure of his dream and withdrew from society. He died in 1912 and was buried in Hollywood Cemetery.

[27]See Oliver Jackson Sands, Jr., *A Story of Sport and the Deep Run Hunt Club* (Richmond, 1977).

[28]*Richmond Daily Dispatch,* June 24, 1871, Jan. 10, 1872; *By-Laws of the Henrico Farmers Club, Organized August, 1884* (Richmond, 1884), p. 3.

[29]*Richmond Daily Dispatch,* June 21, July 24, 1871; Commissioner of Agriculture, *Hand Book of Virginia, 1885* (Richmond, 1885), p. 18.

[30]*Hand Book of Virginia, 1880,* pp. 150, 156–57, 162. Livestock on farms on June 1, 1880, included: 1,790 horses, 815 mules and asses, 60 working oxen, 2,181 milk cows, 814 other cattle, 607 sheep, and 4,889 swine. The total amount of wool produced was 2,054 pounds. The crops produced included 400 bushels of barley, 301,661 bushels of Indian corn, 87,303 bushels of oats, 1,596 bushels of rye, 90,365 bushels of wheat, 101,155 pounds of tobacco, 36,859 pounds of Irish potatoes, 18,690 pounds of sweet potatoes, and 2,882 tons of hay. The value of orchard products was reported as $23,831.

[31]*A Description of Henrico County, Virginia, 1888* (Richmond, 1888), p. 3.

[32]See Solon Justus Buck, *The Granger Movement* (Cambridge, Mass., 1933).

[33]*Minutes of the First Annual Meeting of the State Grange of Virginia, Patrons of Husbandry* (Richmond, 1874).

[34]*Minutes of the Second Annual Meeting of the Virginia State Grange, of the Patrons of Husbandry* (Richmond, 1875); *Minutes of the Third Annual Meeting of the State Grange of the Patrons of Husbandry* (Richmond, 1876).

[35]William du Bose Sheldon, *Populism in the Old Dominion: Virginia Farm Politics, 1885–1900* (Princeton, N.J., 1935); *Proceedings of the Third Annual Session of the State Farmers' Alliance of Virginia* (Petersburg, 1890); *Proceedings of the Fourth Annual Session of the State Farmers' Alliance of Virginia* (Petersburg, 1891).

[36]*Richmond Daily Dispatch,* Jan. 4, 1872.

[37]Wadleigh, "Richmond Coal Field," p. 28; *Acts of the General Assembly, 1897–98,* p. 864.

[38]*Richmond Daily Dispatch,* April 24, 1871.

[39]Ibid., Jan. 26, March 6, April 11, 1872.

[40]Ibid., Oct. 24, 1870; *Acts of the General Assembly, 1881–82,* pp. 29–30.

[41]Carlton N. McKenney of Richmond kindly gave me information on the Seven Pines line. Additional data about this line is in McKenney's soon-to-be published manuscript "Rails in Richmond."

The Richmond and Manchester Railway Company received a charter from the Board of Supervisors in 1891 but did not construct a line into the county. The South Side Railway and Development Company requested permission to operate an electric trolley railway on certain streets in the county including Hermitage Road in June 1898, and permission was granted by the board, but there is no evidence that any construction was started. Henrico County Board of Supervisors Minute Book, no. 2, pp. 7, 91–93, 223, Archives and Records Division, VSL; ibid., no. 3, pp. 87–88.

[42]*Acts of the General Assembly, 1889–90,* pp. 196–98.

[43]Henrico County Board of Supervisors Minute Book, no. 2, pp. 274–75; *Acts of the General Assembly, 1891–92,* pp. 505–6, 721–24, 1,078. The act establishing the new Lee District required that the act be submitted to the voters to determine their wishes for or against the establishment of the district.

[44]*Acts of the General Assembly, 1889–90,* pp. 66–67; McKenny manuscript.

[45]Ibid., *1893–94,* pp.270–76. Barton District was laid out as follows: "Beginning at a point on the corporation line of the city of Richmond, where Saint James street intersects Bacon quarter branch, thence north-wardly up said creek to Houseling's or Griffin's branch; thence north-wardly up said branch to its intersection with the west line of Allen Street, in Duvall's addition; thence north to the intersection of said west line of Allen Street with the north line of Wickham street, thence, northwardly in a straight line to the southwest corner of Rogers street and Griffin avenue, in Barton and Lamb's Brookland park; thence, with the west line of Griffin avenue and the production thereof to the northern line of Barton and Lamb's Brookland park; thence eastward along the boundary line of Bar-ton and Lamb's Brookland park to North avenue; thence southeast across North avenue to the northwest corner of Barton and Fourqurean's North avenue subdivision; thence southeastwardly along north line of Barton and Fourqurean's North avenue subdivision and the south line of P. R. Car-rington's land to the west of the Henrico turnpike; thence southwardly along the west line of said turnpike to its intersection with the Meadow-bridge road; thence westwardly along the north line of said Meadowbridge road to Bacon quarter branch; thence westwardly up said branch to the point of beginning."

[46]Ibid., *1893–94,* p. 272.

[47]Ibid., *1897–98,* pp.322–27. The original act was amended in 1900 to reduce the term of office for the members of the Board of Improvement Commissioners to a period of four years. The boundaries of Fairmount District were established as follows: "Beginning at a point on the east line of Mechanicsville Turnpike, at its intersection with the center of 'Q' street; thence along the said east line of said turnpike northwardly to its intersec-tion with the south line of the property of William H. Brauer; thence along the south line of the property of said William H. Brauer, eastwardly to its intersection with south line of a county road; thence along the said south

line of said county road eastwardly to its intersection with the center of Twenty-third street; thence along the center of Twenty-third street southwardly to the center of 'T' street; thence along the center of 'T' street eastwardly to the center of Twenty-fourth street; thence along the center of Twenty-fourth street southwardly to the center of Carrington street; thence along the center of Carrington street westwardly to the center of 'Q' street; thence along the center of 'Q' street westwardly to the point of beginning." Ibid., *1899–1900,* pp. 62–65.

[48]Henrico County Board of Supervisors Minute Book, no. 2, pp. 412, 415, 417, 420, 421, 453, 456, 458, 462, 472–73, 477–80; ibid., no. 3, pp. 3, 5, 24, 26, 27, 29, 33.

[49]*Acts of the General Assembly, 1897–98,* pp. 570–71.

[50]*Richmond Daily Dispatch,* Jan. 6, 1872; *Acts of the General Assembly, 1881–82,* pp. 287–93; Henrico County Board of Supervisors Minute Book, no. 2, pp. 181–82.

[51]*Virginia School Reports, 1882–83,* pp. 46–47.

[52]Ibid., *1888–89,* pp. 78, 111; ibid., *1893–95,* p. 206.

[53]Ibid., *1890–91,* pp. 84, 91.

[54]Henrico County Board of Supervisors Minute Book, no. 1, pp. 390, 426, 554; ibid., no. 3, pp. 13, 118, 175–76, *Acts of the General Assembly, 1895–96,* pp. 419–20. Except for the sharing of cost for maintaining the hospital and for treating the patients, all costs were paid by the county.

[55]*Acts of the General Assembly, 1897–98,* p. 258; Henrico County Board of Supervisors Minute Book, no. 3, p. 166; *Acts of the General Assembly, 1899–1900,* p. 181.

Chapter IX

[1]E. V. D'Invilliers, "Report on Coalbrook Operation," in Davis and Evans, *Richmond Coal Basin,* pt. 1, p. 29.

[2]Roberts, *Geology of the Virginia Triassic,* p. 97; H. W. Treadwell, "Preliminary Report on the Richmond Coal Basin, 1928," in Davis and Evans, *Richmond Coal Basin,* pt. 1, pp. 120–21; D'Invilliers, "Report on Coalbrook Operation," p. 43.

[3]Davis and Evans, *Richmond Coal Basin,* pt. 2, pp. 130–31; Eavenson, *Coal Industry,* p. 135.

[4]Davis and Evans, *Richmond Coal Basin,* pt. 2, p. 97.

[5]Treadwell, "Preliminary Report on Richmond Coal Basin," pp. 125–26; Davis and Evans, *Richmond Coal Basin,* pt. 2, pp. 98, 102.

[6]*Henrico County Farm Statistics, 1910–1960* (Richmond, 1962), p. 4; *Hand Book of Virginia, 1919,* pp. 144, 145.

[7]*Henrico County Farm Statistics,* pp. 3–4.

[8]Mary Thompson Parks, *"Forget Me Nots": Memories of Rio Vista, Virginia* (Richmond, 1972), p. 4.

[9]*Virginia School Report, 1905–7,* p. 52.

[10]*Programme of the Opening Exercises, Highland Springs High School Building* (n.d., n.p.).

[11]*History, Glen Lea Elementary School* (n.d., n.p.). The present building was built in 1947 at 3909 Austin Avenue. In January 1955 three classrooms were added at each end of the building, and in 1968 seven air-conditioned rooms were added to the west side of the building and the old gym was converted into a library.

[12]*A Brief History of the Long Tradition That Is Ridge School* (n.d., n.p.). The present site of Ridge School was purchased in 1930, and in 1931 a four-classroom building was constructed. The auditorium, cafeteria, three new classrooms, and a basement playroom were added in 1947. The latter was later converted into three classrooms. An annex was built in 1961, and it houses a library, clinic, and ten classrooms.

[13]Henry Lee Nelson, Jr., "The History of Varina School," *Henrico County Historical Society Magazine* 4(1980): 24–30.

[14]*Virginia School Report, 1905–7*, pp. 532–33.

[15]Eliza Stickley Bristow, *Her Level Best (The Story of a Brave Woman)* (n.d., n.p.).

[16]*Richmond Times-Dispatch*, Jan. 31, 1975.

[17]*Virginia E. Randolph and the Anna T. Jeanes Fund* (n.d., n.p.).

[18]*Virginia School Report, 1916–17*, p. 84; ibid., *1917–18*, pp. 56–57.

[19]Bristow, *Her Level Best*.

[20]Parks, *Forget Me Nots*, pp. 2, 3, 11.

[21]Reuben Edward Alley, *History of the University of Richmond, 1830–1971* (Charlottesville, Va., 1977), pp. 133–36.

[22]*The Chamberlayne School, Richmond, Virginia, Catalogue for 1919–1920*, p. 8. See also DeWitt Hankins, *The First Fifty Years: A History of St. Christopher's School, 1911–1961* (Richmond, 1961).

[23]*The Virginia Randolph Ellett School Catalogue, 1917–18; St. Catherine's School Catalogue, 1950–51*.

[24]O'Dell, *Inventory*, pp. 112–13; *Richmond Times-Dispatch*, June 22, 1980.

[25]Henrico County Board of Supervisors Minute Book, no. 3, pp. 315, 223, 363; ibid., no. 4, pp. 6–8, 72, 73, 447, 465; ibid., no. 6, pp. 58–61; State Corporation Commission Charters, Archives and Records Division, VSL; for further information on railways in Henrico and Richmond, see McKenney, "Rails in Richmond."

[26]McKenney, "Rails in Richmond"; Gary M. Banks, *A Directory of Sandston* (Richmond, 1947), pp. 5–6.

[27]Henrico County Board of Supervisors Minute Book, no. 3, p. 234.

[28]William S. Simpson, Jr., "A Henrico County First: William Vaughan's RFD Wagon," *Henrico County Historical Society Magazine* 1(1976): 72–74.

[29]Henrico County Board of Supervisors Minute Book, no. 3, pp. 374–75, 399.

[30]The Virginia War History Commission established a Henrico County branch, and the Reverend E. E. Osgood and George Stoneman served as chairmen. Mrs. T. Asby Wickham served as a member of the committee. Unfortunately, only a few records of this committee survive, and it appears from those records that the history of Henrico in World War I was never written. The records are filed with the Virginia War History Commission Records, Archives and Records Division, VSL.

[31]*Richmond Times-Dispatch*, Aug. 17, 1918.

[32]Ibid., Aug. 16, 17, 18, 1918.

[33]Ibid., Aug. 29, 1918.

[34]Virginia War History Commission Records.

[35]*The History of Sandston School* (n.d., n.p.).

[36]*Henrico Citizens League* (n.d., n.p.), p. 2.

Chapter X

[1]*Richmond Times-Dispatch*, Feb. 2, 1940.

[2]*County of Henrico Annual Report Fiscal Year Ending June 30, 1941* (Henrico, 1941), pp. 6, 8.

[3]Ibid., *1943–44*, p. 6.

[4]See also Francis Earle Lutz, *Richmond in World War II* (Richmond, 1951).

[5]*Dictionary of American Naval Fighting Ships*, 3 vols. (Washington, D.C., 1968), 3:301–2.

[6]*Annual Report, 1945–46*, p. 46; ibid., *1952-53*, p. 70.

[7]Ibid., *1954–55*, pp. 1, 4.

[8]Ibid., *1952–53*, p. 8; ibid., *1953–54*, p. 61.

[9]Ibid., *1955–56*, p.3; ibid., *1956–57*, pp. 8–9.

[10]*Richmond News Leader*, Jan. 26, 1959.

[11]*Richmond Times-Dispatch*, June 13, July 11, 1959.

[12]Ibid., July 11, 1959.

[13]Ibid., July 11, 16 , 1959; *Richmond News Leader*, July 23, 1959.

[14]*Richmond Times-Dispatch*, July 25, 1959.

[15]*Richmond News Leader*, Aug. 7, 1959; *Richmond Times-Dispatch*, Aug. 2, 7, 27, 1959.

[16]*Richmond Times-Dispatch*, Dec. 28, 1959; *Richmond News Leader*, Dec. 29, 1959.

[17]Henrico County Board of Supervisors Minutes, July 28, 1960; *Richmond Times-Dispatch*, July 29, 1960.

[18]*Richmond News Leader*, July 29, Aug. 10, 1960; *Richmond Times-Dispatch*, July 31, Aug. 6, 1960.

[19]*Annual Report, 1960–61*, pp. 15, 40–41.

[20]*Richmond Times-Dispatch*, April 6, 1961; *Richmond News Leader*, May 24, 1961.

[21]*Richmond Times-Dispatch*, Aug. 1, 1961.

[22]Ibid., Aug. 18, 25, Oct. 5, 1961; *Richmond News Leader*, Oct. 10, 1961.

[23]*Richmond News Leader*, Oct. 17, 1961; *Richmond Times-Distpatch*, Nov. 12, 13, 14, 16, 17, 19, 20, 21, 22, 1961. A series of seven editorials from the *Richmond Times-Dispatch* were reprinted by the newspapers in pamphlet format as a public service. Both the *Times-Dispatch* and the *News Leader* supported the merger. The weekly *Henrico County Herald*, which was published in Richmond, opposed the merger and claimed to be "the only newspaper in the world that gives a darn about Henrico County."

[24]*Richmond News Leader*, Nov. 22, 1961.

[25]*Richmond Times-Dispatch,* Dec. 19, 29, 1961.

[26]Ibid., Dec. 28, 1961; *Annual Report, 1962–63,* p. 4.

[27]*Annual Report, 1962–63,* p. 21; ibid., *1963–64,* p. 49; ibid., *1964–65,* p. 15.

[28]*Richmond Times-Dispatch,* April 28, 1964.

[29]Ibid., Jan. 26, 1967.

[30]*Richmond News Leader,* Feb. 28, 1968, Feb. 13, 27, March 10, 1969.

[31]*Henrico County Farm Statistics,* p. 1; *1974 Census of Agriculture,* 2 vols. (Washington, D.C., 1977), 1:253–58.

[32]*Richmond Times-Dispatch,* March 21, 1981.

Bibliography

I. Manuscripts

Henrico County Bicentennial Committee
  McCartney, Martha W. "History of City of Henrico." 1980.
Henrico County Courthouse and Government Center
  Board of Supervisors' Minute Books, 1901–82
  Circuit Court Records, 1940–82
  Civil War Centennial Committee
  County Manager Files
  Pauline P. Warner Publication File
  School Board Minutes and Records
National Archives and Records Service, Washington, D.C.
  Census Records
  Compiled Military Service Records
  Southern Claims Commission
  War Department Collection of Confederate Records
Public Record Office, London
  Entry Book of Letters, Commissions, Instructions, Charters,
    Warrants, Patents, and Grants Concerning Virginia, and Espe-
    cially the Rebellion of Nathaniel Bacon There and the Gover-
    norships of Berkeley and Culpeper and Lieutenant Governor
    Jeffreys, C.O. 5/1355.
  Letters and Papers Concerning American Plantations, C.O. 1/43
  Virginia: Return of Births, Marriages, and Deaths, 1712, C.O.
    5/1316
University of Virginia, Charlottesville
  Thomas Jefferson Papers
Valentine Museum, Richmond
  Henrico County File
Virginia Commonwealth University
  James Branch Cabell Papers
Virginia Historical Society, Richmond
  Henrico County Records
Virginia State Library, Richmond
  Committee on Safety Account Book, General Assembly Records

Davis, Ira Festus, and L. S. Evans, comps. "The Richmond Coal Basin." 1938. Carbon copies of typescripts, bound in three parts.

Bladen, John. "Report on Coal Lands in the Tuckahoe Valley." Undated. Pt. 1:1–11.

D'Invilliers, E. V. "Report on Coakbrook Operation." Undated. Pt. 1:12–36.

Jones, Meriwether. "Some of the Success and Failures in the Richmond Coal Field." 1916. Pt. 1:67–82.

Kimball, I. P. "Report on Richmond Coal Basin and Mines." 1866. Pt. 1:38–99.

McCanna, H. H. "Report to Subscribers to Richmond Syndicate." 1932. Pt. 1:100–116.

Treadwell, H. W. "Preliminary Report on the Richmond Coal Basin." 1928. Pt. 1:117–26.

Wadleigh, Frank R. "The Story of the Richmond, Virginia Coal Field and Its Development, 1700–1934." Pt. 2:1–162.

First Families of Virginia Papers

Henrico County Board of Supervisors' Minute Books and Records, 1870–1900

Henrico County Court and Circuit Court Records, 1650–1940

Henrico County Personal Property Tax Books

Henrico County Proceedings of Commissioners Respecting the Records of Henrico Court Destroyed by the British

Henrico County Real Estate Tax Books

Henrico Parish Records

Historic Records Survey, Works Progress Administration

Latrobe, Benjamin Henry. "An Essay on Landscape"

Legislative Petitions, General Assembly Records

Letters Received, Executive Department Records

Letters Sent, Executive Department Records

Minutes of Monthly Meetings of Quakers, Henrico

Patent and Grant Books, Virginia Land Office Records

Secretary of Virginia Military Records, Department of Military Affairs

Tuckahoe and James River Railroad Correspondence and Report, 1842, Board of Public Works Records

Tuckahoe Canal Company Correspondence, Reports, etc., 1830–35, Board of Public Works Records

The Virginia War History Commission

The Virginia World War II History Commission

Westham Foundry Records

Winder Transcripts from the Public Record Office, London

Writers Project, Works Progress Administration

II. Newspapers

Henrico County Herald
Richmond Daily Dispatch
Richmond Enquirer
Richmond Examiner
Richmond News Leader
Richmond Times and Compiler
Richmond Times-Dispatch
Richmond Whig & Public Advertiser
Virginia Gazette (Dixon and Hunter)
Virginia Gazette (Dixon and Nicholson)
Virginia Gazette (Pinckney)
Virginia Gazette (Purdie)
Virginia Gazette (Purdie and Dixon)

III. Contemporary Sources in Published Form

Acts of the General Assembly of Virginia, 1803–1804, and succeeding sessions to 1922. Richmond: various printers, 1804–1922.

"Acts, Orders, and Resolutions of the General Assembly of Virginia at Sessions of March 1643–1646." *Virginia Magazine of History and Biography* 23 (1915): 225–55.

Annual Reports of the Superintendent of Public Instruction, 1871–1980. Richmond: Superintendent of Public Printing, 1871–1980. Also referred to as *Virginia School Reports.*

"Bacon's Rebellion." *William and Mary Quarterly,* 1st ser., 9 (1900): 1–10.

Bailey, James H. *Henrico Home Front, 1861–1865.* Richmond: Whittet & Shepperson, 1963.

Beverley, Robert. *The History and Present State of Virginia.* Ed. with introd. by Louis B. Wright. Chapel Hill: University of North Carolina Press, 1947.

A Briefe Declaration of the Plantation of Virginia duringe the First Twelve Years, When Sir Thomas Smith Was Governor of the Companie, & Downe to This Present Tyme. By the Ancient Planters Nowe Remaining Alive in Virginia. In *Colonial Records of Virginia, Senate Document (Extra).* Richmond: Public Printer, 1874.

Brock, Robert Alonzo, ed. "Communication from Governor Francis Nicholson of Virginia Dated August 12, 1700." In *Collections of the Virginia Historical Society,* n.s., 6 (1887): 61–67.

———, ed. "Documents, Chiefly Unpublished, Relating to the Huguenot Emigration to Virginia and to the Settlement at Manakin-Town, with an Appendix of Genealogies. Presenting Data of the

Fontaine, Maury, Depuy, Trabue, Marye, Chastain, Cocke, and Other Families." In *Collections of the Virginia Historical Society*, n.s., 5 (1886): 1–204.

——, ed. *The Official Records of Robert Dinwiddie, Lieutenant: Governor of the Colony of Virginia, 1751–1758*. 2 vols. Richmond: Virginia Historical Society, 1883.

——, ed. "The Vestry Book of Henrico Parish, Virginia, 1730–1773, from the Original Manuscript, with Notes and Appendix." *In* J. Staunton Moore, ed. *Annals and History of Henrico Parish and Old St. John's Church, Richmond, Virginia, 1611–1904*. Richmond: Williams Printing Company, 1904.

Brown, Alexander, *The Genesis of the United States*. 2 vols. New York: Houghton, Mifflin and Company, 1890.

Brown, J. "Second Auditor's Report on the State of the Literary Fund, for the Year 1837, and Proceedings of the School Commissioners in the Different Counties, for the Year Ending September 30, 1836." Document 4, *Journal of the House of Delegates, 1838*. Richmond: Thomas Ritchie, 1838.

Browne, William Hand, ed. *Archives of Maryland*. 72 vols. Baltimore: Maryland Historical Society, 1883–1972.

Bruce, Philip Alexander. "Public Officers in Virginia, 1702–1714." *Virginia Magazine of History and Biography* 1 (1894): 361–77, 2 (1894): 1–15.

By-Laws of the Henrico Farmers Club, Organized August, 1884. Richmond: James E. Goode, Printer, 1884.

Byrd, William. "The State of the French Refugees, Dated May 10 and 11, 1701." *Collections of the Virginia Historical Society*, n.s., 5 (1886): 42–44.

Calendar of Virginia State Papers and Other Manuscripts, 1652–1781, Preserved in the Capitol at Richmond. Ed. William P. Palmer. 11 vols. Richmond: Superintendent of Public Printing, 1875.

Carter, Edward C., III, ed. *The Virginia Journals of Benjamin Latrobe, 1795–1798*. 2 vols. New Haven: Yale University Press, 1977.

A Collection of All Laws and Resolutions of the General Assembly of Virginia, Relating to the Board of Public Works; The Report of the Commissioners Appointed to View Certain Rivers within the Commonwealth in 1812; the Reports of 1814–15, from the Committee of Roads and Internal Navigation, to the Legislature, and the Several Annual Reports of the Board of Public Works to the General Assembly, up to 1819. Richmond: Public Printer, 1819.

Colonial Records of Virginia. In *Senate Document (Extra)*, Richmond: Public Printer, 1874.

County of Henrico Annual Report, 1934–1981. Henrico: Office of the County Manager, 1934–81.

A Description of Henrico County, Virginia, 1888. Richmond: Daniel Murphy, Printer, 1888.

Ewald, Johann. *Diary of the American War: A Hessian Journal.* Trans. and ed. Joseph P. Tustin. New Haven: Yale University Press, 1979.

Executive Journals of the Council of Colonial Virginia. Ed. Henry R. McIlwaine et al. 6 vols. Richmond: Virginia State Library, 1925–66.

Fife, R. H., ed. "The Vestry Book of King William Parish, Virginia, 1707–1750." *Virginia Magazine of History and Biography* 11 (1904): 289–304, 425–40, 12 (1904–5): 17–32, 241–56, 369–84, 13 (1905–6): 65–80, 175–90, 265–80.

Force, Peter, ed. *Tracts and Other Papers Relating Principally to the Origin, Settlement, and Progress of the Colonies in North America, from the Discovery of the Country to the Year 1776.* 4 vols. Washington, D.C.: Peter Force, 1836–46.

Ford, Worthington Chauncey. *Journals of the Continental Congress, 1774–1789.* 34 vols. Washington, D.C.: Government Printing Office, 1904–37.

Grammer, John. "Account of the Coal Mines in the Vicinity of Richmond, Virginia." *American Journal of Science* 1 (1818): 125–30.

Hale, Edward E., ed. *Original Documents from the State Papers Office, London, and the British Museum; Illustrating the History of Sir Walter Raleigh's First American Colony, and the Colony at Jamestown, with an Appendix, Containing a Memoir of Sir Ralph Lane, the Governor of the Colony of Roanoke.* Transactions and Collections of the American Antiquarian Society. Boston, 1860. 4:1–65.

Hamor, Ralph. *A True Discourse of the Present State of Virginia.* Reprinted from the London edition of 1615 with an introduction by A. L. Rowse. Richmond: Virginia State Library, 1957.

Handbook of Virginia, 1879–1937. Richmond: Commissioner of Agriculture, 1879–1937.

Hawke, David Freemen. *Captain John Smith's History of Virginia.* New York: Bobbs-Merrill Company, 1970.

Heath, James E. "Auditor's Annual Report, January 1, 1838." Document 2, *Journal of the House of Delegates, 1838.* Richmond: Thomas Ritchie, 1838.

———. "A Table, Shewing the Result of the Assessment of Lands, &c. in the Commonwealth of Virginia." Document 69, *Journal of the House of Delegates, 1838.* Richmond: Thomas Ritchie, 1838.

Hening, William Waller, ed. *The Statutes at Large: Being a Collection of All the Laws of Virginia from the First Session of the Legislature in the Year 1619.* 13 vols. New York, Richmond, Philadelphia: Printed by the Editor, 1819–23.

Henrico Citizens League. N.d., n.p.

Henrico County Farm Statistics, 1910–1960. Richmond: Virginia Cooperative Crop Reporting Service, 1962.

"The History of Bacon's and Ingram's Rebellion, 1676." In Charles McLean Andrews, *Narratives of the Insurrections, 1675–1690.* New York: Barnes & Noble, 1952.

Hotten, John Camden, ed. *The Original Lists of Persons of Quality; Emigrants; Religious Exiles; Political Rebels; Serving Men Sold for a Term of Years; Apprentices; Children Stolen; Maidens Pressed; and Others Who Went from Great Britain to the American Plantations, 1600–1700.* London: Chatto and Windus, 1874.

Johnson, Robert, *The New Life of Virginia. In* vol. 1 of Peter Force, *Tracts and Other Papers Relating Principally to the Origin, Settlement, and Progress of the Colonies in North America, from the Discovery of the Country to the Year 1776.* Washington, D.C.: Peter Force, 1836.

Jones, Hugh. *Present State of Virginia.* London: J. Clarke, 1724.

Journal of the House of Delegates of Virginia, 1828–1829, and succeeding sessions to 1865–66. Richmond: various printers, 1828–66.

"Journal of the Lieut. Governor's Travels and Expeditions Undertaken for the Public Service of Virginia." *William and Mary Quarterly,* 2d ser., 3 (1923): 40–45.

Journal of the Senate, Extra Session, 1861. Richmond: Public Printer, 1861.

Journal of the Senate of Virginia, 1863–1865. Richmond: Public Printer, 1865.

Journal of the Senate of Virginia, 1866–1867. Richmond: James E. Goode, 1867.

Journals of the House of Burgesses of Virginia. Ed. Henry R. McIlwaine and John Pendleton Kennedy. 13 vols. Richmond: Virginia State Library, 1905–15.

Joynes, Thomas R. "Memoranda of Journey to the States of Ohio and Kentucky, 1810." *William and Mary Quarterly,* 1st ser., 10 (1902): 145–58.

Kingsbury, Susan Myra, ed. *The Records of the Virginia Company of London.* 4 vols. Washington, D.C.: Government Printing Office, 1906–35.

La Rochefoucauld-Liancourt, François Alexandre Frédéric, Duc de. *Travels through the United States of North America, the Country of the Iroquoise, and Upper Canada, in the Years 1795, 1796, 1797.* London: R. Phillips, 1800.

Legislative Journals of the Council of Colonial Virginia. Ed. Henry R. McIlwaine. 3 vols. Richmond: Virginia State Library, 1918–19.

"Letters of William Byrd, First." *Virginia Magazine of History and Biography* 26 (1918): 17–31, 124–34, 247–59, 388–92.

"A List of Parishes, and the Ministers in Them." *William and Mary Quarterly*, 1st ser., 5 (1897): 200–202.

"A List of the Number of Men, Women, and Children Inhabitinge in the Severall Counties within the Collony of Virginia, 1634." In *Colonial Records of Virginia, Senate Document (Extra)*. Richmond: Public Printer, 1874.

"Lists of the Livinge & Dead in Virginia, February 16, 1623." In *Colonial Records of Virginia, Senate Document (Extra)*. Richmond: Public Printer, 1874.

McIlwaine, Henry R., ed. "Justices of the Peace of Colonial Virginia, 1757–1775." In *Bulletin of the Virginia State Library*, 14. Richmond: Virginia State Library, 1922.

Mathew, Thomas. "The Beginning, Progress, and Conclusion of Bacon's Rebellion, 1675–1676." *In* Charles McLean Andrews. *Narratives of the Insurrections, 1675–1690*. New York: Barnes & Noble, 1952.

Maxwell, William, ed. "Number of Tithables in Virginia." *Virginia Historical Register and Literary Advertiser* 4 (1851): 19, 67, 74.

The Mineral Resources and Mineral Industry of Virginia. Richmond: Division of Planning and Economic Development, 1951.

Minutes of the Council and General Court of Colonial Virginia, 1622–1632, 1670–1676. Ed. Henry R. McIlwaine. Richmond: Virginia State Library, 1924.

Minutes of the First Annual Meeting of the State Grange of Virginia, Patrons of Husbandry. Richmond, n.p., 1874.

Minutes of the Second Annual Meeting of the Virginia State Grange, of the Patrons of Husbandry. Richmond: J. W. Lewellen, Printer, 1875.

Minutes of the Third Annual Meeting of the Virginia State Grange of the Patrons of Husbandry. Richmond: Clemmitt & Jones, Book and Job Printers, 1876.

Moore, J. Staunton, ed. *Annals and History of Henrico Parish and Old St. John's Church, Richmond, Virginia, 1611–1904*. Richmond: Williams Printing Company, 1904.

Mordecai, Samuel. *Virginia, Especially Richmond, in By-Gone Days; with a Glance at the Present: Being Reminiscences and Last Words of an Old Citizen*. Richmond: Dietz Press, 1946.

Morrison, A. J. *The Beginnings of Public Education in Virginia, 1776–1860: Study of Secondary Schools in Relation to the State Literary Fund*. Richmond: Superintendent of Public Printing, 1917.

Muster Rolls of the Virginia Militia in the War of 1812. Richmond: William F. Ritchie, 1852.

1974 Census of Agriculture. 2 vols. Washington, D.C.: United States Department of Commerce, 1977.

Parks, Mary Thompson. *"Forget Me Nots": Memories of Rio Vista, Virginia*. Richmond: Old Dominion Press, 1972.

Pay Rolls of Militia Entitled to Land Bounty under the Act of Congress of September 28, 1850. Richmond: William F. Ritchie, 1851.

Perry, William Stevens, ed. *Historical Collections Relating to the American Colonial Church.* 3 vols. Hartford: The Church Press, 1870.

Pierce, James. "Practical Remarks on the Shell Marl Region of the Eastern Parts of Virginia and Maryland, and upon the Bituminous Coal Formation in Virginia and the Contiguous Region." *American Journal of Science* 9 (1826): 54–59.

The Proceedings of the Convention of Delegates, Held at the Capitol, in the City of Williamsburg, in the Colony of Virginia, on Monday the 6th of May, 1776. Williamsburg: Alexander Purdie, 1776.

The Proceedings of the Convention of Delegates, Held at the Town of Richmond, in the Colony of Virginia, on Friday the 1st of December, 1775, and Afterwards, by Adjournment, in the City of Williamsburg. Williamsburg: Alexander Purdie, 1776.

Proceedings of the Fourth Annual Session of the State Farmers' Alliance of Virginia. Petersburg: Fenn & Owen, 1891.

Proceedings of the Henrico Agricultural and Horticultural Society. Richmond: P. D. Bernard, 1844.

Proceedings of the Third Annual Session of the State Farmers' Alliance of Virginia. Petersburg: Fenn & Owen, 1890.

Programme of the Opening Exercises Highland Springs High School Building. N.p., n.d.

"Public Officers in Virginia, 1680." *Virginia Magazine of History and Biography* 1 (1894): 225–52.

Quisenberry, A. C. "The Virginia Census, 1624–25." *Virginia Magazine of History and Biography* 7 (1900): 364–67.

Rice, John H., ed. "Sunday School." *Virginia Evangelical and Literary Magazine* 2 (1819): 382–84.

Roberts, Joseph K. *The Geology of the Virginia Triassic.* Richmond: Virginia Conservation and Development Commission, 1928.

Rolfe, John. "Relation of the State of Virginia, 17th Century." *Virginia Historical Register and Literary Advertiser* 1 (1848): 101–13.

——. *A True Relation of the State of Virginia Left by Sir Thomas Dale.* New Haven: Yale University Press, 1951.

——. *A True Relation of the State of Virginia Left by Sir Thomas Dale Knight in May Last 1616 by John Rolfe.* Ed. John Melville Jennings. Charlottesville: University of Virginia Press, 1951.

The Seventeenth, Eighteenth, and Nineteenth Annual Reports of the Board of Public Works to the General Assembly of Virginia. Richmond: Samuel Shepherd, Printer, 1835.

Shoepf, Johann David. *Travels in the Confederation.* 2 vols. Trans. and ed. Alfred J. Morrison. Philadelphia: W. J. Campbell, 1911.

Shepherd, Samuel, ed. *The Statutes at Large of Virginia from October Session 1792 to December Session 1806, Inclusive.* 3 vols. Richmond: Samuel Shepherd, 1835–36.

Skinner, J. S. "The Tree Hill Course." *American Turf Register and Sporting Magazine* 1 (1829): 149–152.

Smith, John. *Captain John Smith's True Relation, 1608.* American History Leaflets Colonial and Constitutional No. 27. Ed. Albert Bushnell Hart and Edward Channing. New York: A. Lowell & Company, 1896.

Stanard, William G., ed. "List of Tithables in Virginia Taken 1773." *Virginia Magazine of History and Biography* 28 (1920): 81–82.

——, ed. "Virginia Legislature Papers." *Virginia Magazine of History and Biography* 18 (1910): 24–44.

Stith, William. *The History of the First Discovery and Settlement of Virginia.* 1747, rept. Spartanburg, S.C.: The Reprint Company, 1965.

Strachey, William. *The Historie of Travell into Virginia Britania (1612).* Ed. Louis B. Wright and Virginia Freund. London: The University Press, Glasgow, 1953.

"A True Narrative of the Late Rebellion in Virginia, by the Royal Commissioners, 1677." *In* Charles McLean Andrews. *Narratives of the Insurrections, 1675–1690.* New York: Barnes & Noble, 1952.

The Twentieth Annual Report of the Board of Public Works to the General Assembly of Virginia. Richmond: Shepherd & Colin, Printers, 1836.

The Twenty-fourth and Twenty-fifth Annual Reports of the Board of Public Works to the General Assembly of Virginia, Richmond: Samuel Shepherd, Printer, 1841.

The Twenty-third Annual Report of the Board of Public Works to the General Assembly of Virginia. Richmond: Shepherd & Colin, Printers, 1839.

Van Schreeven, William J., and George H. Reese, eds. *Proceedings of the General Assembly of Virginia, July 30–August 4, 1619.* Richmond: Whittet & Shepperson, 1969.

Van Schreeven, William J., et al., eds. *Revolutionary Virginia: The Road to Independence.* 7 vols. Charlottesville: University Press of Virginia, 1973–83.

Waddell, Joseph A., ed. "Diary of Captain John Davis, of the Pennsylvania Line." *Virginia Magazine of History and Biography* 1 (1893): 1–16.

War of the Rebellion: Records of the Union and Confederate Armies. 128 vols. Washington, D.C.: Government Printing Office, 1885.

Winfree, Waverly K., ed. *The Laws of Virginia: Being a Supplement to Hening's Statutes at Large, 1770–1750.* Richmond: Virginia State Library, 1971.

Wooldridge, A. S. "Geological and Statistical Notice of the Coal Mines in the Vicinity of Richmond, Virginia [September 1, 1841]." *American Journal of Science* 43 (1842): 1–14.

Wright, Louis B., and Marion Tinling, eds. *The Secret Diary of William Byrd of Westover, 1709–1712.* Richmond: Dietz Press, 1941.

IV. Secondary Works: Books, Articles, and Pamphlets

Alexander, Arthur J. "A Footnote on Deserters from the Virginia Forces during the American Revolution." *Virginia Magazine of History and Biography* 55 (1947): 137–46.

Alley, Rueben Edward. *History of the University of Richmond, 1830–1971.* Charlottesville: University Press of Virginia, 1977.

Andrews, Matthew Page. *Virginia: The Old Dominion.* Richmond: Dietz Press, 1949.

Baird, Charles Washington. *History of the Huguenot Emigration to America.* 2 vols. Rept. Baltimore: Regional Publishing Company, 1966.

Banks, Gary M. *A Directory of Sandston.* Richmond: Keel-Williams Corporation, 1947.

Barbour, Philip L. *Pocahontas and Her World.* Boston: Houghton Mifflin Company, 1970.

——. *The Three Worlds of Captain John Smith.* Boston: Houghton Mifflin Company, 1964.

Berkeley, Edmund and Dorothy S. *John Beckley, Zealous Partisan in a Nation Divided.* Philadelphia: American Philosophical Society, 1973.

Bowman, Larry D. "The Scarcity of Salt in Virginia during the American Revolution." *Virginia Magazine of History and Biography* 77 (1969): 464–72.

A Brief History of the Long Tradition That is Ridge School. N.p., n.d.

Bristow, Eliza Stickley. *Her Level Best (The Story of a Brave Woman).* N.p., n.d.

Brown, Alexander. *The First Republic in America.* Boston: Houghton, Mifflin and Company, 1898.

Bruce, Kathleen. "The Manufacture of Ordnance in Virginia during the American Revolution." *Army Ordnance* 7 (1926–27): 187–93, 385–91.

——. *Virginia Iron Manufacture in the Slave Era.* New York: Century Company, 1931.

Bruce, Philip Alexander. *Economic History of Virginia in the Seventeenth Century.* 2 vols. Rept. New York: Peter Smith, 1935.

——. *Institutional History of Virginia.* 2 vols. New York: G. P. Putnam's Sons, 1910.

———. *Social Life of Virginia in the Seventeenth Century.* Lynchburg: J. P. Bell Company, 1927.

Brydon, George Maclaren. *The Story of Emmanuel Church at Brook Hill in the Diocese of Virginia, 1860–1960.* Richmond: Whittet & Shepperson, 1960.

———. *Virginia's Mother Church and the Political Conditions under Which It Grew.* 2 vols. Richmond: Virginia Historical Society, 1947.

Buck, Solon Justus. *The Granger Movement.* Cambridge, Mass: Harvard University Press, 1933.

Bushnell, David I. *Virginia before Jamestown.* Washington, D.C.: Smithsonian Institute, 1940.

Cabell, N. F. "Some Fragments of an Intended Report on the Post Revolutionary History of Agriculture in Virginia." *William and Mary Quarterly,* 1st ser., 26 (1918): 145–68.

Campbell, Charles. *History of the Colony and Ancient Dominion of Virginia.* Philadelphia: J. B. Lippincott, 1860.

Carson, Jane. *Bacon's Rebellion, 1676–1976.* Jamestown, Va.: Jamestown Foundation, 1976.

The Chamberlayne School, Richmond, Virginia, Catalogue for 1919–1920. Richmond: The Chamberlayne School, 1919.

Chandler, Julian A. C. *The History of Suffrage in Virginia.* Johns Hopkins University Studies in Historical and Political Science, ser. 19, nos. 6–7. Baltimore: Johns Hopkins Press, 1901.

Chesson, Michael B. *Richmond after the War, 1865–1890.* Richmond: Virginia State Library, 1981.

Christian, W. Asbury. *Richmond: Her Past and Present.* Richmond: L. H. Jenkins, 1912.

Cleaveland, Rev. George J. "The Rev. Alexander Whitaker, N.A., Parson of Henrico, Apostle to the Indians, a Savior of Virginia." *Virginia Churchman* 66 (1957): 15–18.

Cocke, Charles Francis. *Parish Lines, Diocese of Virginia.* Richmond: Virginia State Library, 1967.

Coleman, Charles Washington. "The County Committees of 1774–75 in Virginia." *William and Mary Quarterly,* 1st ser., 5 (1896): 94–106.

Dabney, Virginius. *Richmond: The Story of a City.* New York: Doubleday & Company, 1976.

———. *Virginia: The New Dominion.* New York: Doubleday & Company, 1971.

Dew, Charles B. *Ironmaker to the Confederacy: Joseph R. Anderson and the Tredegar Iron Works.* New Haven: Yale University Press, 1966.

Dictionary of American Naval Fighting Ships. 3 vols. Washington, D.C.: Navy Department, 1968.

Dowdey, Clifford. *The Great Plantation.* New York: Rinehart & Company, 1957.

——. *Lee's Last Campaign: The Story of Lee and His Men against Grant, 1864.* Boston: Little, Brown & Company, 1960.

——. *The Seven Days: The Emergence of Lee.* Boston: Little, Brown & Company, 1964.

Drewry, P. H. "Fort Henry: Selection of Site." *William and Mary Quarterly,* 2d ser., 3 (1923): 1–22.

Dunaway, Wayland Fuller. *History of the James River and Kanawha Company.* Studies in History, Economics, and Public Law, vol. 104, no. 2. Whole no. 236. New York: Columbia University Press, 1922.

Eavenson, Howard Nicholas. *The First Century and a Quarter of American Coal Industry.* Pittsburgh: Privately printed, 1942.

——. "Some Side-Lights on Early Virginia Coal Mining." *Virginia Magazine of History and Biography* 50 (1942): 199–208.

Eckenrode, Hamilton James. *The Political History of Virginia during the Reconstruction.* Johns Hopkins University Studies in Historical and Political Science, ser. 22, nos. 6–7. Rept. Gloucester: Peter Smith, 1966.

Edwards, Richard. *Statistical Gazetteer of the States of Virginia and North Carolina.* Richmond: For the proprietor, 1855.

Fausz, J. Frederick. "George Thorpe, Nemattanew, and the Powhatan Uprising of 1622." *Virginia Cavalcade* 28 (1979): 110–17.

Flory, John S. "The University of Henrico." *Southern History Association Publications* 8 (1904): 43.

Freeman, Douglas Southall. *Lee's Lieutenants.* 3 vols. New York: Charles Scribner's Sons, 1951.

——. *R. E. Lee: A Biography.* 4 vols. New York: Charles Scribner's Sons, 1934.

Gaines, William H., Jr. "Courthouses of Henrico and Chesterfield." *Virginia Cavalcade* 17 (1968): 30–37.

Gethyn-Jones, Canon J. E. "Berkeley Plantation, Virginia." *Bristol and Gloucestershire Archaeological Society Transactions, 1976* 94 (1976): 5–17.

Glen Alan, My Community. N.p., n.d.

Gray, Lewis Cecil. *History of Agriculture in the Southern United States to 1860.* 2 vols. Rept. New York: Peter Smith, 1941.

Hankins, DeWitt. *The First Fifty Years: A History of St. Christopher's School, 1911–1961.* Richmond: St. Christopher's School Foundation, 1961.

Harris, John Royall. "The Colonial Royalls of Virginia." *Virginia Magazine of History and Biography* 32 (1924): 411–12, 33 (1925): 103–7, 322–27, 420–23.

Harrison, Fairfax. "The Equine F.F.V.'s" *Virginia Magazine of History and Biography* 35 (1927): 329–70.

Hatch, Charles E. *The First Seventeen Years: Virginia, 1607–1624.* Richmond: Garrett & Massie, 1957.

Heatwole, Cornelius J. *A History of Education in Virginia.* New York: Macmillan Company, 1916.

Hendren, Samuel Rivers. *Government and Religion of Virginia Indians.* Johns Hopkins University Studies in Historical and Political Science, ser. 13, no. 11/12. Baltimore: Johns Hopkins University Press, 1895.

Henry, W. W. "The First Legislative Assembly in America—Sitting at Jamestown, Virginia, 1619." *Virginia Magazine of History and Biography* 2 (1894): 55–67.

History, Glen Lea Elementary School. N.p., n.d.

History Highlights: Henrico County, Virginia. Henrico: Research and Information Office, 1977.

The History of Sandston School. N.p., n.d.

"Horse Meat." *Virginia Magazine of History and Biography* 3 (1895): 90.

Howe, Henry. *Historical Collections of Virginia.* Charleston, S.C.: Babcock & Company, 1846.

Humphreys, Andrew A. *The Virginia Campaign of '64 and '65.* New York: Charles Scribner's Sons, 1883.

Imboden, J. D. *The Coal and Iron Resources of Virginia.* Richmond: Clemmitt & Jones, Printers, 1872.

Johnson, Robert Underwood, and Clarence Clough Buel, eds. *Battles and Leaders of the Civil War.* 4 vols. Rept. New York: Thomas Yoseloff, 1956.

Johnston, F. *Memorials of Old Virginia Clerks.* Lynchburg: J. P. Bell Company, 1888.

Jones, Virgil Carrington. *Eight Hours before Richmond.* New York: Henry Holt and Company, 1957.

Kern, Margaret Ethel Kelley, *The Trail of the Three Notched Road.* Richmond: William Byrd Press, 1928.

Land, Robert Hunt. "Henrico and Its College." *William and Mary Quarterly,* 2d ser., 18 (1938): 453–98.

Leonard, Cynthia Miller. *The General Assembly of Virginia, July 30, 1619–January 11, 1978: A Bicentennial Register of Members.* Richmond: Virginia State Library, 1978.

Little, John P. *History of Richmond.* Richmond: Dietz Printing Company, 1933.

Lowe, Richard C. "Virginia's Reconstruction Convention: General Schofield Rates the Delegates." *Virginia Magazine of History and Biography* 80 (1972): 341–60.

Lutz, Francis Earle. *Chesterfield: An Old Virginia County*. Richmond: William Byrd Press, 1954.

——. *Richmond in World War II*. Richmond: Dietz Press, 1951.

Lyell, Charles. "On the Structure and Probable Age of the Coal Field of the James River, near Richmond, Virginia." *Proceedings of the Geological Society* 3 (1847): 261–88.

McCabe, William Gordon. *The First University in America, 1619–1622*. Richmond: Virginia Society of Colonial Dames, 1914.

——. *Virginia Schools before and after the Revolution*. Charlottesville, Va.: Chronicle Steam Book & Job Office, 1890.

McCary, Benjamin C. *Indians in Seventeenth-Century Virginia*. Richmond: Garrett & Massie, 1957.

MacFarlane, James. *The Coal-Regions of America: Their Topography, Geology, and Development*. New York: D. Appleton & Company, 1873.

Maddox, William Arthur. *The Free School Idea in Virginia before the Civil War*. New York: Columbia University Press, 1918.

Manarin, Louis H. *Richmond at War: The Minutes of the City Council, 1861–1865*. Chapel Hill: University of North Carolina Press, 1966.

——. *Richmond Occupied*. Richmond: Richmond Civil War Centennial Committee, 1965.

——, and Lee A. Wallace, Jr. *Richmond Volunteers, 1861–1865*. Richmond: Westover Press, 1969.

Marambaud, Pierre. *William Byrd of Westover, 1674–1744*. Charlottesville: University Press of Virginia, 1971.

Mason, George Carrington. "The Case against Henricopolis." *Virginia Magazine of History and Biography* 56 (1948): 350–53.

——. "The Colonial Churches of Henrico and Chesterfield Counties, Virginia." *Virginia Magazine of History and Biography* 55 (1947): 45–60, 147–58.

Meade, Bishop William. *Old Churches, Ministers, and Families of Virginia*. 2 vols. Philadelphia: J. B. Lippincott Company, 1857.

Mease, James. *Geological Account of the United States*. Philadelphia: n.p., 1807.

"Miscellaneous Cocke Notes." *Virginia Miagazine of History and Biography* 37 (1929): 230–41.

Moger, Allen W. *Virginia: Bourbonism to Byrd, 1870–1925*. Charlottesville: University Press of Virginia, 1968.

Moore, John H. "Richmond Area Residents and the Southern Claims Commission." *Virginia Magazine of History and Biography* 91 (1983): 285–95.

Mordecai, John B. *A Brief History of the Richmond, Fredericksburg and Potomac Railroad*. Richmond: n.p., 1940.

Morrison, Alfred James. *The Beginnings of Public Education in Virginia, 1776–1860.* Richmond: Superintendent of Public Printing, 1917.

———. "Note on the Organization of Virginia Agriculture." *William and Mary Quarterly,* 1st ser., 26 (1918): 169–73.

Morton, Richard L. *Colonial Virginia.* 2 vols. Chapel Hill: University of North Carolina Press, 1960.

Mossiker, Frances. *Pocahontas: The Life and Legend.* New York: Alfred A. Knopf, 1976.

Neill, Edward D. *The English Colonization of America during the Seventeenth Century.* London: Straham & Co., 1871.

———. *The History of Education in Virginia during the Seventeenth Century.* Washington, D.C.: Government Printing Office, 1867.

———. *History of the Virginia Company of London.* Albany: J. Munsell, 1869.

———. *Virginia Carolorum: The Colony under the Rule of Charles the First and Second, A.D. 1625–A.D. 1685, Based upon Manuscripts and Documents of the Period.* Albany: J. Munsell's Sons, 1886.

Nelson, Henry Lee, Jr. "The History of Varina School." *Henrico County Historical Society Magazine* 4 (1980): 24–30.

Neville, John Davenport. *Bacon's Rebellion: Abstracts of Materials in the Colonial Records Project.* Richmond: Jamestown Foundation, 1976.

O'Dell, Jeff Marshall. *Inventory of Early Architecture and Historic and Archeological Sites, County of Henrico, Virginia.* Richmond: The County of Henrico, 1976.

Pearson, Charles Chilton. *The Readjuster Movement in Virginia.* New Haven: Yale University Press, 1917.

Peters, John O. and Margaret T. *Courts of the Richmond Area: A Primer.* Richmond: Richmond Bar Association, 1969.

Pinchbeck, Raymond B. *Henrico County, 1611–1955.* N.p., n.d.

Pitts, H. Douglas. "Brook Hill Lives." *Henrico County Historical Society Magazine* 2 (1978): 5–6.

Porter, Albert Ogden. *County Government of Virginia: A Legislative History, 1607–1904.* New York: Columbia University Press, 1947.

Prince, Richard E. *The Richmond-Washington Line and Related Railroads.* Salt Lake City: Privately printed, 1973.

Quarles, Marguerite Stuart. *Pocahontas (Bright Stream between Two Hills).* Richmond: Association for the Preservation of Virginia Antiquities, 1939.

Randolph, Richard, "Henrico." *Southern Literary Messenger* 25 (1857): 64–68.

———. "Historical Memoranda." *Southern Literary Messenger* 25 (1857): 121–30.

———. "Varina." *Virginia Historical Register and Literary Advertiser* 1 (1848): 161–62.

Reps, John W. *Tidewater Towns: City Planning in Colonial Virginia and Maryland.* Williamsburg, Va.: Colonial Williamsburg Foundation, 1972.

Robinson, Morgan P. "Henrico Parish in the Diocese of Virginia and the Parishes Descended Therefrom." *Virginia Magazine of History and Biography* 43 (1935): 8–40.

———. *Virginia Counties: Those Resulting from Virginia Legislation.* Bulletin of the Virginia State Library, 9. Richmond: Virginia State Library, 1916.

Rogers, William Barton. *A Reprint of Annual Reports and Other Papers on the Geology of the Virginias.* New York: D. Appleton and Company, 1884.

Rouse, Parke, Jr. *James Blair of Virginia.* Chapel Hill: University of North Carolina Press, 1971.

St. Catherine's School Catalogue, 1950–1951. Richmond: St. Catherine's School, 1950.

Sams, Conway Whittle. *The Conquest of Virginia the Forest Primeval.* New York: G. P. Putnam's Sons, 1916.

Sanchez-Saavedra, E. M. *A Guide to Virginia Military Organizations in the American Revolution, 1774–1787.* Richmond: Virginia State Library, 1978.

Sands. Oliver Jackson, Jr. *A Story of Sport and the Deep Run Hunt Club.* Richmond: Sands, 1977.

Sanford, James K. *Richmond: Her Triumphs, Tragedies, and Growth.* Richmond: Richmond Metropolitan Chamber of Commerce, 1975.

Scott, Joseph. *The United States Gazetteer.* Philadelphia: F. & R. Bailey, 1795.

Sheldon, William du Bose. *Populism in the Old Dominion: Virginia Farm Politics, 1885–1900.* Princeton, N.J.: Princeton University Press, 1935.

Simpson, William S., Jr. "A Henrico County First: William Vaughan's R.F.D. Wagon." *Henrico County Historical Society Magazine* 1 (1976): 72–74.

Sommers, Richard J. "Fury at Fort Harrison." *Civil War Times Illustrated* 19 (Oct. 1980): 12–23.

———. *Richmond Redeemed: The Siege at Petersburg.* New York: Doubleday & Company, 1981.

Southall, James C. "Genealogy of the Cocke Family in Virginia." *Virginia Magazine of History and Biography* 3 (1896): 282–92.

Speck, Frank G. *Chapters on the Ethnology of the Powhatan Tribes of Virginia.* From Indian Notes and Monographs, vol. 1, no. 5. New York: Museum of the American Indian, 1928.

Stanard, W. G. "Racing in Colonial Virginia." *Virginia Magazine of History and Biography* 2 (1895): 293–305.

Tooker, William Wallace. *The Names Chickahominy, Pamunkey, and the Kuskarawaokes of Captain John Smith.* New York: Francis P. Harper, 1901.

Torrence, William Clayton. *The Edward Pleasants Valentine Papers.* 4 vols. Richmond: The Valentine Museum, 1927.

———. "Henrico County, Virginia: Beginnings of Its Families." *William and Mary Quarterly,* 1st ser., 24 (1915–16): 116–42, 202–10, 262–83, 25 (1916): 52–58.

Turner, Charles W. "The Early Railroad Movement in Virginia." *Virginia Magazine of History and Biography* 55 (1947): 350–71.

———. "Virginia Agricultural Reform, 1815–1860." *Agricultural History* 26 (1952): 80–89.

Tyler, Lyon Gardiner. *The Cradle of the Republic: Jamestown and James River.* Richmond: Whittet & Shepperson, 1900.

———. "Education in Colonial Virginia." *William and Mary Quarterly,* 1st ser., 5 (1897): 219–23, 6 (1897–98): 1–6, 71–85, 171–87.

Vaughan, Alden. *American Genesis: Captain John Smith and the Founding of Virginia.* Boston: Little, Brown & Company, 1975.

Virginia E. Randolph and the Anna T. Jeanes Fund. N.p., n.d.

The Virginia Randolph Ellett School Catalogue, 1917–1918. Richmond: The Virginia Randolph Ellett School, 1917.

Ward, Harry M., and Harold E. Greer. *Richmond during the Revolution, 1775–1783.* Charlottesville: University Press of Virginia, 1977.

Warner, Charles Willard Hoskins. *Road to Revolution: Virginia's Rebels from Bacon to Jefferson (1676–1776).* Richmond: Garrett & Massie, 1961.

Warner, Pauline Pearce. *The County of Henrico, Virginia: A History.* Richmond: County of Henrico, 1959.

Washburn, Wilcomb E. *The Governor and The Rebel: A History of Bacon's Rebellion in Virginia.* Chapel Hill: University of North Carolina Press, 1957.

Watson, Thomas Leonard. *Mineral Resources of Virginia.* Lynchburg: J. P. Bell Company, 1907.

Weddell, Alexander Wilbourne. *Richmond, Virginia, in Old Prints, 1737–1887.* Richmond: Johnson Publishing Company, 1932.

Wells, Guy Fred. *Parish Education in Colonial Virginia.* Rept. New York: Arno Press, 1969.

Wertenbaker, Thomas Jefferson. *Bacon's Rebellion, 1676.* Richmond: Garrett & Massie, 1957.

———. *The First Americans, 1607–1690.* A History of American Life Series, vol. 2. New York: Macmillan Company, 1927.

——. *The Shaping of Colonial Virginia.* New York: Russell & Russell, 1957.

——. *Torchbearer of the Revolution: The Story of Bacon's Rebellion and Its Leader.* Princeton, N.J.: Princeton University Press, 1940.

Woodward, Grace Steele. *Pocahontas.* Norman: University of Oklahoma Press, 1969.

Woodward, J. B., and Oswald J. Henrick, "The History and Conditions of Mining in the Richmond Coal Basin, Virginia." *Transactions of American Institute of Mining Engineers* 31 (1901): 477–84.

Wright, Louis B., ed. *The Prose Works of William Byrd of Westover.* Cambridge, Mass: Harvard University Press, 1966.

V. Unpublished Secondary Works

Bullock, Thomas K. "Schools and Schooling in 18th Century Virginia." Ph.D., Duke University, 1961.

Ernst, William Joel. "Gabriel's Revolt: Black Freedom, White Fear." M.A., University of Virginia, 1968.

——. "Urban Leaders and Social Change: The Urbanization Process in Richmond, Virginia, 1840–1880." Ph.D., University of Virginia, 1978.

McKenney, Carlton N. "Rails in Richmond." Manuscript in writer's possession. Richmond.

Roberts, Edward Graham. "The Roads of Virginia, 1607–1840." Ph.D., University of Virginia, 1950.

Sheldon, Marianne Patricia Buroff. "Richmond, Virginia: The Town and Henrico County to 1820." Ph.D., University of Michigan, 1975.

Stoneman, Janet Chase. "A History of Varina-on-the-James." Essay, Longwood College.

Turner, Edwin Randolph, III. "An Ethnohistorical Study of the Powhatan of Tidewater, Virginia." M.A., Pennsylvania State University, 1972.

Index

HENRICO COUN

HANOVER COUNTY